JOHN W. SANTROCK • JANE S. HALONEN

University of Texas, Dallas | James M...

Your Guide to College Success

Strategies for Achieving Your Goals

 WADSWORTH PUBLISHING COMPANY
An International Thomson Publishing Company I(T)P®

Belmont, CA • Albany, NY • Boston • Cincinnati • Johannesburg • London
Madrid • Melbourne • Mexico City • New York • Pacific Grove, CA • Scottsdale, AZ
Singapore • Tokyo • Toronto

COLLEGE SUCCESS PUBLISHER: Karen Allanson
PRODUCT SPECIALIST: Jennie Burger
DEVELOPMENT EDITOR: Alan Venable
EDITORIAL ASSISTANT: Godwin Chu
MARKETING MANAGER: Chaun Hightower
PROJECT COORDINATION: Electronic Publishing Services Inc., NYC
PRINT BUYER: Barbara Britton
PERMISSIONS EDITOR: Electronic Publishing Services Inc., NYC
TEXT DESIGN: Studio Montage
COPY EDITOR: Electronic Publishing Services Inc., NYC
ILLUSTRATOR: Electronic Publishing Services Inc., NYC
COVER DESIGN: Stephen Rapley
COVER IMAGE: Stock Illustration Source, Inc., Tony Novak
COMPOSITOR: Electronic Publishing Services Inc., NYC
PRINTER: Banta, Menasha, WI

COPYRIGHT © 1999 by Wadsworth Publishing Company
A Division of International Thomson Publishing Inc.

I(T)P® The ITP logo is a registered trademark under license.

Printed in the United States of America
2 3 4 5 6 7 8 9 10

For more information, contact Wadsworth Publishing Company, 10 Davis Drive,
Belmont, CA 94002, or electronically at http://www.wadsworth.com

International Thomson Publishing Europe
Berkshire House
168-173 High Holborn
London, WC1V 7AA, United Kingdom

International Thomson Editores
Seneca, 53
Colonia Polanco
11560 México D.F. México

Nelson ITP, Australia
102 Dodds Street
South Melbourne
Victoria 3205 Australia

International Thomson Publishing Asia
60 Albert Street
#15-01 Albert Complex
Singapore 189969

Nelson Canada
1120 Birchmount Road
Scarborough, Ontario
Canada M1K 5G4

International Thomson Publishing Japan
Hirakawa-cho Kyowa Building, 3F
2-2-1 Hirakawa-cho, Chiyoda-ku
Tokyo 102 Japan

International Thomson Publishing Southern Africa
Building 18, Constantia Square, 138 Sixteenth Road, P.O. Box 2459
Halfway House, 1685 South Africa

All rights reserved. No part of this work covered by the copyright hereon may be reproduced or used in any form or by any means—graphic, electronic, or mechanical, including photocopying, recording, taping, or information storage and retrieval systems—without the written permission of the publisher.

Library of Congress Cataloging-in-Publication Data
Santrock, John W.
    Your Guide to College Success: Strategies for Achieving Your Goals /
  John W. Santrock, Jane S. Halonen.
       p.   cm.
    Includes bibliographical references and index.
    ISBN 0-534-53352-3
    1. College student orientation—United States—Handbooks, manuals,
  etc. I. Halonen, Jane S. II. Title.
LB2343.32.S26 1998
378.1'98—dc21
                                  97-47065
                                        CIP

to the Instructor

Of all college courses, no other single course is more important than the one for which this text is written. It is our first and best opportunity to help students learn or improve skills that are fundamental to their academic success and that will continue as life-long skills. To an extent that students themselves often do not fully realize, the problem is two-fold: a problem of both mind and heart. And for every student, every class of students, needs and personal potentials are different.

When we began to conceive of this text, we were aware of the need for improvement in the texts available for the course. Co-author Santrock's years of teaching the college success course at his own college convinced him that no book yet had brought the right balance of heart and mind, breadth of flexibility, and high quality of current, research-proven, sound advice for first-year students. Co-author Halonen's career-long expertise in psychology and teaching of critical thinking skills revealed to her that no college success text yet had done justice to this central focus of academic development. Wide-ranging talks with other instructors of college success confirmed these intuitions. It was those observations that motivated us to pursue this project.

Five qualities of *Your Guide to College Success* make it both truly innovative and worthy of your consideration:

- A content based on the most current, comprehensive research on the principles of effective learning, motivation, and testing; a content worthy of an academic institution and its wide variety of first-year students.
- A conscientious balance of "heart" (understanding and harnessing emotions) and "mind" (mastering academic strategies for thinking and learning).
- A comprehensive, flexible, research-based plan of self-assessments and exercises allowing students and instructors to focus on individual students' priorities, goals, and needs.
- A text that fully supports and provides opportunities for the "portfolio" approach to learning that an increasing number of campuses are adopting.
- Complete full-color customization of the text to fit the needs of every campus, every style of college success course; and a host of other supports, including a unique on-line service, to help your course succeed.

Outstanding Content

We did not take lightly the challenge of writing a book with rich, academically sound content.

How have we infused this text with outstanding content? First, we committed ourselves to presenting concisely the best, most current knowledge on each topic. Then we extensively examined the existing research and literature on a particular topic, such as test-taking strategies, learning styles, or communication skills. We studied the academic literature. We read the best trade books. We thought long and hard about what first-year students really need to know about a topic to succeed in college. Then we wrote.

For each chapter draft we obtained the expertise of a number of consultants—master teachers who examined the content and the pedagogy. They provided suggestions and evaluated the value of the book for their own first-year students. As we continued to revise the manuscript, we also enlisted colleagues at other schools to class-test it extensively, obtaining detailed, written, item-by-item feedback from their students.

Throughout this content-focused process we have kept in mind a central guiding principle:

> **AN OUTSTANDING COLLEGE SUCCESS TEXT MUST ADDRESS BOTH MIND AND HEART.**

Some college success texts strive mainly to address students' academic skills. They go after the student's mind. Others try to connect more with the student's feelings and improve their adjustment to college life. They go after the student's heart. *Your Guide to College Success* seeks a better mix of these two approaches.

Mind and Structure

We reinforce sound academic content with careful and consistent structure. Many college success texts are not organized like other college texts. They also don't look like them. The basic content in *Your Guide to College Success* is logically ordered and clearly presented. Readers will come away from each chapter with a clear, organized understanding of what they need to do to be successful. They also will be able to transfer what they have learned from using this college text to other texts in other courses.

We reinforce the content with careful pedagogy as well. In addition to a complete chapter on critical thinking, we have made sure that each chapter stimulates reflection, good critical thinking and planning, and how to apply these skills throughout the student's college career.

Key learning features within each chapter include:

College Success Checklists An effective way to help students learn is to stimulate their thinking about the skills they currently possess and what they need to learn. The checklist at the beginning of each chapter focuses students on the skills and characteristics needed to succeed in college that the chapter will address. The same checklist appears again at the end of the chapter, where students can evaluate how their thinking may have changed, how much they have learned, and how they have improved in areas where they were weak. It also encourages them to apply what they have learned.

Self-Assessments One or more times in each chapter, students complete a Self-Assessment. This feature helps them to examine themselves more deeply on a specific skill or characteristic. For example, Chapter 3, "Managing Time and Money," includes five self-assessments: "Creating a Term Planner," "My Weekly Plan," "Am I a Procrastinator?," "My Annual Budget," and "My Monthly Budget."

On-Target Tips and Summary Tips for Mastering College The chapters are full of practical strategies for college success. Several times in each chapter the strategies are highlighted in boxed inserts called On-Target Tips. These are handy lists or steps for improving success in some academic life skill. For example, in Chapter 7, "Succeeding on Tests," students will find sets of tips entitled: "Will This Be on the Test?," "How Not to Cram," "Learning to Relax," "Scoring Essay Brownie Points," and "Should I Challenge My Grade?"

The page-long Summary Tips for Mastering College appears at the end of each chapter. It provides a final wrap-up of the main things students need to do to succeed in the areas covered by the chapter.

Our reviewing and class-testing have shown these lists of tips to be extremely popular with both instructors and students. Students report having copied the lists to post them at their desks. Another popular way to use them is to gather copies of them in each student's learning Portfolio (see below).

All pages of *Your Guide to College Success* are perforated. Thus, the checklists, self-assessments, and other features mentioned below can be removed from the book and consolidated in a personal learning portfolio that becomes the student's permanent, personal digest of the course and springboard for applying these skills to other courses and activities on and off campus.

The Learning Portfolio

As the authors of the first introductory psychology text with diversity as its main theme, we have benefited from the input of diversity focus groups and consultants for more than a decade. We have written this text to meet the needs of men and women students representing all ages, ethnic backgrounds, learning styles and abilities. We have taken care to address the needs of commuters as well as campus residents.

The learning portfolio takes as a starting point the fact that students not only have different things to learn, but learn in different ways. Instructors can encourage diverse learning experiences by letting students choose among the different types of exercises. Or instructors can assign different kinds of projects within a chapter to different students. This strategy can address differences in learning styles and in weaknesses needing remediation, as well as the boredom that can set in when instructors find themselves reading too many papers on the same topic.

The learning portfolio that ends each chapter includes five parts, each of which contains further options. The five parts are:

Learning by Reflecting: Journal Entries These exercises can be used for journal writing. Their purpose is to improve the student's self-understanding. Often they ask the student to consider how lessons from prior experience might help them conquer current challenges.

Learning by Doing: Action Projects These are action projects, such as conducting informational interviews, setting up discussions, visiting locations outside class, and making presentations. Many of these projects lend themselves to teamwork and collaborative learning.

Learning by Thinking Critically: Critiques These are mainly writing and discussion exercises to develop students' ability to analyze concepts, solve problems, predict consequences, and offer criticism. Group discussion is often a part of the process.

Learning by Thinking Creatively: Personal Vision These activities help students develop a personal vision, come up with new ways to look at issues, and frequently draw on their creative verbal and visual skills. They often include possibilities for group brainstorming and other creative collaboration.

Learning by Planning: Goal-Setting These give students practice in setting goals and planning achievement strategies in relation to issues and needs that emerge from their reading of the chapter and their use of the checklists and self-assessments.

One advantage of the portfolio approach is that throughout the course, students can collect a personal body of work in which they can see the progress they are making. Another advantage is that instructors can conveniently assess each student's progress and final performance in the course by looking at the accumulating quality of their work throughout the term. We urge you to give the learning portfolio idea your serious consideration. Whether or not you choose to organize your course in this manner, we know you will find the portfolio exercises provide a broad, flexible choice of activities suitable for your students.

Heart, Emotion, and Motivation

Mind isn't all there is to college. A text for this course must engage the heart as well. It must excite and motivate students. It needs to reach their feelings. In every chapter we seek to empower students to become more emotionally resilient, to understand their emotions, to cope with stressful circumstances, and to adopt self-enhancing strategies that will help them to master college.

To do this, we begin each chapter with a high-interest profile of a successful person and their college background. The stories present a mix of famous individuals like Oprah Winfrey, Albert Einstein, Amy Tan, and Arnold Schwarzenegger and other lesser known individuals whose stories are equally revealing and engaging, including graduates of both two- and four-year institutions. The stories are linked with chapter content and start the chapter with positive emotion and inspiration.

The need to motivate and evoke feelings is the rationale behind other features, too. Five chapter features are designed with this in mind:

Feeling Good Students want to feel good. These boxed inserts encourage them to monitor their emotions and use them for their advantage. For example, in Chapter 3, "Managing Time and Money," the insert describes the bad-feeling/good-feeling cycle of emotional buying and offers happier alternatives.

Surprised? Surprise is an important emotion that can motivate. These boxed inserts give information that will surprise many students. One example discusses how many hours students think they should study outside class for every hour they are in class. The surprising results can serve to motivate them to think about their own expectations and to see the need to study more.

Staying Out of the Pits For many students, college is a roller-coaster of emotional highs and lows. In this insert we portray some typical traps, like the serious problem of credit card abuse and suggestions for avoiding it with more effective money strategies.

Amazing But True College Stories Students love and remember dramatic stories. In this feature we present attention-grabbing stories that speak to issues of success. Chapter 1 recounts the remarkable journey of Mary Groda in overcoming numerous obstacles to a college education.

Cartoons Laughter is invaluable behavior that most often springs from positive emotion. Humor helps students relate to a book and its overall message. To this end, each chapter contains a number of cartoons that tie in with the chapter's themes.

We want students to realize that it is not only possible but even preferable to have fun while learning!

Full-Color Customization

Your Guide to College Success comes in a standard version with all fourteen chapters. It also is available in full-color customized versions. Instructors can select the subset of chapters that meet their individual needs, priorities, and values. They can have the chapters bound in any sequence. They can also have the publisher bind materials specific to their campus with the chapters of the text. Students appreciate and benefit from customization, especially since they pay only for the chapters the instructor chooses to use.

Acknowledgments

We would like to thank the many respondents to our recent course survey. This book benefitted greatly from the ideas of a carefully selected panel of reviewers and class-testers, all of whom are experienced instructors of college success courses at their institutions. Their guidance was invaluable in the development of this text. We especially thank our in-depth class-testers, who worked with manuscript chapters on a day-to-day basis with their students and provided superb feedback to the entire book team.

Reviewers and Class Testers

Carolyn B. Berry, Winston-Salem State University
Mary K. Bixby, University of Missouri-Columbia
Bill Blank, Laramie County Community College
James Eastgate Brink, Texas Tech University
Janet Cutshall, Sussex County Community College
Heidi Gregg, Sussex County Community College
Karan Hancock-Gier, University of Alaska-Anchorage
Gary G. John, Richland College
Kathryn K. Kelly, St. Cloud State University
Alice Lanning, University of Oklahoma
Judith Lynch, Kansas State University
Scott McAward, University of Utah
Lauren Pernetti, Kent State University
Sharon Robertson, University of Tennessee at Martin
Judith D. Schriefer, Franklin Pierce College
Joy W. Shortell, Cayuga Community College
Cynthia C. Turner, St. Philip's College

Particular thanks to Karan Hancock-Gier, Alice Lanning, and their students for their outstanding class-testing work. In addition to reviewing and class-testing, Dr. Lanning also shouldered the sizable task of writing an outstanding Instructor's Resource Manual for the text. We hope you will be as impressed as we are by the sound practicality of its advice, its creative suggestions, and its ease of use.

Survey Respondents

Britt Andreatta, University of California-Santa Barbara
Victoria Angis, Castleton State College
Jim Barr, Laramie County Community College
Janet Baxter, Belmont Abbey College
Tim Beardsley, West Virginia University-Parkersburg
Rennie Brantz, Appalachian State University
Norman Binder, University of Texas-Brownsville
Dorothy Clark, Montgomery Community College
Linda Rosa Corazon, Skyline College
Francoise Corey, California State University-Long Beach
Terese K. Conway, Oakton Community College-Des Plaines
E.B. Cox, Blue Ridge Community College
Ray Davis, University of South Carolina
Roberta L. Delgano, Santa Rosa Junior College
Mary Edwards, Trident Technical College
Lowell Frame, Indiana Business College
Ellen Galligan, Sullivan County Community College
Phil Griffin, Tacoma Community College
Maryann Greenwood, Modesto Junior College
John Harwood, Richland College
Gladys Hauton, Nebraska Methodist College
Jann Hickey, University of Southern Indiana
Jim Hiett, Volunteer State Community College
Bettie Horne, Abraham Baldwin College
David Hosman, Valencia Community College
Judy Jackman, Amarillo College
Bill Jones, Monterey Peninsula College
Eileen Korpita, University of South Carolina
Scott Kaplan, University of South Carolina
Naomi Karetnick, Middlesex County College
Laurel Kracen, Kishwaukee College
Mary Conley Law, Saint Martin's College
Willie Lawrence, Langston University
Deborah Lowe, Nassau Community College
Natalie Miller, Joliet Junior College
Ralph Miller, College of Du Page
Lynne Norris, Embry-Riddle Aeronautical University
Bruce Peterson, Sonoma State University
Pam Pudelka, Del Mar College
Kate Saudberg, University of Alaska-Anchorage
David Sundberg, Central Missouri State University
Darlene Thomas, Midlands Technical College
Linda Timmerman, Navarro College
Myron Umerski, St. Cloud State University

Ancillaries

For more details on how to order each of the following, see the preview pages at the front of your Instructor's Edition, or contact your local ITP sales representative.

Instructor's Edition Includes a visual walk-through of features and chapter-by-chapter grids to show how self-assessments, lists of tips, portfolio exercises, videos, and other resources can be used in connection with specific topics within chapters.

Instructor's Resource Manual Prepared by Dr. Alice Lanning of the University of Oklahoma. Includes additional ice-breakers and other exercises, how to structure group and collaborative learning, alternative teaching strategies, specific suggestions for teaching each topic, chapter quizzes, and many other resources.

The Wadsworth College Success Course Guide A resource for instructors and administrators on creating and running a first-year course.

College Success Internet-At-A-Glance A one-page laminated pocket reference for students. Gives URL sites related to college success.

Franklin Quest Planner, College Edition The best professional time management system in a special student version, including an audio training tape for the student. Available at a very low cost if purchased bundled with each text.

Success Online (http://www.success.wadsworth.com) An Internet service including professional resources, opportunities for online discussion, online library offerings and services, virtual conference center opportunities, sample syllabi, e-mail to authors, electronic access the Keystone newsletter. For students, the site provides interactive exercises and tutorials, links to web resources, and access to a virtual community of other students to extend their learning.

InfoTrac College Edition Online access to complete articles from over 600 scholarly and popular publications.

CNN College Success Today, Vol. I Timely segments on key topics in college success, produced by the award-winning educational team at CNN and only available from Wadsworth!

The Wadsworth Video Series An extensive selection of videos on AIDS, stress management, improving grades, healthful eating and nutrition, substance abuse prevention, and maximizing mental performance.

World of Diversity A powerful two-video set on communication and conflict resolution between cultures.

AT&T WorldNet Service Free Internet access for one month, with customized links to college success-related sites.

College Success Guide to the Internet, by Daniel J. Kurland A practical guide for students and instructors.

to the Student

This book has a number of devices that will help you learn the material more effectively and make your learning more enjoyable. Below are brief descriptions and examples.

Beginning of Chapter

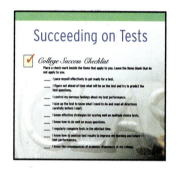

College Success Checklist

A checklist opens each chapter. The items listed are the main skills and characteristics that you need to succeed in college related to the chapter. Completing the checklist will get you thinking in terms of aims of the chapter and how to apply them.

Preview

This brief section helps you preview the chapter's main themes.

Chapter Outline

This tells you the main headings of the chapter so you can get a quck visual overview of the main topics that are covered.

Images of College Success

Each chapter opens with an interesting personal story related to the chapter's topic.

Within Chapter

Self-Assessments

One or more times in each chapter, you will be asked to complete a Self-Assessment. This features helps you to examine yourself in relation to a skill or problem.

On-Target Tips

These appear as boxed inserts in each chapter, and they provide a number of specific strategies for you to apply.

Feeling Good, Surprised?, Staying Out of the Pits, and Amazing But True Stories

Each of these appears once per chapter. They describe real students' experiences that can give you insights about college life.

Cartoons

Each chapter has a number of cartoons related to the content that we hope you enjoy.

End of Chapter

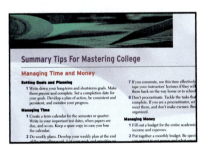

Summary Tips for Mastering College

This section provides a final wrap-up of the main things in each chapter. It's a summary outline of the chapter's key suggestions.

College Success Checklist

This will be the same checklist you filled out at the beginning of the chapter. By completing it again, you can see how much you have learned, how your views may have changed, and what you need to work on further.

Review Questions

These test your knowledge of what you learned in the chapter.

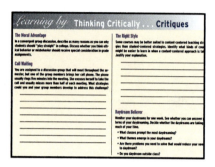

Learning Portfolio Exercises

This section includes five different types of exercises: Learning by Reflecting, Learning by Doing, Learning by Thinking Critically, Learning by Thinking Creatively, and Learning by Planning. In consultation with your instructor you can select and complete appropriate exercises and collect the results in a Learning Portfolio that you can use in your other classes and on the job!

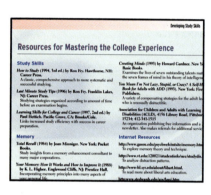

Resources for Mastering the College Experience

This final section includes a wide range of useful resources that you will find handy in and out of the classroom. They include books, brochures, Internet locations, addresses, and phone numbers.

Table of Contents

Chapter 1 Adapting to College 1

Images of College Success: Marian Wright Edelman 2

Changing Contexts and the Changing You 3
- Making the College Transition 3
- Your Developing Identity 3

Getting Motivated, Setting Goals, and Planning 9
- Getting Motivated 9
- Setting Goals and Planning 10

What College and This Book Can Help You to Do 11
- Expand Your Thinking Skills and Knowledge 11
- Improve Your Basic Academic Skills and Work Habits 13
- Develop Your Communication Skills, Relationships, and Personal Qualities 14
- Improve Your Chances of Achieving Financial Success and Living Longer 14

Your Learning Portfolio 15
- College Success Checklists 15
- Self-Assessments 15
- Learning Portfolio Resources 15

Self-Assessments
- 1.1: Where Are You Now? Exploring Your Identity 8
- 1.2: The Areas of College in Which I Need to Improve the Most 16

On-Target Tips
- Developing a Positive Identity 9

Chapter 2 Thriving in the Classroom 25

Images of College Success: Robert Fulghum 26

Exploring Learning Styles 27
- Defining Learning Styles 27
- Adapting Learning Styles 29
- Building Your Learning Portfolio 29

Making the Class Work 30
- Creating a Good First Impression 30
- Being There 32
- Staying Focused 34
- Participating in Class 34
- Stoppers 35

Collaborating with Others 37
- Types of Group Work 37
- Making Groups Work 38

Relating to Instructors 39
- The Many Roles of Instructors 40
- Instructors and Seniority 42
- Getting to Know Instructors 42
- Content-Centered Versus Student-Centered Teaching Styles 43
- Solving Problems with Instructors 44

Self-Assessments
- 2.1 How Do I Learn Best?: A Learning Style Profile 31
- 2.2 What Is My Class Participation Style? 37
- 2.3 How Do I Make Groups Work? 41

On-Target Tips
- Overcoming Distraction 35
- Chatterbox Solutions 38
- Working with Study Partners 39
- Becoming a Distinctive Student 43

Chapter 3 Managing Time and Money 53

Images of College Success: Eric Papczun 54

Setting Goals and Planning 55

Managing Time 56
- Using Time Effectively 56

Balancing College, Work, Family, and Commuting 62
Tackling Procrastination 64

Managing Money 65
Budgeting 66
Banks, Checks, and Credit Cards 70
Financial Aid 72

Self-Assessments
3.1: Creating a Term Planner 57
3.2: My Weekly Plan 60
3.3: Are You a Procrastinator? 65
3.4: My Annual Budget 67
3.5: My Monthly Budget 69

On-Target Tips
Four Steps in Setting Priorities 62
Effective Ways for Commuters to Use Their Time 64
How to Overcome Procrastination 66
Pinching Pennies 68

Chapter 4 Connecting with Campus and Community 81

Images of College Success: Marc Andreessen 82

Surveying Resources 83
Campus Resources 83
Staying Healthy 83
Staying Safe 85

Living Arrangements 85
On-Campus Living 85
Commuter Life 86
Family Matters 87

Getting Connected 88
Extracurricular Activity 88
Cultural Enrichment 88

Getting Help 89
Academic Advising 90
Academic Support Services 91
Personal Concerns 91
Overcoming Limitations 92

Tapping Library Resources 93

Mastering Technology 95
Getting Up to Speed 95
Technophobia 96
Academic Work and Technology 97
The Internet 99

Computer Addiction 101

Self-Assessments
4.1: Knowing the Campus 84
4.2: Homesick? 89
4.3: A Library Treasure Hunt 94
4.4: Computer Addiction 103

On-Target Tips
The Roommate from Hell 85
A Format for Success 90
Overcoming Computer Fears 97

Chapter 5 Taking It All In: Listening, Reading, and Taking Notes 111

Images of College Success: Talia Falkenstein 112

Classroom Listening 113
Commit to Class 113
Concentrate and Listen 114
Capture Key Ideas 114
Connect Ideas 115

Taking Notes from Lecture 117
Note-Taking Strategies 117
Note-Taking Formats 119

Reading 124
Commit to Reading 124
Find Time and Space to Concentrate 124
Plan to Capture and Connect 124
Reading Primary and Secondary Sources 127
Reading Different Disciplines 128
More Strategies to Improve Reading 129

Marking Text and Taking Notes from Text 133
Highlighting Text 133
Personalizing Text 134
Creating External Notes 134
More Tips for Successful Notes on Readings 134

Self-Assessments
5.1: Auditing Your Note-Taking Style for Lectures 120
5.2: What's Your Reader Profile? 130
5.3: How Fast Do You Read? 133

On-Target Tips
Taming the Tough Lecture 116
To Tape or Not to Tape 118
Mixing Books and Kids 125
The Best Reading Plan 126

Chapter 6 Developing Study Skills 143

Images of Success: Yo-Yo Ma 144

Why Study? 145
 Where to Study 145
 When to Study 147

Improving Your Memory 149
 How Memory Works 149
 How to Memorize 150

Study Strategies for Complex Ideas 155
 The Humanities 157
 Natural Science and Math 158
 Social Science 159
 Foreign Language 159

Factors That Influence Study Success 160
 Academic Strengths and Weaknesses 160
 Gender and Learning 161
 Learning Differences 162

Self-Assessments
 6.1: Early Bird or Night Owl? 148
 6.2: Am I Ready to Learn and Remember? 156
 6.3: What Is My Frame of Mind? 162
 6.4: Could I Have a Learning Disability? 165

On-Target Tips
 After Class Is Over 146
 Abstract Art 157
 Deep Study Strategies for the Humanities 158
 Becoming Better at Science and Math 159
 Thriving in Social Science 160
 Learning Languages 161
 Breaking the Silence 163

Chapter 7 Succeeding on Tests 173

Images of College Success: Albert Einstein 174

"Why Do I Have to Take All of These Tests?" 175
 Preparing for the Test 175
 Sensible Study Strategies 175
 Last-Minute Strategies 179
 It's Test Day 180
 In Case of Emergency 180
 Controlling the Butterflies 181

Taking the Test 184
 General Strategies 184
 Multiple Choice 185
 True–False 186
 Fill-in-the-Blank 187
 Short Answer 187
 Essay Questions 187

Reviewing the Test 191

About Grades 191
 College Versus High School Grades 192
 Grading Systems 192

Integrity in Taking Tests 193
 How Widespread Is Cheating? 193
 Why Do Students Cheat? 193
 Why Shouldn't Students Cheat? 194

Self-Assessments
 7.1: Do I Have Test Anxiety? 183
 7.2: How Well Do I Test? 190
 7.3: How Honest Am I? 195

On-Target Tips
 How Not to Cram 176
 Will This Be on the Test? 177
 Learning to Relax 182
 Scoring Essay Brownie Points 189
 Should I Challenge My Grade? 191

Chapter 8 Thinking 203

Images of College Success: Temple Grandin 204

Critical Thinking 205
 Bloom's Taxonomy 205
 Some Keys to Good Critical Thinking 208

Creative Thinking 217
 Individual Creativity 217
 Csikszentmihalyi's Ideas on Creativity 219
 Breaking Mental Locks 220

Holistic Thinking 221
 Right-Brained Thinking 221
 The Medicine Wheel 223
 Mindfulness 224

Self-Assessments
 8.1: Where Do I Bloom? 209
 8.2: The Critical Difference 210
 8.3: How Systematically Do I Solve Problems? 213
 8.4: My Creative Profile 219

On-Target Tips
 Decoding Assignments 206

Coming Up with Alternatives 212
I Have a Question 215
Making Good Decisions 217
Making Sound Judgments 218

Chapter 9 Writing and Speaking 233

Images of College Success: Amy Tan 234

Self-Expression, College, and Careers 235

Writing 235
Learning to Write and Writing to Learn 235
Expressive Writing 236
Formal Writing 236
Habits of Effective Writers 237
Writing Problems 244

Speaking 245
Speaking Your Mind 245
Good Speaking 247
Overcoming Problems 249

Self-Assessments
9.1: What Are My Writing Strengths and Weaknesses? 243
9.2: What Are My Speaking Strengths and Weaknesses? 250

On-Target Tips
Organizational Behavior 240
The Saving Grace 242
Anti-Theft Protection 245
Surviving the Home Stretch 249

Chapter 10 Communicating and Developing Positive Relationships 259

Images of College Success: Oprah Winfrey 260

Communicating Effectively 261
Developing Good Listening Skills 261
Barriers to Effective Verbal Communication 261
"You" Messages and "I" Messages 262
Communicating Nonverbally 263
Gendered Communication 264

Resolving Conflict with Others 265
Being Assertive 266
Negotiating Effectively 267

Relationships 270
With Parents 270
With Partners 270
With Children 271
With Roommates 272
Loneliness and Friends 272
Dating 274

Self-Assessments
10.1: Do You Blow Up, Get Down and Dirty, Cave In, or Speak Up? 268

On-Target Tips
Developing Active Listening Skills 262
How to Become More Assertive 269
Getting Along with a Roommate 2720
Coping with Heartbreak 274

Chapter 11 Living in a Diverse World 283

Images of College Success: Ana Bolado de Espino 284

Diversity in Culture and Ethnicity 285
Collectivism, Individualism, and Diversity Within Groups 285
Ethnic Identity, and Diversity on Campus 285

Diversity in Gender 288
Gender Controversy 288
Androgyny 289
Improving the Lives of Women and Men 289

Diversity in Sexual Orientation 293

Diversity in Age 295

Strategies for Improving Relations with Diverse Others 295
Assess Your Attitudes 296
Work on Taking the Perspective of Others 296
Seek Intimate Contact 296
Respect Differences and Don't Overlook Similarities 296
Seek More Knowledge 297
Treat People as Individuals Instead of Stereotyping Them 297
Show Enthusiasm 297
Resolve Conflicts 297

Self-Assessments
11.1: Are You Androgynous? 290

On-Target Tips
Communicating More Effectively with People from Individualist and Collectivist Cultures 286
International S.O.S. 288
Gender-Based Strategies for Self-Improvement 293
Returning Student Strategies 295
Communicating Across Ability Levels 296

Chapter 12 Being Physically and Mentally Healthy 305

Images of College Success: Arnold Schwarzenegger 306

Physical Health 307
Know Your Health Style and Your Body 307
Exercise 310
Sleep 310
Eat Right 311
Don't Smoke 313
Avoid Drugs 314
Make the Right Sexual Decisions 317

Mental Health 320
Cope with Stress 321
Have High Self-Esteem 325
Be Emotionally Intelligent 327
Get Rid of Depression 327
Understand Suicide 329
Seek Help for Mental Health Problems 329

Self-Assessments
12.1 What Is Your Health Style? 308
12.2 Do You Abuse Drugs? 316
12.3 How Emotionally Intelligent Are You? 328
12.4 Is Depression a Part of Your Life? 330

On-Target Tips
Motivating Yourself to Exercise 310
How to Sleep Better 311
Improving Your Self-Efficacy 323
What to Do When Someone Is Contemplating Suicide 329

Chapter 13 Pursuing Academic and Career Success 339

Images of College Success: Bernard Shaw 340

Achieving 341

Designing an Academic Path 341
Getting the Right Courses 341
How Important Is the College Catalog? 345
Majors and Specializations in Two-Year and Four-Year Institutions 345
Finding a Mentor 350

Exploring Careers 352
Occupational Outlook 352
Finding the Right Career Match 352
The Ideal Job Candidate 355
Getting Positive Work Experiences During College 357

Self-Assessments
13.1: How Goal Directed Am I? 342
13.2: Am I a Perfectionist? 344
13.3: Planning Your Coursework for an Associate Degree or Certificate 349
13.4: Mapping Out a Four- or Five-Year Academic Plan 351
13.5: Matching Your Career Interests with the Fastest-Growing Jobs 354

On-Target Tips
Getting Yourself Going 345
Getting Rid of Perfectionist Tendencies 346
Getting More Satisfaction Later 348
Getting What You Want 350
Knocking 'Em Dead in an Interview 357

Chapter 14 Practicing Integrity 365

Images of College Success: Emmitt Smith 366

Personal Values 367
What Are Values? 367
Value Conflicts 367
Clarifying Your Values 367
The Values of First-Year College Students 369
The Right Values 372

Academic Values 375
Academic Integrity and Ethics 376
Disciplines and Values 377

Putting It All Together 379
Looking Back 379
Looking Forward 381

Self-Assessments
14.1: What Are My Values? 368
14.2: Where Am I Now? Re-examining My Identity 376
14.3: How Do I Resolve Value Conflicts on Campus? 378
14.4: Am I Mastering the College Experience? 380

On-Target Tips
Covey's Strategy for Clarifying Your Values 374
Putting It All Together Now and in the Future 378

References 388

Credits 393

Index 395

Adapting to College

CHAPTER 1

 College Success Checklist

Place a mark beside the items that apply to you. Leave the items blank that do not apply to you.

____ I have a good idea of how college differs from high school.

____ I recognize which aspects of the life I had before college must change for me to succeed in college.

____ I can describe how well-formed my identity is in a number of areas of my life.

____ I understand how important motivation, goal-setting, and planning are in mastering college.

____ I can predict how some of my thinking skills will improve during college.

____ I know which basic academic skills will help me tackle many different courses.

____ I am aware of the most effective work habits for college success.

____ I realize that positive involvement with peers plays an important role in college success.

____ I know some gratifications I need to delay to succeed in college.

____ I can estimate how much I will benefit financially from completing college.

____ I know how many years on the average I will add to my life by graduating from college.

Preview

This chapter will give you a sense of the most important aspects of adapting to college. You will be stimulated to think about what it's like to go from your previous life to your new college life. Adapting to college also involves getting motivated, setting some goals, and planning. We will examine some strategies for this. You will read about what college and this book will do for you. We will profile how to put together a Learning Portfolio that will help you master college.

Chapter Outline

Images of College Success: Marian Wright Edelman

Changing Contexts and the Changing You
  Making the College Transition
  Your Developing Identity

Getting Motivated, Setting Goals, and Planning
  Getting Motivated
  Setting Goals and Planning

What College and This Book Can Help You to Do
  Expand Your Thinking Skills and Knowledge
  Improve Your Basic Academic Skills and Work Habits
  Develop Your Communication Skills, Relationships, and Personal Qualities
  Improve Your Chances of Achieving Financial Success and Living Longer

Your Learning Portfolio
  College Success Checklists
  Self-Assessments
  Learning Portfolio Resources

Self-Assessments
  1.1 Where Are You Now? Exploring Your Identity
  1.2 The Areas of College in Which I Need to Improve the Most

On-Target Tips
  Developing a Positive Identity

Images of College Success
Marian Wright Edelman

Marian Wright Edelman founded the Children's Defense Fund in 1973. For more than two decades she has worked to advance the health and well-being of America's children. When Marian was fourteen, her father died. The last thing he told her was not to let anything get in the way of her education. Four years later she entered Spelman College in Atlanta. Marian was challenged by college and she responded by working hard to master the challenge. Beginning in her junior year, she won scholarships to study in Paris and Moscow. Edelman later commented that the experiences abroad gave her the confidence that she could navigate the world and do just about anything.

In her book *The Measure of Our Success*, Edelman (1992) highlighted a number of lessons for life. The lessons are directed at her college-aged sons and other students. Among the worthwhile lessons are

■ **There is no free lunch.**

Don't feel like you are entitled to anything you don't sweat and struggle for. Take the initiative to create opportunities. Don't wait around for favors. Don't assume a door is closed. Push on it until you get it open.

■ **Don't be afraid of taking risks or of being criticized.**

Everyone makes mistakes. It's the way you learn to do things right. It doesn't matter how many times you fall down. What matters is how many times you get up. We need more courageous shepherds and fewer sheep.

■ **Don't ever stop learning and improving your mind, or you will get left behind.**

College is a great investment. However, don't think you can just park your mind there and everything you need to know will be poured into it. Be an active learner. Be curious and ask questions. Explore every new horizon you can.

Marian Wright Edelman (left) mastered the college experience and went on to become a tireless advocate for improving the lives of children. Among her recommendations are (1) There is no free lunch, (2) Don't be afraid to take risks or be criticized, and (3) Don't ever stop learning and improving your mind or you will get left behind. Do Edelman's recommendations have meaning for your own life?

Changing Contexts and the Changing You

*Life is change.
Growth is optional.
Choose wisely.*

**Karen Kaiser Clark
American author, 20th century**

You already have shown that you can adapt to changes in your education. Remember when you entered the first grade? When you started middle or junior high school? When you started high school? The transition to college is challenging. It involves changing on many fronts at the same time.

Making the College Transition

Whether you have entered college right out of high school or as a returning student, you'll need to adapt in certain ways. These can include learning better study habits, figuring out how to manage your time and money better, getting involved in campus activities, making new friends, adjusting to new living conditions, and coping with roommate problems.

If you are a traditional-aged college student who went to high school last year, think about how your first college year might be different from your senior year of high school. You already may recognize that

- **Colleges are often much larger,** more complex, and more impersonal. You probably knew the principal of your high school, who may have greeted you in the hall. Your teachers in high school probably knew your name and maybe your family. In college, your instructors may not know you by name or recognize your face outside class.

- **College classes are often much larger.** Although some of your instructors will require attendance, many will not. If you miss class it is your responsibility to find out what you missed. Most instructors do not allow make-up work without a reasonable, well-documented explanation.

- **College instructors give fewer tests** and may hold you responsible for more than what they say in class. Some won't let you make up tests.

- **Nobody treats you like a kid anymore.** You have more independence, choice, and responsibility. You are more on your own about how to use your time.

- **You have to do much more reading now** in college and do more work outside class.

- **Good grades may be harder to get.**

- **Your college classmates may be more diverse.**

If you are a nontraditional-aged college student who has been away from college for a while, how is your life going to be different from before you returned to college? Some possible changes include

Staying Out of the Pits

Are You Reminiscing Too Much?

When the stresses of college begin to mount, you may find it easy to spend a lot of time reminiscing about the way things used to be. In the space below, write down three features of your life before college that you are glad you are leaving behind:

1 _____

2 _____

3 _____

If you start feeling blue about college pressures, review this list. It may help you firm your resolve to continue your studies.

If you are a first-year student just out of high school, what kind of transitions do you have to make? If you are a returning student, what transitions are you experiencing?

- **Less free time.** You're probably working and may have children also. It's tougher finding enough hours in the day.
- **Greater financial pressures.** The cost of getting an education probably is greater than you imagined. You also may have had to reduce your work hours to take college classes.
- **New classroom experiences.** The classroom may be different from what you remember from high school or college earlier in your life. Relationships and dress codes may be more casual than you remember. There's more technology now, especially computers.
- **Doubts about abilities.** Being out of the classroom for so long and then returning can be stressful. Because they have been out of school for a period of time, some returning students may doubt their abilities. However, returning students bring a wealth of experience to college and should feel good about the contributions they can make.
- **Feeling like an outsider on campus.** It will be important to get to know other students, your own age or younger. Join or create a study group. Ask about organizations for returning or commuting students. Consider joining to become more involved in college life.

More information and tips for returning students are presented in various parts of the book, including Chapter 11, "Living in a Diverse World."

No matter where you've come from, college is a change. Usually we think of transitions as between a beginning and an end. Let's do the opposite, going from an ending to a beginning. Think of transitions such as those you are experiencing now as having three parts (Bridges, 1991):

1. An *ending*, followed by
2. A period of *change* that can be stressful and confusing, followed by
3. A *new beginning*

What has ended? You may have left a lot behind: the security of living at home with parents who took care of many of your everyday needs; friends you saw daily, the comfort of being known as a successful student; teachers who knew you; pets!

You may have left behind the security of full-time work to attend college. You may be combining work and college. Or you may be trying to combine work, family, and college.

In a recent national survey of first-year students, 1 of every 4 said they "felt overwhelmed with what I have to do" (Sax & others, 1997). Many of the first-year students said that the pressure to succeed was especially present in their lives.

Out of change, though, comes a *new beginning*. Like every other period of life, your college years will be filled with highs and lows, successes and failures. Succeeding in the transition to college will give you self-confidence and increase your self-esteem.

Psychologist Carl Rogers (1980) said that each of us has the ability to cope with problems and reach our full potential. One day he was walking along the coastline of northern California. As he looked out at the waves beating furiously against the jagged rocks and shooting mountains of spray into the air, he noticed the breakers pounding a sea palm, a kind of seaweed about 2 to 3 feet tall. The plant appeared fragile and top-heavy. The waves crashed against it, bending its slender trunk almost flat and whipping its leaves in a torrent of spray. Yet the moment the wave passed, the plant became erect, tough, and resilient once again. The amazing plant took this incessant pounding hour after hour, week after week, and year after year. Yet all the time it was nourishing itself, maintaining its position, and growing. In this palmlike seaweed, Rogers saw the tenacity and forward thrust of life. He saw the ability of a living thing to push itself into a challenging environment and not only hold its own, but adapt, develop, and reach its full potential.

The living self has one purpose only: to come into its own fullness of being; as a tree comes into full blossom or a bird into spring beauty.

D. H. Lawrence
English novelist, 20th century

How might your first-year experience be like that of the sea palm pictured here? When the going gets tough and you feel like you are being pounded into the ground, what strengths can you call on to make it through these difficult times?

During your first year of college, you may feel as if you are being pounded like the sea palm. Work can pile up. You initially may not get the grades you hoped for. Sometimes people will get under your skin. If the going gets tough, come back to this passage about the sea palm. Think about how you share its resilience and its ability to grow and reach its full potential.

Your Developing Identity

What Is Identity? The concept of identity is the masterpiece of famous psychotherapist Erik Erikson (1968). He described *identity* as who you are, what you are all about, and where you are going in life. Your identity is the whole of you, a self-portrait of many pieces. One of life's most important tasks is to integrate all of these pieces into a meaningful identity. Identity's pieces include

- **Vocational identity** (the career and work path you want to follow)
- **Religious identity** (your spiritual beliefs; how important religion is in your life)
- **Achievement, intellectual identity** (the degree to which you are motivated to learn and achieve; your curiosity and intelligence)
- **Political identity** (whether you are conservative, liberal, middle-of-the-road, or somewhere else on the political spectrum; how politically active you are)
- **Sexual identity** (whether you are heterosexual, homosexual, or bisexual)
- **Gender identity** (how masculine, feminine, or androgynous you feel you are; how strongly you identify with the traditional norms of your sex)
- **Relationship identity** (whether you are single, married, divorced, and so on)
- **Ethnic and cultural identity** (which part of the world or country you come from and how strongly you identify with your ethnic and cultural heritage)
- **Personality characteristics** (for example, whether you are introverted and like doing things by yourself or extraverted and like

"Who are you?" said the caterpillar.

"I—I hardly know, Sir, just at present—at least I knew who I was when I got up this morning, but I think I've changed several times since then."

Lewis Carroll
English writer, 19th century

to do things with others; or the extent to which you are anxious or calm, hostile or friendly)

- **Interests** (the kinds of things you like to do; this could include sports, art, music, reading, and so on)

Your Identity Status   Canadian identity expert James Marcia (1980, 1998) believes your identity status can be measured along two dimensions: exploration and commitment. *Exploration* is the work you do in examining meaningful alternatives. *Commitment* is the personal investment you show in some aspect of your identity.

The extent of your exploration and commitment gives you one of four identity statuses:

- **Identity diffusion.** Your identity is diffused if you have not yet explored meaningful alternatives and have not yet made a commitment.
- **Identity foreclosure.** You experience identity foreclosure if you have made a commitment to an identity without exploring alternatives.
- **Identity moratorium.** You are in an identity moratorium if you are exploring meaningful alternatives but have not yet made a commitment.
- **Identity achievement.** You have an identity achieved status if you have explored meaningful alternatives and made a commitment.

Where are you now? What is your identity like at this point in your life? To explore your identity, turn to Self-Assessment 1.1.

How College May Change Your Identity   Alan Waterman (1989) was curious about whether a student's identity changes during college. He asked first-year students, juniors, and seniors about their identity and found that juniors and seniors were more likely to have an identity-achieved status. However, they were more likely to be identity-achieved in the vocational/career area than in

Explore thyself. Herein are demanded the eye and the nerve.

**Henry David Thoreau
American essayist, poet, and naturalist, 19th century**

"Do you have any idea who I am?"

Edward Koren © 1988 from The New Yorker Collection. All Rights Reserved.

Self-Assessment 1-1

Where Are You Now? Exploring Your Identity

Your identity is made of many different parts. Some of the most important components are your vocational identity, religious identity, achievement/intellectual identity, political identity, sexual identity, gender identity, lifestyle identity, ethnic and cultural identity, personality characteristics, and interests. Think deeply about your exploration and commitment in each of these areas. For each area, check your identity status as diffused, foreclosed, in a moratorium, or achieved.

IDENTITY COMPONENT	IDENTITY STATUS			
	Diffused	Foreclosed	Moratorium	Achieved
Vocational identity	____	____	____	____
Religious identity	____	____	____	____
Achievement/intellectual identity	____	____	____	____
Political identity	____	____	____	____
Sexual identity	____	____	____	____
Gender identity	____	____	____	____
Relationship identity	____	____	____	____
Lifestyle identity	____	____	____	____
Ethnic and cultural identity	____	____	____	____
Personality characteristics	____	____	____	____
Interests	____	____	____	____

You may want to keep this Self-Assessment and return to it at the end of the term. You should enjoy looking back at yourself to see how you have changed or remained the same. If you checked "Diffused" or "Foreclosed" for any areas, take some time to think about what you need to do to move into a moratorium identity status in those areas.

the religious and political areas. Many were foreclosed in relation to religious and political identity. Waterman's findings suggest that many college students especially might benefit from deeper exploration of their religious and political identities.

College plays such an important role in a person's identity development because it is a setting where exploration and different views are encouraged (Evans, Forney, & Guido-DiBrito, 1998). Your views will be challenged by your classmates and instructors. Listen to these different views carefully. Don't reject them immediately just because they are different. Think about the ideas. Massage them. Bounce your own thoughts and feelings off others. Try not to be afraid of criticism. Your identity will expand and grow with every challenge you undertake.

As a first-year student, you probably will be in moratorium for many areas of your identity. That's good. Keep exploring, keep searching. The answers will come. It's easy to take the secure route and wimp out. If you do this, you risk missing out on the rich, diverse experiences that can move you to more complete identity achievement.

MAMA Cycles Once you achieve an identity, do you keep that identity the rest of your life? No, your life will change and so will you. If you are a returning student, you may have achieved an identity in a career or area of work, but now have decided to pursue a different avenue. Marcia (1996) says that we go through MAMA cycles of moratorium, achievement, moratorium, and achievement. Your first identity is just that: your first. It is not and should not be your final identity.

What can you do to move your identity forward? For some helpful tips, turn to the insert, "Developing a Positive Identity."

Getting Motivated, Setting Goals, and Planning

A young Canadian, Terry Fox, completed what had to be one of the greatest runs in history. Fox averaged a marathon a day for five months, running 3,339 miles across Canada. What made Fox's run so great? An amputee and a victim of cancer, he was running to raise money for cancer research. Before his run, Terry had set a goal and was intensely motivated to reach it. He wanted his life to have a purpose and to make a difference in this world. He surpassed his goal.

Getting Motivated

It is hard to match Terry Fox's motivation, but the lesson is clear. When you want something badly enough, you will expend the energy and effort to get it. We will describe many strategies that will help you to succeed in college in this book,

On Target Tips

Developing a Positive Identity

- Remember that for many people the college years are the most important years in life for developing an identity.
- Your identity doesn't come in a sudden surge of awareness. It develops in bits and pieces over many years.
- Your identity is complex, with many components. One of your tasks is to integrate all of these parts into a positive, integrated whole.
- Some college students have not explored their identity adequately. They may have foreclosed on a particular identity without considering enough alternatives. In some cases, they may have accepted their parents' views without deeply examining whether they want to be clones of their parents. You eventually may come back to adopt an identity similar to that of your parents. Along the way, though, your identity will be moved forward if you evaluate different paths.
- Your identity will advance if you turn inward to examine your thoughts and feelings. However, developing an identity is not done in isolation from others. Your identity will move forward if you bounce your views off others. Take advantage of the opportunities college provides to get feedback from others about your identity.
- Even when you think you have achieved an identity you feel comfortable with, it will change at some point in the future. Your identity will stay with you the rest of your life, but it won't be cast in stone. Through the college years and beyond, you will change and your world will change, especially if you explore new opportunities and challenges.

but all the strategies in the world won't help you unless you become motivated to learn them and use them.

How can you become motivated to succeed in college?

- **Be confident and enthusiastic.** When you face something difficult, it is easy to think that you can't do it. Believe in yourself. You never will reach your dreams or attain your goals if you don't think you can. View problems and hurdles as challenges, not stresses. Think about how good you will feel when you face challenges rather than avoid them, when you achieve rather than quit.

- **Feel in command.** Don't be trapped by the difficulty of your college experiences. Students who feel trapped say things like, "I'm not very good at this." When you start talking to yourself like this, you only add fuel to the fire. You will become even more anxious and you probably will do worse. Instead, say positive things to yourself. Believe in yourself and your ability. Tell yourself, "I'm going to make it. I can do it. This is a challenge I'm going to face and overcome."

- **Be internally motivated.** If you were in high school last year, your parents may have motivated you to study hard. Your teachers also may have given you a push now and then to succeed. In college, the responsibility is on your shoulders. Now your parents and teachers are less likely to motivate you on a regular basis. You have to take the challenge of mastering college yourself.

Being internally motivated means seeing yourself as responsible for your achievement and believing it is your effort that makes you reach your goals. If you don't do well, you don't say it is because of bad luck or that it was someone else's fault. You face the music and assess what you can do better to accomplish what you want. You don't mope around for days. You develop a plan.

Being internally motivated does not mean doing everything in isolation. Surround yourself with other motivated people. Ask people who are successful how they motivate themselves. Find a mentor, who might be an older student, an instructor, or a teaching assistant that you respect, and ask for advice on getting motivated, setting goals, and planning.

Setting Goals and Planning

For each of us, setting goals and planning can be the difference between success and failure. When we don't set goals, don't plan, and don't map out how we are going to use our time, time tends to slip away until it's too late to accomplish what we want. Students vary a lot in how much they set goals, plan, and manage their time. Some do little about it. Others realize that the time they take to set goals, plan, and organize their time pays off in helping them get done what they need to in a timely fashion.

Goal-setting and planning go hand in hand. When you set goals, you need to develop a plan to reach them. After you have made the plan, you have to motivate yourself day by day or week by week to carry it out.

What kind of goals should you set? Your goals should be challenging, reasonable, and specific. When you set challenging goals, you commit yourself to improving yourself. Be realistic but stretch yourself to achieve something meaningful. Also, when you set goals, be precise. A diffuse goal is, "I want to be successful." A precise, concrete goal is, "I want to achieve a 3.5 average this term."

Terry Fox exemplifies how important getting motivated, planning, and setting goals in life are. The highly motivated Fox set a goal of running more than 3,000 miles across Canada to raise money for cancer research. He spent considerable time planning his run. Although he faced some unforeseen obstacles, such as ice storms, he reached his goal. The amazing thing about Fox's run: He is an amputee.

No bird soars too high if he soars with his own wings.

William Blake
English poet, 19th century

Have both long-term and short-term goals. Some long-term goals take years to reach, such as becoming a successful teacher or getting into medical school. Other goals are more short-term, such as doubling study time next week or not drinking this weekend.

Sometimes on the way to our goals, unforeseen obstacles get in the way. Although Terry Fox had planned his trans-Canada run flawlessly, he did not anticipate some of the circumstances that arose: severe headwinds, heavy rain, snow, and icy roads. After his first month of running, Fox was averaging only 8 miles a day, far below his plan. But he kept going and picked up the pace in the second month to the point at which he was back on track to reach his goal. So it may be for you. As you go through the weeks and months ahead, check your progress toward your goals. If obstacles arise, motivate yourself to overcome them and push forward.

Make long-term and short-term goals. Commit to them. A true commitment is a heartfelt promise to yourself that you will not back down. Too many of us have dreams and good intentions, but lack the commitment to reach our dreams. If this sounds like hard work, consider the alternative: Living your life being uncommitted. A person who is uncommitted sees no compelling reason to get up in the morning. One day follows another, with the only goal being to make it through the day.

Good planning means getting organized. It means getting your life in order. It means controlling your time and life, instead of letting your world and time control you.

The author of *Even Eagles Need a Push*, David McNally (1990), suggests that as you set goals and plan, you should also live your life one day at a time. Make your commitments in daily bite-sized chunks. The artist paints one stroke at a time. Don't let long periods of time slip by when you aren't working on something that will help you reach your goals.

Get started today on your goals for the term, next week, and tomorrow. Map out your plan. Put the plan into action. You will reap the benefits. Chapters 3 and 13 deal with goal-setting in greater detail. We believe that planning and goal-setting are so important to college success that goal setting/planning exercises appear toward the end of each chapter in this book.

What College and This Book Can Help You to Do

College and this book can do a lot for you if you put your head and your heart into them. This book will give you a feel for the areas that you can work on and will lay out strategies.

Expand Your Thinking Skills and Knowledge

Your instructors and fellow students will challenge you to analyze, to evaluate, to solve problems, to poke holes in arguments. They will challenge you to show "why" and to back up your opinions. Your instructors also will help you to develop your creative talents. For example, they will ask you to generate unique rather than common solutions to problems and issues. Exercises in this

Feeling *Good*

Saying "Thank You"

Identify two people who have had an important influence on your decision to go to college. Contact them via a personal visit, a phone call, or e-mail. Express your gratitude for their influence. Be specific about what they contributed to your motivation. As you communicate with them, they may comment about what they saw in you that made them feel good about your ability to succeed in college.

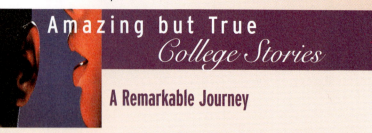

Amazing but True College Stories

A Remarkable Journey

Mary Groda did not learn to read or write as a child. She was labeled mentally retarded. During her teenage years, she was described as incorrigible and was sentenced to two years in a reformatory. During her stay there, she decided to do something with her life. She started working harder at school and received her high school diploma.

Before she left the reformatory, more problems arose in her life. She had an unwanted pregnancy without marriage. Then, a stroke took away the reading and writing skills she had mastered. With her father's support, Mary regained these important academic skills.

In serious financial difficulty, she contacted appropriate agencies and was paid to rear seven foster children. She started taking classes at a community college. Mary got her college degree and eventually was accepted into medical school. Mary Groda is now a practicing physician (Conner, 1984).

Hold on to this story about Mary Groda. There will be times when you feel like the whole world is caving in on you. The obstacles will seem impossible to overcome. The stresses will feel awful. When this happens, think about the challenges Mary Groda faced. Like Mary Groda, you have the motivation and will to overcome any obstacle.

---

book will stimulate you to engage in critical and creative thinking.

Above all else, college is a place where you can *learn*. *Learning* means adapting and changing because of experience. Make it a high priority to learn from both success and failure. Make a commitment not to make the same mistake twice.

Good learners adapt and improve by

- **Getting Motivated.** All the right learning strategies make no difference if you aren't motivated to use them. This book will challenge you to motivate yourself.

- **Focusing their talents and skills.** Some courses can put you to sleep. Others can spark your interest, even make you passionate about a subject. Where you "catch fire" will show you where to take your future.

- **Understanding and using their preferred learning style.** Some of us learn by doing things ourselves. Others learn by watching or listening to someone lecture. Some of us are better at field projects. Others prefer to do laboratory observations or experiments.

  Your college work will help you sort through the ways you prefer to learn. This book will discuss learning styles and help you to determine your preference.

- **Expanding knowledge about many topics and increasing expertise in a particular area.** College offers enormous opportunities to expand your skills and interests. Take advantage of the opportunities to diversify yourself. Learn more about art, culture, history, literature, and science by taking classes in these areas. Feel good about your willingness to venture into unfamiliar territory.

  As you expand your knowledge about many topics, also increase your expertise in a particular area. One of your tasks in college is to find one or two areas that you are passionate about. In the next few years, zero in on a major that excites you. Consider choosing one or two minor areas as well.

- **Coping effectively with stress.** College presents a lot of stress: tests, grades, pressures for success, interacting with new and different people, being overwhelmed with all you have to do, feeling isolated (Levine & Cureton, 1998). In this book you will learn how to view taxing circumstances as challenges to master rather than as overwhelming stressors. You will learn how to call on others to help you cope with stress. At the end of each chapter of the book is a valuable section called "Resources for Mastering the College Experience." The resources include books, brochures, agencies, telephone numbers, and Internet addresses that are related to the chapter's content. For example, the Resources section can steer you in the right direction if you are down to your last penny; get depressed; hate computers but have to learn to use them; have trouble with a roommate; start overeating and gain too much weight; or need help with other problems.

This book will encourage you also to examine your health lifestyle and find ways to improve it.

Improve Your Basic Academic Skills and Work Habits

College courses will expand your basic academic skills. Mastering basic math and reading skills early in college gives you a strong foundation. These strategies will refine your basic academic skills:

- **Improve your ability to learn and memorize.** College confronts you with many different learning demands from many different teachers. This book encourages you to evaluate your strengths and weaknesses as a learner. Our goal is to help you get to the point at which learning is a natural pleasure.

   Playwright Tennessee Williams once remarked, "All of life is memory except for that one moment that goes by so fast you can hardly catch it." When you try to remember something you read in a text or heard in a lecture, you need some good strategies to recall this information. We will provide you with these strategies.

- **Improve your reading, writing, and speaking skills.** Reading, writing, and speaking effectively are critical for success in college and beyond. Many students feel overwhelmed by all the reading they have to do. Others feel held back by weak writing. Some need to work on their speaking skills. We will describe some practical ways to improve in these areas.

- **Use campus resources to your advantage.** Every college has resources and services to help students master college. This book will make you more aware of them. You also will learn how to use off-campus resources effectively.

- **Master technology.** If you don't develop good computer skills, you will be left behind. This book will examine technological challenges and especially focus on using e-mail and the Internet.

- **Learn more effective work skills.** College and success thereafter require self-discipline and good work habits. These habits will help you be a valuable employee, a skilled professional, or a resourceful entrepreneur after college. This book describes strategies to manage personal resources effectively. You will learn the best ways to stay on task, on time, and under budget. These strategies will give you more hours not only for study and work but for play and sleep as well.

   This book also will help you develop effective classroom strategies with lots of tips on taking notes, participating in class, collaborating with other students, and interacting with instructors. It will help you adopt more effective study and test-taking habits. You will learn the best ways to review notes and prepare for tests, and how to manage test anxiety.

Surprised

What Are the Odds?

A ritual occurs on many campuses during first-year orientation. A college representative says, "Look to your left. Look to your right. Only one in three of you will make it to college graduation." Many students are shocked that such a low percentage of their classmates will earn their diplomas. How can you make sure you are the one in three who survives? Note that the one in three figure is the average across all campuses in the United States. Your college may have a lower or higher rate of first-year students who graduate.

DILBERT reprinted by permission of United Feature Syndicate, Inc.

Develop Communication Skills, Relationships, and Personal Qualities

Alexander Astin (1993), a professor at UCLA, was interested in finding out what factors predict whether students will be happy and stay in college. Of all the factors he studied, the most important for students' happiness and continuation in college was their positive involvement with other students. Student organizations, social groups, college dormitories, classes, the student union, the library, and many other campus settings provide extensive possibilities for meeting and getting to know people.

Good communication skills improve your chances of becoming positively involved with other students. Communication skills also are critical for success in the work world. In a recent national survey, employers rated communication skills (such as listening skills, speaking skills, and collaborating with others) as the most important characteristics of an ideal job candidate (Collins, 1996). In this book, you will learn many strategies for communicating effectively with others.

College helps you to discover that people are diverse and have diverse ideas and opinions. You are likely to interact with students and instructors from different backgrounds from yours—people with different religious beliefs and different opinions on issues. They may come from a different culture or ethnic group. In this book, we will explore effective ways to live in a diverse world.

Many of the things we want most in life don't come easily and immediately. To get A's, we have to grind it out week by week. We have to trade off immediate pleasure for delayed gratification. College will give you opportunities to practice delay of gratification. Put yourself in for the long haul. In the end, you will look back and be proud of resisting the urge to get all of your pleasures now. The biggest and best rewards *will come*.

College is also a place where you can identify and refine your personal values. College may challenge your values. Some of them may change.

Improve Your Chances of Achieving Financial Success and Living Longer

Counting on winning the lottery? A $5 million bonus to sign with a pro football team? Getting a college degree won't guarantee you as much money as these unrealistic star-struck notions, but college graduates do make considerably more money in their lifetimes than those who do not go to college. People with a bachelor's degree make over $1,000 per month more than people who only have a high school diploma in the United States (U.S. Bureau of the Census, 1990). And people with two years of college and an associate degree make over $500 a month more than those who only graduated from high school. Think about how valuable a college degree is to you over a lifetime. Also, college graduates are happier with their work and have more continuous work records than their counterparts who don't go to college or don't finish college.

And how would you like to give yourself a couple more years of life on this planet? One of the least known ways to do this is to graduate from college. If you do, you are likely to live longer than your less educated counterparts! How much longer? At least one year longer. And if you go to college for five or more years, you are likely to live three years longer than if you only finished high school.

This section noted some areas in which this book can help you. To evaluate which areas you believe you need to improve on the most, complete Self-Assessment 1.2.

Your Learning Portfolio

Each chapter includes the following exercises for you to complete.

College Success Checklists

You already should have filled out one of these in this chapter. It stimulates you to think about the main skills and characteristics you need that are related to the chapter's content. At the end of each chapter, you will see it again. By filling out the checklists *before* and *after* you have read a chapter, you can evaluate how much you learned.

Self-Assessments

One or more times in each chapter, this feature will help you to evaluate yourself on a specific skill or set of characteristics. You already should have completed two Self-Assessments in this chapter.

Learning Portfolio Resources

To help you experience many different kinds of learning, we developed five types of exercises for the end of each chapter.

- **Learning by Reflecting.** These will help you improve your self-understanding by completing journal entries. Doing so will give you practice at the important skill of writing and other benefits of keeping a journal. In a number of research studies, James Pennebaker (1990), a professor at Southern Methodist University, found that first-year students who write in a journal or portfolio cope more effectively with stress and are healthier than those who don't.
- **Learning by Doing.** These exercises involve action projects: interviews, discussions, field trips, presentations, and so forth. Most action projects help you solve problems and practice report writing. Some include collaborating with others.
- **Learning by Thinking Critically.** These exercises help you to develop your ability to apply concepts, solve problems, predict consequences, and offer criticism. Your critical insights will be expressed in critiques, memos, reports on group discussions, or other

Self-Assessment 1-2

The Areas of College in Which I Need to Improve the Most

This book can help you adapt to college and master many areas of your college life. From our discussion of what college and this book can do for you, we have pulled out the main things we believe this book can help you to do. One of the areas listed—making accurate assessments of your strengths and weaknesses as a learner—is highlighted in the exercises you will do in the book.

To evaluate which areas of college you think you need to improve on the most, rate yourself from 1 to 5, with 5 = Don't need to improve on at all, 4 = Need a little improvement, 3 = Need moderate improvement, 2 = One of my weaknesses—I need to improve in this area considerably, and 1 = I am very weak in this area and need to improve extensively.

DEVELOP MY LEARNING AND THINKING SKILLS
- ___ Get motivated
- ___ Focus my talents and skills
- ___ Understand and use my preferred learning style
- ___ Make accurate assessments of my strengths and weaknesses as a learner
- ___ Cope effectively with stress

IMPROVE MY BASIC SKILLS AND WORK HABITS
- ___ Improve my ability to learn and memorize
- ___ Improve my reading, writing, and speaking skills
- ___ Identify available resources and use them to my advantage
- ___ Master technology
- ___ Manage personal resources, such as time and money, effectively
- ___ Develop effective classroom strategies
- ___ Adopt effective study and test-taking habits

DEVELOP MY COMMUNICATION SKILLS, RELATIONSHIPS, AND PERSONAL QUALITIES
- ___ Improve my communication skills
- ___ Develop more positive relationships
- ___ Connect with diverse people and ideas
- ___ Delay gratification
- ___ Practice positive values

Look back the list and evaluate the areas you need to work on the most (those that you marked 1, 2, and 3). Put your head and your heart into improving in these areas this term.

formats that will give you further practice in writing, speaking, and collaborating.

- **Learning by Thinking Creatively.** These exercises stimulate you to develop a personal vision as you pursue novel insights alone and with other students. The creative thinking exercises may require you to express your insights in writing. You also may try your hand at drawing images, creating slogans, crafting posters, or other activities. Some exercises will encourage you to brainstorm with other students to arrive at creative solutions.

- **Learning by Planning.** Planning is crucial to college success. In these exercises you will set goals that may build on the Self-Assessments and College Success Checklists. Completing these exercises will give you more concrete objectives and plans for mastering college.

Your instructor will help you decide which assignments to complete as part of your Learning Portfolio. For example, some instructors will emphasize particular skills. Some may select critical thinking or journal exercises. Others may rotate assignments across categories. Still others may stress setting goals at the end of each chapter. To make it easy for you to collect College Success Checklists, Self-Assessments, and Learning Portfolio Resources in your Learning Portfolio, the book's pages are perforated. You also may want to tear out the pages with the On-Target Tips and the Summary Tips for Mastering College and put them in your Learning Portfolio.

Throughout the term, your Learning Portfolio will grow. You can add to it other work related to mastering college. This will be valuable to you in two ways. First, the portfolio will serve as a concrete reminder of what your beginning experiences in college were like. You may enjoy looking back at where you were today and how you have changed. You especially can benefit from re-examining your goals and seeing whether you met them. Second, keeping the portfolio will help you develop the habit of keeping important papers. In fact, you may want to keep adding to the portfolio as you go through college to help you chart your path as a learner.

MISS PEACH By Mell Lazarus

© 1973 News America Syndicate

Summary Tips For Mastering College

Adapting to College

Making the College Transition
1. Give some thought to how college differs from high school. Recognize that regardless of your environment, the transition to college involves change. Remind yourself that the change can be challenging and requires you to adapt.
2. Let go of some old ties and securities. Develop new friends. Look at your new life as a constructive challenge rather than as a source of overwhelming stress.

Developing Your Identity
1. Explore your identity in a number of different areas of your life. Examine what you want to do with your life. Refine and fine-tune your identity as you move forward. Understand that you will make some mistakes. Try on some new hats; keep some of them, discard others. Learn from your mistakes and wrong turns.
2. Recognize that the college years play an important role in your identity development.

Getting Motivated, Setting Goals, and Planning
1. You can know all of the right things to do to succeed in college, but if you are not motivated you never will get anywhere. Being confident and enthusiastic, feeling in command, and being internally motivated can help you succeed in college.
2. Set goals, get organized, and plan. Set some long-term and short-term goals. Develop some goals you want to reach at the end of the term. Put together a plan to attain them. On Saturday or Sunday, map out your schedule and what you hope to accomplish for the following week. Make your goals concrete and specific.

What College and This Book Can Do for You
1. Expand your thinking skills and knowledge. Good learners adapt and improve by getting motivated, focusing their talents and skills, understanding and using their preferred learning style, expanding knowledge about many topics and increasing expertise in a particular area, and coping effectively with stress.
2. Improve your basic skills and work habits. The following strategies will help you: improve your ability to learn and memorize, improve your reading, writing, and speaking skills, identify available resources and use them to your advantage, master technology, and learn more effective work skills such as managing personal resources effectively, developing good classroom strategies, and adopting effective study and test-taking strategies.
3. Develop communication skills, relationships, and personal qualities. This includes connecting with diverse people and ideas, learning to delay gratification, and practicing positive values.
4. Remember that college can improve your chances of financial success and living longer.

Your Learning Portfolio
1. Put your heart and head into the exercises in this book. Answer the questions and fill in the items honestly. Your motivation and integrity in doing the exercises will help you to learn a great deal about yourself and improve your chances of college success.
2. The College Success Checklists will give you a picture of where you are before you read the chapter and where you are after the chapter. Examine your strengths and weaknesses. Develop a plan to improve on your weaknesses.
3. Fill out the Self-Assessments. They will further your self-understanding. The Self-Assessments you filled out in this chapter should give you a sense of your identity in a number of different areas of your life.
4. Do some or all of the Learning Portfolio, based on your instructor's preferences. The Learning Portfolio will help you to experience different types of learning. The learning exercises can help you improve your ability to engage in reflective thinking, carry out action projects, think critically, develop creative strategies, and engage in planning and goal setting.

College Success Checklist

Have your views changed since you completed this checklist at the beginning of the chapter? Place a check mark beside any item for which you feel good about your current practice. Also check any item for which you have new ideas about how to improve.

____ I have a good idea about how college differs from high school.

____ I recognize which aspects of the life I had before college must change for me to succeed in college.

____ I know how well-formed my identity is in a number of areas of my life.

____ I understand how important motivation, goal-setting, and planning are in mastering college.

____ I can predict how some of my thinking skills will improve during college.

____ I know which basic academic skills will help me tackle many different courses.

____ I am aware of the most effective work habits for college success.

____ I realize that positive involvement with peers plays an important role in college success.

____ I know some gratifications I need to delay to succeed in college.

____ I can estimate how much I will benefit financially from completing college.

____ I know how many years on the average I will add to my life by graduating from college.

In the space below, list items that you still need to work on the most. This list may help you complete the goal-setting exercise in the Learning Portfolio.

Review Questions

1 How is the college context you are in now different from the context you were in before college? For example, how is college different from high school?

2 What is the nature of identity? How is your identity likely to change during your college years?

3 What benefits do students gain from college?

4 What are some of the benefits that you should get from studying this book and taking a college orientation class?

5 Why is it important to keep a journal?

Learning Portfolio

Learning by Reflecting... Journal Entries

Risky Business

Marian Wright Edelman offered this worthwhile lesson regarding adapting to college: "Don't be afraid to take risks or be criticized." By starting college, you have demonstrated that you can take a risk. Think about your past academic work, especially a time when you took a risk. Then record in your journal

- What was the risky situation?
- How did you overcome any fears you may have had about not being successful?
- Did you accomplish what you wanted? Why or why not?
- What lessons can you learn from this experience to help you feel empowered about the risks you will be facing now?

Launching Your New Life

Think about the changes that have taken place in your life since you started college.

- What have you left behind?
- Are you clinging to anything that you need to let go?
- What will your life be like without the familiar routines you are used to?
- What can you do to cope with these losses?
- What excites you most about starting over in your new environment?

Overcoming Orientation Stress

Describe the most stressful experience you have had so far in college.

- What makes it so stressful?
- How did you initially cope with it?
- How did you resolve the problem?
- If the problem still bothers you, how do you plan to resolve it?

Learning by Doing... Action Projects

Finding Your Way

Find the section in your student handbook that describes the services available to you. Then turn to the map of your campus that shows where the services are located. Identify two services from which you think you might benefit. Go to the services, find out about the services provided, and bring back their brochures that describe their services. Write a memo to your instructor describing what you found out and place it in your portfolio.

Sharing Your Reality

Get together with a group of two or more students and discuss your impressions of college so far. How does the reality compare with the ideas you had about what college would be like? When you report this experience in your journal, be sure to describe how your experience compares with other students'.

Goal-Tending

To help you make progress in college, your goals must be challenging, realistic, and specific. Most people create diffuse goals. These goals are so vague that they don't give you a clear sense of what to do next. Transform the following diffuse goals into goals that are challenging, realistic, and specific:

I want to be popular.
_____
_____

I want to make lots of money.
_____
_____

I want to improve my learning.
_____
_____

I want to be healthier.
_____
_____

Learning by Thinking Critically... Critiques

Was It Good for You?
As part of a group discussion, evaluate the quality of the orientation your college provided. What was especially effective about the experience? What should be changed? Write a summary of your recommendations in a memo to the person responsible for planning orientation. Your instructor should be able to provide the person's name.

Risk Management
Many college students don't get past their first year. Think about your own risks for staying in college. Make a list of the factors that could undermine your ability to be successful. What can you do to minimize these threats so you can thrive in this new world?

Way Beyond Navel-Gazing
Identity expert James Marcia suggested that forging an identity requires hard work. Look at Self-Assessment 1.1 and identify the areas in which you have achieved your identity. In your portfolio analyze why you might feel so sturdy in these areas. Next, look at the areas where you haven't felt the same high level of commitment. Speculate why these areas have not been as easy for you to resolve.

Learning by Thinking Creatively... Personal Vision

As Sturdy as a Sea Palm
Carl Rogers used the poignant metaphor of sea palm, thriving despite being battered by the winds and seas, to capture the resilience of the human spirit. Metaphors are comparisons that provide concrete examples of ideas. Create your own metaphor that communicates your experiences about this stage of your college career. Draw and explain your metaphor in your portfolio.

The Magic Wand
Suppose your teachers granted you a magic wand to make three changes to improve your academic life. What three changes would you make and why?

1 _____
_____
_____
2 _____
_____
_____
3 _____
_____
_____

My Hero
As you read about the inspiring example of Terry Fox, you probably recognized how heroic his fund-raising efforts were, given his physical disability. Fox demonstrated that motivated people can overcome even severe limitations. But Fox is not the only inspirational example you may know. Find a picture of someone you would consider inspiring. Describe why you selected this person as your role model and how you may be similar to your hero.

Learning by Planning... Goal Setting

Review the results of the Self-Assessments you completed in this chapter. Also review the College Success Checklist. What can you conclude about things you need to do to improve your skills?

What goal should you select from this chapter for making positive changes that will help you master the college experience? *(Hint: Is your goal challenging, reasonable, and specific?)*

_____
_____
_____
_____

What strategies will you use to achieve your goal? *(Hint: Can you organize your strategy into a series of smaller goals?)*

_____
_____
_____
_____
_____
_____
_____
_____

What obstacles may be in your way as you attempt to make these positive changes?

_____
_____
_____
_____

What additional resources might help you succeed in achieving your goal?

_____
_____
_____
_____

By what date do you want to accomplish your goal?

_____

How will you know you have succeeded?

_____
_____
_____
_____

Resources for Mastering the College Experience

Changing Contexts and the Changing You

Identity: Youth and Crisis (1968) by **Erik Erikson. New York: Norton.**
Encourages you to think about your identity and explore different options.

How to Deal with Your Parents (1991) by **Lynn Osterkamp. New York: Berkeley Books.**
Specific strategies for dealing with your parents, by a nationally recognized authority on family conflict and communication.

Letting Go: A Parent's Guide to Today's College Experience (1992, 2nd ed.) by **Karen Coburn and Made Treeger. Bethesda, MA: Adler & Adler.**
Tells parents of students what the college experience is like and how the student is changing.

Managing Change: Making the Most of Change (1991) by **William Bridges. Reading, MA: Addison Wesley.**
Excellent strategies for coping with the change involved in transitions, such as high school to college and work to college.

What College Can Help You to Do

College: The Undergraduate Experience in America (1987) by **Ernest Boyer. New York: HarperCollins.**
Explores the benefits of college and what the college experience is like for many students.

Getting Motivated, Setting Goals, and Planning

Even Eagles Need a Push (1990) by **David McNally. New York: Dell.**
An inspiring, motivating, uplifting, stimulating book for thinking about the kind of life you want to live. Lots of ideas for success.

Stephanie Winston's Best Organizing Tips (1995) by **Stephanie Winston. New York: Simon & Schuster.**
Invaluable tips for planning and organizing your time from a leader in the field of time management.

Strategies for Making Your College Experience a Success

Throughout this book, we recommend hundreds of different resources—books, agencies, pamphlets, phone numbers—that can help you succeed in college. Following are two such resources.

Intimate Connections (1985) by **David Burns. New York: Morrow.**
Supports the important strategy of becoming involved and connected with other students. Excellent on learning how to make positive connections with others.

The Measure of Our Success (1992) by **Marian Wright Edelman. Boston: Beacon.**
Stimulates thoughts about what kind of person we want to be. Twenty-five worthwhile lessons of life.

Writing in a Journal/Learning Portfolio

Opening Up (1990) by **James Pennebaker. New York: Avon.**
How you can benefit from writing about your experiences in a Learning Portfolio. Insights into why writing about troubling thoughts protects you from the internal stresses that can cause physical illnesses.

Internet Resources

Warning: copy the Internet address exactly as it is written. Adding spaces or making other changes will cause an address not to work. Websites often change address. Also, they go off-line now and then. We have visited these sites but can't guarantee that they'll still be there when you try them. Try not to get frustrated if you find the site is down or gone. Try your Internet search feature.

http://www.internetuniv.com
News, features, entertainment, travel tips, "knowledge for college," sports, money, etc.

http://www.psych-web.com/mtsite
Career, study, and survival help. Georgia Southern University.

http://pegasus.cc.ucf.edu/~rla/fillers/collegeismorethan.htm
Encouraging words.

http://www2.environs.com:443/talbot/liberalarts1.html
Explains why liberal arts education is important for career preparation and life enrichment.

http://www.psych-web.com/mtsite/page6.html
Ideas about goal-setting.

http://www2.environs.com:443/talbot/coping1.html
General strategies for coping with college.

Thriving in the Classroom

CHAPTER 2

College Success Checklist

Place a check mark beside the items that apply to you. Leave the items blank that do not apply to you.

____ I can describe my preferred learning styles.

____ I use strategies for dealing with different teaching styles.

____ I use the course syllabus regularly to organize my work for a course.

____ I usually attend class or try to find out what I missed.

____ I stay focused during class.

____ I make positive contributions to the class.

____ I know how to collaborate with others.

____ I build positive relationships with my instructors.

____ I know what areas I need to improve to be successful in the classroom.

Preview

This chapter will help you learn to make the most of your classroom experiences. You will explore how your own learning style affects how you learn and why some classes are easier for you than others. You will discover how positive behaviors in the classroom facilitate your learning, including how to collaborate effectively with other students during group work. You also will see what it takes to build and maintain strong relationships with instructors.

Chapter Outline

Images of College Success: Robert Fulghum

Exploring Learning Styles
- Defining Learning Styles
- Adapting Learning Styles
- Building Your Learning Portfolio

Making the Class Work
- Creating a Good First Impression
- Being There
- Staying Focused
- Participating in Class
- Stoppers

Collaborating with Others
- Types of Group Work
- Making Groups Work

Relating to Instructors
- The Many Roles of Instructors
- Instructors and Seniority
- Getting to Know Instructors
- Content-Centered Versus Student-Centered Teaching Styles
- Solving Problems with Instructors

Self-Assessments
- 2.1 How Do I Learn Best?: A Learning Style Profile
- 2.2 What Is My Class Participation Style?
- 2.3 How Do I Make Groups Work?

On-Target Tips
- Overcoming Distraction
- Chatterbox Solutions
- Working with Study Partners
- Becoming a Distinctive Student

Images of College Success
Robert Fulghum

Robert Fulghum's amazing writing career started with a column for a newsletter at the church where he was pastor. One of his columns talked about the life-long value of the ideas contained in simple sayings directed toward children. For example, "Share everything," "Play fair," and "Clean up your own mess" were lessons that Fulghum believed to be as important in helping adults get along as they were for children.

A kindergarten teacher in the congregation was so impressed by one essay that she sent it home with the children in her class. One child's parent was a literary agent who thought that Fulghum's writing would have broad appeal in such complex times. She was right. *All I Really Need to Know I Learned in Kindergarten* topped the New York Times hard-cover bestseller list for 96 weeks, followed by the paperback bestseller list for 133 weeks. Fulghum continues to enlighten us by simplifying life's experience in other best-selling, homespun, anecdotal books.

Robert Fulghum, author of the best-selling book *All I Really Need to Know I Learned in Kindergarten.* Did Fulghum really learn everything he needed to know in kindergarten?

Is it true that Fulghum really learned everything he needed to know in kindergarten? No. But his earliest school experiences laid a foundation for the wisdom that would evolve through the rest of his education and his life. Fulghum began at the University of Colorado. Then his father became ill and, to be closer to home, Fulghum transferred to Baylor University. In these and later experiences, he developed a rare capacity to analyze his own experiences and mine them for the simple truths his essays communicate. College also helped him to learn to write and to build the self-discipline to pursue a challenging career as a writer.

The self-described "philosopher of ordinary experience" promotes the use of common sense and kindness to meet the challenges of modern life. His ideas are relevant from the sandbox to the college classroom and beyond. We will adapt many of his simple strategies to make suggestions about how to succeed in the classroom.

Many people look back on the first few months of college as one of the most exciting periods in their lives. Why? Not only did they discover new experiences, ideas, and people, but they discovered new aspects of themselves. Many of these discoveries can happen in the classroom.

Every course, every class will be different, based on such factors as your instructor's teaching style and strategy; your preferences for ways of learning; the nature and difficulty of the course; the learning climate you, your peers, and your instructor create together; and the quality and commitment of everyone in the class.

Let's consider what will help you make the most of your time in the classroom.

> *All this bumbling means something.*
>
> **A. A. Milne**
> **British children's author, 20th century**

Exploring Learning Styles

People differ in how they prefer to learn. These different preferences are sometimes called *learning styles*. Learning styles evolve through formal learning in school and informal learning outside. The classes you will enjoy most are probably the ones that best match your preferred style.

Defining Learning Styles

Learning styles are a learner's preferred methods or formats for acquiring new information and developing intellectual skills. Actually, you may hear the term *learning style* used in several ways throughout your education. Let's examine several different approaches to learning style that may help you identify your preferred kinds of learning experiences.

Sensory Styles Information comes into your awareness through different senses (Skinner, 1997). You may not have many opportunities in college to use your sense of smell and taste as ways to learn. However, hearing, seeing, touching, and moving are different sensory modes that learners may come to prefer. Some people are good *auditory* learners. They can absorb a lecture without much effort. Others may be *visual* learners. Give them a graph, an outline, or a video and they learn more efficiently. People who learn most easily using touch or movement may learn the most in courses that involve physical movement (such as dance class or nursing) or other hands-on experience. They are sometimes called *kinesthetic* learners.

Deep Versus Surface Learning Some courses that you will take in college will be so intriguing that you will be naturally drawn in to understand the course ideas in depth. However, in some courses you may find yourself devoting just enough time and energy to get by. These contrasting examples illustrate *deep* (studying to comprehend the course ideas) versus *surface* (studying the minimum of what needs to be learned) learning styles (Marton, Hounsell, & Entwistle, 1984).

Surface learning styles are much less likely to be successful in college courses. Surface learners are passive. They rely primarily on rote memorization and don't explore how immediate learning in a course may be helpful beyond the classroom. Surface learners tend to be motivated by grades and positive feedback from the teacher. In contrast, deep learners actively construct their learning experiences. They enjoy the process of learning for its own sake (Snow, Corno, & Jackson, 1996).

Learning and Study Strategies Inventory The Learning and Study Strategies Inventory, or LASSI (Weinstein, 1987), describes learning style as preferred strategies for successful learning. This approach was developed at the University of Texas at Austin to help students who were coming to college academically underprepared. LASSI assesses attitude and motivation, time management patterns, anxiety and concentration, study skills (including how to process information from different media, how to select main ideas, and what kinds of study aids to use), and test-preparation and test-taking skills. LASSI can lead to recommendations about strengthening deficient areas.

> *Just knowing has meant everything to me. Knowing has pushed me out into the world, into college, into places, into people.*
>
> **Alice Walker**
> **Contemporary American novelist**

Myers-Briggs Type Indicator Many college success programs evaluate personality factors and thinking styles that influence how people learn. The Myers–Briggs Type Indicator assesses characteristics on four scales (Myers, 1962):

- **Extraversion-Introversion (EI):** Do you focus on the outer world of people or the inner life of ideas? Extraverts like to be the life of the party and enjoy social affairs and connecting with others. By contrast, introverts prefer more solitary activities.

- **Sensing/Intuiting (SN):** Do you like to work with known facts or with possibilities? Sensing persons like to gather lots of information through their senses before taking action. By contrast, intuiting individuals trust their intuition when making up their mind.

- **Thinking/Feeling (TF):** Do you like to evaluate evidence or are you comfortable going with your emotions? Thinkers pride themselves on their ability to systematically reason and resist letting their emotions dictate their conclusions. Feelers trust their emotions. When viewing a play, thinkers might focus on whether the elements of the play make sense while feelers react more emotionally.

- **Judging/Perceiving (JP):** Do you prefer order and planning or spontaneity and flexibility? Judgers are systematic in making judgments and offering criticism. They enjoy logic, debate, and other settings where systematic reasoning can apply. By contrast, perceivers thrive on opportunities to use their perceptions and develop their aesthetic appreciation. They like humanities classes where they can learn about a wide range of opinions and expand their experience.

Taking the Myers–Briggs inventory produces scores on these pairs of qualities and shows which ones you prefer. Each four-letter code designation (for example, *ENTJ* stands for *extraverted–intuitive thinking–judging*) corresponds to an academic style with its own strengths and weaknesses. Many instructors believe that knowing your Myers–Briggs profile can help you anticipate and solve academic problems.

Sternberg's Thinking Styles Robert J. Sternberg (1994, 1997) suggested another set of learning styles that describe how students mentally govern themselves. He associates the dominant styles of thinking in his model with different functions of government: *legislative, executive,* and *judicial.*

Students who prefer a *legislative* style tend to be inventive and nonconforming. They prefer assignments that have minimal structure so they can maximize the individual impact they can have on their work. They like conducting science projects, writing stories, and solving problems in creative ways.

In contrast, students with an *executive* style thrive when given specific instructions about what to do to be successful. For them, unstructured assignments produce chaotic conditions that frustrate them and prevent them from doing their best. They prefer to write papers on topics assigned by the instructor rather than coming up with their own ideas. They like to build models from existing designs or see examples of successful performances rather than breaking new ground.

Those with *judicial* learning styles prefer situations that allow them to demonstrate critical thinking skills. They like to judge and evaluate. They find it easy to spot the flaws in an argument or to do a critical analysis of a work of art or fiction. They prefer sitting in judgment of the work of others to creating new works of their own or following someone else's suggestions.

Kolb's Learning Styles Another popular approach to learning styles was proposed by David Kolb (1984). He suggested that people learn in four different ways:

- Concrete experiencing: learning by being directly involved in a situation
- Reflective observing: looking at the situation and thinking about its meaning
- Abstract conceptualizing: forming theories about why things happen the way they do
- Active experimenting: testing theories by making a plan and carrying it out

Kolb believes that one person may use all four styles. However, over time people tend to prefer certain learning styles over others. These styles reflect the kinds of learning that are more efficient or easier for each person to master. Taking Kolb's *Learning Style Inventory* can help you identify which of the learning styles you prefer. Kolb believes that preference for one learning style over another can roughly predict the majors and even future occupations that college students choose.

If the environment permits it, anyone can learn whatever he chooses to learn.

**Viola Spolin
Contemporary American theater director**

Adapting Learning Styles

Understanding your own learning style can give clues about how to succeed in any classroom. For example, not only will you be more comfortable, but you will probably thrive in classes where the climate appeals to your learning style. Awareness that learning styles differ among their students has prompted many instructors to include different kinds of activities in their courses and to suggest various study strategies that may be helpful for that course. When it is time to register for classes, it's a good idea to invest some time researching which instructors have a teaching style that suits your learning style. Go beyond questions about whether the instructor is "good." Ask *how* they teach. Find out whether the instructor will be a good match for your learning style.

What happens if your learning style does not match your instructor's teaching style? You may have to work hard to develop strategies that bridge the gap. For example, if your instructor simply lectures, you may have to find ways to make your learning more visual or more hands-on. Another strategy is to form a study group with students who have different learning styles so you can benefit from each other's perspectives.

Building Your Learning Portfolio

As noted in Chapter 1, the Learning Portfolio Resources at the end of each chapter reflect five types of learning designed to help you become a deeper learner. The types are a hybrid of many of the learning style systems you just read about. Four of them are discussed in more detail, including the kinds of assignments and courses that promote each learning style, in Table 2.1. Complete Self-Assessment 2.1 to identify your own preferences based on this scheme.

The Learning Portfolio Resources end with **Learning by Planning,** which provides systematic practice in goal-setting and achievement. Regardless of your other learning style preferences, setting realistic goals and planning effective strategies for achieving them can improve your chances of college success.

Table 2-1
Learning Styles

LEARNING BY REFLECTING

Reflective learners are in touch with emotional content in learning. They thrive in classes such as the humanities in which they can learn by observing rather than participating in direct action.

Preferred activities: logs, journals, essay questions, films, and small and large group discussions.

LEARNING BY THINKING CRITICALLY

Careful observation, analyzing relationships, evaluating quality, and making decisions are all components of critical thinking. Classes that are theoretical in nature may be especially effective in promoting critical thinking.

Preferred activities: lecture, writing papers, conducting debates, executing projects, building models, or evaluating theories.

LEARNING BY DOING

Many kinds of classes are ideal for learning by doing. These include science and math classes as well as career-oriented classes, such as business or nursing.

Preferred activities: laboratory work, applied projects, field work, modeling, games and simulations, and problem sets

LEARNING BY THINKING CREATIVELY

Students sometimes neglect their own creativity during college. But chances to think creatively aren't found only in "creative arts" classes.

Preferred activities: writing stories, brainstorming, solving problems in original ways, designing research, creating collages, and making posters.

Making the Class Work

Your earlier experiences in school, from kindergarten through high school, have taught you much about what makes classrooms work. This section explores how your personal presence, concentration, and class participation bolster your learning at the *college* level.

Creating a Good First Impression

College instructors usually assume that you arrive at college already possessing academic common sense. Knowing how to develop positive classroom relationships with instructors is an important part of that common sense. Some guidelines—which sound suspiciously like Robert Fulghum's rules—can help you create a good first impression:

- **Buy the right stuff.** You won't look like a serious student if you don't have the required books. Seriously consider also buying or borrowing the "recommended" books, depending on your priorities.

- **Be prepared.** Prepare *before* class. If you read assignments before class, you will ask better questions and impress your instructors with your motivation to learn. You will also get more out of the lecture or discussion.

- **Do the work on time.** Coping with deadlines is serious business in college. Many students are surprised when they learn that college deadlines are not as flexible as they were in high school.

  If you miss a deadline, you may not be able to negotiate an extension. Most instructors do not extend deadlines to individual students without justification. Many believe that doing so gives an unfair advantage over students who do their work on time.

Common sense is perhaps the most equally divided, but surely the most underemployed, talent in the world.

Christiane Collange
Contemporary French writer

Self-Assessment 2-1

How Do I Learn Best?: A Learning Style Profile

Each choice below captures an aspect of how people prefer to learn. Think about each choice in relation to yourself.

Choose all items that apply. Circle the number in front of the item.

WHEN I HAVE TO LEARN HOW TO OPERATE A NEW PIECE OF EQUIPMENT, I
1. Watch someone who knows how to operate the equipment.
2. Carefully study the owner's manual.
3. Fiddle with the dials until I produce a desired effect.
4. Ignore the instructions and make the equipment suit my purposes.

THE ASPECTS OF LECTURE I APPRECIATE MOST ARE
1. The chance to record the ideas of an expert.
2. A well-constructed argument about a controversial issue.
3. Illustrations using real-life examples.
4. Inspiration to come up with my own vision.

MY CLASS NOTES USUALLY LOOK LIKE
1. Faithful recordings of what the instructor said.
2. Notes embellished with my own questions and evaluations.
3. Outlines that capture key ideas.
4. Notes with drawings, doodles, and other loosely related ideas or images.

I PREFER ASSIGNMENTS THAT INVOLVE
1. Emotional expression.
2. Analysis and evaluation.
3. Solving practical problems.
4. Creative expression.

IN CLASS DISCUSSION
1. I am a watcher rather than a direct participant.
2. I am an active, sometimes argumentative participant.
3. I am an involved discussant, especially related to real-life issues.
4. I like to contribute novel ideas that no one else thinks about.

I WOULD RATHER WORK WITH
1. Stories about individual lives.
2. Abstract ideas.
3. Practical problems.
4. Creative ideas.

MY LEARNING MOTTO IS
1. "Tell me."
2. "Let me think this out for myself."
3. "Let me experiment."
4. "How can I do this uniquely?"

Interpretation: Look over your responses. Use the following code for each question to determine your preferred learning style:

1 = *Learning by reflecting*
2 = *Learning by critical thinking*
3 = *Learning by doing*
4 = *Learning by creative thinking*

The alternative with the most checks is your preferred learning style. You may discover that you strongly favor a particular type of learning over others. Or you may find that your preferences are spread across several categories. Your experiences in college will help you develop your skills in all areas so you will become more flexible and more resourceful.

Amazing but True College Stories

Beyond "The Dog Ate My Paper"

Professor Doug Bernstein (1993) keeps a running tally of excuses students give to get a break from their teachers. Some of his favorites are listed below:

- I can't take the test Friday because my mother is having a vasectomy.
- I had an accident, the police impounded my car, and my paper is in the glove compartment.
- I need to take the final early because the husband of the woman I am seeing is threatening to kill me.
- I can't take the exam on Monday because my mom is getting married on Sunday and I'll be too drunk to drive back to school.
- I broke my nose on my alarm clock when I got up for the exam.
- I had a split brain operation, and the side that knew the answers was not connected to the side that controlled my speech.
- I suffer from multiple personalities and one of my bad personalities threw the good side's paper away.
- My husband recycled my paper. That's why I couldn't hand it in.

UNITED FEATURE SYNDICATE. 200 Park Avenue. New York. N.Y. 10166 (212) 692-3700

Missing deadlines gives an instructor the wrong signal. It suggests that the class is low on your list of priorities. When you do run into difficulties meeting a deadline, notify your instructor as soon as you can to talk about possible options.

- **Use the syllabus.** A course syllabus comprehensively describes how the instructor expects the course to proceed. The syllabus can include the course objectives, reading list, grading policies, and other information that applies throughout the term. When you have questions about the direction of the course, the syllabus can help you see what lies ahead.

   The syllabus also can give hints about the instructor's unique point of view and insights about what is most important. It may contain helpful hints on how to study for the tests. Some instructors hold students responsible for reading all materials listed in the syllabus. This can be a surprise at test time if you thought that your class notes would be enough.

- **Play straight.** The syllabus may or may not discuss cheating or other moral issues. However, your college's student handbook will outline the code for academic integrity on your campus. If you are caught violating this code, you face a range of unpleasant consequences, from severe (expulsion from school) to more lenient (zero on the work submitted).

- **Stay cool.** The best classes run on respectful and civil behavior. Respect does *not* mean that you cannot challenge or ask questions. In fact, many instructors (but not all) regard student questions as an essential part of classroom learning. However, all instructors expect participation to be civil (calm, polite, and efficient rather than prolonged, pointless, or profane). Table 2.2, "How to Get on the Wrong Side of an Instructor," describes other behaviors that can get in the way.

Being There

Tom couldn't believe it when the alarm went off. He felt like he'd just gone to bed. He had meant to read the chapter for his introductory biology class last night but then he met that interesting woman when he went for coffee. Because he didn't read the assignment and his instructor had not scheduled a quiz, Tom thought, "I'll just sleep in and try to catch up on the reading later."

College involves a higher level of personal responsibility than most students experienced in high school. This freedom can be alluring and intoxicating.

Table 2-2
How to Get on the Wrong Side of an Instructor

Some behaviors that disturb and distract instructors and students alike (Appleby, 1990).

BEHAVIORS THAT SHOW QUESTIONABLE MATURITY
- Talking during lectures
- Chewing gum, eating, or drinking noisily
- Being late and leaving early
- Creating disturbances
- Wearing hats
- Putting feet on desks or tables
- Being insincere or "brown-nosing"
- Complaining about work load
- Acting like a know-it-all
- Wearing headphones

BEHAVIORS THAT SHOW INATTENTION
- Sleeping during class
- Cutting class
- Acting bored or apathetic
- Not paying attention
- Being unprepared
- Packing up books and materials before class is over
- Asking already-answered questions
- Sitting in the back rows when there are empty seats in front
- Obviously yawning
- Slouching in seats
- Asking "Did we do anything important?" after missing class
- Not asking questions
- Doing work for other classes in class
- Reading the newspaper in class

MISCELLANEOUS IRRITATING BEHAVIORS
- Cheating
- Asking "Will this be on the test?"
- Being more interested in grades than learning
- Pretending to understand
- Blaming teachers for poor grades
- Giving unbelievable excuses
- Wearing tasteless T-shirts

Especially when instructors do not require attendance, you may be tempted to skip classes.

Occasionally you may have to miss a class. Make arrangements then to copy someone else's notes. Exchange phone numbers now with a friend in class as part of a backup system.

Skipping classes frequently is dangerous to your well-being in a class. One problem is that you may come to over-rely on borrowing notes from others. Class notes are highly personal. What the instructor says in class is filtered, and perhaps distorted, by the note-taker. Even when you know for certain that the student who took the notes is a superb listener, you almost certainly will get less from borrowed notes than from being there and taking your own.

If you do not come to class, most instructors believe that you put your learning at risk by losing the chance to participate in active learning experiences, missing hints about which information is most likely to show up on tests, and preventing the instructor from getting to know you (in classes where this is possible). Another reason to avoid missing classes is financial. Do the calculations in Table 2.3 to determine how much money you waste each time you miss a class. Ouch! When you think about how much time it takes to earn that amount of money, it seems foolish to waste it by choosing to skip class.

Another compelling reason for attending class is that it affects your grades. One research study compared the absentee patterns of successful students (grades of B and above) and unsuccessful students (grades C and below) (Lindgren, 1969). The results were not surprising. Successful students regularly attended class; 84% of those who got B or above made a habit of going to class.

Staying Out of the Pits

Ask It This Way

When you cannot attend a class, don't ask your instructor, *"Did I miss anything important?"* Although your question may be innocent, your instructor may hear something entirely different. Your question implies that your instructor regularly spends time on unimportant information or trivial detail. Instead, ask *"Can I make up any of the work I missed during my absence from class?"* Or you can talk with a peer to help you get caught up.

Table 2-3 The Cost of Cutting Class

How much tuition did you pay for this term?

How many credits must you take on your campus to be considered full-time?

Divide the full-time hours into your tuition dollars (cost per credit hour):

How many hours is the course you are most tempted to avoid?

Multiply the course credit hours by the cost per credit hour (cost of the course):

How many classes meet in this course over the term?

Divide the cost of the course by the number of classes:

The final calculation represents the financial loss that happens every time you cut this class.

Fewer than half of the students who did not attend regularly were able to achieve a B or better.

Staying Focused

Poor concentration can have many causes. For example, you might feel distracted because

- You are thinking too much about your classmates or worried about what they think of you
- You think the course has limited value to you, especially if it is outside your major
- You may not be as healthy or well-rested as you need to be
- You dislike the instructor or the ideas being presented

Of course, you won't be able to focus if you are using class time to catch up on other obligations, such as doing homework for your next class.

The key to concentration is staying actively involved with the course. Think of the instructor's input as one end of a conversation: Debate with the instructor in your notes, capture the key ideas in your own words, and come up with your own examples.

Daydreaming can be costly. Some is normal. If you find that you daydream so much that you have trouble tracking what is going on, you'll need to take steps to deal with it. "Overcoming Distraction" suggests what you can do to overcome daydreaming and improve your concentration.

Participating in Class

Instructors have different goals regarding student participation. Some expect you to concentrate on listening, thinking, and taking notes. Others want you to be actively involved in other ways as well. Participating in various ways will develop your academic skills. Asking or responding to questions can make a class much more worthwhile for you and your classmates. Questions and answers help you

- **Practice relevant course concepts.** When you contribute concept-based comments to the discussion, you show that you are integrating the course ideas in how you think.
- **Make appropriate links to past class experience, other courses, or current events.** This, too, reinforces your learning.
- **Identify and clarify confusing ideas.** Your tactful questions can expose confusion and lead to better explanations. Other members of the class will appreciate this, as may your instructor.
- **Illustrate concepts with relevant but brief personal experience.** Personal stories sometimes can add a dimension to concepts that make them easier to learn. However, such experiences must be brief and clearly relevant.
- **Offer criticism.** Some instructors present controversial material to promote critical thinking. Others don't. However, even if they don't, you may be able to offer critical thinking responses at other appropriate times in the course. For example, you can respond to an instructor's request for feedback, comment about a flawed

theory, or challenge others to back up their opinions with evidence or reasoning.

- **Stimulate further relevant discussion.** The value of some students' comments may not be clear at first. If your comments cause others to join in, that may improve the quality of the class. Sometimes even wrong answers can clarify confusing ideas or prompt further important discussions.

Stoppers

Some "contributions" hinder rather than help a class. For example, when a student or instructor acts aggressively, learning suffers. It is hard to concentrate on the subject at hand when the air bristles with bad feelings, regardless of who is angry.

Some instructors clearly are hostile to students. They may be disappointed in how their students are responding to class. They may have become disenchanted with college teaching and may take it out on their students. The hostility can be expressed in formidable assignments, harsh grades, or belittling remarks.

Students also show hostility in the classroom. They may be disappointed with the quality of the class. They may feel overwhelmed by the work and angry at instructors they hold responsible for their stress. Students demonstrate hostility in a number of ways, including angry remarks, threatening behavior, skipping class, or stony silence.

If you feel the urge to attack, take a deep breath. Focus on the course content rather than on class dynamics. Steer clear of aggressive tactics (attacking, insulting, judging, swearing) that increase social discomfort.

What can you do if your anger distracts from your performance in the course? Think about talking directly to the source of your anger, whether this is your instructor or some other person. You may be able to avoid hostile climates by asking about instructors' reputations before you register for classes. Choose the ones who are well-respected for their considerate attitudes toward students.

Some students, though not hostile, reflect a need to dominate and use the classroom like a stage. They feel obliged to answer every question in a relentless, driven fashion. Students who overwhelm the class probably need feedback from the instructor and their classmates to hold back and let others participate. Check the frequency of your own contributions and hold back when you find yourself doing most of the talking. Education should not be a solo act. It should be an ensemble.

Some students forget that a classroom is a formal place. They may tell stories in too much detail or they may take discussion in obscure directions that other members of the class can't or do not want to go. When you contribute to the class, pay attention to the body language of your classmates and the instructor. If others get restless, lose interest, or avoid eye contact, perhaps you should tell the moral of the story first and then forget the story.

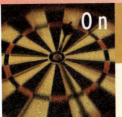

On Target Tips

Overcoming Distraction

- *Sit near the front.* If you cannot see or hear clearly, move until you can.
- *Eliminate distractions in the environment.* If other noise develops, take action. Close windows or doors to shut out distraction. The instructor may not realize the level of interference in the room.
- *Reduce the pressures that are pulling you off task.* Write down unrelated concerns separately from your notes so that you can address them later.
- *Practice stress management.* Develop and use some stress management strategies to clear your mind when you need to concentrate.
- *Try not to shut down when you don't like what you hear.* When you are distressed by lecture content or delivery style, try to concentrate on identifying more precisely what bothers you and what you can challenge. You also can try to focus on hearing what you most likely will be tested on.
- *Track your progress.* Keep regular track of how much time you are paying attention. At the end of each class, use the upper right-hand corner of your notes to record an estimate of what percentage of time you were on track. As you practice concentrating, notice your progress.

To ask questions of a wise person is the beginning of wisdom.

German proverb

Surprised

Where Do Your Daydreams Take You?

The work of one instructor documented how extensive daydreaming can be (Adler & Towne, 1996). During lecture, he randomly fired a gun (of course, he used blanks!) to ask his students to record what they were thinking about at that moment.

The results? At any random point in the lecture, only 20% were paying attention to the activities of the class. Only 12% were listening actively. Others were reminiscing (20%) and thinking erotic thoughts (20%). The rest were thinking about things outside class, reflecting on religious concerns, or anticipating lunch.

Interrupting is another dominating behavior. When a person interrupts, the negative impact appears in the angry or disorganized responses of others. Interruptions may cause the prior speaker to lose track of a point. If you tend to interrupt others, monitor your patterns more closely. Learn to pause before speaking. The pause may give you time to improve your contribution.

Some students lean out of their seats and vigorously wave, wanting to be called on first. This is inappropriate in college. If you tend to do this, compare your behavior to how others are acting in class. Lowering your intensity will help the class as a whole to feel a little more relaxed.

Speaking up in class is a painful prospect for many students, just as teaching or leading a class is a challenge for a new instructor. It is especially painful for people who are shy, who lack confidence in their ideas, or who have been hurt by past experiences in the classroom. If you have trouble expressing yourself or refuse to talk in class, confer with your instructor about your doubts. Then negotiate an agreement to participate in a manner that the instructor thinks is reasonable. For example, some sympathetic instructors may be willing to give you questions ahead of time. This gives you time to compose an answer that you feel comfortable contributing to the class.

Keep a public focus while in the classroom. Whether they occur during lecture or during class discussions, private chats disrupt the classroom. The noise makes hearing difficult for everyone. The instructor has no way of knowing whether the private chat is course-related; most assume otherwise. See "Chatterbox Solutions" for some ways to avoid getting drawn into these situations.

To assess your current participation patterns, complete Self-Assessment 2.2.

It may be intimidating to ask a question in class, but after you have done it once, it feels less scary to do it again.

Self-Assessment 2-2

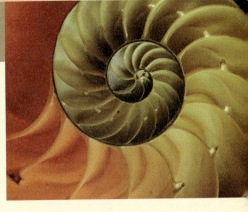

What Is My Class Participation Style?

Think about your own style of participation in classes that encourage student contributions. Review the behaviors below and mark the column that represents how you tend to be.

	USUALLY LIKE ME	SOMETIMES LIKE ME	NEVER LIKE ME
Positive contributions: When I speak in class . . .			
I talk directly about the ideas and concepts I am learning in the course.	_____	_____	_____
I make appropriate links to past class experience, other courses, or current events.	_____	_____	_____
I apply course ideas to new situations.	_____	_____	_____
I usually try to identify and clarify confusing ideas.	_____	_____	_____
I tell brief personal experiences that illustrate course concepts.	_____	_____	_____
I show critical thinking about the course.	_____	_____	_____
I try to stimulate further relevant discussion with my comments.	_____	_____	_____
Negative contributions: When I speak in class . . .			
People act like I have said something attacking or hostile.	_____	_____	_____
I talk more than everyone else in class.	_____	_____	_____
I lose track of the point I originally started to make.	_____	_____	_____
I find it hard to resist talking to classmates during class.	_____	_____	_____
I am so eager to speak in class that classmates tease me about my intensity.	_____	_____	_____
I don't participate in class discussion.	_____	_____	_____

As you review these patterns, which ones do you need to change the most? Consider having a peer rate you on these participation styles to see whether your perceptions match.

Collaborating with Others

Working in groups adds a vital element to your education. It improves your ability to communicate, develops your project skills, and makes you better at dealing with conflict. This section describes what you can do to make group work efficient and effective.

Types of Group Work

Working with your peers can take many forms. Instructors may ask you to join a group discussion during class or assign you to a project group outside of class.

On Target Tips

Chatterbox Solutions

What can you do if your urge to talk to a classmate interferes with your ability to stay on track? You can

- Defer your discussion until after class. Make a note to jog your memory about the topic.
- Move away from your companion.
- Imagine that your instructor can hear exactly what you are saying.
- Translate your social impulse toward one person to consideration for the whole class.

They also may ask you and a classmate to confer briefly to share reactions with each other about some concept presented in class.

Brainstorming Brainstorming is group work that combines both divergent thinking (exploring different points of view) and convergent thinking (working toward a consensus or shared solution). In the initial stages of brainstorming, group members

- Come up with as many ideas as possible
- Keep all ideas on the table without dismissing any ideas as too crazy
- Postpone criticizing anyone's ideas
- Expand on the ideas of other members

Once the group has generated a lot of ideas, members can judge their quality, narrow the options, and work to solve a problem. Brainstorming can be stimulating, sometimes even wild. The playful momentum of the group encourages everyone's creativity.

Study Groups Study groups tend to be convergent and task-oriented. You do not have to wait for an instructor to convene a study group. Recruit interested classmates to meet regularly and talk about a challenging course. Your commitment to your classmates will help motivate you to stay on top of the coursework. Your group discussions can help you identify key concepts and confusing ideas to pursue with your instructor in the next class. "Working with Study Partners" offers some ideas on how to structure study groups.

Making Groups Work

Whether the group is working on a 10-minute discussion project in class or a challenge that spans several weeks, effective groups usually work in stages. Three common stages are described here (Alverno College Faculty, 1994; see Figure 2.1).

Planning the Task As the group convenes, members lay the groundwork for working together efficiently by doing four things:

- Introduce group members and the purpose of meeting ("Who are we? Why are we here?")
- Agree on goals and objectives ("What tasks do we need to do?")
- Create a plan for working together ("How can we work together efficiently?")
- Set criteria for success ("How will we know we have succeeded in our task?")

Completing the Task Once the ground rules have been established, your group can shift to addressing the specific task at hand. Although leadership does not have to be appointed formally, usually group members who ask questions to move the group along assume leadership. As differences of opinion emerge, your group may encounter conflicts. When it does, members can advocate their own viewpoints, ask for clarifications, or mediate disputes between other members.

University of Texas at Austin professor Philip Treisman. His research found that collaborative learning strategies helped ethnic minority students succeed in math and science classes.

Evaluating the Results In the final stage of the discussion, your group should summarize what has been accomplished and evaluate whether the group has been successful. Examine how well the group has performed so you can improve its efficiency in the future. You also may need to plan another meeting or plan how the group will communicate its findings.

Group work can provide some of your most exciting learning—and some of your most frustrating. When you join with others to solve a problem or explore the meaning of a work of art, your pooled brainpower can result in insights you might never have had on your own. Effective groups tend to bring out the best in their members. However, people regularly have problems being effective in groups. Table 2.4 describes some common problems and what to do about them.

To explore the ways you can help a group meet its objectives, complete Self-Assessment 2.3.

On Target Tips

Working with Study Partners

Involving others to explore course ideas with you can improve your college success. Several ways your study group can approach the material from a course are

- Identify the hardest concepts or ideas you have encountered.
- Talk about the problems or ideas you especially like or dislike.
- Discuss which parts of the readings interest you the most.
- Help group members share and clarify their understanding of the material.
- Discuss strategies for remembering course material.
- Generate questions from course content to prepare for testing.

Relating to Instructors

Before your education is over, you will have all kinds of instructors. They will vary not only in their disciplines, but also in their enthusiasm, competence, warmth, eccentricities, and humor. Some will clearly demonstrate their concern

Planning the task → Completing the task → Evaluating the results

Figure 2-1 Three Stages of Effective Group Collaboration. Efficient groups accomplish their work in three stages: planning how they will work together, solving the problem or exchanging points of view, and reviewing the quality of their work, which may include planning for future meetings.

Table 2-4
Common Problems and Sensible Solutions in Groups

PROBLEM	SOLUTION
Failing to do ground work Group members may be so eager to get on with the task that they jump right into a chaotic and unsatisfying discussion.	**Establish some ground rules** Your group will collaborate more efficiently if you have a clear picture of what the group wants to achieve and how you hope to achieve it.
Rushing to consensus When group members are not very invested in the task, they may be uncritical and hasty in completing it.	**Ask for commitment to good work** Point out that slowing down might produce better results than a hasty discussion.
Avoiding conflict Some groups become disorganized as disagreements emerge. Conflict is valuable because differences of opinion can lead to a better-quality discussion or well-considered solution.	**Legitimize difference of opinion** When conflict emerges, ask group members to support their opinions with evidence. Let the quality of support persuade the group.
Committing groupthink Groupthink occurs when group members yield to pressure to agree publicly with a position when they disagree privately. They may not want to rock the boat.	**Play the devil's advocate** Announce your intention to play devil's advocate. Search for anything that is being left out of consideration. Detect flaws that have not been identified yet.
Failing to involve all members When groups are large and some members take charge, shy or unprepared members may be less likely to participate.	**Specify useful roles** Ask quiet members to serve the group by taking notes or summarizing the key ideas. Ask them directly about their opinions.
Allowing domination Sometimes leaders push too hard and end up alienating other group members. They may not recognize the value of involving all members to improve the quality of the group's conclusion.	**Ask for space and cooperation** When leaders get too pushy, suggest that other members need more time and space to express their ideas. If this gentle confrontation does not work, be more forceful. Point out what the group may lose when some don't participate.
Tolerating off-task behavior Less committed members may engage in behaviors (such as popping gum) that distract from the working climate of the group.	**Ask for concentrated effort** Suggest that the offending person change the behavior to help promote a more favorable, quiet working environment.
Preparing inadequately When discussions are sluggish, you may suspect that preparation has been lax. If there are no consequences for good or bad preparation, conditions are ripe for chronic underpreparation.	**Challenge the intention** Ask members how they intend to help the group. Your requests may be unsuccessful at that time, but their embarrassment may motivate preparation for the next group meeting.
Coping with coasters Some group members may not contribute once they sense that the group will succeed by the work of the more energetic or motivated members.	**Clarify expectations** Express your disappointment and anger about the unfair distribution of work. Propose some consequences for those who aren't doing their fair share.
Running out of time Deadlines can creep up fast, especially if you don't have time to do project work in class, where it would be most convenient.	**Plan a process calendar** Work backward from the due date to give yourself ample time to complete all the steps. Plan to meet outside class for best results.
Circumventing trouble-makers Many students appeal to teachers to reconfigure the groups so that their new group (without the trouble-maker) can get along and get the task done smoothly.	**Focus on the task at hand** You don't have to love your group members to do effective work. However, you need to establish ground rules for respect in groups where there are personality conflicts.

> *Muddle is the extra unknown personality in any committee.*
>
> **Anthony Sampson**
> **Contemporary British social historian**

about helping you succeed. Others may appear indifferent. Often this is because they are swamped by other commitments that come with a college faculty job.

The Many Roles of Instructors

For many faculty, their role as instructor is their number-one priority. Many people who choose college teaching are dedicated to helping students learn. They enjoy watching their students develop new perspectives. However, even when

Self-Assessment 2-3

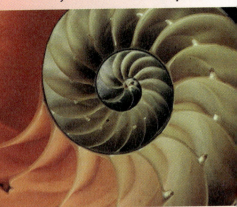

How Do I Make Groups Work?

You can do many things to help the group achieve its goals. Based on your past experiences in groups of all kinds, which of the following are you likely to do when you are in college groups?

	I do this regularly	I do this sometimes	I have not done this
I form groups to solve problems.	___	___	___
I arrange where a group should meet.	___	___	___
I propose the group goals.	___	___	___
I show leadership in moving the group in different directions.	___	___	___
I focus on bringing out the opinions of quieter members.	___	___	___
I challenge other members to defend their ideas.	___	___	___
I keep track of the time and let the group know how much time is left.	___	___	___
I monitor the group's progress toward the goal.	___	___	___
I mediate disputes between group members.	___	___	___
I summarize the agreements we have made.	___	___	___
I advocate for the ideas that are the best.	___	___	___
I make sure everyone understands our objective.	___	___	___
I keep track of what is happening and report these events to the group.	___	___	___
I praise other people's positive contributions.	___	___	___
I evaluate the effectiveness of our decisions.	___	___	___
I challenge misbehavior to keep the group on track.	___	___	___
I thank group members for their hard work and contributions.	___	___	___

If you checked off that you regularly do the things that help groups move toward their goals, you are demonstrating the kind of leadership that will make you a strong collaborator. You may notice that you contribute some things regularly to groups but still have some room to grow in strengthening your leadership skills. If you mostly checked the column on the right, there are many ways in which you can improve. Start with skills that are less demanding. For example, make it a point to keep track of the time for the group or praise the positive contributions of others. Once you feel comfortable making contributions at this level, you can increase the level of challenge in the goals you set for yourself.

their interest in teaching is genuine, instructors are most likely to take a special interest in students who show enthusiasm for the course and take their work seriously.

Some instructors, especially at universities where classes are large, may seem more invested in their role as researchers in their disciplines. These instructors may be assigned to teach fewer classes to enable them to conduct research and secure grants to help earn funds for the college. For this reason, many classes at larger schools may be staffed by graduate assistants who are supervised by regular faculty.

Many community colleges and liberal arts colleges are known for high-quality teaching. Both types of colleges usually claim effective teaching as central to their missions. However, teaching loads are often heavier in these institutions. For example, some community college instructors may teach 15 or more credits per term.

Faculty roles also involve other tasks to keep the college functioning. Many instructors serve as advisors to help students design their academic paths, learn efficiently, and prepare for the future. Some instructors provide service to the college by participating on committees, such as Admissions, or raise funds for the college. Others may donate time to the nearby community through public service, or sit on the board of directors of a nonprofit agency. Some instructors are active in professional groups within their disciplines. And just like you, instructors have full personal lives. As you can probably guess, your instructors are busy even when they are not in the classroom.

Instructors and Seniority

As you get to know the faculty, you may be able to distinguish instructors who have been around for a while from those who are new. Members of the faculty include senior instructors, junior faculty who are in their first few years, and part-time (adjunct) instructors who have temporary appointments (Leatherman, 1997). Students sometimes report frustration in asking questions about the campus to instructors, who may have as little experience with the college as the students do.

Most liberal arts colleges and universities use a ranking system for their faculty that reflects seniority and responsibility. For example, a full-time faculty member may be an assistant, associate, or full professor. Faculty members get promotions from one level to the next based on their teaching quality, research productivity, and service to the community. Many faculty earn *tenure*, which means that the person has secured a valued and virtually permanent place on the faculty.

On some campuses, academic rank is meaningful and prominent. For example, instructors may list their rank on their course syllabi. Some senior faculty may even expect you to show more deference to them based on their rank and status. On other campuses, especially at community colleges, academic ranks don't mean as much. In fact, academic rank may not be conferred at all.

Getting to Know Instructors

Regardless of their rank or seniority, many instructors enjoy getting to know who you are. Instructors respond most positively to students who show interest and enthusiasm for their courses. If you get into a jam later in the term, instructors have

> *Knowing and learning are communal acts. They require a continual cycle of discussion, disagreement, and consensus over what it all means.*
>
> **Parker Palmer**
> **Contemporary American sociologist**

an easier time cutting some slack for students who have been responsive and responsible. When test scores fall between two grades, students who seem to care about their work are the ones who are bumped up instead of down. However, other advantages of getting to know your instructors may be even more important. Research indicates that seeking contact with faculty outside the classroom is associated with staying in college and graduating with honors (Astin, 1993).

How can you help your instructors take a special interest in your intellectual growth? "Becoming a Distinctive Student" gives some tips.

Is it possible to get acquainted with your instructors in large classes? Although it may be challenging, the answer is yes. By asking intelligent questions during class or visiting during office hours, chances are good you will stand out even *more* in very large classes. If you have an assignment in this course to interview an instructor, it can help you start to get to know one instructor on an informal basis.

Content-Centered Versus Student-Centered Teaching Styles

Instructors differ in their teaching styles and the learning climates they foster (Duffy & Jones, 1995). Some instructors are *content-centered*. They typically use lectures as the major way of transmitting knowledge. The learning climate in lecture-based courses tends to be highly structured, paced by the lecturer's strategy for covering material in a meaningful way. Instructors expect that students will faithfully reproduce the material covered in their notes in test situations. The majority of college classes are taught using the lecture method (Svinicki & Dixon, 1986).

Other instructors are *student-centered*. They focus mainly on developing students' intellectual growth using active learning strategies to promote collaboration (Silverman, 1997). They may use small group discussions, film clips, and student performances to draw in students with differing learning styles. Their classes may be more spontaneous because they are willing to depart from their plans if they think a new direction serves their students.

Students tend to fare better in certain classroom climates than others. For example, if you are really good at memorizing and critical thinking, then you may prefer the structure and efficiency of a lecture, the content-centered approach. When you find yourself in student-centered classes that feel less comfortable, impose as much structure on the experience as possible to make it more consistent with your own learning preference. Outline your reading. Try to anticipate what the class will cover. Form a study group to work systematically on the course ideas.

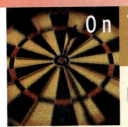

On Target Tips

Becoming a Distinctive Student

Some strategies for distinguishing yourself as a student with academic promise are:

- ***Sit in the front.*** The most motivated and interested students often sit close to the instructor to minimize distractions and create the opportunity for informal discussion before or after class.

- ***Bring articles or clippings to class related to the course.*** Instructors like to see you make independent connections between what you are learning and your life outside the classroom. They may incorporate your ideas into the class and remember you for making the contribution.

- ***Take advantage of existing opportunities to get to know your instructors informally.*** On some campuses, faculty sponsor informal gatherings to help you network with others. You also can join student interest clubs with faculty sponsors. These are great opportunities to get to know the faculty as people.

- ***Visit during your instructor's office hours.*** Most instructors identify their office hours when the course begins. Check in with your instructor about something you found interesting or were confused about from class discussion. Ask the instructor to review your notes to see whether your note-taking skills are on-target.

- ***Use e-mail to connect, if that is an option.*** Many instructors like to communicate with their students via e-mail. This is a great option if you tend to be shy or if the instructor seems hard to approach.

- ***Actively seek a mentor.*** After you engage an instructor's interest in you, find out about the instructor's availability to serve as your mentor, someone who can give you guidance beyond the classroom and help you find other opportunities to develop. This can be the most meaningful connection you will make in college.

Feeling *Good*

About Making the Connection

Think about the instructors whose classes you have this term. Now select the one you think might be hardest to talk to. Check your syllabus for that instructor's office hours. Then go. Ask the instructor to clarify a point that is confusing or share an insight you have gotten that related to class. Most instructors are surprised that more students don't take advantage of office hours. Once you have made a connection to the "tough" instructor, building a positive relationship with your other instructors will be a piece of cake!

If you learn best when you have the opportunity to apply course concepts to practical examples, then student-centered approaches probably will appeal more to you. When you find yourself in a content-centered or lecture-based class, you may need to make systematic notes during the course, but work with the notes more creatively when you study. Using study strategies that are more consistent with your learning style may help your learning to endure longer.

Solving Problems with Instructors

If you are lucky, you may not have to solve relationship problems with your instructors. However, four problems may prompt you to take self-protective action:

- When there is a serious mismatch between your abilities and the level of the course
- When appropriate personal boundaries with instructors are challenging to manage
- When you and your instructor disagree about the completion status of your work
- When you need to make a complaint about an instructor's actions

Mismatch   Courses sometimes are unsatisfying because the instructor does not teach at a level the students can handle. In some of these courses students feel overwhelmed by an instructor who is talking over their heads. In other cases, instructors offer too little challenge and students feel cheated out of learning.

To resolve either problem, first talk with your classmates to verify that others are struggling, too. Then (preferably with one or two other concerned students) request an appointment with the instructor and present your concerns directly. Many instructors will be pleased with your initiative and grateful for the feedback. Others will be less enthusiastic but can give you suggestions about how cope with their demands. If you can't resolve the mismatch through talking with the instructor, consider withdrawing from the course and taking it again later with a different instructor.

Managing Boundaries   Most instructors give clear signals about how and when they can be contacted. Instructors usually have office hours. They can and should respond to student questions or concerns during those periods as part of their professional responsibilities.

Instructors differ in their enthusiasm about being contacted outside class or office hours. Some provide home phone numbers and encourage you to call whenever you have questions. Others request not to be disturbed at home because they want to separate their professional and personal lives. It is easy to see how students get confused about how and when to contact their instructors. If your instructors have not specified that they can be reached at home, use memos, voice mail, office hour visits, or questions after class to ask questions or maintain contact.

Friendships between instructors and students pose an especially complex boundary problem. Many instructors believe that friendship with students is a bad idea. They don't want to do anything that could compromise their objectivity. Other instructors believe that they can be objective in their grading even if they are evaluating the work of a student-friend. Friendships can sometimes go awry even among people with the best intentions. A general self-protective

> *The university is not engaged in making ideas safe for students. It is engaged in making students safe for ideas.*
>
> **Clark Kerr**
> **Former president**
> **of Stanford University**

strategy is to avoid friendships with instructors as long they have power to make decisions that could affect your progress in college, since friendships can go away.

Keeping Copies of Your Work When an instructor and student dispute whether work has been completed, the burden of proof falls on the student. Get in the habit of making copies of your papers. Then, if a paper gets lost or misplaced, you can easily replace it. Keep returned projects in a safe place so you can retrieve them if the instructor has failed to record and grade them. When the term is over and your instructor has filed your grades, retain your best work for your academic portfolio. This will help you track your progress over time and will give you samples that may help in future job applications.

Making Complaints You have several options when you are upset by an instructor's conduct. First, recognize that the instructor is the authority in the class. The instructor usually has a longer history at the college than you have. A longer history and academic credentials do not mean that the instructor's actions cannot be criticized. But weigh carefully whether you are upset enough that it is worthwhile to proceed when the instructor holds greater power and probably more credibility.

If you think you should complain, start by explaining your concerns directly to the instructor. Ask for an appointment. Present your concern and offer evidence that supports it. If this is unsuccessful, appeal in writing for assistance to the instructor's immediate supervisor. In most cases, this supervisor is the department head or coordinator, who will hear you out and determine what next steps to take. If the supervisor fails to take action and you still need further resolution, ask for an appointment with that person's supervisor, most likely the academic dean. At each stage of the chain of command, the person will ask what attempts you have made already to resolve the problem before attempting to do anything further about it.

As one cautionary note, you are unlikely to have much luck appealing a final grade unless you can identify a specific error in the instructor's judgment. Most colleges regard instructors as the final authority in grading and rarely or never overturn their grades.

If you have a complaint about a class, start by talking directly with your instructor. By describing the problem and offering your interpretation, you may be able to solve the problem quickly and fairly.

Summary Tips For Mastering College

Thriving in the Classroom

Exploring Learning Preferences
1. Work to understand your own learning preferences. This will help to you cope with the variety of assignments you will encounter.
2. Try to adapt your learning strategies in situations that are not a perfect match for your learning style.
3. Accept and muster some enthusiasm for assignments that stretch your style or ability. This will help you develop intellectual flexibility.

Making the Class Work
1. Prepare for classes to engage your instructors' interest in your learning. Keep up with your reading, ask questions, show curiosity about class activities, and refer to your syllabus for help.
2. Work with your instructor and classmates to build a positive environment in the classroom. Everyone in the class must be responsible for making it a good experience.
3. Attend class regularly. Asking others to take notes for you puts your grade and your learning at risk.
4. Identify and eliminate distractions that interfere with your concentration. Some daydreaming is normal. Don't let it get out of control.
5. Watch your peers and instructor to determine whether your contributions are well-received. Compare how students respond to your input versus the input of others. Get an idea of your impact.

Collaborating with Others
1. Form study groups to understand and learn course concepts. Don't wait for the instructor to suggest this option.
2. Make ground rules for groups to improve efficiency. Assign roles, plan your tasks, and set criteria for meeting your goals.
3. Tolerate conflict to improve the quality of group conclusions. Differences of opinion can produce better solutions.

Relating to Instructors
1. Recognize that instructors differ in how much they enjoy the classroom. Most will be interested in helping you grow intellectually even if they don't always act that way.
2. Expect that your instructors will be diverse in age, seniority on campus, duties on campus, and teaching style. Ask your advisor or experienced students about an instructor before you register for the class. Read syllabi carefully for hints about instructors' styles and preferences. Get to know them informally if you can.
3. Act self-protectively when you develop a conflict with an instructor. Maintain good records about your completed work and avoid developing friendships that could compromise your progress.
4. Follow established procedures if you make a formal complaint against an instructor. Talk first with the instructor. If that does not solve the problem, talk with the instructor's supervisor.

✓ College Success Checklist

Have your views changed about any of the following items since you filled out this checklist at the beginning of the chapter? Place a check mark beside any item for which you feel good about your current practice. Also check any for which you have new ideas about how to improve.

____ I can describe my preferred learning styles.

____ I use strategies for dealing with different teaching styles.

____ I use the course syllabus regularly to organize my work for a course.

____ I usually attend class or try find out what I missed.

____ I stay focused during class.

____ I make positive contributions to the class.

____ I know how to collaborate with others.

____ I build positive relationships with my instructors.

____ I know what arewwas I need to improve to be successful in the classroom.

In the space below, list the items that you still need to work on the most. This list may help you complete the goal-setting exercise in the Learning Portfolio.

Review Questions

1 What are some ways in which learning styles have been defined?

2 What are some strategies for getting your instructor to take an interest in your learning?

3 What happens in the three stages of effective group work?

4 What are some strategies for overcoming problems that interfere with group effectiveness and efficiency?

5 What are some typical problems that occur between student and instructor and how can you solve them?

Learning Portfolio

Learning by Reflecting... Journal Entries

Changing Your Investment
Review the results of Self-Assessment 2.2 on your class participation style. Most students have some room for improvement. Select two behaviors that you think you should improve to make a better investment in the class. Describe what strategies you could use to make those improvements. What risks are involved? What might you gain? What might you lose?

What Did You Learn in Kindergarten?
You have already invested many years in your education. Think about the kinds of classroom experiences you had before college.
- How are college classes similar to your earlier educational experiences?
- How are they different?
- Are teachers different in college than at earlier levels?
- Will any lessons from kindergarten, grade school, or high school serve you well in college?

The Deep End of the Pool
You probably recognized when you read about deep and surface learning that how comfortable you are as a learner may depend on the context. For example, you may easily comprehend complex ideas in a subject that you find intrinsically interesting. When subjects don't intrigue you, your efforts may feel shallow.

Think about the courses you are registered for this semester:
- In which ones are you likely to be a natural deep learner?
  _____
  _____
- Which ones are more likely to produce shallow learning where you will probably do just enough to get by?
  _____
  _____
- What implications does this have for how you plan to study?
  _____
  _____

Learning by Doing... Action Projects

Interviewing a Teacher
Arrange a 30-minute appointment with one of your instructors during the instructor's office hour. Tell your instructor that your task is to get to know more about the instructor. The topics you may want to cover include
- How did the instructor become interested in teaching?
- What is the instructor's educational philosophy?
- What kind of research or special scholarship interests does the instructor pursue?
- What does the instructor especially like about this learning environment?
- What interests do you and the instructor have in common?

Write a report of your interview for your portfolio or give a short speech on what you learned.

Reviewing a Syllabus
Consult the syllabus from the course you expect to be your most difficult. Examine it carefully. Try to make predictions about how the class will proceed based on the hints offered in the syllabus. For example:
- How labor-intensive will the course be?
- Where will the peak periods of effort occur?
- How student-centered is the instructor?
- How flexible will the instructor be if you have trouble?
- What are some good strategies for preparing for exams?

Social Engineering
Select a group that meets to complete a task and watch them work. What recommendations would you give them about how to improve their group dynamics?
- Did they define their task clearly enough at the outset of the meeting?
- Was the leadership in the group adequate for the task?
- Did they work efficiently or waste time being off-task?
- Could the quality of their decisions have been improved?
- Did they complete the task in the allotted time?
- Did they evaluate the quality of their work at the end of the meeting?

Assessing Your Learning Style
If you haven't completed a learning style inventory in connection with class activities, locate a copy of one of the inventories described at the beginning of this chapter. Complete the inventory. Evaluate whether the results are consistent with your own intuition about your learning style.

Learning by Thinking Critically... Critiques

The Moral Advantage
In a convergent group discussion, describe as many reasons as you can why students should "play straight" in college. Discuss whether you think ethical behavior or misbehavior should receive special consideration in grade assignments.

Call Waiting
You are assigned to a discussion group that will meet throughout the semester, but one of the group members brings her cell phone. The phone usually rings five minutes into the meeting. She excuses herself to take the call and usually misses more than half of each meeting. What strategies could you and your group members develop to address this challenge?

_____
_____
_____
_____
_____
_____
_____

The Right Style
Some courses may be better suited to content-centered teaching strategies than student-centered strategies. Identify what kinds of courses might be easier to learn in when a content-centered approach is taken. Justify your explanation.

_____
_____
_____
_____
_____
_____
_____

Daydream Believer
Monitor your daydreams for one week. See whether you can uncover patterns of your daydreaming. Decide whether the daydreams are taking too much of your time.
- What classes prompt the most daydreaming?
- What themes emerge in your daydreams?
- Are there problems you need to solve that would reduce your need to daydream?
- Do you daydream outside class?

Learning by Thinking Creatively... Personal Vision

A Whole New You
Write down the kinds of positive contributions you normally make to class discussion. Then try to participate using a different positive strategy. Describe the impact of your experiment. Did classmates respond to you differently in some way? How?

Everything I Need to Know I Plan to Learn in College
Look through Robert Fulghum's book, *Everything I Need to Know I Learned in Kindergarten*. Write down 10 simple truths that might serve as the draft for a college-level version of the book.

Your Learning Metaphors
Think about what it feels like for you to learn in the college classroom. Do you feel like a sponge, soaking up every detail you can? Do you feel like a juggler? A prisoner? A butterfly? Are there other metaphors that describe your student experience? Describe or draw your metaphor and explain its significance.

Learning by Planning... Goal Setting

Based on what you have read and done in this chapter, what are your goals for making positive changes that will help you master college? Review the results of the Self-Assessments you completed in this chapter. Also review the College Success Checklist. What can you conclude about things you need to do to improve your skills?

What goal should you select from this chapter for making positive changes that will help you master the college experience? (*Hint: Is your goal challenging, reasonable, and specific?*)

_____
_____
_____
_____

What strategies will you use to achieve your goal? (*Hint: Can you organize your strategy into a series of smaller goals?*)

_____
_____
_____
_____
_____
_____
_____
_____

What obstacles may be in your way as you attempt to make these positive changes?

_____
_____
_____
_____

What additional resources might help you succeed in achieving your goal?

_____
_____
_____
_____

By what date do you want to accomplish your goal?

_____

How will you know you have succeeded?

_____
_____
_____

Resources for Mastering the College Experience

Getting to Yes: Negotiating Agreement Without Giving In (1981) by R. Fisher and W. Ury. Boston: Houghton Mifflin.
A handbook on negotiation, applicable to problems that develop in college, such as persuading an instructor to grant you an extension of a deadline or accept an excuse.

Influence: Science and Practice (1993, 3rd ed.) by Robert Cialdini. New York: HarperCollins.
Basic tactics to improve your ability to persuade. May be useful in negotiating with instructors.

Wise Choices (1996) by Richard Zeckhause, Ralph Keeney, and James Sebenuis, eds. Boston: Harvard Business School Press.
Expert discussions of how to craft diplomatic settlements, seek cooperation, and communicate effectively in negotiation.

Learning Through Discussion (1977) by W. F. Hill. Beverly Hills, CA: Sage.
How to improve the quality of group discussion. Examines how different disciplines exchange information through discussion.

Cooperative Learning (1983) by R. E. Slavin. New York: Longman.
Shows how learning can be improved by forming collaborative groups to explore and expand course ideas. A classic.

Tips for Teams (1995) by Kimball Fisher, Steven Raynor, and William Belgard. New York: McGraw-Hill.
How groups can overcome resistance, handle laggards, hold sessions that save rather than waste time, steer clear of trouble from the beginning, and build an effective collaboration.

Internet Resources

http:www.luminet.net/~jackp/survive.html.
For a survival guide.

http://www.byu.edu/cfac/advisement/professors.html
How to cope with instructors who are more demanding and "less tolerant of your best excuses."

http://rateyourprof.com
Helps track down information about matching your learning style to a specific profesor's teaching style.

http://www.utep.edu/ingle/learning.html
Illustrates the various learning styles described by David Kolb.

http://www.howtolearn.com/personal.html

http://www.hcc.hawaii.edu/hccinfo/facdev/lsi.html
Two sites with tests for auditory, visual, kinesthetic, or tactile sensory preferences in learning.

http://www.hcc.hawaii.edu/hccinfo/facdev/30things.html
Explores advantages that adult learners bring to college.

Managing Time and Money

CHAPTER 3

College Success Checklist

Place a check mark beside the items that apply to you. Leave the items blank that do not apply to you.

____ I set long-term and short-term goals related to time and money, then plan how to reach them.

____ I have created a calendar for this term.

____ I regularly do weekly plans.

____ I allocate adequate time for studying and assignments outside of class.

____ I set priorities on what I do with my time.

____ I regularly make to-do lists.

____ I know my biological rhythms and use this awareness to plan effectively.

____ *For students who work or have a partner/family:* I effectively balance my work/family/relationship obligations with college demands.

____ *For students who commute:* I effectively use commuting time.

____ I'm good at doing things on time and rarely procrastinate.

____ I have filled out a budget for the academic year.

____ I put together a budget for this month.

____ I am prepared to handle unexpected expenses.

____ I know lots of ways to save money.

____ I know how to use banks, checks, and credit cards responsibly.

____ I am aware of the financial aid that is available to me.

Preview

Time and money are two things that many college students think they don't have enough of. Time and money are precious resources. Harness them and they can make your life more satisfying and productive.

Chapter Outline

Images of College Success: Eric Papczun

Setting Goals and Planning

Managing Time
- Using Time Effectively
- Balancing College, Work, Family, and Commuting
- Tackling Procrastination

Managing Money
- Budgeting
- Banks, Checks, and Credit Cards
- Financial Aid

Self-Assessments
- 3.1 Creating a Term Planner
- 3.2 My Weekly Plan
- 3.3 Are You a Procrastinator?
- 3.4 My Annual Budget
- 3.5 My Monthly Budget

On-Target Tips
- Four Steps in Setting Priorities
- Effective Ways for Commuters to Use Their Time
- How to Overcome Procrastination
- Pinching Pennies

Images of College Success
Eric Papczun

During college, Eric Papczun lost his car, drum set, and credit rating to the Repo Man. How did he get into such serious financial jeopardy? Eric had no trouble obtaining more than 20 credit cards. He had an American Express card, bank cards, gasoline credit cards, and department store cards. Among his purchases were a $6,000 car and a $2,000 drum set. Even though he worked at a grocery store 25–40 hours a week, the credit card debts became overwhelming. The bill collectors started appearing and things started to get embarrassing. An American Express collector showed up at the fraternity house where Eric lived. Eric hid out from him but four months later the fraternity itself posted an eviction notice on his door because he was long overdue on his rent.

Reality did not completely set in until a Monday morning when Eric went out to get into his car to drive to class. It was gone. At first he thought someone had stolen it so he called the police. They told him that it had been repossessed. When his friends asked him where his car was, he lied and said he had taken it to his parents' house and was going to have it sold.

As all of this was unfolding, Eric was academically successful and, ironically, majoring in finance. There's more irony. He was a high-profile student on Kent State University's campus and became treasurer of the student body. His worst fear was that the campus newspaper would get word of his financial disasters. Fortunately for Eric, it never did.

Eric started accumulating credit cards in his first year and by his junior year he owed more than $30,000 in today's dollars. When his car was repossessed in his senior year he finally began cutting up his credit cards and throwing them away. Eric graduated from college when he was 22 but it took him until he was 27 to pay off all of the credit card debts he had accumulated as an undergraduate. Even though he has paid all of his bills in a timely fashion since he graduated from college, his credit history won't be clear until he is 31.

After college, Eric took a job with a consumer credit union. He became one of the founders of the Kent State Student Credit Union. Hoping that other college students won't get into the deep trouble he did, Eric gives talks to beginning college students about the importance of managing their money. When he talks to college students, he concludes by making two points:

- A lot of people think that only "losers" get into financial trouble. Eric was a high-profile, successful college student who got into financial ruins.
- Don't bury your head in the sand. Recognize when you have a financial problem and do something about it.

Setting Goals and Planning

The first step in successfully managing time *and* money is to ask yourself what your goals are and plan how to reach them. In Chapter 1, we briefly touched on setting goals and planning. Here we expand on these extremely important aspects of your college success and tie them more closely to managing time and money.

Do you have a list of clearly defined goals that you want to achieve in your life? Some people do, but many don't. Why do many people avoid setting goals? Some people don't set goals because they fear that they won't attain them. Or they have set unrealistic goals they cannot reach and have become disappointed.

Why should you set goals? When you set goals, you make a commitment to improve yourself. Setting goals also encourages you to think about what is important to you. And setting goals gives direction to your life and helps you to focus your energy. Without setting goals and trying to reach them, you risk working long hours on less important tasks or drifting aimlessly with little purpose to your life.

Following are some helpful strategies in setting goals and reaching them:

- **Make your goals specific and concrete.** Sharpen your focus when you create goals. Some general, fuzzy goals are "I want to be happy" and "I want to have more money." Be more precise in crafting goals. Instead of having a general goal of wanting to be happy, you might establish several more specific goals. These might include getting a 3.2 average this term and resolving an argument with your best friend. Rather than saying you want to have more money, you might set a goal of saving $20 a week by reducing your spending on entertainment and clothing.

- **Set a completion date for your goals.** A good idea is to attach a completion date at which time you expect to reach a particular goal. If your goal is to save $100, you might set a date of 5 weeks from now to achieve that goal. If your goal is to make one good new friend, you might set a goal of 6 weeks for achieving this.

- **Set both long-term and short-term goals.** Start by setting some long-term goals, then turn to your short-term goals. How long is a long-term goal? It could be what you want to achieve 20 or 30 years from now. But let's not begin that far in the future. Let's start with 5 years from now. What are your 5-year goals? Think about different domains of your life when you create goals, such as your goals for personal development, lifestyle, school, and career.

- **Thinking more short-term, what are your goals for this term?** What do you want to attain in your personal life? Academic life? In your personal life, you might set a goal of becoming more involved in community service and state that you will spend three hours or more each week helping others. In your academic life, you might set goals of not missing any classes, doing weekly plans to map out study time, and making the dean's list of honor students.

Every morning if you plan the day's transactions and follow that plan, you carry the thread that will guide you through the maze of the busiest life. But if you make no plan, chaos will reign.

Victor Hugo
French novelist and playwright,
19th century

- **Develop a plan of action.** After you have set your long-term and short-term goals, develop a plan of action to attain them. Shortly, we will ask you to map out your plans for the term, for next week, and for tomorrow.
- **Be consistent and persistent.** It's easy to slack off and not stay on track to attain goals. Keep after your goals. Expect that some obstacles will appear that you did not anticipate. Look at the obstacles as challenges to overcome.
- **Monitor your progress.** Periodically, examine how you are doing on your way to your goals. After you have written down your goals, you might want to place them where you will see them from time to time. A good place to list your goals is in a term calendar, or you might tape them to the inside of your personal address book. If after a week or month you are falling behind, evaluate what you can do to get on track.

Managing Time

Many college students feel overwhelmed with all they have to do. Yet some of the busiest and most successful students get good grades *and* find enough time for play and leisure. How do they do it? They

- Control their life by controlling their time
- Set goals
- Develop systematic plans and follow them
- Set priorities
- Don't procrastinate

If you don't manage time effectively, this chapter can make a big difference in your life. You will learn how to control your life by controlling your time.

Using Time Effectively

There's a saying: "If you fail to plan, you plan to fail." A key to success is to develop systematic plans for managing time. Then follow them.

Developing Systematic Time Plans   Successful planning can be divided into knowing what needs to be done and when to do it, or task and time. A six-part task and time plan includes the following (Douglass & Douglass, 1993):

What Needs to Be Done

- **Goals** (What do I expect to accomplish?)
- **Activities** (What will I have to do to reach the goals?)
- **Priorities** (Which tasks are more important than others?)

The Time to Do It

- **Time estimates** (How much time will each activity take?)
- **Schedules** (When will I do each activity?)
- **Flexibility** (How flexible do I have to be to allow for unexpected things?)

Creating a Term Calendar   You will benefit by mapping out a time plan for the entire term. Get a calendar that has the current month and the next three to four months on it. Some colleges provide a term calendar that identifies breaks and holidays. If you don't have a calendar for the term, Self-Assessment 3.1 provides the days and weeks to create one. Write in vacations and holidays. Then get out

> *You've got to be careful if you don't know where you are going because you might not get there.*
>
> **Yogi Berra**
> **American baseball star,**
> **20th century**

Self-Assessment 3-1

Creating a Term Planner

First, list your main goals for the term:

_____
_____
_____

Then, fill in the planner according to the instructions on pages 56–58. The upper left corner of each box is for the day of the month.

Week of	MONDAY	TUESDAY	WEDNESDAY	THURSDAY	FRIDAY	SATURDAY	SUNDAY
_____							
_____							
_____							
_____							
_____							
_____							
_____							
_____							
_____							
_____							
_____							
_____							
_____							
_____							
_____							
_____							

your course syllabi and write down all of the important dates for tests, homework assignments, and papers.

Code different courses in different colored pencil. History might be in red, English in blue, biology in green, and so on. Pencil allows you to revise schedules easily. Highlight exams with a marker or write them in large letters.

After you have written down your exam and other task dates on the calendar, look at the dates. Think about how many days or weeks you will need to study for major exams and write major papers. Mark the days or weeks in which these tasks will be your main priorities. Before you make out your weekly plan each week, examine your term plan to identify your week's main priority.

Keep a spare copy of your term calendar in case you lose the original. You might want to carry one calendar with you when you go to classes. Post the other one on your bulletin board or keep it in your desk.

Your term calendar is not etched in stone. Monitor it regularly and evaluate whether you need to modify it. Your circumstances may change. An instructor might add another assignment or two, change a test date, and so on. You might find out that you need more study time than you originally predicted for a particular course.

The Weekly Plan Students benefit from making weekly plans. Former Chrysler Corporation chairperson Lee Iacocca (1984) credits his weekly plan as the key to his success.

Self-Assessment 3.2 provides a grid that you can use to map out your weekly plans. Photocopy the grid before you complete your first full weekly plan. In the *Planning* column on the xeroxed grid, which can serve as your master weekly calendar, fill in your class hours, regular work commitments, and other routine tasks. Then use the blank Self-Assessment 3.2 to complete your first weekly plan. As you do, ask yourself the six questions we described earlier:

- What do I expect to accomplish?
- What will I have to do to reach these goals?
- What tasks are more important than others?
- How much time will each activity take?
- When will I do each activity?
- How flexible do I have to be to allow for unexpected things?

A good strategy is to create this plan at the end of the preceding week. Put it together on Friday afternoon, or at the latest Sunday evening. The plan takes no more than a half hour for most students. Yet it can save you at least an hour a day of efficient time use that week. Just 30 minutes of effective planning can save you 7 hours next week!

Now that you have mapped out next week's tasks and when you plan to do them, it is very important to monitor your weekly schedule closely all week to see whether you carried out your plans. A good strategy is sit down at the end of each day and write in the *Actual* column what you actually did that day. Compare what you planned to do with what you actually did. Analyze the comparison for problems and plan some changes to solve the problems.

Remember to use the weekly planner in concert with your term planner each week of the term. Every Friday, pull out your term planner and see what your most important priorities are for the following week. Make any changes that are needed on the term planner. Then get out your xeroxed copy of the weekly planner and write down what you plan to do next week.

Allocating Time for Studying and Other Activities A critical time management task is putting enough time aside for studying or doing assignments outside of class. In a national survey (Astin, 1993), the more hours students

spent studying or doing homework, the more they
- Liked and stayed in college
- Improved their thinking skills
- Graduated with honors
- Got into graduate school

Students who have higher grades and graduate with honors are less likely than students who have lower grades and don't graduate with honors to watch TV or spend time partying (Astin, 1993).

Evaluate how much time you have allocated in your weekly time plan for activities such as studying, watching TV, and partying. The majority of first-year students report that they spend less than six hours per week studying or doing assignments outside of class (Sax & others, 1995). According to the Surprised? box, that is not nearly enough to get high grades. Students who make solid grades study far more hours per week: two or three hours outside of class for every hour in class.

Swiss Cheese and Set Time Two strategies for getting the most out of your weekly time are called *Swiss cheese* and *set time*. Time management expert Alan Lakein (1973) describes the Swiss cheese approach as poking holes in a bigger task by working on it in small bursts of time or at odd times. For example, if you have 10–15 minutes several times a day, work on a math problem or jot down some thoughts for an English paper. You will be surprised at how much you can accomplish in a few minutes.

The set time approach is virtually the opposite of Swiss cheese. In the set time approach, you set aside a fixed amount of time to work on a task. In mapping out your weekly plans, you may decide that you need to spend six hours a week studying biology and doing biology homework. You could set aside 4–6 P.M. Monday, Wednesday, and Saturday for your out-of-class biology work.

Setting Priorities and Doing To-Do Lists What makes a good time manager? A critical skill is figuring out what the most important things are to get done and when to do them—in other words, *setting priorities*. A very effective way to set priorities is to make up a daily to-do list that is manageable. Your goal is to complete all of the tasks on the to-do list. If that turns out to be impossible, make sure you get the most important tasks completed. A no-miss day is one after which you can cross off every item as completed.

Time management expert Stephanie Winston (1995) recommends four steps when setting priorities (see insert on page 62).

Surprised

Are You Studying Enough?

How much time do you spend studying or doing homework each week? 5 hours? 10 hours? 15 hours? 20 hours? 25 hours? 30 hours? If you want to get high grades, how many hours do you need to study?

Many students underestimate the number of hours they need to study. A guideline is that if you want to get average grades, for every hour in class you may need to study two to three hours outside class. Thus, if you are taking 12 hours of classes, you need to study 24–36 hours a week. High grades may require even more time.

Write in the blank how many hours you currently spend on studying and assignments outside of class each week: _____.

Write in the following blank how many hours you are in class each week: _____ x 2 or 3 = _____.

How are you doing? Are you spending enough time studying to get the grades you want?

Self-Assessment 3-2

My Weekly Plan

For the following week, write down how you plan to use your time in the *Plan* column, using the guidelines described in the text. At the end of each day next week, write down how you actually used your time that day in the *Actual* column.

		MONDAY		TUESDAY		WEDNESDAY	
		Plan	Actual	Plan	Actual	Plan	Actual
AM	6:00						
	7:00						
	8:00						
	9:00						
	10:00						
	11:00						
	12:00						
PM	1:00						
	2:00						
	3:00						
	4:00						
	5:00						
	6:00						
	7:00						
	8:00						
	9:00						
	10:00						
	11:00						
	12:00						
AM	1:00						
	2:00						
	3:00						
	4:00						
	5:00						

Managing Time and Money 61

THURSDAY		FRIDAY		SATURDAY		SUNDAY	
Plan	Actual	Plan	Actual	Plan	Actual	Plan	Actual

On Target Tips

Four Steps in Setting Priorities

- **Step 1: Make up your daily to-do list before you go to bed at night.** Or do the list first thing the next morning. Set priorities. Estimate how much time it will take to complete each task.

- **Step 2: Identify the top-priority tasks list and try to do these first.** Do them in the morning if possible.

- **Step 3: Raise your time consciousness.** Periodically look at or think about your list. Maybe you have a few items that take only a little time. Knock them off in 10 minutes here, 15 minutes there. Keep your priorities in focus. Make sure you get your number-one priority done before it is too late in the day.

- **Step 4: Toward the end of the day, examine your to-do list.** Evaluate what you have accomplished. Challenge yourself to finish the few remaining tasks.

Winston (1995) also recommends blocking out time each day for the one task that will have the most potential benefit. For example, you might have a major paper in English class due in three weeks that counts for one-third of your grade. Each day, assign yourself one task concerned with the paper; for example:

- First day: Go to library and survey topics.
- Second day: Narrow topics.
- Third day: Select topic.
- Fourth day: Construct outline.
- Fifth day: Write first two pages.
- And so on.

Do successful people really use to-do lists in their everyday lives? Most successful people certainly do. By doing the lists, they don't lose track of the tasks they want to complete.

Unnecessary interruptions, such as telephone calls and drop-in visitors, can undermine setting your priorities. To avoid such unwanted intrusions,

- Unplug the phone.
- Get an answering machine.
- Hang a DO NOT DISTURB sign on the door.
- Tell visitors that you are too busy to talk with them. Then say, "I'll get back to you when I've finished what I am doing."

Tuning In to Your Biological Rhythms Some of us are "morning people," others "night people." That is, some students work more effectively in the morning. Others are at their best in the afternoon or evening. Evaluate yourself. What time of the day are you the most alert, the most focused?

If you are a night person, plan more of your classes in the afternoon. Conduct your study sessions at night. If you are a morning person, plan your classes in the morning. Get most of your studying done by early evening.

What can you do if you hate getting up and get stuck with morning classes? Start your day off properly. Many students begin their day with too little sleep and poor nutrition. They wake up tired. Does this description fit you? If so, try getting a good night's sleep and eating a good breakfast before you tackle your morning classes. You may discover that you are not a "night person" after all.

Balancing College, Work, Family, and Commuting

Time management includes some challenges for students who work, have a partner or children, or commute. What are some good time management strategies for these students?

Balancing College and Work Managing time can be difficult for students who work to pay their college expenses and support themselves. For both part-time and full-time students, those who work full-time are less likely than students who work part-time or not at all to complete college, have high grade-point averages, graduate with honors, or go on to graduate or professional school (Astin, 1993).

Whether part-time work is positive or negative for college students depends on where they work. In general, a part-time job *off campus* is an academic minus. However, a part-time job *on campus* is an academic plus. Why does it matter whether you work part-time off campus or on campus? The answer has to do with *involvement*. Students who work part-time on campus are more likely to be connected with other students and faculty. The greater on-campus immersion more than compensates for the time students devote to the part-time job.

How much can you work before it brings down your grades? It's best not to work more than 10–20 hours. Full-time students who work more than 20 hours a week get lower grades than students who work fewer hours. They also are much more likely to drop out of college.

What can you do improve your chances of college success if you have to work more than 20 hours per week and go to college? The following strategies may help:

- Carefully evaluate how many classes you are taking. Consider taking a reduced class load to allow for more study time for each class.
- Be organized, plan, and use the time management strategies we have discussed on an everyday basis. Do weekly plans every week. Use to-do lists every day.

Time Management for Students with Partners and Children Time is especially precious commodity if you have a partner or children. Communication and planning are important assets in balancing your relationship or family time with your academic time.

Talk with your partner about his or her importance in your life. Set aside time for your partner as well as for your academic life. Plan ahead for tests and crunch study time. Then inform your partner about these dates. After you have created your weekly and term calendars, let your partner see how you plan to use your time. If your partner also is a student, you may be able to coordinate your study times so you will have free time for each other after you have studied. If one person works and another is in school, perhaps work-related activities can be coordinated with your school/study time.

If you have a partner or child, try to build some study time into the time you have at school before you come home. Use time between classes for study. Possibly arrive at school 30 minutes before your first class and stay 30 minutes after your last class to squeeze in uninterrupted study time. If your child has homework, use this time for your own study. Take a break for 10 minutes or so for each hour you study at home and play or talk with your child. Then, go back to your studying. If your children are old enough to understand, tell them what your study routine is and ask for their cooperation. Consider having your children play with other children in the neighborhood during your study hours. Also check into child care and community agencies that may provide services and activities for your children in the before-school and after-school hours.

Managing the time demands of college may mean reorganizing how you spend time with significant others in your life. Being a commuter also means facing special time demands.

On Target Tips

Effective Ways for Commuters to Use Their Time

- Save time by consistently using to-do lists and weekly plans.
- Audiotape your instructors' lectures if they will let you. Play them back on the way home or on the way to school.
- Rehearse what you learned in class today on your way to work or school.
- If you carpool with others who are in one or more of your classes, use the commuting time to discuss class material with them.
- Use a backpack or briefcase to carry your books and papers that you use each day. Organize the materials you plan to use the next day at school the night before. Then put them in your satchel.
- Exchange phone numbers with other students in your classes early in the semester. Call them if you need to discuss class issues. Or you might get their notes in case an emergency comes up and you miss a class.
- Create a personal commuter telephone directory. Write down important numbers that you might need. These might include
    - Office phone numbers of your instructors and their secretaries or teaching assistants
    - Library
    - Student services
    - Study partners
    - Other campus resources
- Schedule your classes at the earliest possible time during registration. This will get you the classes you want at the times you want.

> Better three hours too early than a minute too late.
>
> **William Shakespeare**
> **English playwright and poet,**
> **16th–17th century**

Effective Use of Commuter Time If you commute to class, you already know how much time disappears on the road. Commuting students also are more likely to have family and work commitments that cut into study time. Courses may be available only at inconvenient times. Schedule conflicts can make it difficult for commuters to take part in study sessions and other learning opportunities. Solving such scheduling problems requires good time management. See the box, "Effective Ways for Commuters to Use Their Time."

Tackling Procrastination

"I know I've got to get my math homework done but I've got all weekend." Sound familiar? We procrastinate when we avoid a task that needs to be accomplished. To evaluate whether you are a procrastinator, complete Self-Assessment 3.3.

Procrastination can take many forms (University of Illinois Counseling Center, 1984):

- **Ignoring the task, hoping it will go away.** A midterm test in math is not going to evaporate, no matter how much you ignore it.
- **Underestimating the work involved in the task or overestimating your abilities and resources.** Do you tell yourself that you are such a great writer that you can grind out a 20-page paper overnight?
- **Deceiving yourself that mediocre performance or less is acceptable.** For example, you may tell yourself that a 2.8 grade point average will get you into graduate school or a great job after graduation. This mindset may deter you from working hard enough to get the GPA you need to succeed after college.
- **Substituting a worthy but lower-priority nonacademic activity.** For example, you might clean your room instead of studying for a test. Valuing cleanliness is fine, but if that value becomes important only when you need to study for a test, you are procrastinating.
- **Believing that repeated "minor" delays won't hurt you.** For example, you might put off writing a paper so you can watch your favorite TV program for 30 minutes. Once the one-eyed monster has grabbed your attention, you may not be able to escape its clutches.
- **Dramatizing a commitment to a task rather than doing it.** For example, you take your books along on a weekend trip but never open them.
- **Persevering on only one part of a task.** For example, you write and rewrite the first paragraph of a paper, but you never get to the body of it.
- **Becoming paralyzed when having to choose between two alternatives.** For example, you agonize over whether to do your math homework or your English homework first. You don't get either done. See also Table 3.1.

Self-Assessment 3-3

Are You a Procrastinator?

For each question, circle T or F as it applies to your behavior right now. If you have trouble choosing true or false, pick the one that best fits your most recent experience.

1.	I often find myself performing tasks that I had intended to do days before.	T F
2.	I often miss concerts, sporting events, or the like because I don't get around to buying the tickets on time.	T F
3.	When planning a party, I make the necessary arrangements well in advance.	T F
4.	When it is time to get up in the morning, I most often get right out of bed.	T F
5.	A letter may sit for days after I write it before I mail it.	T F
6.	I generally return phone calls promptly.	T F
7.	Even with jobs that require little else except sitting down and doing them, I find they often don't get done for days.	T F
8.	I usually make decisions as soon as possible.	T F
9.	I generally delay before starting on work I have to do.	T F
10.	When traveling, I usually have to rush in preparing to arrive at the airport or station at the appropriate time.	T F
11.	When preparing to go out, I am seldom caught having to do something at the last minute.	T F
12.	In preparing for some deadline, I often waste time by doing other things.	T F
13.	If a bill for a small amount comes, I pay it right away.	T F
14.	I usually return an R.S.V.P. request very shortly after receiving the invitation.	T F
15.	I often have a task finished sooner than necessary.	T F
16.	I always seem to end up shopping for birthday or Christmas gifts at the last minute.	T F
17.	I usually buy even an essential item at the last minute.	T F
18.	I usually accomplish all the things I plan to do in a day.	T F
19.	I am continually saying "I'll do it tomorrow."	T F
20.	I usually take care of all the tasks I have to do before I settle down and relax for the evening.	T F

Scoring:
Give yourself one point each for questions 1, 2, 5, 7, 9, 10, 12, 16, 17, and 19 that you answered true. Give yourself one point each for questions 3, 4, 6, 8, 11, 13, 14, 15, 18, and 20 that you answered false. Add up the points. If your total score is 9 or more, you are above average in your tendency to procrastinate. If your score is 13 or above, you are having extreme difficulty with procrastination.

Which, if any, of these behaviors is a problem for you? Recognizing the problem is a first step toward solving it. The box "How to Overcome Procrastination" offers some additional tips.

Managing Money

Managing money and managing time are similar in many ways. Term and weekly time plans are much like annual and monthly budgets. Both time and money plans involve setting priorities so that you do or pay the most important

> *Money can be translated into the beauty of living, a support for misfortune, an education, or future security. It also can be a source of bitterness and worry.*
>
> **Sylvia Porter**
> **Leading financial advisor,**
> **20th century**

Table 3-1
Excuses for Procrastinating

Do these sound familiar?

"I'm too tired to study right now. I'll take a rest and then I'll feel more like studying."

"I've got plenty of time to do it later."

"It is too nice a day to spend time on this."

"I've been working so hard, I need to take a few days off from studying."

"I'll wait until I become inspired and motivated."

"It's too late in the week to start."

"Ten years from now, will it really matter if I get this finished?"

"It might not be good enough."

How to Overcome Procrastination

- **Set a deadline and put it on your calendar.** This creates a sense of urgency where previously none existed.
- **Become better organized.** Some procrastinators don't organize things effectively. Develop an organized strategy for tackling the work.
- **Make a game of it.** This is an effective plan for turning something you dread into something more enjoyable.
- **Divide the task into smaller jobs.** Sometimes we procrastinate because the task seems so complex and overwhelming. Divide a large task into smaller parts. Set subgoals of finishing one part at a time. This strategy often can turn what seemed to be an unmanageable task into a doable one. For example, imagine that today is Thursday and you have 15 math problems due on Monday. Set a goal of doing 5 by Friday evening, 5 by Saturday evening, and 5 by Sunday evening.
- **Build in a reward for yourself.** This gives you an incentive to complete all or some part of the task. For example, treat yourself to a movie you have been wanting to see tonight if you get all of your math problems done.

things first so that you will have successful outcomes. Time and money management both include estimations, such as how much time or money you will need for various activities or expenditures. Both involve taking a set amount of something and scheduling or allocating it for maximum effectiveness. Managing time and money also requires flexibility to allow for unexpected obstacles. And whether you are managing time or money, the most important aspect of a good plan is how well you follow through and carry out the plan.

Many college students have money concerns. In the recent national survey of first-year college students more than half had some concerns about financing college; about one in five students had major concerns (Sax & others, 1995).

Let's explore the nature of budgeting, checks and credit cards, and financial aid available to college students.

Budgeting

A budget is a plan that lets you see whether your input of money (total income) meets your output of money (total expenditures). It also helps you to manage cash so that the timing of income and expenditures matches. A good budget anticipates cash-flow problems (which arise when you don't have enough money to pay your bills when they are due) and alerts you to make necessary adjustments such as postponing expenditures, getting more income sooner, and using credit to better advantage.

Evaluating Your Income and Expenses for the Academic Year Self-Assessment 3.4 helps you to identify your income and expenses for the entire academic year. In thinking about your income, evaluate its sources. They probably consist of one or more of the following: family, spouse, grandparents; savings; financial aid; and work.

Self-Assessment 3-4

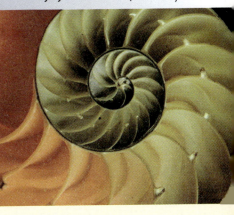

My Annual Budget

Fill in the blanks below in pencil. Use a separate sheet of paper for your preliminary calculations. How much income, fixed expenses, and variable expenses do you expect to have for this academic year?

Resources and Income for the Year from ____ to ____
(Date) (Date)

Income
- Family _____
- Savings _____
- Financial aid _____
- Work _____
- Other _____
  - Total resources _____

Fixed Expenses
- Tuition and fees _____
- Books _____
- Supplies _____
- Housing _____
- Child care _____
- Other _____
  - Total fixed expenses _____

Variable Expenses
- Food _____
- Transportation _____
- Phone and other utilities _____
- Clothing _____
- Laundry/dry cleaning _____
- Entertainment _____
- Hair care/beauty treatments _____
- Other _____
  - Total variable expenses _____

Summary

Add up your total fixed and variable expenses. Then subtract this total from your total income. This allows you to determine whether your balance at the end of the academic year will be positive or negative.

Resources and Income for the Year from ____ to ____
(Date) (Date)

- Total fixed expenses _____
- Total variable expenses _____
- Total expenses _____
- Total income _____
  - Minus
- Total expenses _____
- Balance _____
- **(Which you want to be zero or greater than zero)**

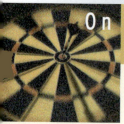

On Target Tips

Pinching Pennies

Following are 21 ways to pinch pennies (McDonald, 1994):
- Make your own lunch.
- Shop around. Fight the urge to buy the first item you see.
- Don't allow yourself to be pressured. Resist high-powered sales tactics.
- Learn when to say no. Ask yourself whether you can really afford what you are thinking about buying. Will it fit in your budget?
- Try bartering instead of spending. For example, agree to watch a friend's children for a few hours in return for a good meal.
- Reduce the number of shopping trips you make; every time you walk into a store, you may be tempted to spend money.
- Clip coupons, keep them organized, and use them when needed.
- Borrow or accept hand-me-down clothes from friends and relatives.
- Buy clothes only on sale, never at full retail.
- Visit a cosmetology or barber school to have students cut your hair for less money.
- If you have to pay extra for utilities, use fans instead of air conditioning in warmer months.
- If you have a car, plan your excursions to get the most efficient use of gas.
- Check newspapers for special prices on lunches or dinners.
- Many colleges have discounts on movies, sporting events, musicals, plays, and so on. Take advantage of these discounts, which often are substantial, if you go to these types of events.
- Attend campus entertainment events, which are usually cheaper than commercial entertainment.
- Take advantage of your college's library services. Read their books, magazines, and newspapers instead of buying them, for example.
- Use your college's exercise facilities rather than joining a health club.
- Regularly leaf through the campus newspaper to find discounts on food, movies, and so on. Just because it is listed as a discount, though, doesn't mean you are getting a good deal. Be sure to compare prices if you are going to indulge.
- Ask other students about the least expensive supermarkets, drug stores, restaurants, and so on.
- Ask yourself whether what you are buying is practical. Peer pressure, fads, and trends can become very expensive.
- Be prepared to change your attitude when necessary. For example, some people think that the most expensive item is the best item. That is not always true. You don't always get what you pay for.

Putting together a budget also requires you to examine your expenses. A good strategy is to list fixed expenses and variable expenses separately. Fixed expenses are unavoidable costs. For college students they usually include tuition and fees, books, supplies, housing, and for parents of young children, child care.

Variable expenses are flexible costs that you can modify if necessary. Variable expenses include things like food, transportation, phone and utilities, clothing, laundry/dry cleaning, entertainment, and hair care/beauty treatments.

Does your estimated annual budget show a negative balance after you have summarized your total income and total expenses? If so, you need to find ways to increase your income or decrease your variable expenses. If you want to decrease your variable expenses, a good way to start is to put together a budget for a shorter time frame. A monthly budget is a good strategy.

Creating a Monthly Budget By creating a budget each month for a while, you can get a better feel for whether your annual budget is working. Self-Assessment 3.5 provides you with an outline for creating a monthly budget. This is your specific plan for where you expect to get your money in the next month and what you plan to spend it on. When you add up your income and expenses for the next month, is your balance negative? If so, look at ways you can reduce your variable expenses. The box "Pinching Pennies" lists a number of money-saving tips.

Being Prepared for Unexpected Expenses No matter how hard we try, we can't anticipate every little thing that crops up. Life has a way of presenting us with unexpected expenses or diminished income: Your car might break down. Your utility rates might go up. Someone might break into your room and steal your money. Your part-time job might end. Someone might offer you the chance to buy tickets to the Super Bowl "cheap." Friends may ask you along on a weekend trip.

In many cases, you can't predict these circumstances or keep them from happening. What you can do is to consistently stay on a positive budget month to month. Then, you will have more money coming in than going out when a financial emergency arises. Also, try to anticipate any financial roadblocks that might arise down the road. You probably will be more emotionally prepared to handle them than if you did not expect them.

Self-Assessment 3-5

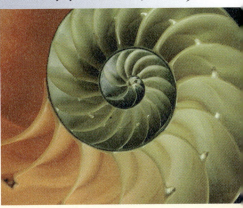

My Monthly Budget

Fill in your budget plan for the next month in the *Planning* column. Then monitor your income and expenses in the next month. A good monitoring strategy is to keep track of all your expenses in a small notebook each day. Keep a running tab of all your expenses for the next month then at the end of the month write down your actual income and expenses in the *Actual* column.

	PLANNING	ACTUAL
Income and Resources for the Next Month		
Family	_____	_____
Savings	_____	_____
Financial aid	_____	_____
Work	_____	_____
Total income for next month	_____	_____
Fixed Expenses for the Next Month		
Tuition and fees	_____	_____
Books	_____	_____
Supplies	_____	_____
Housing	_____	_____
Child care	_____	_____
Total fixed expenses for the next month	_____	_____
Variable Expenses for the Next Month		
Food (at home or prepaid school cafeteria)	_____	_____
Food (snacks, lunches, and other meals out)	_____	_____
Transportation	_____	_____
Utilities	_____	_____
Clothing	_____	_____
Laundry/dry cleaning	_____	_____
Entertainment	_____	_____
Hair care/beauty treatments	_____	_____
Miscellaneous	_____	_____
Total variable expenses for the next month	_____	_____

Add up your total fixed and variable monthly expenses, then subtract this total from your total monthly income. This determines whether your balance at the end of the next month will be positive or negative.

	PLANNING	ACTUAL
Budget Summary for the Next Month		
Total monthly fixed expenses:	_____	_____
Plus		
Total monthly variable expenses	_____	_____
Total monthly expenses:	_____	_____
Total monthly income	_____	_____
Minus		
Total monthly expenses	_____	_____
Balance for the next month	_____	_____

Amazing but True College Stories

The Case of the Pizza Addiction

First-year student Robert loved pizza. He ordered pizza every night, had it delivered to his room, and paid for it with a check.

The first month or so this didn't pose any problem. But Robert wasn't very good at balancing his checkbook. And the pizza chain wasn't very forgiving about the string of bad checks Robert began to write.

A policeman showed up at Robert's dorm one night with a warrant for his arrest. Robert was escorted to the police station and locked up. It cost his parents $200 to bail him out.

If you have a checking account, keep track of how much money is in your account. Write down the amount of each check you write. Keep track of the totals.

> *I finally know what distinguishes man from the other beasts: money worries.*
>
> **Jules Renard**
> **French novelist, 19th century**

Banks, Checks, and Credit Cards

Becoming an effective money manager involves knowing how to use checking accounts and credit cards to your advantage.

Checking Accounts The checkbook lets you keep a running summary of your transactions. How can you open up a checking account? By choosing a bank and

- Depositing money (cash, check, or money order)
- Providing some form of identification, such as a driver's license
- Presenting your social security number
- Filling out a signature card to identify yourself when you cash a check

Banks compete for customers, so they offer many different deals on checking accounts. Some accounts are free. Others can involve monthly charges against your account and a charge for each check you write. Look around and compare banks before you open a checking account. Even if you don't keep a certain minimum balance in your account, you may be able to get free checking. Some checking accounts also include other services such as

- A MasterCard or Visa card.
- An ATM (automatic teller machine) card that allows you to obtain money 24 hours a day; if you use your ATM card at another bank's machine, you may be charged a fee for that transaction.
- Overdraft protection in case you write a check without adequate funds in your account.

Credit Cards Credit cards let you buy things by temporarily using the credit card company's money. Most of them let you pay back this "loan" at your own

Become knowledgeable about how banking, checking, and credit cards work. The knowledge can make you a more effective money manger.

DILBERT reprinted by permission of United Feature Syndicate, Inc.

pace, provided you pay a monthly minimum amount, including interest. The amount of principle you repay each month becomes available for reuse. Some credit cards also charge annual fees. American Express works a little differently regarding interest. You pay an annual fee. You don't pay monthly interest, but have to pay your bill in full each month.

Don't be misled by low interest rates or small annual fees. Be sure to check the *grace period* as well. A grace period is the amount of time in which you are allowed to pay your bill before a finance charge is added. Know how the grace period is figured. Some banks that charge lower interest rates have no grace period. A typical grace period is 25 days. This means you essentially get a cash float of 25 days from the time you get billed until the time you have to pay. If there is no grace period, you start paying interest from the day you make your purchases. With this type of card, you are charged interest even if you pay your bill on time. Avoid this type of credit card.

Credit card annual fees usually range from $15–$50 for regular cards to $75–$300 for premium cards that offer special services. As a rule, you won't be able to find a credit card with a long grace period, low interest rates, and no annual fee. You will have to make a decision about which choice is cheapest for you. If you do get one or more credit cards, try to pay in full each month. At least pay more than monthly minimums. Also avoid late payment. The most common fee for late payment is $15 but some companies charge up to $20.

Feeling *Good*

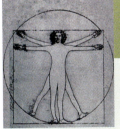

Now, Bad Later

Many people feel good when they buy something. So when they feel bad, what do they do? They go out and buy something. It makes them feel good.

When some people get their credit card bill, it makes them feel bad. So what do they do to make themselves feel better? They go out and buy something else.

It doesn't take a rocket scientist to figure out what eventually happens. Big, overwhelming debts. Sooner or later the feel good part drops out of the feel bad–feel good cycle.

Don't be an emotional shopper who buys things to feel good. Separate your emotional life from your buying habits. Managing your money effectively can help you to avoid emotional buying and the yo-yo bad-good feeling cycle.

Staying Out of the Pits

The Lure of Free and Easy Plastic

Free and easy plastic. What could possibly go wrong with getting a few credit cards? For starters, the average college student graduates with $10,000 in debt. In many cases, part of the debt is on credit cards.

Sixty-four percent of students have credit cards. It is all too easy for students to get credit cards. And it is all too easy to run up big debts on them.

Many students have more than one credit card. *Don't*, say financial advisors. The more credit cards you have, the easier it is to run up big debts. Too often students use credit cards to compensate for their lack of financial planning.

What are some alternatives to credit cards?

- Debit cards
- Prepaid long-distance calling cards
- Sending e-mail instead of making long-distance calls using credit cards
- A checking account in which parents deposit funds each month

Students today often are inundated with offers to obtain credit cards. The offers may seem like they are too good to be true and they usually are. Like Eric Papczun, whose story opened the chapter, many students are lured into living beyond their means because of all the things they can charge on the cards. Before they know it, they have charged large sums of money. The interest mounts up and they are deep in debt.

Credit cards usually do not cause problems when used in moderation. However, always keep in mind what credit really is. Credit is paying for the privilege of using someone else's money. Don't abuse credit cards by charging beyond your budget. If you do, you will place yourself in serious financial danger.

Protect your credit cards just as you would cash. Write down the credit card numbers. Keep the numbers in a safe place. Put the phone numbers to contact in case of theft or loss in the same safe place. Cardholders are usually liable for some charges (such as the first $50) if the theft is not reported immediately. Keep credit card receipts and compare them with your monthly statement. This tells you whether the charges are accurate.

Financial Aid

Table 3.2 shows the sources of educational expenses for first-year students. Notice that students call on many different sources to fund their college education, such as family, summer work, other savings, part-time jobs, loans, and scholarships.

Table 3-2
Sources of Funds for First-Year College Students

SOURCE	RECEIVED ANY AID FROM	RECEIVED $1,500 OR MORE FROM	SOURCE	RECEIVED ANY AID FROM	RECEIVED $1,500 OR MORE FROM
Parents or family	76%	52%	College work-study grant	13	1
Spouse	1	1	Other college grant	26	15
Savings (summer work)	50	8	Vocational rehabilitation funds	1	1
Savings (other)	30	7	Other private grant	10	3
Part-time job (on campus)	22	2	Other government aid (ROTC, BIA, etc.)	3	2
Part-time job (off campus)	23	2			
Full-time job while in college	3	1	Stafford/Guaranteed Student Loan	30	14
Pell Grant	23	5	Perkins Loan	9	2
Supplemental Educational Opportunity Grant	6	1	Other college loan	10	6
			Other loan	7	4
State scholarship or grant	16	4	Other	4	2

More than 7 million undergraduates—slightly less than half—receive some form of financial aid. The federal government provides approximately $25 billion of financial aid for undergraduates each year. Table 3.3 provides an overview of federal loans that are available to college students.

The most important factor in determining how much money a college student can receive is the expected family contribution (EFC). The EFC is how much money a family can afford to pay toward the cost of education. This is based on family income and the value of assets such as savings accounts, stocks, and real estate. To figure out how much aid a student should be given, colleges subtract this amount from how much a student has to pay for tuition, books, and living expenses.

Be honest when filling out financial aid forms. Applicants who knowingly provide false or misleading information on federal forms can be fined up to $10,000 and be sent to prison!

In addition to federal loans and grants, many scholarships are available to college students. A good initial strategy is to contact the financial aid office at your college. Find out what scholarships are available. Many national organizations, businesses, churches, and other agencies have scholarships for students. At the end of the chapter, we list some places to find out about scholarships.

Credit cards are easy for college students to get. No job, no credit history—you can still get them. However, running up big debts on credit cards has become a major problem for many college students. What are some alternatives to credit cards?

Table 3-3
Federal Grants or Loan Programs

PELL GRANT

A Pell Grant, unlike a loan, does not have to be repaid. For many students a Pell Grant provides a financial aid foundation to which other aid can be added. The maximum award for the academic year 1997-1998 was $2,700. How much money you can obtain through a Pell Grant depends on several factors: your EFC, the cost of attending college, whether you are a full-time or part-time student, and whether you attend school for a full academic year.

FEDERAL STAFFORD LOANS

These are low-interest (just under 7%) loans that are available from banks, other lenders, and even some schools. The loans are backed by the federal government and are available regardless of your need. Needy students can apply for what is called a subsidized loan. This means that the government pays the loan's interest while the student is enrolled in college. As of 1997, Stafford loans for first-year students ranged from $2,625 to $6,625.

FEDERAL PLUS LOANS

Parents with good credit can borrow up to the entire amount of an education (tuition, books, and living expenses, minus any estimated financial aid received by the student) from banks or credit unions. Interest rates on these loans are set each June.

FEDERAL PERKINS LOANS

These are low-interest (5%) loans that are administered through the college's financial aid office. They provide needy students with up to $3,000 a year to help with tuition costs. The total amount you can borrow as an undergraduate in this program is $15,000. Payback begins nine months after you leave school.

FEDERAL SUPPLEMENTAL EDUCATIONAL OPPORTUNITY GRANTS

These grants are campus-based and award from $100 to $4,000 a year to needy students.

FEDERAL WORK-STUDY PROGRAM

This program provides jobs on or off campus for students who need financial aid. The program encourages community service work and work related to the student's course of studies.

Summary Tips For Mastering College

Managing Time and Money

Setting Goals and Planning

1. Write down your long-term and short-term goals. Make them precise and complete. Set a completion date for your goals. Develop a plan of action, be consistent and persistent, and monitor your progress.

Managing Time

1. Create a term calendar for the semester or quarter. Write in your important test dates, when papers are due, and so on. Keep a spare copy in case you lose the calendar.
2. Do weekly plans. Develop your weekly plan at the end of the preceding week. List your goals and priorities on your weekly plan.
3. Make sure you schedule enough time for studying and doing homework.
4. Set priorities and do daily to-do lists. Make your to-do lists before you go to bed at night or the first thing the next morning. Be sure to block out time each day for the one task that will benefit you the most.
5. Know your biological rhythms—whether you are a "morning" person or an "evening" person. Use this awareness to plan your most important classes or study at the times when you are at your best.
6. Balance your work, family/partner, and college obligations. Try not to work more than 10–20 hours per week. Try to work on campus rather than off.
7. If you commute, use this time effectively. For example, tape your instructors' lectures if they will let you. Play them back on the way home or to school.
8. Don't procrastinate. Tackle the tasks that you need to complete. If you are a procrastinator, set deadlines, meet them, and don't make excuses. Become better organized.

Managing Money

1. Fill out a budget for the entire academic year. List your income and expenses.
2. Put together a monthly budget. Be specific about where you expect to get money and what you plan to spend it on.
3. Be prepared for unexpected expenses. The best way to do this is to stay on a positive budget.
4. Be frugal and use money-saving strategies. Read about ways to cut expenses.
5. Use checking accounts and credit cards responsibly. Balance your checkbook each month to keep track of your cash flow. Don't let credit cards lure you into living beyond your means.
6. Be aware of what financial aid is available to you. Contact the financial aid office at your college to find out sources of financial aid.

College Success Checklist

Have your views changed since you completed this checklist at the beginning of the chapter? Place a check mark beside any item for which you feel good about your current practice. Also check any item for which you have new ideas about how to improve.

____ I set long-term and short-term goals related to time and money, then plan how to reach them.

____ I have created a calendar for this term.

____ I regularly do weekly plans.

____ I allocate adequate time for studying and assignments outside of class.

____ I set priorities on what I do with my time.

____ I regularly make to-do lists.

____ I know my biological rhythms and use this awareness to plan effectively.

____ *For students who work or have a partner/family:* I effectively balance my work/family/relationship obligations with college demands.

____ *For students who commute:* I effectively use commuting time.

____ I'm good at doing things on time and rarely procrastinate.

____ I have filled out a budget for the academic year.

____ I put together a budget for this month.

____ I am prepared to handle unexpected expenses.

____ I know lots of ways to save money.

____ I know how to use banks, checks, and credit cards responsibly.

____ I am aware of the financial aid that is available to me.

In the space below, list items that you still need to work on the most. This list may help you complete the goal-setting exercise in the Learning Portfolio.

Review Questions

1 Why are goal-setting and planning so important in managing time and money?

2 What are the key components of developing systematic plans for managing time?

3 How can setting priorities help you manage your time?

4 What are some time management strategies for students who work, have a partner or children, or commute?

5 What are some strategies for tackling procrastination?

6 What factors are involved in budgeting for college students?

7 What are some good strategies for using checking accounts and credit cards?

Learning Portfolio

Learning by Reflecting... Journal Entries

Evaluating Your Time Management Skills

We discussed many different ideas about managing time, such as developing a term plan, creating a weekly plan, setting priorities and consistently creating to-do lists, and tackling procrastination.

- What are your strengths and weaknesses with regard to managing time?

- What do you plan to do to improve your weaknesses?

Linking Goals with Time Spent in Activities

- In what waking activities do you spend more than three hours a week?

- How does each of these activities relate to your goals?

- Examine your reasons for participating in these activities that are unrelated to your goals.

Improving Your Budget

List the three most important things you can do that will improve your ability to balance your budget this term.

1. _____

2. _____

3. _____

Learning by Doing... Action Projects

Doing To-Do Lists

Do to-do lists each of the next seven days. Put the list together in the late evening before you go to bed each night. Prioritize the items and jot down how much time each activity is likely to take. Then periodically review the list the next day and check off the activities you have completed. Remember to complete your number-one priority before it gets too late in the day. After completing to-do lists for a week, evaluate how much the lists made your days more manageable and organized.

Putting Swiss Cheese into Action

The Swiss cheese approach involves poking holes in bigger tasks by working on them in small bursts of time or at odd times. List your biggest task for next week. You should have some set time to work on it. However, also try to work on it in small bursts when you have a little time here, a little time there. At the end of next week, come back to this activity and write down how much more time you were able to sneak in on the big task by taking the Swiss cheese approach.

Exploring Campus Jobs

Probably the fastest way to do this is to go to the financial aid office on your campus. Ask for a list of the part-time jobs that are available. Do any of these jobs appeal to you?

Learning by Thinking Critically... Critiques

Learning How to Be More Precise About Time and Plans
Following are some vague plans. Make them more specific.

Vague: I'm going to start getting to school on time.

Precise: _____

_____

Vague: I plan to watch TV less and study more.

Precise: _____

_____

Vague: I'm going to quit wasting my time.

Precise: _____

_____

Procrastinating Less
Procrastination is a big problem for a lot of college students. Earlier in the chapter we described some strategies for reducing procrastination. Get together with several other students and try to come up with additional problem-solving strategies for reducing procrastination.

Analyze Your Credit Rating
Investigate what makes a person have a good or bad credit rating. Ask a reference librarian where you can find this information. Summarize the main factors that influence a person's credit rating.

Learning by Thinking Creatively... Personal Vision

Creating Time or Money Proverbs
Ben Franklin wrote "Early to bed, early to rise, makes a man healthy, wealthy, and wise." Create your own quote about managing time or money that is meaningful for you. Put the quote in your Learning Portfolio and possibly on your bulletin board. Your personal quote about managing time or money is: _____

_____

_____

Beyond Swiss Cheese
We described the Swiss cheese and set time approaches to using your time more productively. In the Swiss cheese approach, you poke holes in a big task by working on it in small bursts and at odd moments. In the set time approach, you set aside a specific number of hours to work on a task on a regular basis. Gear up your imagination and come up with a catchy title for a time management approach that works for you. Write down its title and briefly describe it below.

Title of approach: _____

Description: _____

_____

_____

_____

_____

_____

Brainstorming About Cutting Expenses
Collaborate with several other students about the best ways to cut expenses and save money this term. You might want to refer to the list of tips on page 68 regarding how to pinch pennies. Add your own insights to the list.

Learning by Planning... Goal Setting

Review the results of the Self-Assessments you completed in this chapter. Also review the College Success Checklist. What can you conclude about things you need to do to improve your skills?

What goal do you want to select from this chapter for making positive changes that will help you master the college experience? (*Hint: Is your goal challenging, reasonable, and specific?*)

_____
_____
_____
_____

What strategies will you use to achieve your goal? (*Hint: Can you organize your strategy into a series of smaller goals?*)

_____
_____
_____
_____
_____
_____
_____
_____

What obstacles may be in your way as you attempt to make these positive changes?

_____
_____
_____
_____

What additional resources might help you succeed in achieving your goal?

_____
_____
_____
_____

By what date do you want to accomplish your goal?

_____

How will you know you have succeeded?

_____
_____
_____
_____

Resources for Mastering the College Experience

Developing a Systematic Plan for Managing Time

How to Gain an Extra Hour Every Day (1992) by Ray Joseph. New York: Plume.
An excellent time management book with more than 500 time-saving tips.

Stephanie Winston's Best Organizing Tips (1995) by Stephanie Winston. New York: Simon & Schuster.
How to combat procrastination, prioritize, file effectively, and many other time management strategies. Author runs a time management firm whose clients include American Express and Xerox.

Organizers/Schedulers

Although you may be able to find calendar blanks/planners published on your own campus, the following companies offer excellent time management organizers/schedulers. You can request a catalog that describes their system and materials.

Day-Timers, One Day Timer Plaza, Allentown, PA 28195-1551; 215-395-5884

Franklin International Institute, 2460 Decker Lake Blvd., Salt Lake City, UT 84119-0127; 800-767-1776

Time Management Center, 1590 Woodlake Dr., Chesterfield, MO 63017; 800-458-6468

Managing Your Time by Using a Computer

A number of software packages are available to help you manage your time by using a computer.

Lotus Organizer, Lotus Development Co.; 800-343-5414

SideKick, Borland International; 800-331-9877

Who-What-When, Chronos Software; 800-777-7907

Tackling Procrastination

Procrastination (1983) by Jane Burka and Leonora Yuen. Reading, MA: Addison Wesley.
A good resource for understanding why you procrastinate and how you can overcome it.

Living Without Procrastination (1995) by M. Susan Roberts. Oakland, CA: New Harbinger.
Excellent and up-to-date on how to stop postponing your life. How to identify your procrastination style. Tips for conquering procrastination.

Budgeting

The Consumer Reports Money Book (1992) by Janet Bamford, Jess Blyskal, Emily Card, Aileen Jacobsson, and the editors of Consumer Reports Books. New York: Consumer Union of the United States.
Excellent information about checking accounts, savings accounts, loans, charge cards, budgeting, financial planning, and credit ratings.

How to Pinch a Penny Till It Screams (1994) by Rochelle McDonald. Garden City, NY: Avery.
Hundreds of common-sense and creative ideas for making your money go further.

Checking Accounts and Credit Cards

The Wall Street Journal Guide to Understanding Personal Finance (1992) by Kenneth Morris and Alan Siegel. New York: Dow Jones & Co.
An easy-to-read roadmap for everyday financial matters such as banking, credit, and financial planning.

Financial Aid

Financial Aid: The Student Guide (1998–1999). Washington, DC: U.S. Dept. of Education.
Free, published yearly. Tells about federal student financial aid programs and how to apply for them. Also, call 800-433-3243 for the address and telephone number of the appropriate state agency regarding federal aid. Also contact your college's financial aid office.

Your Personal NET College: How to Get Into the College of Your Dreams (1996). New York: Wolf New Media.
Lists Internet and online services regarding financial aid for college students. Includes federal aid, scholarships, and loans. Describes and evaluates the services. Free updates at *Your Personal NET* Web site, http://www.ypn.com.

USA Today Credit Card Checklist
Monthly Money section feature of *USA Today*. Lists banks and savings institutions that offer the best terms for credit cards. The list is based on whether you carry a balance or pay off the balance each month. Information provided by CardTrak of Frederick, MD, which surveys hundreds of credit card issuers each month.

Internet Resources

http://personal31.fidelity.com:80/decisions/college/calculator.html
Helps you estimate your college degree expenses.

http://www.finaid.org
All aspects of financial aid, including funds available for athletes, nontraditional age, minority students, etc.

http://www.collegeguides.com
Includes quality ratings of all resources listed. Offers book purchasing service to make you more financially savvy.

http://www.jayicom.Fishnet/Money
"Admissions guru" directs your financial aid quest.

http://www.signet.com/collegemoney/
Financial advice for college students from Signet Bank.

http://www.tglsc.org
Information about avoiding financial woes.

http://www.geocities.com/SouthBeach/Palms/9205
Procrastination Central offers light observations on bad habits.

http://www.carleton.ca/~tpychyl
Canadian site describes current research on procrastination.

http://www.balancenet.org/
Includes time management on "straight talk about school."

http://www.noguelph.cal/csrc/learning/homepage.html
Consult with peer helpers about management issues.

Connecting with Campus and Community

CHAPTER 4

 College Success Checklist

Place a check mark beside the items that apply to you. Leave the items blank that do not apply to you.

____ I know about the specific services that are available on my campus.

____ I do not engage in behaviors that put me at risk.

____ I know the advantages and disadvantages of the living arrangement I have chosen.

____ I understand the value of extracurricular activities as a way to enhance college success.

____ I plan to consult with my academic advisor on a regular basis.

____ I know where to get help with personal problems.

____ I am familiar with the campus library and take advantage of its resources.

____ I make use of technological services available on campus when necessary.

____ I am comfortable using the Internet to find information and communicate with others.

Preview

The challenges of college will help you become a masterful problem-solver. However, you will be much more effective in solving problems if you know how to make the best use of the resources available to you. This chapter acquaints you with typical problems faced by beginning students and suggests strategies for resolving them. Because information technology is becoming an essential tool for gathering information, we will look at what you need to know about it. One aim of technology is to help you connect effectively with others on and off campus.

Chapter Outline

Images of College Success: Marc Andreessen

Surveying Resources
- Campus Resources
- Staying Healthy
- Staying Safe

Living Arrangements
- On-Campus Living
- Commuter Life
- Family Matters

Getting Connected
- Extracurricular Activity
- Cultural Enrichment

Getting Help
- Academic Advising
- Academic Support Services
- Personal Concerns
- Overcoming Limitations

Tapping Library Resources

Mastering Technology
- Getting Up to Speed
- Technophobia
- Academic Work and Technology
- The Internet
- Computer Addiction

Self-Assessments
- 4.1 Knowing the Campus
- 4.2 Homesick?
- 4.3 A Library Treasure Hunt
- 4.4 Computer Addiction

On-Target Tips
- The Roommate from Hell
- A Format for Success
- Overcoming Computer Fears

Images of College Success
Marc Andreessen

During his senior year at the University of Illinois, Marc Andreessen supported himself as a lab technician on campus, making $6.85 per hour. Within two years, he was worth more than $50 million. This change in finances resulted from the public offering of stock in Netscape Communications, the company he cofounded in 1994. Obviously not all on-campus employment leads to making a fortune. But Andreessen's story is a great example of making the best of campus resources.

The Internet is an international network of computer systems connected by telephone lines. It's been around for a long time, but in the past it was a troublesome array of disorganized information that was difficult for most users to navigate. In his senior year, Andreessen worked with six other students to create Mosaic software, the first browser that facilitated access to the Web. A subsequent partnership with Jim Clark produced *Netscape*, a browser that could search the Web 10 times faster than *Mosaic*. When the company offered *Netscape* shares to the public, the stock price zoomed from $28 to $75 per share. In 18 short months *Netscape* grew to 1,100 employees. By 1996, eighty million users were visiting the *Netscape* Web site daily.

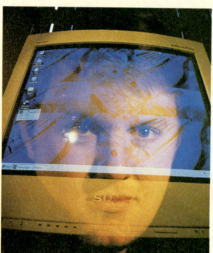

Marc Andreessen's taming of the Internet demonstrated masterful problem-solving skills.

Some computer experts suggested that Andreessen's *Netscape* was like a David going up against the Goliath of Bill Gates's Microsoft. The volatility of the computer industry will lead to a risky and exciting future for *Netscape* and for Andreessen. But for now, let's simply salute a problem-solving genius and learn to use a tool he gave us.

Surveying Resources

When Roger arrived on campus for the first week of classes, he was amazed by how complicated it seemed. Now less than one month into his first term, he is amazed at how easily he navigates the campus that at first was so confusing. At the same time, he continues to make new discoveries about the campus and how it works.

Campus Resources

You probably have visited some resource centers already. One of your first stops was probably the bookstore for textbooks, study supplies, and snacks to support your work. You may have passed through a bustling student center or commons where you can check out bulletin boards or pick up the campus newspaper.

One of your primary goals in college should be developing self-sufficiency in solving problems and getting your needs met. You can accomplish a lot on your own if you understand how to gather information and if you are not afraid to ask questions. Using your resource materials and finding out what is available will go a long way toward making you an independent learner. Complete Self-Assessment 4.1, "Knowing the Campus," to become even more aware of the services that may be available.

Staying Healthy

Many campuses have fully equipped medical centers for their students. Health care services may offer blood testing, health screenings, pregnancy tests, flu shots, and educational programs, as well as regular physician care. Smaller campuses may offer access to a nurse or health specialists trained in emergency care. Find

> *I'm not afraid of storms, for I'm learning how to sail my ship.*
>
> **Louisa May Alcott**
> **American novelist, 19th century**

ZIGGY © 1982, 1995 ZIGGY AND FRIENDS, INC. Dist. by UNIVERSAL PRESS SYNDICATE. Reprinted by permission. All rights reserved.

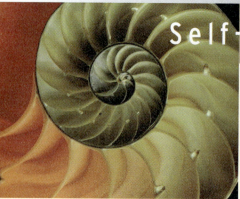

Self-Assessment 4-1

Knowing the Campus

DOES MY CAMPUS HAVE	YES OR NO	LOCATION/NOTES
Career services center?	_____	_____
Student testing center?	_____	_____
Math laboratory?	_____	_____
Performing arts center?	_____	_____
Campus security?	_____	_____
Financial aid office?	_____	_____
ROTC service?	_____	_____
TV or radio station?	_____	_____
Work-study program?	_____	_____
Planetarium?	_____	_____
Banking center?	_____	_____
Computer labs?	_____	_____
Multimedia and graphics lab?	_____	_____
Car rental agency?	_____	_____
Writing lab?	_____	_____
Art gallery?	_____	_____
Health center?	_____	_____
Travel agency?	_____	_____
Mental health services?	_____	_____
Language lab?	_____	_____
Intramural sports office?	_____	_____
Student government office?	_____	_____
Post office?	_____	_____
Lost and found?	_____	_____
Printing service?	_____	_____
Museum?	_____	_____
Foreign studies office?	_____	_____
Honors program?	_____	_____
College newspaper office?	_____	_____
Religious services?	_____	_____
Campus cinema?	_____	_____
Lost and found?	_____	_____
Alumni center?	_____	_____

Compare your information with that of others in the class. How are you doing in discovering the resources on your campus?

out the phone number for these services. Carry them with you. When health emergencies arise, contact an employee of the campus or call the campus switchboard to explain the situation and request urgent help.

Staying Safe

Personal safety is an important concern on all campuses. Security personnel monitor the campus for outsiders and sometimes provide escorts after dark. If you feel unsafe or spot activities that you think may threaten the well-being or property of others, call the campus switchboard or security and report your suspicions or concerns.

Most campuses teem with activity. Unfortunately, they do attract people who find busy places ideal for stealing. No matter what the size of your campus, possessions that can be converted to cash can disappear. Keep your personal belongings locked up when you are not around. Consider taking out an insurance policy on valuable property that might be the target of thieves.

Exercise good judgment about the risks you take. You will be meeting many people. Most of them will enrich your life, but some may try to take advantage of you. Be careful about lending money or equipment, especially to people you have just met. Exercise your street smarts on campus to avoid potential exploitation.

You sometimes may feel pressured by friends to take safety risks, such as drinking inappropriately, taking drugs, or hanging out in clubs that don't feel safe. Don't succumb to friendly pressures to do things that place you at risk. True friends have your best interests at heart. If you find that you are under pressure to take risks, it's time to re-evaluate your friendships.

On Target Tips

The Roommate from Hell

What can you do if you get an impossible roommate?

- *Focus on specific conflicts, rather than negative character.* As conflicts arise, focus on concrete descriptions of problems instead of judging and labeling your roommate's character or motives.

- *Find a mediator.* You may be able to involve a trusted third party to help you talk through your problems and develop some new strategies for coping with one another.

- *Check with your residence hall advisor about your options.* You can usually shift roommates at either the end of term or the end of the school year. You also can ask for help with your most pressing concerns from the residence assistant, usually a senior-level student.

- *Spend as little time as possible with your roommate.* Pursue independent activities or study outside your room.

- *Seize the learning opportunity.* College life may be filled with challenging characters. Think about an unfortunate roommate assignment as an opportunity to improve your skills in dealing with difficult circumstances.

Living Arrangements

One of the biggest problems you may need to solve during college is finding the living arrangement that best supports your college success. You may join other students in residence on campus, live off-campus, or figure out how to make the most of combining academic work with life at home.

On-Campus Living

Many students live in residence halls while they study full-time. In most situations this means having one or more new acquaintances as roommates. Residence halls have rules to manage life for all their residents, but they can also provide a great sense of community and a source of new friendships.

Roommates need to create a supportive community. For example, you may have to negotiate fair space in the room or turn-taking for necessary chores. Usually residence life includes meals provided on campus; however, some residence rooms have kitchens, further complicating the negotiations and sharing you need to do with roommates. What happens if you end up with a challenging roommate? "The Roommate from Hell" offers some strategies.

"Yes, you are a square peg in a round hole. Precisely."

On some campuses, a popular choice is joining a sorority or fraternity. Although Greek housing is more expensive than residence housing, Greek organizations provide a cohesive social network and more structured expectations for how to live and succeed in college. For example, Greek houses usually require study table hours in the evening to help you establish good study habits.

Greek organizations hold rush periods in which they invite prospective members to visit their houses. They ask people they think will fit their social organization best to become pledges. Many sons and daughters pledge the same organization as a parent or grandparent did. Legacies (students with relatives who were members before them) have an easier chance of being selected. After graduation, a Greek affiliation may continue to serve you well by offering a network of acquaintances from the fraternity or sorority that can help you with jobs and internships.

Greek organizations used to ask pledges to demonstrate their commitment by completing arduous or embarrassing tasks in a ritual called *hazing*. More recently, hazing has been softened or eliminated on most campuses.

Commuter Life

Many students live near campus in apartment housing. Apartments may have many advantages (Dobkin & Sippy, 1995), such as greater privacy, more space, greater variety in cooking (your own and your roommates'), and possibly less expense. However, you also lose potential study time on maintaining your apartment, arranging meals, and commuting. The expenses of furnishing an apartment and transportation may wipe out what you hoped to save.

You will discover that commuting requires extra planning. For example, you may have to arrive on campus much earlier than your first scheduled class

Take your life in your own hands, and what happens? A terrible thing: no one to blame.
Erica Jong
Contemporary American novelist

to find a parking place. This may be a blessing in disguise. Forcing yourself to get to campus early can create blocks of study time that you can use to your advantage. Find a quiet place where you can concentrate until it's time for class.

If you choose apartment life, you need to watch how you use your time. Freedom from rules and regulations can entice you into wasting time. Whether you room alone or with roommates, create and use a schedule to manage your time.

Family Matters

Combining school with family life is hard, but manageable. Your challenge at home involves helping family members cope with your new priorities and reduced involvement in the family. Some family members may be supportive, pitching in wherever they can to make your balancing act successful. Some may resent having to compete with your studies for your attention. Schedule some time with them to help them understand how your education will benefit the family in the long run. Plan some special periods when you can give them your full attention. Schedule family time to promote their cooperation and support.

If you are combining parenthood with college, finding good-quality child care is important. Most colleges operate child care centers. Fees for child care services are often lower than babysitting costs off-campus. Child care may be a source of employment for college students or education majors, so the quality of care usually is exemplary. In addition, such services are overseen by the state agency in charge of day care licensing.

You may be able to visit your child during the day, which can help both of you stay connected to each other. Where staff-to-child ratios are small, child care workers may be able to give you specific reports about the kind of activities your child did that day. In addition, they may be able to continue special programs you have started at home to help develop your child's good behavior and habits.

Students sometimes discover that their own parents have trouble letting go. Overinvolved parents may try to intervene in their child's college experience, especially if their child is having difficulties. "Surprised? By a Student's Power" shows you one way to help overinvolved parents learn to respect some reasonable boundaries.

On the other hand, some students find their new independence disconcerting. Many are living away from home for the first time. Some long for the comfort and security of their parents' homes so much that the early weeks of the first semester are painful. Homesick students report that they have trouble concentrating in their classes (Burt, 1993). Most often, homesickness recedes as they become more involved in and connected with activities on campus. Some students feel disabled by the intensity of their homesickness and drop out of school rather than endure the pain. To evaluate the severity of your homesickness, complete Self-Assessment 4.2.

If you suffer from homesickness, contacting people at home probably will make you feel better. You can feel reassured to hear how things are going and you can plan when your next physical contact will be. Some students use e-mail to contact home for regular, nonintrusive, and inexpensive contacts that may prevent homesickness altogether. However, contacting home can also intensify homesick feelings. In this case, distract yourself from contacting home by immersing yourself in study or planning some fun activities with new friends.

The best way to keep children home is to make the home atmosphere pleasant—and let the air out of the tires.

Dorothy Parker
American writer, 20th century

Surprised By a Student's Power

Nosy relatives know only what you choose to tell them about your college success. According to the Family Education Responsibility and Privacy Act (FERPA), the college cannot release your records to anyone but you. Instructors can discuss your progress or difficulties only in your presence or with your permission. This legal constraint encourages your family members to let you resolve your own problems.

Getting Connected

Finding meaningful new relationships and activities may be one of your highest priorities right now. A report on first-year students' activities found that involvement in even one extracurricular activity was associated with the decision to stay in school longer (Astin, 1993). There are many ways to go about finding your niche on campus and off.

Extracurricular Activities

Participating in extracurricular activities improves your chances of meeting people who share your interests.

Many choices for activities are usually listed in the campus handbook or advertised in the student newspaper. Many majors sponsor clubs that allow you to explore career concerns through field trips or special speakers. Journalism majors (and others) can work on the college newspaper or yearbook. Drama students (and others) can audition for plays. Business majors may join an entrepreneur's group to examine how successful business people manage their lives and work. Intramural and campus sports are available. Some clubs promote service and contribute in meaningful ways to the welfare of others. Extracurricular activities help you develop leadership skills and manage multiple commitments.

It may seem like your study life is too full to accommodate fun. However, leisure activities are important for balance in your life. The campus may hold dances, concerts, campuswide celebrations, or other events to help you meet people, relax, and have fun.

As valuable as extracurricular activities are in giving your life balance, your involvement can also create some problems. Some activities are expensive. If your income is limited, look for ones that let you meet others without wiping out your cash. Another challenge lies in becoming too involved. Before you know it, you may have more commitments than you can manage and too little time to study. Have fun, but don't let that become your first priority.

Cultural Enrichment

Because most campuses are training grounds for artists and performers, they often operate an art gallery for student work or the work of invited artists. They also host live performances in music, dance, and theater to showcase student and faculty talent, as well as outside professional performers.

Don't overlook cultural opportunities in the community. Nearby museums, galleries, theaters, the symphony, and political gatherings can all enrich your learning.

Most college students have spiritual concerns. Campus ministries usually coordinate religious activities for various denominations. These may be formal religious services or social groups where you can simply get together with others of similar faith. You will be able not only to practice your faith, but also to expand your network of friends with common values. Of course, religious services are also available off-campus.

As you get connected to the campus and community through extracurricular and cultural activities, you have a great opportunity to sample new pursuits.

Self-Assessment 4-2

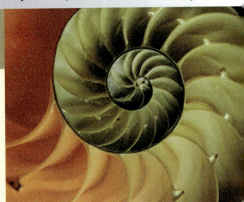

Homesick?

For many traditional-aged students, going away to college may be the first opportunity and challenge they face in living apart from their families. If you are living away from home for the first time, evaluate how homesick you are.

	YES	NO
I often have fantasies about what my family members are doing while I am at school.	___	___
I have trouble studying because thoughts of my family and life at home interfere.	___	___
I miss the comfort and security of my home.	___	___
Sometimes during the day I feel unusual aches and pains in my chest and stomach.	___	___
If I were not afraid of the disapproval of my parents and friends, I would probably go home right now.	___	___
None of the people I am meeting seem as friendly or as interesting to me as my friends at home.	___	___
I am not sure I really need a college degree to be happy.	___	___
I call home twice a week or more.	___	___
I dream about being at home a lot and feel a little disoriented when I wake up from such pleasant dreams.	___	___
I think people at home are probably having a difficult time getting along without me.	___	___
I feel a tremendous sense of relief when I anticipate going home for a vacation from school.	___	___
I often feel empty.	___	___

The more questions to which you responded "yes," the more significant are your feelings of homesickness and the more likely you are to drop out of school. Although homesickness is usually a transitional feeling, you may be at risk if you checked more than a few characteristics. Talk with someone you trust on campus about homesickness as a threat to your well-being and your intentions to stay in school. They can suggest some activities that will help to distract you until the feelings lessen and you make new attachments. On the other hand, if you answered "no" to all the questions, call home. Your parents may be struggling a bit with your new-found independence and your success in getting along without them.

Think of this period as a time when you can explore life as an "amateur anything." Explore a broad range of experiences.

Getting Help

College should help you become an independent learner. However, especially in the early stages of your learning, most people on campus will be eager to help

On Target Tips

A Format for Success

When you need to contact instructors or academic staff members to help you solve a problem, give them some advance notice about your needs. A standard memo format will help you set the context for the meeting. Be sure to include your telephone number and good times to reach you so the person can contact you in case a change in scheduling is necessary. For example:

Memo
To: Dr. Charles
From: Tyrell Wilkins
Re: Changing majors
Date: 9/27

I would like to meet with you during your 11 A.M. office hour on Monday, 10/5. I am thinking about changing majors but I want to find out whether this could delay my graduation. Please e-mail me or call me any weekday evening after 7 P.M. if the proposed time doesn't work for you. Thank you!

Phone: 555-3300
E-mail: tykins@omninet.edu

---

you launch a successful academic career. Whether you are just seeking information or requesting training, there are several things you can do to get the help you need (Canfield & Hansen, 1995):

- **Ask as if you expect to get help.** Your tuition dollars pay for assistance in the classroom, the library, or even the cafeteria line. Ask with authority. You may be able to enter that restricted part of the library merely by acting like you know what you are doing.

- **Ask someone in a position to help you.** You may have to do some homework to find out who can help you best. If someone you approach can't deliver, ask whether that person has any ideas who might be able to help you solve your problem.

- **Ask questions that are clear and specific.** Even those who enjoy helping students don't like to have their time wasted. Think ahead about what you need and what level of detail will satisfy you. Take notes so you won't have to ask to go over the same ground twice.

- **Ask with passion, civility, humor, or creativity.** Enthusiasm goes a long way toward engaging others to want to help you. A polite request is easier to accommodate than a loud, demanding one. Sometimes problems yield more readily to a playful request. A clever request is just plain hard to turn down. Although this approach can entail more risk, the results can be very satisfying. Size up whether your instructors will appreciate a humorous approach. If not, your good intentions and creativity may backfire.

Academic Advising

Perhaps the most important helper you will discover on campus will be your academic advisor. Navigating academic life by yourself is not a good idea. Your academic advisor will know important information about your course requirements that will help you realize your plans. Advisors can explain why certain courses are required and can alert you to instructors who may be more suited to your preferred learning style.

Plan to confer with your advisor regularly. When it is time to register for next term's courses, schedule a meeting with your advisor early in the registration period. Bring a tentative plan of the courses that you think will satisfy your requirements. Be open to other suggestions if the advisor can offer you compelling reasons for taking those courses. For example, your advisor may suggest that by taking some harder courses than you had planned, you can prepare yourself better for the career you have chosen. Your advisor will help you reach your career objective as efficiently as possible, but not by compromising solid preparation.

What do we live for, if it is not to make life less difficult for each other?

George Eliot
English novelist, 19th century

Some advisors may not have regular office hours. To maximize your effectiveness and efficiency, call your academic advisor for an appointment before dropping by. If you put your concerns in writing before the appointment, your advisor will have some time to work on your specific issues before you come to your appointment. See "A Format for Success" to help you get started.

If the personal chemistry between you and your academic advisor isn't good, confront that problem with your advisor. Say what behaviors make you feel uncomfortable. Recognize that your own actions may have something to do with the problem. You need an advisor you can trust. If you can't work out a compromise, request a change to find an advisor who is right for you.

Academic Support Services

Most campuses provide access to specialists who can assist you with academic problems. If you are struggling, you might want to go to this office now and learn what kinds of services it offers. For example, many study skill specialists are qualified to do diagnostic testing to determine the nature of your learning difficulties, or they can refer you to specialists who can provide this service. They can suggest compensating strategies for your assignments and may be able to give you some directions about taking courses with instructors who are more sympathetic with your struggle to learn. They can also set up and monitor additional study supports, including tutoring and study groups, to get you accustomed to the demands of college-level work.

Personal Concerns

College life is often challenging on a personal level. Talking to a counselor or therapist may provide the relief you need. Large campuses have mental health departments or psychology clinics. They may have therapists and counselors on site who will give you the support you need on a one-to-one or a group basis. The fee for such services either will be on a sliding scale (meaning that the cost is

Man's unique reward is that while animals survive by adjusting themselves to their background, man survives by adjusting his background to himself.

Ayn Rand
American philosopher and novelist, 20th century

Dana Fradon © 1991 from The New Yorker Collection. All Rights Reserved.

> *Either I will find a way or I will make one.*
>
> **Sir Philip Sidney**
> **English poet and soldier,**
> **16th century**

proportional to your income), covered by your health insurance policy, or included as part of the services paid for by your tuition.

Some student services offer topic-specific support groups. For example, you may find a support group for single mothers who are returning to college later in life. Or perhaps you are a student struggling with English as a second language. Support groups offer you the opportunity to meet with others who have similar issues. Their advice and experience may be helpful. Ask the counseling center or dean's office about support groups you might join.

If you do not find a group that addresses your concern, consider creating one. Most support groups start from the concerns of one or two students. The student services office usually will assist you with the advertising and the room arrangements to help your group get off the ground.

Overcoming Limitations

Brooke Ellison is a first-year college student who gets around her campus in a motorized wheelchair. Paralyzed from the neck down, she also needs a portable respirator to breathe. She has been this way since she was struck by a car six years ago. When she was a child, before her spinal cord was damaged, Brooke was very active. She played the cello, sang in the church choir, danced, and practiced karate. Now her physical disability keeps her from doing any of these things.

Brooke isn't alone. In the last decade, the number of college students with a disability has increased dramatically. Today more than 10% of college students have some form of physical or mental impairment that substantially limits their major life activities.

Many individuals overcome the limitations of their physical abilities to become successful college students.

Colleges are required to make reasonable accommodations to allow students with a disability to perform up to their capacity. Accommodations can be made for motor and mobility impairments, visual and hearing deficits, physical and mental health problems, and learning disabilities.

If you have a disability, determine what support you need to succeed in college. The level of service a college provides can be classified as follows:

- **Minimal support.** Students generally adapt to the college and advocate for their own services and accommodations.
- **Moderate support.** The campus offers a service office or special staff member to help students with advocacy and accommodations.
- **Intense support.** The campus provides specific programs and instructional services for students with disabilities.

Among the academic services that may be available on your campus are

- **Referrals for testing, diagnosis, and rehabilitation.** Specialists who can help in this area may be on or off campus.
- **Registration assistance.** This involves consideration regarding the location of classrooms, scheduling, and in some cases waivers of course requirements.
- **Accommodations for taking tests.** Instructors may allow you to have expanded or unlimited time to complete tests. You may be able to use a word processor or other support resources during the test.
- **Classroom assistance.** Someone may be assigned to take notes for you to translate lectures into sign language. Or instructors may allow their lectures to be taped for students with impaired vision or other disabilities.
- **Special computing services and library skills.** Support services on campus are finding inventive new ways to interpret written texts to overcome reading and visual limitations.

Tapping Library Resources

Libraries may not seem a likely site for adventure. But think about it. Each visit to the library may feel like a treasure hunt. The treasure might be a bit of information, an opportunity to go online, or a chance to check out a new book from your favorite author. The sooner you get a feel for how the library works, the more use it will be.

One of your classes may arrange a tour as part of its activities. If not, ask a librarian for help in getting oriented. Librarians can give you the schedule of library tours or provide you with maps or pamphlets to help you search independently. Although librarians may look busy when you approach them, step up and ask for help. Most of them enjoy teaching others how to use the library. If you find an especially friendly librarian, cultivate the relationship. A librarian friend can be a lifesaver.

What will you need to know to be effective in using the library? The following questions may help you organize your first tour of the library:

- How can I check out materials? What are penalties for late returns?

Self-Assessment 4-3

A Library Treasure Hunt

Where would you find the following treasures in your library?

A copy of your college's mission statement? _____

The call number of a novel by Jane Austen? _____

A copy of the most recent issue of *Discover* magazine? _____

A surgeon general's report on the effects of smoking? _____

Painter Salvador Dali's birthdate? _____

A book by Dr. Seuss? _____

The call numbers for the books in your prospective major? _____

A picture of Attorney General Janet Reno? _____

A biography of scientist Carl Sagan? _____

A map of your home town? _____

A criticism of Mark Twain's writing? _____

The number of books written by Sigmund Freud? _____

You may already know where many of these treasures are hiding. Look over your answers. Which resources do you have some confidence in using? Which treasures were you unable to find? Ask a librarian to help you locate the information and develop your skills as a treasure hunter.

- Do instructors place materials on reserve? If so, how does this process work?
- Does the library have a broad range of journals in my interest area?
- Is the library catalog online or on cards? Are some things online and others not?
- Can I arrange interlibrary loan to get materials not available in my college library?
- What kinds of reference materials are available? Are the abstracts of published research electronic or in paper-bound volumes?
- Where are the stacks and when can I use them?

There is a lot to learn about the library. Technological advancements in information science mean that libraries regularly introduce new procedures. There is always something new to learn about using the library. Self-Assessment 4.3 can get you started learning how.

Mastering Technology

Expert use of technology can make your college life easier (Reich, 1998). Technology can improve your access to information and your efficiency and effectiveness in completing assignments. Thanks to the efforts of people like Marc Andreessen, technology can also connect you to an electronic community that can enrich your work and your life.

Students differ in their desire to use computers. Some thrive on knowing the latest technological developments. Others feel intimidated and avoid situations that might betray their limited experience. Socioeconomic factors, including their family's education and income levels, influence whether students develop technological expertise. Researchers have found that students who grow up with college-educated parents are more likely to use computers than students with less-educated parents (Rocheleau, 1995). Unfortunately, students whose backgrounds provide only limited access to computers or who have had little opportunity to practice computer skills are at a serious disadvantage in college.

The future world of today's college students will be increasingly technology-dependent. Technology is transforming the educational landscape of colleges.

Getting Up to Speed

If your own background has given you little chance to become familiar with computers, you can use several strategies to get up to speed. You should be able to become computer literate by making good use of the free computer labs on campus. Many campus computer labs are open early and close late to promote student access. Some campuses have computer labs in the residence halls. Take a beginning computer class to start learning the skills you will need in a computer-dependent world. Or find part-time work that involves computer processing so you can earn a paycheck while you learn these valuable skills.

Although it's expensive, another strategy is to buy your own computer system. Select the platform, either IBM or Macintosh, that is most commonly used by students and professionals in the area you are considering as a major. If you do not have enough money to buy a computer, contact the student services office at your college to find out whether special student loan or grant arrangements are available for this purpose. If you are returning to college to improve your skills for current work, purchasing a computer system for college will be tax deductible.

No one system can address all of your needs, but there are some basic features that will help you conquer problems in the academic world. A good basic system includes the computer, a monitor, a printer, and sufficient memory. Many software programs require a great deal of memory to work. If you choose a laptop, you will have the additional convenience of being able to take notes anywhere.

To maximize the use of your computer for gathering and exchanging information, you also need a modem and a CD-ROM. A modem sends and receives information via phone lines. It allows you to use the Internet to visit Web sites, download valuable research information, and correspond with others via e-mail, listserves, and chatrooms. CD-ROMs let you play CDs that contain encyclopedias, atlases, large address directories and other large reference works. Some textbooks now come with CD-ROMs.

The purchase price of a computer will include some software programs. The variety of programs is staggering. Certainly you will need a word processing program. You also may want a graphics program for creating images, presentation package for making computer-based presentations, or spreadsheet for processing numbers.

He that will not apply new remedies must expect new evils; for time is the greatest innovator.

Francis Bacon
English scientist and philosopher, 16th century

Staying Out of the Pits

Minutes You Can't Get Back

Computer games can be a great source of relaxation and stimulation. Programmers have created very involving gaming situations. However, once you enter those worlds, you may not be able to get out. Consider carefully how you manage your time. From the outset of your studies, limit how much time you spend gaming. It might even be a smart idea to avoid purchasing games that could create too much interference, or at least defer your purchase until you have a break from school.

I, a stranger and afraid
In a world I've never made.

A. E. Housman
English poet, early
20th century

Technophobia

Technophobes are people who are highly anxious about and therefore tend to avoid technology. Technological jargon intensifies the problem because it makes the new technology harder to accept, understand, and embrace.

Technophobes carefully avoid any situations in which they are confronted with increased technological demands (Hellman, 1976). For example, they are slow to use new telephone features. They may cling to the typewriter rather than switch to word processing on a computer. Although technophobes might be preserving some romance in their lives by sticking with old methods, they are sacrificing time and energy. They may justify their avoidance by saying that the rate of change is just too hard to cope with: Why learn a new technology when it is likely to be replaced in short order by something else?

Technophobia appears to be more common among women. As girls become teenagers, many of them tend to lose interest in technology. They may think that if they show an interest in it, they will be seen as less feminine or they will be lonelier and not have as much time to spend in social relationships. Also, they come to perceive that computers are mainly for males (Sadker & Sadker, 1994). Boys are more likely than girls to have a computer in their home, attend a summer computer camp, have a parent (usually their father) teach them computer skills, and take computer classes in elementary and secondary school.

In college, the computer gender gap continues. In a recent national survey of first-year college students, males consistently said that they probably would pursue computer-related majors and careers more than females did (Sax, 1995).

"I'M ONLY ATTENDING SCHOOL UNTIL IT BECOMES AVAILABLE ON CD-ROM."

Communities on the Internet and the computer industry itself appear to be organized more for men's interests than women's (Kerr, 1990). For example, women report discomfort with the nature of exchanges on many bulletin boards. In reaction, some women have started discussion groups where flaming is actively discouraged. Few computer games are designed specifically for women, and many women dislike the violence typically shown in these games. In addition, few computer companies are headed by women.

If you have fears about technology—whether you are female or male—what can you do to conquer them? See "Overcoming Computer Fears" for some ideas. But it may also be comforting to know that many others share your predicament.

Academic Work and Technology

Your academic life will be easier if you learn how to use technology. Some forms of technology help you retrieve information. Others help you express what you have learned. Whenever possible, use these tools to reach your goals more efficiently or professionally.

Word Processing Word processing programs on a computer make the process of writing and rewriting papers easier because you can make changes without having to retype most of your work (Maddux, Johnson, & Willis, 1997). You can also select different print types, called *fonts*, and use other features to highlight or underline key sections of your work. Also, you can incorporate headers (standard headings at the top of each page), page numbers, and footnotes easily with most word processing programs. Many will also develop your reference list, placing it in the conventional format for the discipline in which you are writing. Perhaps most helpful of all are the features that allow you to check spelling, grammar, and word count when your paper is completed. Of all of the tips for success in this book, one of the most important is *Learn to use a word processor and write all your papers on it.*

Word processing also involves some hazards. If you don't make a habit of saving your work often, you can end up with nothing to print. Spell-checkers do not substitute for good proofreading, because spell-checking will identify words that are misspelled but not words that are misused. For example, most won't catch the difference between *there* and *their* or *to, too,* and *two*. The worst problem associated with word processing is that it might encourage you to procrastinate because your first draft can look very professional. This is a mistake because you won't be able to take full advantage of your revising capacity. Better papers are better because the writer allowed some time to think again and revise.

Spreadsheet Programs Spreadsheet programs perform calculations on numeric data. For example, if you conduct an experiment in chemistry, you can enter your numbers in the columns of a spreadsheet. Then the spreadsheet program can do the math to calculate and summarize results. Students who

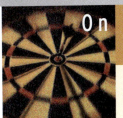

On Target Tips

Overcoming Computer Fears

- ■ *Learn to use the keyboard.* You can probably tell how much the world has shifted toward computer literacy when you try to retrieve a book from the library or even interact with museum displays. Until the technology progresses to voice-driven means, efficient keyboarding skills will be the key to solving problems quickly on the computer.

- ■ *Find a good computer mentor.* Your mentor should be able to communicate clearly about computers at a level you can understand. If they don't, let them know it, or find a different mentor. Your mentor should also show patience in helping you overcome your difficulties. The computer resource center at your college may provide services to beginning computer users.

- ■ *Identify what frightens you.* Many fears are irrational and can be overcome. You might be concerned about looking foolish or stupid, for example. A surprising number of people harbor fears about inadvertently hurting the machine. Once you face such feelings, you can more easily figure out how to defuse them.

- ■ *When you feel frustrated, take a break.* All new computer users feel awkward and uneasy. If you begin to feel frustrated and run out of patience, take a break, go for a walk, do something else. Come back to the computer later when you feel refreshed.

- ■ *Practice, practice, practice.* If you commit yourself to learning how to use a computer and are willing to practice, your computer abilities will grow.

> *Science and technology multiply around us. Either we use those languages or remain mute.*
>
> **J. G. Ballard**
> **Contemporary British science fiction author**

> There are women who spout techno-speak in their sleep and plenty of men who think a hard drive means four hours on the freeway, but the computer culture is created, defined, and controlled by men.
>
> **Barbara Kantrowitz**
> **Contemporary American journalist**

"A highway? Isn't there a path for those of us who would like just a nice easy stroll?"

major in business are likely to use spreadsheets in marketing analyses, business plans, and financial projections. Your instructors will probably tell you which spreadsheet programs will best suit your needs.

Graphics and Presentation Software Graphics packages let you express yourself visually. They allow you to copy and design images, create animations, develop charts and graphs, and make impressive computer-driven presentations. Some of your courses may have graphic requirements. In other classes, your initiative in providing graphics can improve the content and aesthetic appeal of work you submit.

Databases Your campus library houses electronic databases that you can use for research assignments. Each database uses key words, years, or authors to direct you to specific articles in the professional literature. Table 4.1 lists some of the most frequently used academic databases. You may find other uses for databases as well. For example, business classes may explore how to keep track of inventory or potential customers. If you get a part-time job at the college, you may be working with databases of alumni addresses or bookstore inventories.

Fax In an emergency, you may be able to fax a completed assignment to an instructor. Both parties must have access to a phone line and a fax machine. Faxing allows your document to be transmitted in the format in which you wrote it, in contrast to e-mail, which may remove format cues from the documents it transmits. However, it is important to check out your instructor's rules about electronic submission. Some refuse to accept faxed papers because it is often inconvenient for them to retrieve your assignment. They may also be concerned that such practices will give those with fax machines an unfair advantage over those who can't fax their work.

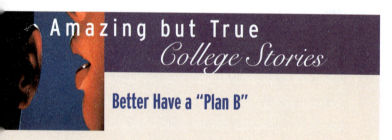

Better Have a "Plan B"

Once again Alan had left his research for a term paper until the last minute. He had sworn that he would never get in that spot again, but now he found himself in a race with the clock. He had just a few more articles he needed to xerox so he could take them home and do a fast construction. He spent two hours tracking down just what he needed.

Unfortunately, when he went to make copies of the articles, he found this sign on the machine:

> This copier is broken. We called for service placed yesterday. Please don't ask me any more questions. (Just because you have an emergency doesn't make it my emergency.)
>
> – The Librarian

Table 4-1
Popular Electronic Abstracts

RESEARCH COVERAGE	ABSTRACT TITLE
Behavioral sciences	PsychInfo/PsychLit
	Sociological Abstracts
Business	PROMT
	ABI/INFORM
Education	ERIC
Humanities	Economic Literature Index
	Historical Abstracts
	Humanities Abstracts
	Philosopher's Index
Natural science	BIOSIS
	MEDLINE
News reports	Associated Press
	NEXUS
	Reuters
Nursing	CINAHL (Cumulative Index Nursing/Allied Health)
Reference	Books in Print
	Dissertation Abstracts
	Academic Index
	Britannica Online

The Internet

The Internet is a major force in the academic world and elsewhere (Poole, 1998). You probably have noticed the new, widespread use of World Wide Web addresses in advertising. If you are an experienced surfer of the Net, you know

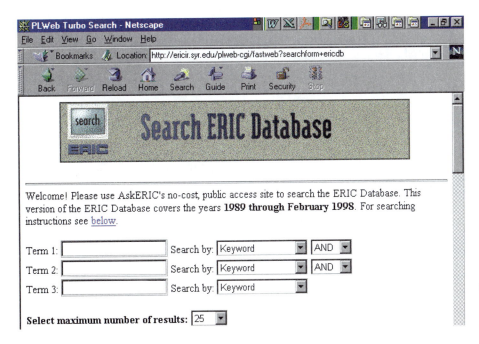

When you use an online database, such as ERIC, you have many choices about how to search for the information you want.

It is characteristic of all deep human problems that they are not to be approached without some humor and some bewilderment.

**Freeman Dyson
Contemporary American physicist**

how your own work patterns have changed since you began using this tool. If you have not personally experienced the astounding capabilities of the Net, find ways to get access and become competent to enhance your problem-solving skills using the tools discussed in this chapter.

E-Mail Electronic mail allows ongoing Internet conversations with people who share your interests (Murray, 1998). For example, you may have classes in which your instructors require discussions online using a class listserve. Such discussions allow you to practice the language of the course and can improve your understanding of course concepts. Some instructors welcome questions via e-mail because it is often more convenient for both parties than office hour visits. Technologically oriented instructors are often remarkably open to developing online relationships with their students. Some may be even more open to online chat than in-person discussions.

Your campus may provide you with a free e-mail account. Most campuses that have not yet provided this service are hard at work raising funds to do so. If your campus does not offer e-mail accounts, you can join a full-range commercial service for about $20 per month. If you have an e-mail address, consider getting some cards printed with your name and e-mail address to facilitate building your own electronic community. Once you have your own e-mail address, it will be easy to send private mail to others, participate in listserves, visit Web sites, and download a variety of resources available on the Net.

E-mail has expanded our horizons but also has introduced a whole new terrain of interpersonal communication challenges (Halonen & Santrock, 1997). Electronic communication is a hybrid of speaking (in its casual, spontaneous nature) and writing (in its use of the keyboard) in conversations that are usually spread out over time rather than occurring in real time. Three problems result:

- **Electronic communications promote a "first draft" mentality.** Many software programs for constructing messages online do not easily allow the writer to edit the message, unlike most ways of writing in the past. This forces greater thoughtfulness, but sometimes only after the words get away from their author. Using e-mail, we tend to send a message as soon as we type it, without re-reading it for possible errors in fact or judgment. Also, in some e-mail programs the online writer cannot conveniently edit more than the current line of text. In that case, the entire message must be rewritten when the writer discovers a mistake well into the message. (It is possible to compose a message in other word processing formats that allow editing. Then cut and save the message so you can paste it when you open your e-mail and address the message.)

- **Body language and speaking cues are absent.** New users find that language subtleties cannot be communicated easily in e-mail. Humor and sarcasm, for example, are especially difficult to communicate clearly in this new medium. Users have compensated for this problem in interesting ways. For example, some add emphasis by typing important words in capital letters. This helps the reader see how VERY important the message might be. A recent Internet exchange led one user to respond to a less experienced writer who used only capitals, "Stop yelling at me!"

Other users add symbols to suggest emotion. For instance, these combinations of characters help clarify the writer's meaning; turn the book sideways for full effect (Reid, 1995):

"All this E-mail... I miss schmoozing."

:-)	smiling face	:-(	unhappy face
:-p	tongue sticking out	:-(*)	someone about to throw up

- **Virtual communities may be unwelcoming.** Some users are distressed at how quickly the emotional tone of electronic forums can sour. Others enjoy the intensity of the heated exchange among network members. Some users dominate newsgroups with overlong and self-centered posts. Others enjoy "flame-baiting" more committed users, hoping to derail the community from the more meaningful exchanges they might have had if they had not felt compelled to "flame" the intruder. Some intruders "spam" user groups by cluttering mailboxes with unwanted advertisements and messages. Such degeneration into hostility might be caused by the absence of human cues online, the unlikelihood that hostile posts will be punished, and the contagious quality of flaming (McLaughlin, Osborne, & Smith, 1995).

World-Wide Web The World Wide Web is both the most exciting and the most frustrating development on the Internet (Grabe, 1998). The excitement comes from the impressive variety of information presented in pictures, sounds, and dazzling graphics available to anyone with a browser. The Web lets you move easily from one piece of information to other related information by clicking hot buttons on a Web site. In this way you can search through a "web" of connected sites. When you find a site that you especially like and wish to revisit, you can create bookmarks that let you return there directly.

The frustration comes from the sheer quantity of information now available on the Web. Entering a key word on the search engine of a browser may result in the browser listing thousands of possible resources, or hits. You may have no easy way to separate the valuable ones from the "noise." Visiting every site takes too long. This explains why some students report that they spend hours on the Web and still are not able to answer the questions that prompted their search.

Many organizations and businesses offer information on the Web that pertains to college subjects. For example, a class studying AIDS may find a lot on the Web about AIDS, including current research on medication, legal concerns, and support groups. Because many Web pages are updated frequently, this information may be among the most current professional research that you can review. Unfortunately, some Web sites don't get updated and their information may be out of date. The Web contains a lot of junk. The Web does not currently have the same quality control procedures that you would find in the academic journals in your college library. Get in the habit of examining the information about the maintenance of the Web site. It will help you judge the currency and value of the information posted.

Surfing the Web can be a wonderful experience. Sometimes, maybe too wonderful. Most users report that hours can slip away while they are using the Web. Be prepared to invest some time if you choose to use this helpful tool.

Computer Addiction

It is hard to pry some people away from their computers. Some computer technology fans are so dedicated to their computers that they neglect their work or studies. How can a computer be so preoccupying? Computers can be addictive in several ways:

- **The compelling opportunity to explore the world.** Casual surfing of the Net can take you in many directions. Anyone with healthy

Computer addiction is a more and more common problem. How can a computer become so engrossing?

curiosity can find it hard to stay away from the vast and varied information sources that computers can reach.

- **The obsessive attraction of computer games.** The thrill of good performance is rewarding. It is easy to begin to bargain with yourself to play "just one more time" to see whether you can better your score. Hours slip by as you gradually refine your game skill and lose your real social connections.

- **The seduction of electronic relationships.** An electronic relationship between two people can feel profound even though it is only words. The absence of physical cues may allow you to connect to others in a novel way. Without the other elements of real life intruding, such exchanges can lead to deeper emotional involvement and reward than a user may currently experience in face-to-face relationships.

With Self-Assessment 4.4, you can see whether you might be too dependent on your computer. Conquering computer addiction first requires understanding

Self-Assessment 4-4

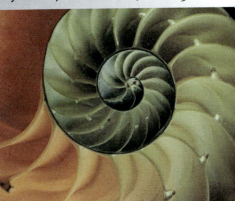

Computer Addiction

These behaviors are characteristic of intense computer use. Mark those that are true with a "T" and those that are false with an "F."

_____ I think about things related to my computer even when I'm not online.

_____ I have missed social engagements that I have looked forward to because I lost track of time while on the computer.

_____ I devote the major portion of my recreational spending to programs or equipment for my computer.

_____ I have a stronger sense of belonging with a virtual community (such as a newsgroup) than I do with any other of my acquaintances.

_____ I usually turn on the computer before I have breakfast or greet the people I live with.

_____ I feel major disorientation from my regular life when my computer is out of commission.

_____ I have the best-equipped computer system of all my peers.

_____ I hate it when people ask to use my computer because I'm afraid they may mess things up.

_____ I can easily go without sleep for long periods if I'm involved in something interesting on the computer.

_____ I have a hard time letting someone have the last word in an online computer group discussion.

_____ I have had arguments with significant others in which my computer use was a central topic.

_____ I can't stand thunderstorms because they interrupt my use of the computer.

If you found yourself identifying more true than false statements, you may have a problem with computer addiction. Examine the patterns of true answers and evaluate why your computer connection is more reinforcing than other aspects of your life. You may want to consult with a counselor at college if this awareness is distressing to you.

why you spend so much time at it. You may need to abandon some current computer sources of pleasure and seek similar joys in your immediate surroundings. Some colleges offer support groups for people who have trouble separating from their machines. If this is a problem in your life, ask at your student affairs office whether support is available.

Summary Tips for Mastering College

Connecting with Campus and Community

Surveying Resources
1. Get used to feeling confused in the beginning. Complex campus environments take some time to learn.
2. Make a point to learn how to navigate the campus. Don't be surprised if you continue to learn new things about the campus well into your first term.
3. Prevent problems by staying safe and healthy. Learn about campus resources that will help you avoid problems and protect your property as well as your physical and mental health.

Choosing a Living Arrangement
1. Choose a living arrangement that will help you succeed academically and socially. Don' be afraid to change an arrangement if you find that your first choice doesn't work.
2. Off-campus living may provide too many freedoms. Carefully consider the advantages and disadvantages before you move away from activities that will support your success.
3. Prepare to negotiate new connections to family members. Homesickness, overprotective parents, demanding children, and discouraging partners all require attention and careful handling.

Getting Connected
1. Make time for extracurricular activities and leisure. Choose activities that make you feel relaxed and fulfilled as a complement to the hard work you will do in your courses.
2. Explore new cultural experiences, both on and off campus, including religious services. College is a great time to try out your new role as an "amateur anything."

Getting Help
1. Vigorously pursue a strong relationship with your college advisor. Your advisor should know a lot about how the college runs, who the best teachers are, and what your wisest path will be to graduation.
2. Seek consultation early if you start to feel unsuccessful. Your campus probably provides support groups and diagnostic testing to help you identify some strategies to overcome academic challenges.
3. Don't be shy about seeking help from counselors. People employed in campus counseling centers will have many ideas about helping you feel more satisfied with your efforts.

Tapping Library Resources
1. Think about the library as a store of treasures. The sooner you understand its resources, the sooner you'll be able to tap them.
2. Ask librarians for help when you can't find what you need. Librarians usually welcome the chance to help you find the right resources.

Mastering Technology
1. Get comfortable with using technology. You can use it to obtain information, write, calculate, and even develop a social group.
2. Use technology whenever you can to complete assignments. Technology can help you work smarter, not harder.
3. Make adjustments if you spend too much or too little time using computers. Either problem can interfere with your academic achievement.

☑ College Success Checklist

Have your views changed about any of the following items since you filled out this checklist at the beginning of the chapter? Place a check mark beside any item for which you feel good about your current practice. Also check any for which you now have new ideas about how to improve.

____ I know about the specific services that are available on my campus.

____ I do not engage in behaviors that put me at risk.

____ I know the advantages and disadvantages of the living arrangement I have chosen.

____ I understand the value of extracurricular activities as a way to enhance college success.

____ I plan to consult with my academic advisor on a regular basis.

____ I know where to get help with personal problems.

____ I am familiar with the campus library and take advantage of its resources.

____ I make use of technological services available on campus when necessary.

____ I am comfortable using the Internet to find information and communicate with others.

In the space below, list the items that you still need to work on the most. This list may help you complete the goal-setting exercise in the Learning Portfolio.

Review Questions

1 What are some ways to enhance your personal safety?

2 How does your living arrangement influence your ability to study?

3 Why does extracurricular involvement improve academic success?

4 What are some strategies for working with your academic advisor?

5 What are some problems you can solve in the library?

6 How does technological competence enhance your ability to do assignments?

Learning Portfolio

Learning by Reflecting... Journal Entries

Developing Your Leadership

One important outcome of extracurricular activity can be stronger leadership skills. Think about all the situations you have been in where you could have exhibited leadership.

- When have you been able to act as a leader?
- If you have been unable to exert leadership, what has prevented you?
- What leadership skills are most important for you to work on?
- How might a specific extracurricular or volunteer activity develop your leadership skills?

Ranking the Risks

In a collaborative group, make a top-ten list of the reasons you think students tend to drop out of college. Use the list to reflect in your journal on how "at risk" you might be in your own adjustment to college. Consult with your advisor if your evaluation warrants action.

Technology and You

How comfortable are you with the changes in technology that have happened in your lifetime? Think about the following as the basis for a journal entry on your comfort with technology:

- Are you a technological "have" or "have-not?"
- Is technological change usually something you welcome? Why?
- What kinds of change are hardest for you to adapt to?
- What kinds of change do you anticipate eagerly?
- How sympathetic are you with those who resist change?

Shopping for Services

From the list of services that have been mentioned in this chapter, identify the services that you think will be most useful to you. Explain why these services appeal to you.

Learning by Doing... Action Projects

Exploring Extracurricular Opportunities

Locate or create a list of available extracurricular events or meetings. Identify those that appeal to you most. Then attend one event. Write a memo to your instructor in which you describe your reactions to the activity. Would you attend again? What obstacles would you have to overcome to make this a regular part of your campus life?

Knowing Where

Your success this year may depend on being able to locate resources that will make it easier for you to perform academically. Interview trusted students who have been on campus longer than you to see whether you can identify and locate the following:

- Cheapest photocopies
- All-night drug store
- Best ice cream
- Local businesses offering student discounts
- Discount bookstores
- Best cheap, hot breakfast
- Best software for sale
- Live music
- Best pizza
- Coffee
- Free or cheap film series
- Best tree
- Place for quiet conversation
- Best bulletin board
- Place to dance
- View of the stars

Visiting Your Computer Center

Make an appointment to visit the computer facility on your campus that is most convenient to you. Whether you own a computer or not, make a list of the kinds of functions you might be able to do at the center that you can't do on your own system. While you are at the computer center, try to get access to the Web to find out whether your school has its own site.

Uncovering Web Treasures

Select a concept that you are learning about in one of your classes. Enter this concept as the key word in a Web search. Identify how many resources the search uncovered. Then select one Web site and visit it. Use the Web site's available hot buttons to see where else your search can take you. Be prepared to talk about the results of your Web search in class.

Learning by Thinking Critically... Critiques

Breaking Down Resistance

Many people object to the idea of seeking outside assistance when they have a hard time in school. Suppose your best friend in college is beginning to have doubts about the wisdom of staying in school but refuses to talk to anyone. What arguments could you propose that might make seeking help less objectionable?

_____
_____
_____
_____

Girls (and Boys) Just Wanna Have Fun

You read about the importance of trying to incorporate leisure activities to round out your experience in college. Describe the advantages and disadvantages of weekly recreation and leisure pursuits.

Civilizing the Internet

Describe some strategies that would be helpful in handling uncivil responses on the Internet. How could you respond effectively to someone who hogs a newsgroup? What would be an effective way to rehabilitate a "flame-baiter" (someone who makes critical, sometimes demeaning comments on an Internet newsgroup)? Write your recommendations on a word processing program if you need practice with this tool.

Learning by Thinking Creatively... Personal Vision

Your Cognitive Campus Map

You probably received a copy of your campus map as part of orientation materials. Draw your own map but emphasize the important aspects of campus by drawing them larger and in a more stylized fashion. You may also find it interesting to return to your cognitive map at the end of the semester to see how your view may have changed. (Try constructing your map using a computer graphics program for additional practice.)

Creative Commuting

If you are a commuter, you spend a lot of valuable time on the road getting to and from campus. Brainstorm some creative alternatives that would exploit this captured time more effectively.

_____
_____
_____
_____

Oh, What a Tangled Web

You have probably had an opportunity to visit a web site on the Internet. If you haven't, go to your computer center and ask for assistance in learning how to navigate this remarkable information technology. Think about what your own web site might look like. What aspects of yourself or other information might you want to let other people know through the web?

Learning by Planning... Goal Setting

Review the results of the Self-Assessments you completed in this chapter. Also review the College Success Checklist. What can you conclude about things you need to do to improve your skills?

What goal do you want to select from this chapter for making positive changes that will help you master the college experience? (*Hint: Is your goal challenging, reasonable, and specific?*)

___

What strategies will you use to achieve your goal? (*Hint: Can you organize your strategy into a series of smaller goals?*)

___

What obstacles may be in your way as you attempt to make these positive changes?

___

What additional resources might help you succeed in achieving your goal?

___

By what date do you want to accomplish your goal?

___

How will you know you have succeeded?

___

Resources for Mastering the College Experience

General Problem-Solving Strategies

Rising Above: A Guide to Overcoming Obstacles and Finding Happiness (1996) by Jerry Wilde. San Jose, CA: Resource Publications.
Uses rational-emotive therapy as the basis for strategies when confronting problems.

Power Lines: What to Say in 250 Problem Situations (1991) by Lynn Weiss and Loran Cain. New York: Harper.
Solving problems by preparing a good verbal offense.

Life and How to Survive It (1994) by Robin Skynner and John Cleese. New York: Norton Publishers.
A light-hearted approach to solving problems by a psychiatrist and an ex–Monty Python member.

Family Matters

When Kids Go to College: A Parents' Guide to Changing Relations (1992) by Barbara M. Newman and Phillip R. Newman. Ohio State University: Sandstone Press.
A helpful guide to changes that happen to students when they live away from home. Explores resulting family strains.

Freedom from the Ties that Bind: The Secret of Self-Liberation (1996) by Guy Finley. St. Paul, MN: Llewelyn Press.
Comprehensively reviews how coping with loss sets the stage for increased independence. Addresses how family relationships change when family members change.

Getting Help

Inside College: New Freedom, New Responsibility (1990) by Henry C. Moses. New York: College Entrance Examination Board.
Explores adjustments to the new freedoms of college life, both academic and social aspects.

Beating the College Blues (1992) by P. A. Grayson and P.W. Meilman. New York: Facts on File.
Helpful about various aspects of college life. Easy-to-read question-and-answer format.

Mastering Technology

The Little PC Book: A Gentle Introduction to Personal Computing (1996, 2nd ed.) by L. J. Magid. Berkeley, CA: Peachpit Press.
A comprehensive book assuming no prior knowledge of computers. Like having a computer buddy for learning how to use a personal computer.

Multimedia and CD-ROMS for Dummies (1995, 2nd ed.) by A. Rathbone. Foster City, CA: IDG Books.
An easy-to-read book. Explores how multimedia can enhance learning. Includes a CD-ROM that shows you, step by step, how a CD-ROM works. Includes tips and warnings.

Using Your Mac: The User Friendly Reference (1996) by Todd Stauffer. Indianapolis: Que Corp.
A plain English reference guide to a Macintosh computer. Straightforward tutorial text and pictures of computer screens. Tells how to get the most from the Mac.

Infosurfing Through the Internet (1995) by D. Alexander and J. Preisler. New York: Avon Books.
A comprehensive guide to the Internet, including review of popular online services. Valued-priced.

Internet Yellow Pages (1995) by C. Maxwell. Indianapolis: New Rider.
Describes the broad-based services available on the Internet, and rates their quality. Solidly organized.

Life on the Screen: Identity in the Age of the Internet (1995) by Sherry Turkel. New York: Simon & Schuster.
A provocative analysis of how computers may encourage a fractured sense of self. Looks at the implications of a computer-based society and multiple realities.

Internet Resources

http://www.collegenews.com
On-line college news to promote a nationally networked community of students.

http://www.student.com
Current news, sports, campus features, and travels; from current movie release dates to dorm room decorating.

http://www.collegefreshman.com
Help related to financial aid, career search, and travel.

http://www.rankit.com
Information about where to find opinions related to campus life, from the best local Chinese food to students' favorite media personalities.

http://www.cybercampus.com
Various student resources and advice.

http://www.collegebowl.com
Play an electronic version of "The College Bowl" and make connections across the country.

http://surfcsn.com
"The ultimate shopping adventure" from your dorm room.

Taking It All In: Listening, Reading, and Taking Notes

CHAPTER 5

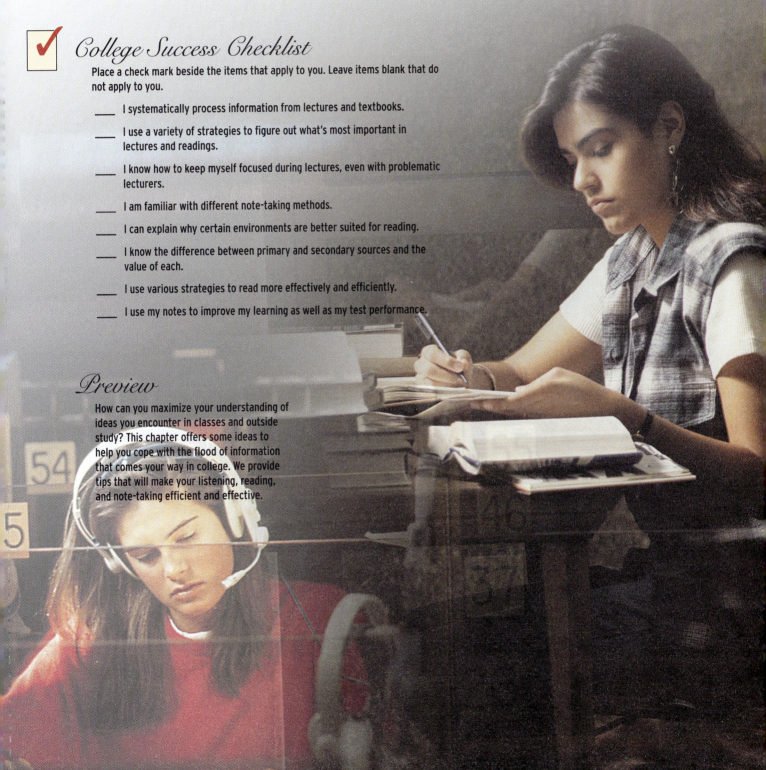

✓ College Success Checklist

Place a check mark beside the items that apply to you. Leave items blank that do not apply to you.

____ I systematically process information from lectures and textbooks.

____ I use a variety of strategies to figure out what's most important in lectures and readings.

____ I know how to keep myself focused during lectures, even with problematic lecturers.

____ I am familiar with different note-taking methods.

____ I can explain why certain environments are better suited for reading.

____ I know the difference between primary and secondary sources and the value of each.

____ I use various strategies to read more effectively and efficiently.

____ I use my notes to improve my learning as well as my test performance.

Preview

How can you maximize your understanding of ideas you encounter in classes and outside study? This chapter offers some ideas to help you cope with the flood of information that comes your way in college. We provide tips that will make your listening, reading, and note-taking efficient and effective.

Chapter Outline

Images of College Success: Talia Falkenstein

Classroom Listening
 Commit to Class
 Concentrate and Listen
 Capture Key Ideas
 Connect Ideas

Taking Notes from Lecture
 Note-Taking Strategies
 Note-Taking Formats

Reading
 Commit to Reading
 Find Time and Space to Concentrate
 Plan to Capture and Connect
 Reading Primary and Secondary Sources
 Reading Different Disciplines
 More Strategies to Improve Reading

Marking Text and Taking Notes from Text
 Highlighting Text
 Personalizing Text
 Creating External Notes
 More Tips for Successful Notes on Readings

Self-Assessments
 5.1 Auditing Your Note-Taking Style for Lectures
 5.2 What's Your Reader Profile?
 5.3 How Fast Do You Read?

On-Target Tips
 Taming the Tough Lecture
 To Tape or Not to Tape
 Mixing Books and Kids
 The Best Reading Plan

Images of College Success
Talia Falkenstein

When she started her first year at the College of DuPage, a large community college in the suburbs of Chicago, Talia Falkenstein knew a hard road was ahead. Not only was she new to college and to study in the United States, but she also had a learning disability that made her an "extremely slow reader." Raised in her native Israel by her American mother and Israeli father, Falkenstein had spoken English at home, just not the English she was hearing in her beginning courses and seeing in her assignments.

Falkenstein often felt lost when instructors introduced new terms in her first year, particularly when her instructors used a lot of slang. She recalled, "In my first writing class, we were supposed to write a paragraph about 'arcades.' That assignment wouldn't have been too hard—*if* you knew what 'arcades' were. So I learned to stop the instructor or ask the student next to me when I didn't understand the words." She also attended all her classes, developed a keen sense of listening for what was important, and took notes that would help her remember *how* the instructor had spoken in class, strategies that are characteristic of good auditory learners.

As she learned to process information at the college level, Talia Falkenstein overcame challenges from her dyslexia and her use of English as a second language.

College reading was even more of a challenge. For example, in an English class Falkenstein was mystified by the language in Shakespeare's play *Twelfth Night*. This may be when she developed "side listening and reading" strategies. She downloaded an interpretation of *Twelfth Night* from the Internet, saw a production of the play, and read whatever she could that would help her grasp Shakespeare's meaning. At her reading speed, she just didn't have time to read texts two or three times to understand them like a lot of her friends. Sometimes she couldn't even read everything that was assigned. So she regularly made appointments with her instructors to discuss the problem. Falkenstein asked some variation of this question: "I have *all* this material to learn for your course and I'm a slow reader—What's the best thing to do?" In most cases, she found that her instructors were very responsive to her requests for help.

Falkenstein understood when she started at DuPage why her advisor told her that her language skills weren't strong enough for some of the courses she wanted. "But," she said with a smile, "If you challenge me, I'll prove you wrong." She aced the courses that she was discouraged from taking, and when she graduated from DuPage and later from Elmhurst College, she achieved a 3.9 average. Not only did she excel academically, but her information-processing strategies were so efficient that she had time to serve on DuPage's Board of Trustees and teach Hebrew at her temple.

Taking It All In: Listening, Reading, and Taking Notes   113

By now you recognize that college requires you to process an extraordinary amount of information. In this chapter we describe a simple, easy-to-remember model of efficient information processing:

- *Committing* yourself to do your best work
- *Concentrating* to eliminate distractions and focus on the material
- *Capturing* critical information
- *Connecting* new ideas to what you already know

> *Learning is not attained by chance. It must be sought with ardor and attended to with diligence.*
>
> **Abigail Adams**
> **U.S. First Lady, 18th century**

Classroom Listening

First let's apply the model of information processing to getting the most from classes.

Commit to Class

Obviously, you can't benefit from lecture if you aren't there. It is even more important to make yourself attend the classes that you are less enthusiastic about because learning will be harder in these courses. But being there involves more than being just physically present. Commit to the work involved, clear your mind of distractions, and focus on the job.

Be psychologically ready to learn. Arrive a few minutes early and review the notes from the last class or glance over your reading assignment. Identify any areas that are difficult to understand and think about questions that could clarify them. These activities will help you build some expectations about how the class will flow.

Be on time. Well-organized instructors often use the first few minutes of class to review what happened in the last class (which allows you to rehearse what

Surprised

You've Got Some Spare Time

Normal speakers talk at a rate of about 150 words per minute. Normal listeners can process words at least three times faster, or about 500 words per minute (Nichols, 1966). Even when instructors talk very fast, you should have time to spare in making sense of what they have to say. Although this difference in processing time gives you an advantage as a listener, it can also derail your efforts by making it easier to daydream.

you have been learning) and to set the agenda for the current class (which helps you get organized for new learning).

Concentrate and Listen

Concentration is influenced by a lot of things. If you are well-rested, you won't be tempted to nod off in slower stretches of lecture. Minimizing other distractions, such as noisy classmates or a growling stomach, will help you perform at your best. When you find yourself beginning to lose track, refocus to stay with the flow of class. Think of related examples or try to make connections with what you have learned in class before.

Throughout your college education, you will spend many hours listening, most often to lectures. Instructors differ in their ability to lecture. Some make learning easy; others make it tough. Sometimes students react differently to the same lecturer. For example, some are enchanted by a lecturer who shares personal anecdotes, while others find these examples annoying and time-wasting. Regardless of the talent of the instructor, you have to muster your best listening skills to learn all you can in the classroom.

Define your listening role as an active one. When you passively record each word the instructor says, you listen to *duplicate* rather than to *comprehend*. Passive recording can produce a fine reproduction of the instructor's words without true understanding. This shifts the burden of actual learning to a later time after class, when the ideas may already have faded. It is much more efficient to use your time in class to master lecture ideas through active involvement. Don't delay the job to a later homework period, when you probably should be moving on to the next assignment.

Capture Key Ideas

Listening to lecture is a hard job. Some instructors may help you by starting with a preview, outline, or map of the material that a lecture will cover. Others won't; they expect you to grasp their organization (even when it is obscure) and recognize key ideas. What are some strategies you can use?

Identify Key Words and Themes Often these are ideas that the instructor repeats, highlights, illustrates with examples, or displays on a blackboard or projection. Most courses are organized around a central set of terms. When you hear a term or phrase that is unfamiliar, chances are good it is a new idea you need to learn. Unfamiliar terms probably represent the specialized language involved in the discipline you are studying.

Recognizing broader themes may be more challenging. Sometimes your instructor will give you an overarching theme to help you organize what you will hear. If the instructor does not, make a point to think about how the details point to a theme that your instructor has been developing across class periods. Try to keep the big picture in mind so you don't feel overwhelmed by details.

Relate Details to the Main Point Instructors use stories, examples, or analogies to reinforce your learning of the main points. Their stories are usually intended to do more than entertain. Check to make sure you understand why the instructor chose a particular story or example.

> When you go to school, you're supposed to learn how to listen.
>
> **Annie Dodge Wauneka**
> **American Navajo leader,**
> **20th century**

Work on Your Sixth Sense   Some students just know when an instructor is covering key ideas, especially material that is likely to be on the test. They sit, pencil poised, and wait for the instructor to get to the good stuff. Actively categorize what your instructor is saying by asking questions such as

- Is this statement central to my understanding of today's topic?
- Is this an example that helps clarify the main ideas?
- Is this a tangent (an aside) that may not help me learn the central ideas?

Save Your Energy   Don't write down what you already know. When instructors require a text, they usually structure their lectures to overlap with the textbook. Instructors also supplement what the textbook doesn't cover. If you have read your assignment, you should be able to recognize when the instructor overlaps with the text. Open your text and follow along, making notes in the margins if you know the instructor stays close to the text. Pay closer attention when what you hear sounds unfamiliar.

Listen for Clues   Pay special attention to words that signal a change of direction or special emphasis. For example, note when a concept or topic comes up more than once. This topic is likely to show up on an exam. Transition speech, such as "in contrast to" or "let's move on to" or even "this will be on the next exam" signals changing topics or new key points. Lists usually signify important material that is also easy to test. Instructors are most likely to include ideas on a test that they consider to be most exciting, so listen for their excitement in class.

Connect Ideas

Colin couldn't figure out why Jim did so much better on his exams. "It's like this," Jim explained with a smile, "I think about the ideas I'm learning in class like they are helium balloons. They will float away from me unless I throw them a line to secure them. And the more lines I throw up there to secure the idea, the better."

The best listeners don't just check in with the speaker from time to time. They actively use processing strategies to create more enduring impressions of the lecture and to escape impulses to daydream.

Paraphrase What You Hear   Translating lecture content into your own words helps you to be certain that you really understand. If you can't translate the ideas into your own words, you may need to do more reading or ask more questions until you are able to do so.

Relate Key Ideas to What You Already Know   When you can see how the course ideas connect to other aspects of your life, including your experiences in other courses or contemporary events, the ideas will be easier to remember. For example, if you are studying in sociology how societies organize into different economic classes, think about how those ideas apply to the neighborhood where you grew up.

Look Up Unknown Words   Use a dictionary in class to look up words you don't know. Or if the instructor is moving fast, write the word at the top of your notes and look it up right after class.

Anticipate   When you guess the direction that the class will take, you can come up with examples that make ideas more compelling. You can also ask questions. No matter what form your anticipation takes, you will stay actively involved with the ideas in the lecture.

The first duty of a lecturer—to hand you after an hour's discourse a nugget of pure truth to wrap up between the pages of your notebooks and keep on your mantelpiece forever.

**Virginia Woolf
British novelist and literary critic, 20th century**

On Target Tips

Taming the Tough Lecture

The Boring Lecturer. Instructors give boring lectures for a number of reasons. They may have lost interest in their work. They may have a limited understanding of classroom dynamics. Some instructors even may suffer from speech fright. Some antidotes for the boring instructor:

- *Make more connections to what you hear.* Rather than allowing monotonous tones to seduce you into drifting away from the point of the lecture, listen harder. When you apply what you hear to what you already know, you will breathe more life into the lecture.

- *Ask questions that encourage examples.* Stories have a natural appeal. They can arouse and sustain attention. By requesting an illustration of a key point, you may help the instructor add life to the lecture. Although this may be easier to accomplish in small classes, you can ask for examples in visits to your instructor during office hours.

- *Give encouraging body language.* Show active interest in the lecture. Maintaining good eye contact, nodding your head, or even smiling occasionally can motivate teachers to give more to the class.

The Fast-Talking Lecturer. Enthusiastic instructors may talk too fast for you to catch what they are saying. When you are confronted with a fast talker,

- *Ask the instructor to slow down.* Most fast-talking instructors know that they talk too fast. Many appreciate getting some feedback so they can adjust their pace.

- *Encourage the instructor to write down the key terms.* Seeing them written down will help you decode the terminology and key ideas. And while the instructor writes on the board, you may be able to catch up.

- *Focus on the major thrust of the presentation, not the detail.* Fast talkers are hardest for students who attempt to take notes word for word. Concentrate on the major ideas rather than getting down every word.

The Obtuse Lecturer. You may have difficulties understanding some instructors because they simply use more sophisticated language than you are used to hearing. Some strategies for coping with instructors who are hard to understand:

- *Prepare for class carefully.* If you get some idea of the subject by doing the assigned readings before class, then you'll have an easier time in class. You'll already be familiar with many key terms.

- *Ask for restatements.* If you persist in asking for interpretations when instructors' language is too complex, many will simplify. They will adjust the level of their language to avoid losing the time that it takes to re-explain.

- *Change your attitude.* Think about this kind of instructor as eloquent rather than obtuse. They give you extra education for your tuition dollar. You will emerge from their classes with an enriched general vocabulary as well as a greater understanding of the language of their field.

The Disorganized Lecturer. Some lecturers organize poorly. They go off on tangents or don't teach systematically from an organized plan. Some strategies for coping with chaotic instructors:

- *Look at the big picture.* Concentrate on the larger themes so you won't feel overwhelmed by disconnected detail.

- *Form a study group.* Pool your resources to make sense of the teaching.

- *Increase connections.* Use note-taking strategies that will help you see the connections between the ideas. See how much organization you can impose on the lecturer's input.

Adapt to Challenging Lecture Styles In a truly inspired lecture, time flies. However, some lecturers cause time to crawl and almost stand still. See "Taming the Tough Lecture" for what to do when the teacher's style falls short.

Evaluate the Quality of Your Listening Keep track of how much of the time you are staying on task. Give yourself feedback on how well you are listening and try to address whatever keeps you from listening.

Taking Notes from Lecture

Note-taking serves many purposes. It provides a summary of information and experience in the class. It also helps you to track the discussion and thereby stay involved.

Note-Taking Strategies

Successful students take good notes. Less successful students tend to take notes on automatic pilot. They don't give much thought to how to make note-taking serve their learning. You can create superior notes by practicing a few simple strategies.

Adapt Your Notes to the Context You may find that some note-taking styles work better than others in some kinds of classes or with certain kinds of instructors. Size up the instructor's style and organization. Adopt a format that suits these factors and the subject's degree of complexity. Some students like to tape the lecture as a backup for their notes. "To Tape or Not to Tape?" tells when taping is a good idea.

Review Your Notes Often Rather than waiting until the night before a test, it pays to make regular use of your notes. For example, review your notes right after class if you can. Some students like to rewrite their notes after class as a way of consolidating information. If you don't rewrite, at least reread your notes to

> *Laziness may appear attractive, but work gives satisfaction.*
>
> **Anne Frank**
> **German diarist killed in the Holocaust**

Used by permission of UNIVERSAL PRESS SYNDICATE. All rights reserved.

On Target Tips

To Tape or Not to Tape

Many students wonder whether it's a good idea to tape record lectures. Tape the lecture

- If you feel more confident having access to the complete text of the lecture
- If you have a learning disability that hinders your ability to listen carefully or accurately
- If you have a system planned for how to listen to the tapes regularly
- If you can take advantage of commuting time to listen to tapes
- If you must be absent but can get a classmate to do the recording.

Without a plan or special need to justify taping, you probably will end up with a pile of cassettes that you never listen to.

---

add whatever might be missing. You may also want to highlight certain phrases, identify the key points, or revise notes that are unclear.

Reviewing your notes between classes can also help consolidate your learning. Some students review notes from the previous class just before the next meeting of the course as a way to get back into the subject.

Organize Your Materials for Easy Retrieval A separate notebook or compartment in a binder for each subject can improve your efficiency. Three-ring binders allow you to rearrange and add pages. Write on only one side of the page to make your notes easier to arrange and easier to review later. Some students use index cards because they are easy to carry, organize, and review.

Identify the Lecture Clearly Be sure to include the topic or title of the lecture, if any, along with its date. This makes it easier for you to track down specific information when it is time to review.

Take Notes from All Relevant Input Some students believe only the instructor's input is worth recording. However, the instructor may treat any class material as fair game for testing, even when it is introduced by other students. Remember to summarize the relevant details from videos or films that are shown in class.

Use Abbreviations You can use standard abbreviations to record information more quickly. Table 5.1 shows some common abbreviations. You also can develop your own abbreviations for words that you need to write often. For example, you can abbreviate academic disciplines, such as *PSY*, *BIO*, *EN*, and *LIT*. When terms are used regularly throughout the course, develop abbreviations for them as well. For example, *EV* might stand for *evolution* or *A/R* for *accounts receivable*. When you use personalized abbreviations, write their

Table 5-1
Common Abbreviations for Notes

Practicing the use of your own abbreviations or the standard abbreviations in this table will save time as you construct your notes.

i.e.	= that is (to clarify by restating a point)	<	= less than
e.g.	= for example (to clarify by adding a typical case)	>	= more than
vs.	= versus (to identify a contrasting point)	k	= 1,000 (as in 10 k for 10 thousand; k = kilo)
∴	= therefore (to come to a conclusion)	~	= approximately
∵	= because	??	= I'm confused
w/	= with	*	= important, testable
w/o	= without	@	= at
→	= leads to		

meanings inside the cover of your notebook as a handy reference.

Personalize Your Notes Regard your note-taking as a creative opportunity. Consider adding sketches to illustrate concepts and make them more memorable. Use color creatively. For example, write down instructors' ideas in blue and valuable student comments in red. Try to think of other strategies that will help you stay invested in creating the work, but avoid paying so much attention to your note-taking style that you get distracted from the content.

Request Feedback About Your Notes Especially in classes in which note-taking is a struggle for you, consult with your instructor during office hours and ask for assistance in developing more effective notes. Ask whether you are capturing the main ideas.

Don't Erase Mistakes Erasing takes more time than simply drawing a line through an error. Drawing a line also lets you restore the information later if you need it.

Evaluate Your Note-Taking Strategy When a test is returned, examine the structure of your notes to see what accounted for your success. Continue to practice the strategies that served you well. Modify practices that may have made it hard for you to learn or to test well. You can also audit your own style of listening in lecture by completing Self-Assessment 5.1. The results will show where you can improve.

Staying Out of the Pits

It's Not Dictation

The worst strategy students can adopt when taking notes in lecture is trying to get down every word the instructor says. They become transcribers, trying to reproduce the lecture verbatim (word-for-word). This approach to note-taking pays off only for secretaries, not for students.

Recall the time advantage that the listener has in processing information. At 500 words per minute you can usually think and listen more than three times faster than a speaker can talk. Transcribers do well if they can get down 80 to 90 words a minute using shorthand. On the other hand, students who transcribe instructor's words without benefit of shorthand may write at a rate of less than 20 words per minute (Kierwa, 1987). By concentrating on capturing individual words, you will get only a portion of the message and will certainly miss the big picture.

Note-Taking Formats

Once you get beyond the idea of taking notes verbatim, you have numerous good options. Here are several popular methods.

Outlining An outline summarizes key points and subpoints (see Figure 5.1). The summary of headings at the outset of each chapter of this book is also an outline. When you use an outline form, the results are neat and well-organized. Naturally, outlines are easiest to create when the lecture itself is well-organized. Some outliners dispense with the numbers and letters because the task of numbering may distract from listening. They simply use indentations to signify subpoints.

Summary Method In this approach, you monitor the lecture for critical ideas and pause at intervals to summarize what you think is most important. Writing summaries may be somewhat time-consuming, but it helps you take greater responsibility for judging what is crucial and relating that to other aspects of the course. It is also an effective way to handle a disorganized lecturer.

Concept Maps A concept map provides visual cues about how ideas are related (see Figure 5.2). You can try mapping for both organized or disorganized lectures. You may find that it works or that it gets too messy. Some students construct concept maps after class from lecture notes as a way to review the material.

Fishbone Diagram Some students use a conceptual map called a fishbone diagram (see Figure 5.3). This method is used by business managers to explore

Self-Assessment 5-1

Auditing Your Note-Taking Style for Lectures

	ALWAYS	SOMETIMES	NEVER
I approach listening as an active learner.	____	____	____
I select a format to suit the purpose.	____	____	____
I organize my notes in one place.	____	____	____
I label the lecture with title and date.	____	____	____
I take notes from all participants in class.	____	____	____
I concentrate during the class.	____	____	____
I work to build my vocabulary.	____	____	____
I strike errors instead of erasing them.	____	____	____
I try not to write dense notes. I leave space for adding more notes later.	____	____	____
I listen for directional cues or emphases.	____	____	____
I avoid shutting down when I have a negative reaction to what I hear.	____	____	____
I highlight key ideas or themes.	____	____	____
I use abbreviations to save time.	____	____	____
I personalize my notes to stay invested.	____	____	____
I review my notes after class.	____	____	____
I pay attention to the quality of my note-taking process as I go.	____	____	____
I would consider asking the instructor for help in constructing better notes.	____	____	____

Review the areas that you have marked "sometimes" or "never." Develop some goals for improvement.

Chapter 5   Taking It All In

I. Classroom Listening
   A. Commit
      1. Attend
      2. Be ready
         a. Arrive early
         b. Review prior classes
         c. Identify confusion from assignments
      3. Don't be late or you will miss
         a. Review of past classes
         b. Schedule for the day
   B. Concentrate and Listen
      1. Concentration keys
         a. Get enough rest
         b. Avoid noisy classmates
         c. Eat to prevent stomach growls
         d. Refocus by thinking of related examples
      2. Listening to different lecturers
         a. Instructors differ in skill
         b. Student preferences differ
           in appreciation of teaching style
      3. Avoid passive recording
         a. Does not produce real learning
         b. Shifts learning burden to later
      4. Listening outside of lecture
         a. Student speeches and presentations
         b. Films
         c. Informal groups
         d. Audiotapes
   C. Capture Key Ideas
      1. You are responsible; some profs may help with outlines or maps
      2. Listening strategies
         a. Identify key words, themes
           1) words repeated
           2) new words or terms
           3) look for the "big picture"
         b. Relate details to main point
         c. Categorize lecture elements
           1) Central ideas
           2) Supportive examples
           3) Tangents
         d. Don't record what you know already
         e. Listen for cues
           1) Language
           2) Body language
   D. Connect Ideas
      1. Paraphrase lecture content
      2. Relate key ideas to prior knowledge from
         a. Other classes
         b. Contemporary events
         c. Personal experience
      3. Anticipate class direction
         a. Ask questions
         b. Make predictions
      4. Evaluate the quality of listening
         a. Test results as basis
         b. Note-taking audit
      5. Adapt to challenging lecturers
         a. The bore
           1) Make connections
           2) Ask questions
           3) Give encouragement
         b. The fast-talker
           1) Ask for slow-down
           2) Ask for written examples
           3) Don't record detail
         c. The obtuse
           1) Prepare carefully
           2) Ask for restatement
           3) Change appreciation
         d. The disorganized
           1) Look at the big picture
           2) Form a study group
           3) Increase connections

II. Notes from Lecture . . .

Figure 5.1 A Partial Outline of This Chapter

how problems have developed (Ishikawa, 1986). First, the problem or outcome is identified and printed in the head of the fish. Then primary factors are identified and connected like ribs to the backbone of the "fish". Finally, each rib is elaborated with spurs showing more detail. The method is often used by groups because individual contributions are easy to insert into the diagram. It can also be used for individual note-taking or reviewing.

The Cornell System   Divide your notepaper by drawing a vertical line about two inches from the left-hand margin (Figure 5.4). On the right-hand side take

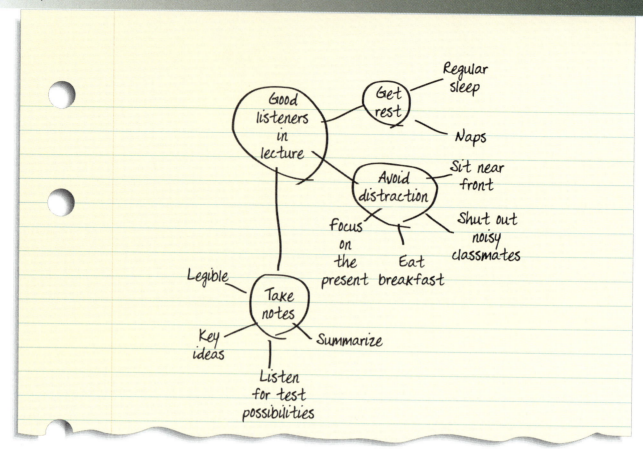

Figure 5.2 **The Concept Map.** A concept map is a helpful tool for visual learners. It displays the key ideas in a lecture or resource and shows how the ideas relate to each other.

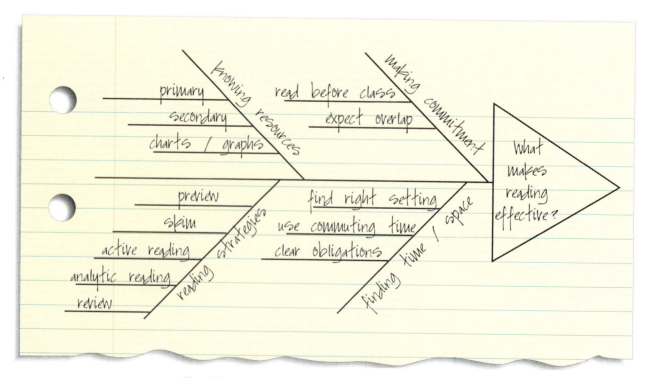

Figure 5.3 **The Fishbone Diagram.** A fishbone diagram is a helpful note-taking format to address cause-effect relationships or to use when you are working in a group with other students. Write the problem or topic in the fish's head and identify the main factors as the large bones in the fish skeleton. Elaborate each factor to complete the diagram.

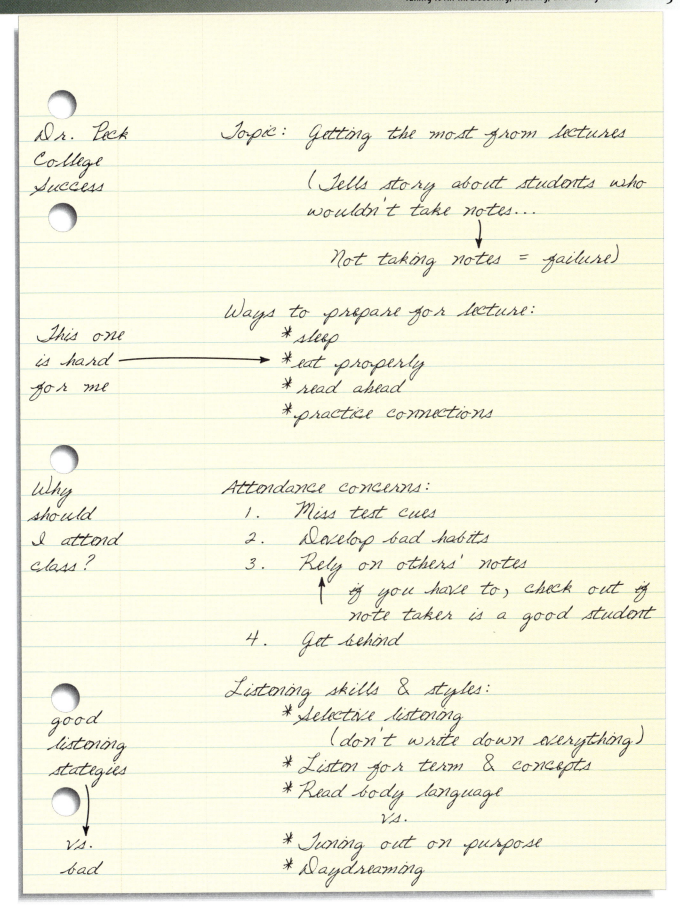

Figure 5.4 The Cornell Method. The Cornell method separates your records of the class from your impressions about the records. The use of key words and comments in the left margin makes your notes easy to review.

People say that life is the thing, but I prefer reading.

**Logan Pearsall Smith
American essayist,
20th century**

down information you hear in the class. On the left side, write key words and phrases that will make your work easier to review later. On the left side you can also jot down questions, comments, or examples that occur to you as you listen to a speaker. Reserve a few lines at the bottom of each page where later you can write a summary of the page.

The Cornell system creates a great tool for reviewing. Cover up the right-hand portion of the page and use the organizers at the left as sample test questions. When you can recite the notes on the right in response to the cues on the left, you should be ready for the test.

Reading

Not all of your learning will take place in the classroom. In this section we explore how to get the most out of your reading assignments. Again, we follow our four-part model.

Commit to Reading

Some students assume that reading assignments is not essential because (they think) the instructor will review the reading during lecture. This is not a wise assumption. Many instructors assign reading as a related but independent resource. They do not review the readings; they expect you to read it and know what it said. Successful students complete assigned readings *before* class to prepare to understand the lecture. Connections and overlaps between lecture and reading reinforce their learning. Another reason to complete reading assignments is that it is embarrassing when you are called on to report your impressions of the reading and haven't a clue what to say.

Find Time and Space to Concentrate

College reading takes concentration. Schedule blocks of time for reading in a place where you won't be interrupted often. On your master schedule, set aside times for study. Clear other obligations from your mind so you can concentrate.

Students differ about where they prefer to read. Many like the library. Others find it *too* quiet or too full of distracting people. Residence halls often set aside quiet rooms for reading. Some students do their best reading at their own desks. Others prefer to read in bed, as long as they can ward off the impulse to sleep. Many students say they can read effectively wherever they can get into a comfortable position and can concentrate. You may want to experiment to find out which settings work best for you.

If you can spend only minimal time on campus, you face other challenges in securing quiet space and uninterrupted time. Some commuters on public transportation can read and review while they travel. If you are stuck with reading an assignment in a noisy environment, you may want to wear headphones with familiar instrumental music just loud enough to block distractions. If you have a long drive to school, you can use it to review audiotapes. If you have to combine studying with child care, see "Mixing Books and Kids."

Plan to Capture and Connect

How you read will depend on your interest level, the complexity of the material, and the time you have to do the reading. If you are very interested in a topic

If you have to do some of your reading in distracting environments, take some steps to minimize the distraction. For example, if you want to read on a crowded, noisy bus, you might want to listen to music played at a low level on your stereo headphones.

and already know something about it, you may not need disciplined strategies to comprehend the reading. Just dive in and take notes.

But what if the reading is unfamiliar and difficult? As suggested in our opening profile of Talia Falkenstein's struggle with reading, you will want to read both selectively and systematically. Your system probably will include some of the following types of reading: preview, skimming, active reading, analytic reading, and review (see Figure 5.5). "The Best Reading Plan" describes some combinations we recommend for different situations.

Preview   Dave, an education major, always previews his reading assignment no matter what the subject. Previewing helps him estimate how intense his effort will need to be to complete the assignment. During the preview, Dave looks at

- **The context for the assignment.** He thinks about the class activities that have led up to the assignment to see how it fits into the course.
- **The length of the reading.** Dave can estimate how long he will need to devote to the job by applying his reading speed to the number of pages in the assignment.
- **The structure and features of the reading.** Dave knows that some readings are structured in sections at the end of which he may take a break. Textbook features such as summaries will help him rehearse his learning.

Mixing Books and Kids

What are some strategies for securing reading time if you are responsible for children?

- Plan to read during nap times, after the children have gone to bed, or before they get up.
- Set a timer for 15 minutes and provide activities that your children can do at the table with you. Let them know that at the end of 15 minutes—when the timer goes off—everyone will take a play break!
- Find other students with similar child care needs. Pool your resources to hire a regular babysitter or trade babysitting services to free up more time for reading.

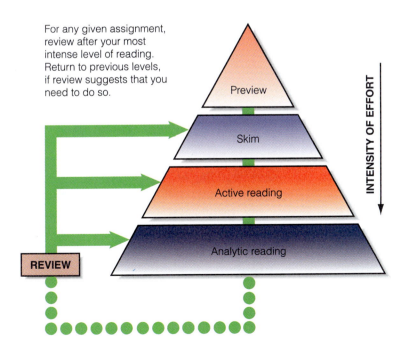

Figure 5.5 Elements of Your Reading Plan. Approaching your reading assignments strategically means adopting different reading strategies. The type of reading you choose will depend on your available time, the complexity of the material, and your own motivation to master the ideas. As you go from top to bottom of the pyramid, the intensity of your effort increases. That is, you become more involved with the material and the reading task becomes more demanding. The consequences of your review may return you to the reading to skim, read actively, or read analytically.

On Target Tips

The Best Reading Plan

Here are several combinations of reading strategies for different situations:

- When you want to develop understanding of the ideas:
  Preview → Active reading → Review
- When you want to get practice in critical thinking about your reading: Preview → Analytic reading → Review
- When you have trouble retaining what you read:
  Preview → Skim → Active reading → Review → Review
- When you don't have time to read for mastery:
  Skim → Review (pay close attention to summaries and boldface terms)

- **The difficulty of the reading.** Dave knows that higher-level material may require more than one reading.

Skimming Whereas previewing helps you size up the reading, skimming covers the content at a general level. When you skim, you read at about twice your average rate. You focus on introductory statements, topic sentences (usually the first sentence in the paragraph), and boldface terms. Slow down to examine summaries carefully.

Karen, a management major, likes to skim a text before she settles down to read more intensely. Skimming give her a sense of the kind of information her reading assignment contains. She recognizes that many of her courses overlap in the concepts that she learns. By skimming the material, she can see where the assignment contains new ideas that she will have to read more carefully.

Markie, a full-time communications major with a half-time job, doesn't always have the time to read her assignments as thoroughly as she should. Rather than abandoning her reading, she skims some assignments. She usually reserves the strategy for easier courses so she can concentrate more intensely on her tougher courses.

One study skill specialist agrees that you don't need to read every word of every assignment (Frank, 1966). Your ability to read selectively improves as you become accustomed to how readings relate to a course and how your instructor chooses test material from a combination of readings and lecture. Skimming provides you with the surface structure of the ideas in the text when that is all you have time for. Successful skimmers can usually participate in class discussions with some confidence if they rehearse the main ideas and have read some key passages.

Active Reading Tamika, a music major, was distressed to reach the bottom of the page of her science reading only to discover that no information had come across. You have probably experienced something similar. It is easy to engage in *empty* reading. Your eyes track across the lines of text but your brain fails to register anything meaningful.

One way to prevent the wasted time of empty reading or to avoid having to read the same material over and over is to read texts actively. As an active reader, you immerse yourself in what the author is trying to say. You focus on identifying the main ideas and on understanding how supporting points reinforce those ideas. When you read actively, you also work at constructing the meaning in what you read by linking the information to your own personal knowledge or experience. For example, you may use these questions as guidelines to promote active reading:

- Have I ever experienced anything similar to what is described in the reading?
- How does this relate to other things I already know?
- How might this be useful for me to know?

- Do I like or agree with these ideas?
- What relationship does the reading have to current events?

Active readers form as many linkages as possible between their personal experience and knowledge and what they are reading.

Analytic Reading   Joshua, majoring in pre-med, likes to read his assignments at an even more intense level. Like other analytic readers, he likes to break ideas open or dig underneath their surface. He tries to spot flaws in the writer's logic. He compares the quality of the work to that of other works he has read. He examines whether the materials are persuasive enough to change his own viewpoint. He identifies which elements are clear and which are confusing. Good analytic readers question both the author and themselves as they dig their way through the reading. The following questions may help you become an analytic reader:

- What are the author's background and values? Do these influence the writing?
- Does the author's bias taint the truthfulness of what I'm reading?
- What implicit (unstated) assumptions does the author make?
- Do I believe the evidence?
- Is the author's position valid?
- Are the arguments logically developed?
- What predictions follow from the argument?
- What are the strengths and weaknesses of the argument?
- Is anything missing from the position?
- What questions would I want to ask the author?
- Is there a different way to look at the facts or ideas?
- Would these ideas apply to all people in all cultures or in all situations?

Review   Anthropology major Sanjay likes to review his reading assignments to help consolidate his learning. He reviews his notes immediately after class and before he begins his next reading assignment. Reviewing the assignment makes the main points stand out and makes them easier to remember. Think of reviewing as an opportunity to test yourself on your own comprehension. Question yourself on details or write out summaries of what you have read.

The quality of notes you have taken can make all the difference when it's time to study for a test. With well-constructed notes that you have reviewed systematically after your classes, your final review should be a breeze.

Reading Primary and Secondary Sources

There are two general types of readings for courses: primary sources and secondary sources. A primary source is material written in some original form. Autobiographies, speeches, research reports, scholarly articles, government documents, or historical journal articles all might be viewed as primary source readings. For example, you may read the *Constitution* as a primary source in your political science class.

Secondary sources summarize or interpret primary sources. A magazine article that discussed politicians' interpretations of the *Constitution* generally would

> *Reading a book is like re-writing it for yourself. You bring to a novel, anything you read, all your experience of the world. You bring your history and you read it in your own terms.*
>
> **Angela Carter**
> **British writer and educator, 20th century**

> *Some books are to be tasted, others to be swallowed, and some few to be chewed and digested.*
>
> **Francis Bacon**
> **English statesman and philosopher, 16th century**

Those who cannot remember the past are condemned to repeat it.

**George Santayana
American poet and philosopher, 20th century**

be considered a secondary source. Textbooks are secondary sources that try to give a comprehensive view of information from numerous primary works.

You have many more opportunities to read primary sources in college than you did in high school. Most people find reading original work to be exhilarating. For example, reading a speech by Frederick Douglass about the abolition of slavery usually will stimulate you more than reading his critics' interpretations of his speeches. However, the reading level of primary sources is often more difficult than the level of secondary sources. Original works must be chewed and digested.

Doing your own interpretation of original scholarship is also more challenging than accepting others' interpretations. When reading primary sources, learn as much as you can about the intentions of the authors and the context in which the writings first appeared. Understanding the historical period will help you with interpretation.

Reading Different Disciplines

As you have already discovered, your reading assignments in different courses vary in level of difficulty. Some assignments will be laden with technical terms that tend to slow you down. Others require your imaginative engagement for you to get the most from them.

Reading in Literature Any author who intends to share experiences through poetry, novels, plays, or short stories creates a narrative that invites you into the action (Skinner, 1997). If you allow yourself to participate in your reading by visualizing the action, you participate at the level the author intended. If the story is complex, make a list of the key figures as they are introduced so you can easily reacquaint yourself with who they are. Think about the motivations of the characters and see whether you can predict what they will do next. Try to use as many senses as the author used—*tasting, smelling, hearing*—as you recreate the author's world in your imagination.

Reading in History Some students dislike history because they believe that events of the past are unrelated to them. What a mistake! We are all the walking expression of history. Reading history is a great opportunity to use your imagination. Think about whether you would react in the same way to the circumstances of the historic figures you are reading about. Try to make predictions about what consequences must have followed for certain key events. History will come alive if you dare to let it.

Reading in Science and Math Many disciplines, especially mathematics and social and natural sciences, use mathematical notation, graphs, tables, and other visual information to illustrate important ideas. Usually authors include visual depictions of information to make important and complex ideas easier to understand. It is probably a good idea to spend more time studying charts and graphs so that you understand the concepts behind them rather than glancing over them as filler in the text.

Make notes about the concepts and formulas you are reading about. For example, use an index card for each new formula and make notes about its appropriate uses. Or maintain a running glossary of terms if that will help you keep things straight.

The sciences can be especially challenging because of the level of abstraction scientists often incorporate in their writing. Strive to develop the practice of

The world may be full of fourth rate writers but it's also full of fourth rate readers.

**Stan Barstow
British novelist, 20th century**

"All very well and good—but now we come to chart B."

coming up with concrete examples to take some of the mystery out of reading in the sciences.

More Strategies to Improve Reading

Use Self Assessment 5.2 to evaluate your current reading profile. Then consider these additional strategies for improving it.

- **Practice a positive attitude.** College reading can be extremely challenging. If you approach your reading with a feeling of defeat, you may give up at the first sign of difficulty. Keep a positive attitude. Others have succeeded before you. If they could manage, so can you.

- **Make the author your companion.** Most authors envision themselves talking to their readers as they write. As you read, imagine talking to the author as a way of making your reading more lively. When you approach the reading as one end of a conversation, it may be easier to make comments, to see relationships, and to be critical.

- **Pace yourself according to difficulty level.** When you are naturally drawn to some kinds of reading, you may not have to struggle to get the key ideas. However, some difficult writing may need to be read three or four times before it begins to make sense. This kind of struggle with complex material or abstraction is normal.

- **Take breaks to restore concentration.** Plan to take breaks at regular intervals throughout a reading session. How long you can read between breaks depends on how hard you have to work to grasp the ideas. Examine the material to see whether there are natural breaks, such as the end of a section, that correspond with your attention span.

    Reward yourself when you have completed your target reading: Go for a walk, talk briefly

Staying Out of the *Pits*

Watch What You Say

One bad habit that many students fall into is *subvocalizing*. This involves concentrating on sounding out the words as you read. Some students mouth words as they read, which provides clear evidence of inefficient reading. However, others subvocalize with their mouths closed. The problem with subvocalizing is that it dramatically slows down your reading because it limits your reading speed to how fast you talk. Instead, concentrate on reading phrases or passages rather than this verbatim strategy. Your reward for "keeping your mouth closed" is faster reading with more time to spare.

Self-Assessment 5-2

What's Your Reader Profile?

Check the alternative that best describes you as a reader:

1. When I have an assignment to read
   - ____ a. I am usually enthusiastic about what I will learn.
   - ____ b. I like to wait to see whether what I have to read will be valuable.
   - ____ c. I am generally apprehensive about reading assignments because I'm afraid I may not understand them.

2. My attitude toward the authors of my college books is
   - ____ a. I think of them as human beings with an interesting story to tell.
   - ____ b. I haven't really given the writers much thought.
   - ____ c. I think of them as people who will probably talk over my head.

3. When I plan my reading
   - ____ a. I think about how the assignment fits in with the objectives of the course.
   - ____ b. I review the prior assignment to set the stage for current work.
   - ____ c. I plunge in so I can get it done.

4. I take breaks
   - ____ a. To consolidate the information I read.
   - ____ b. To help extend the length of productive study time.
   - ____ c. Whenever I lose interest in my reading.

5. When I don't know a word
   - ____ a. I look it up, write it down, and practice it.
   - ____ b. I try to figure it out from the context of the sentence.
   - ____ c. I usually skip over it and hope it won't make too much difference in the meaning.

6. When I can't understand a sentence
   - ____ a. I reread the sentence more carefully.
   - ____ b. I try to figure out the sentence from the context of the paragraph.
   - ____ c. I skip the sentence, hoping it will make sense later.

7. When the whole assignment confuses me
   - ____ a. I try to find more materials that will shed some light on my confusion.
   - ____ b. I ask the instructor or someone else for ideas about how to cope with the assignment.
   - ____ c. I tend to give up on it.

8. When I read
   - ____ a. I concentrate on reading as fast as I can while still understanding the meaning.
   - ____ b. I try to sweep as many words as I can at a glance.
   - ____ c. I take it one word at a time—speed doesn't matter to me.

Results: *Alternatives a and b of each question are more indicative of success patterns for college readers. If you have marked many c alternatives, you might benefit from a visit with a reading specialist on campus who can help you develop more successful strategies.*

with someone in person, on the phone, or by e-mail, or do some pleasure reading. When you have two or more kinds of reading to complete, do the harder or duller one first, while your concentration is stronger.

- **Shift gears when you do not make progress.** A fresh start may be required if you find yourself reading and rereading the same passage. Try writing a note on the reading. Take a break. Get something to drink. Call a classmate to confer about your struggle. Return to the passage with an intention to read more slowly until the clouds part.

- **Read other sources if the reading is confusing.** Sometimes an author's style is hard to comprehend. As Talia Falkenstein (in our opening profile) discovered when she was trying conquer *Twelfth Night*, browsing the Internet may be helpful. For non-fiction, find a clearer book on the same topic at the library or bookstore. Make sure that its coverage is comparable to your assigned text.

    Some bookstores sell guides to certain disciplines that may help to clarify basic ideas. Keep your introductory textbooks as references for when you are challenged in later, tougher courses. Get help from an instructor or tutor in finding other sources.

- **Build your vocabulary.** College is a great place to expand your vocabulary. In the process of learning the specialized languages in the discipline, you will also expand your general vocabulary. Get a dictionary and use it often for words you don't know. Once you look up a word, practice using the word to help you remember it. On an index card, keep a list of new words and their meanings. Use it as a bookmark.

    If you do not have a dictionary nearby when you need it, you may be able to use word attack skills to understand a word. You can often divide a word into parts that give you hints about the meaning (see Table 5.2). You also may be able to figure out the meaning of the word from the rest of the sentence.

- **Work on reading faster.** Fast readers tend to be more effective learners than slow readers, not only because they remember more of what they read but because they also save valuable time (Armstrong & Lampe, 1990). Learn your reading speed by completing Self-Assessment 5.3.

    You can improve your reading speed by concentrating on processing more words with each sweep of your eyes across a line of text. For example, if you normally scan three words at a time, practice taking in four words with each scan or scan to read whole phrases instead of individual words. You can also ask to have your reading abilities tested formally by reading specialists at the college. They can help you identify specific problems and solutions.

- **Increase your accountability for reading.** Make commitments that will help you feel more accountable for what you have read. Join a study group or promise to tutor another student who needs help. Some students negotiate with their instructors about how they can contribute to class on a given day. This strategy is especially helpful for shy students.

Table 5-2
Word Attack Skills

Root words (core of the meaning), prefixes (word beginnings), and suffixes (word endings) provide clues about word meanings. Here are some common examples from Latin and Greek.

ROOT WORDS	MEANING	EXAMPLES
capere, cap, capt	to take or seize	captive: one who is taken
duco, duct	to lead	deduce: to conclude or solve
facere, fac, fact	to make or do	factitious: made up
fero, fer	to bear	offer: to provide
graphein, graph	to write	telegraph: to send message
mittere, mit	to send	transmit: to send across
plicare	to connect	implicate: to suggest involvement
specio, spec	to see	specimen: observable sample

PREFIXES	MEANING	EXAMPLES
a, ab	without or not	atheist: nonbeliever in God
ad	to	advocate: to speak for
ambi	both	ambivalent: uncommitted
con	together	convention: formal gathering
de	from or down	despicable: abhorrent
dis	not	disinterest: boredom
ex	over	exaggerate: to magnify
hyper	above	hyperactive: overactive
hypo	under	hypodermic: under skin
mono	single	monolingual: speaking one language
non	not	nonresponsive: not reacting
pro	forward	production: process of making
re	back, again	revert: return to former state
sub, sup	under	subordinate: in a lower position
trans	across	transpose: to change places

SUFFIXES	MEANING	EXAMPLES
-able, -ible (adjective)	capable of	responsible: in charge
-ac, -al, -il (adjective)	pertaining to	natural: related to nature
-ance, -ence (noun)	state or status	dalliance: playful activity
-ant, -end (noun)	one who does	servant: person who waits on others
-er, -or (noun)	one who does	contractor: one who builds
-ive (adjective)	state or status	festive: party-like
-ish (adjective)	quality of	foolish: like a fool
-less (adjective)	without	heartless: harsh, unfeeling
-ly (adjective/adverb)	like	miserly: like a miser
-ness (noun)	state of	peacefulness: state of peace

Self-Assessment 5-3

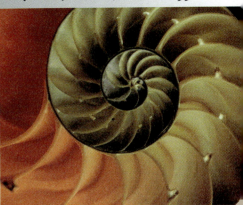

How Fast Do You Read?

Select a text from one of your courses. Set a timer for five minutes and start reading. When the timer goes off, stop reading. Count the number of lines you have read in the five-minute period. Pick several lines at random in the text and count the number of words in the lines. Multiply the number of lines you read by the average number of words per line. This will give you an approximation of the total of words you read in the five-minute period. Finally, divide by 5 to produce your reading speed in words per minute.

Content area: _____

Date of assessment: _____

Number of lines read: _____

× Number of words per line: _____

= Approximate total words _____

Divided by 5 (minutes) _____

Approximate words per minute _____

How does your reading speed compare to these average speeds for different kinds of reading (Skinner, 1997)?

Skimming	800 words per minute	_____
Active reading	100–200 words per minute	_____
Analytic reading	Under 100 words per minute	_____

Use this estimate as a baseline for your reading speed. Consider repeating this evaluation a few weeks from now after you have practiced. (Conscientious practice at increasing your reading speed should produce higher reading rates.) Remember, your reading speed also should vary according to the difficulty of the material.

Marking Text and Taking Notes from Text

Just as there is no one correct way to take notes from lecture, there is no one sure-fire method for taking good notes for readings. There are three general strategies. The first two are for books you own. The third involves creating an external set of notes.

Highlighting Text

Using a highlighter helps many students concentrate as they read and makes it easier for them to review for tests. Ideally, you should highlight topic sentences,

I had the worst study habits and the lowest grades. Then I found out what I was doing wrong. I had been highlighting with a black magic marker.

Jeff Altman
Contemporary American comedian

key words, and conclusions, which will usually make up much less than one-quarter of the text.

Although this strategy may keep you engaged with the reading, there are several hazards. You may highlight too much material so that you are faced with rereading nearly the entire text when you review. Also, simply highlighting does not show *why* you highlighted a passage. And when it is time to review, you still need to carry the complete text with you. Finally, if you sell your text after the course is over, the highlighting may make it worth less.

Personalizing Text

Some students find that they can absorb a text more easily by drawing pictures and writing summary notes in the margins. To make your learning more vivid, you can draw arrows or thumbs-down signs when you disagree, and circle key terms. Of course, this also may make the book worth less if you sell it back.

Creating External Notes

Creating a set of external notes on what you read gives you more flexibility in how you study and review later. You can use many of the lecture note methods (such as outlining or the Cornell system) to digest readings.

An alternative structure for external notes on readings involves recording six types of information:

- The source by title and author
- The purpose of the reading
- Key terms
- Controversies
- Important lists
- Conclusions

More Tips for Successful Notes on Readings

How else can you improve your reading notes?

- **Write your notes in your own words.** There are two reasons to translate the author's words into your own. First, it increases the personal connections you make to the material and makes it easier to remember. Second, it avoids plagiarism when you use the notes to write a paper. When you literally lift the words of an author from a text and later present these words as your own, you are stealing the thoughts and expressions of another. Instructors may view this as laziness or deceit and may penalize you. You can avoid this complication by paraphrasing as you take notes on your reading.

- **Avoid writing things down that you do not understand.** Some ideas you just won't understand on first reading. You may feel tempted to write down unclear ideas with the intention of returning to them later. Do not write things down that don't make sense to you and move on. Instead, mark the passage with a question and do what you can to clarify it before you move on.

- **Think and record in pictures.** Try to turn text information into some other form to help you remember. If you can make a list or table, create a graph, or draw a picture, it may be easier for you to recall. Diagrams and tables can also be tools for summarizing.

- **Periodically evaluate the quality of your notes.** Especially after an exam, review your notes to see how well they worked.

- **Explain yourself.** College reading often is very complex and abstract. It is easy to read a mass of material and think you understand what you have read when you really didn't grasp the concepts in the passage at all. Imagine that you have a study companion who doesn't read as well as you do and struggles to understand the central ideas in assignments. Regularly explain the key ideas in the reading to your "friend," particularly when the material is harder or less interesting for you. When you can't explain the passage easily, this signals your need to review the passage again. Of course, if you use this strategy, you may need to advise those with whom you are living that you are using a study strategy or they may think the pressures of college are getting to you!

Taking effective notes means not only from lecture, but also from your readings. What are some good strategies for taking notes from your readings?

Summary Tips For Mastering College

Taking It All In

Classroom Listening

1. Commit yourself to the class. You will benefit more from classes where you have prepared than those where you go in cold.
2. Concentrate on listening by using different listening strategies in different situations. Listening actively during lecture is the most efficient way to learn in class.
3. Capture the key ideas from class. Interpret the instructor's language and body cues to help you determine what is more likely to be tested.
4. Connect what you hear to what you know already to make lecture easier to learn. The more connections you make, the better.

Taking Notes in Class

1. Size up what kind of note-taking strategy will work best in a given class. The same strategy may not be effective in all settings.
2. Use your notes for review. Promote mastery by reviewing right after class, between classes, and before class.
3. Use abbreviations. Make up your own, but be sure to record what the symbols mean.
4. Evaluate the effectiveness of your note-taking strategies from the results of your tests. You can figure out which approaches work well and where you need to change.

Reading

1. Find a place where you can read with few interruptions. Do what you can to clear your obligations so you can concentrate.
2. Expect primary sources to be harder to read than secondary sources. You will need to make your own interpretations and understand the context in which the primary source was written.
3. Plan a reading strategy for each class that fits the material's complexity, your reading capacity, and your available time. Use textbook features such as in-chapter summaries to plan your approach.
4. Take a positive attitude toward your reading. Others have been successful and you will be, too.
5. Reward on-task reading behavior but try to avoid snacking. Pace yourself to make your reading time efficient.
6. Consult other sources if your assignments or readings are hard to decipher. Find similar textbooks or other library materials that can help.

Marking Texts and Taking Notes from Text

1. Be selective when you highlight text. If you highlight too much, you may need to reread most of the text later.
2. Write your notes in your own words. This practice will show you what you understand and lay a good foundation for avoiding plagiarism when you write.
3. Select a note-taking format that makes it easy to review and succeed. Get help with learning how to take more effective notes if your system does not work.

✓ College Success Checklist

Have your views changed about any of the following items since you filled out this checklist at the beginning of the chapter? Place a check mark beside any item for which you feel good about your current practice. Also check any for which you now have new ideas about how to improve.

____ I systematically process information from lectures and textbooks.

____ I use a variety of strategies to figure out what's most important in lectures and readings.

____ I know how to keep myself focused during lectures, even with problematic lecturers.

____ I am familiar with different note-taking methods.

____ I can explain why certain environments are better suited for reading.

____ I know the difference between primary and secondary sources and the value of each.

____ I use various strategies to read more effectively and efficiently.

____ I use my notes to improve my learning as well as my test performance.

In the space below, list the items that you still need to work on the most. This list may help you complete the goal-setting exercise in the Learning Portfolio.

Review Questions

1 What are the basic ingredients of a good system for processing information?

2 What are some strategies for listening when lecturers are challenging?

3 What styles of note-taking make the most sense for classes you are taking?

4 What is the difference between a primary and a secondary source?

5 When would you use different reading styles in college courses?

6 How can you modify your reading technique to improve retention?

7 What are some important features of good note-taking from text?

Learning Portfolio

Learning by Reflecting... Journal Entries

Getting Insights from Success
Think about a course you are taking this semester in which taking notes is easy for you.

- What about the teacher's style contributes to your success?
  _____
  _____
- How do you make your notes a personal reflection of your learning?
  _____
  _____
- How might your note-taking improve if you adopted some of the ideas in this chapter? Which ideas could work for you?
  _____
  _____

Expand these notes in your journal.

Evaluating Your Reading Path
You have had enough experience with academic reading to recognize that some kinds of reading are really challenging for you while other kinds of reading feel easy.

- What kinds of reading are easiest for you to do?
  _____
  _____
  _____
- What kinds of reading are hardest?
  _____
  _____
  _____
- Can you think of any strategies that might carry over from the easier reading to the harder reading?
  _____
  _____
  _____

The Perfect Place to Read
Try to imagine what kind of environment would best support your reading. Describe the qualities you would need to have in the environment. How far off is the ideal you have just described from your current reality? What can you do to make your current arrangement better?

Learning by Doing... Action Projects

Exploring Interpretation
Read a newspaper account (a secondary source) of a current scientific project. Then ask a librarian to help you track down the original work (the primary source) in a scientific journal. Compare the length of the reports, the language level difficulty, the order of importance of ideas, and any other contrasting features. Based on your observations, how would you say that primary and secondary sources differ?

How Do You Read?
Monitor how you read your assignments for one week. Then rate how regularly you engage in different kinds of reading:

	I do this regularly	I sometimes do this	I rarely do this
Previewing	____	____	____
Skimming	____	____	____
Active reading	____	____	____
Analytic reading	____	____	____
Reviewing	____	____	____

In which categories might you improve your overall performance?

On a New Note
Try out a new note-taking method for two weeks. At the end of that period compare your old and new methods in relation to how confident you feel about mastering the material. Should you continue your new method or go back to your old one?

Learning by Thinking Critically... Critiques

A Shared Path to Success

Convene a small group in your college success class to compare your strategies for taking notes. Try to select a course that you have in common even if you don't have the same instructor. See whether as a group you can determine which approaches are more effective in capturing the critical ideas and in promoting appropriate learning for that type of course.

Working from Memory

Suppose you found yourself in a class where the instructor forbade you from taking notes. Suppose he claimed that note-taking interfered with your capacity to pay full attention to the activities in the class.

- Is his idea believable?
  _____
  _____
- Would you accept this? Why or why not?
  _____
  _____
  _____
- How might your listening skills change as a result of this class?
  _____
  _____
  _____
- What course of action do you have?
  _____
  _____
  _____

Analyzing the Sixth Sense

Some students excel in their ability to figure out what information given in class will show up on the tests. Speculate about what kinds of cues they are interpreting to make their instructor's behavior so predictable.

- What voice cues are helpful?
  _____
  _____
  _____
- What kinds of words reveal an instructor's intent?
  _____
  _____
  _____
- What behaviors show an instructor's excitement about concepts?
  _____
  _____
  _____

Learning by Thinking Creatively... Personal Vision

On the Side

In our opening profile, we saw some side strategies that helped Talia Falkenstein succeed when assignments seemed hard to manage. Select an assignment that lies ahead in one of your classes that feels challenging. Brainstorm about five side strategies you could use if you run into difficulties in completing the assignment. (Remember, there is a difference between a side strategy and an unethical practice.)

Your Own System

You have read about several systems for taking notes. The system you developed before coming to college may be similar to one of them. Based on everything you have learned in this chapter, design a note-taking system that you think will work for you in the course where you seem to be having the most strain. What are the basic features of your new design?

Taking Advantage

Effective organizational strategies will serve you well in college, but they will also benefit you in your life after graduation. Think about the future you are preparing for by pursuing a college education. In what ways will the capacity to process information effectively and efficiently influence the quality with which you do your work? Speculate about the advantages you can gain by developing good information processing skills now.

Learning by Planning... Goal Setting

Review the results of the Self-Assessments you completed in this chapter. Also review the College Success Checklist. What can you conclude about things you need to do to improve your skills?

What goal do you want to select from this chapter for making changes that will help you master the college experience? (*Hint: Is your goal challenging, reasonable, and specific?*)

_____
_____
_____
_____

What strategies will you use to achieve your goal? (*Hint: Can you organize your strategy into a series of smaller goals?*)

_____
_____
_____
_____
_____
_____
_____
_____

What obstacles may be in your way as you attempt to make these positive changes?

_____
_____
_____
_____

What additional resources might help you succeed in achieving your goal?

_____
_____
_____
_____

By what date do you want to accomplish your goal?

_____

How will you know you have succeeded?

_____
_____
_____

Resources for Mastering the College Experience

Listening

The Lost Art of Listening (1995) by Michael P. Nichols. New York: Guilford Press.
Examines the many challenges that complicate listening.

Listening in Everyday Life: A Personal and Professional Approach (1991) by Deborah Borisoff and Michael Purdy (Eds.). Lanham, MD: University Press of America.
Explores the link of accurate listening to career development and professional success.

Listen Up: Hear What's Really Being Said (1991) by Jim Dugger. Shawnee Mission, KS: National Press Publications.
Written for journalists, with principles that apply to classroom information processing.

Reading

Reading Smart (1994) by Nicholas Reid Schaeffer. New York: Princeton Books.
Many techniques for building speed and retention in learning, based on paying attention to the context of the reading. Describes a "reading racetrack" for monitoring personal progress.

Reading for Success (1996) by Laraine Flemming. Boston: Houghton-Mifflin.
Emphasizes attitude and motivation in developing effective study skills. Provides example selections from textbooks from different disciplines.

How to Read a Book: The Art of Getting a Liberal Education (1940) by Mortimer Adler. New York: Simon & Schuster.
Includes a list of "great books" deemed essential to a good liberal education.

Note-Taking

Advanced Listening Comprehension: Developing Listening and Note-Taking Skills (1982) by Patricia Dunkel and Frank Pialorsi. Rowley, MA: Newburgy House Publishers.
Written exercises and audio activities to practice listening and note-taking skills. May especially help those who speak English as a second language.

Getting Straight A's (1995) by G. W. Green Jr. New York: Lyle Stuart Publishers.
Emphasizes rewriting notes to improve retention and promote preparedness for tests.

Internet Resources

http://world.std.com/~emagic/mindmap.html
Mind-Mapping.

http://www.csbsju.edu/advising/help/eff-list.html
Ideas on effective classroom listening.

http://ecuvax.cis.ecu.edu/academics/schdept/unstud/asc/notetake.htm
Tips and examples for effective note-taking.

http://www.dartmouth.edu/admin/acskills/cornell.html
More details on using the Cornell method.

http://www.coun.uvic.ca/learn/hndouts.html
More advice and models for how to organize your notes.

http://www.dartmouth.edu/admin/acskills/index.html#study
Ways to improve reading, listening, and note-taking; tips for international students.

http://www.ucc.vt.edu/studysk/notetake.html
Solid tips for note-taking and in-class skills.

http://hkuhist2.hku.hk/firstyear/semina4.htm
Illustrates by examples how to record important ideas from readings.

http://www.utexas.edu/student/lsc/handouts/1422.html
How to read textbooks efficiently.

Developing Study Skills

CHAPTER 6

✓ College Success Checklist

Place a check mark beside the items that apply to you. Leave the items blank that do not apply to you.

____ I know the benefits of good study habits.

____ I choose appropriate places and times to study.

____ I review regularly to learn course information better.

____ I organize materials to make them easier to learn and remember.

____ I use strategies to improve my memory related to coursework.

____ I recognize when I'm being asked to think abstractly.

____ I adapt my study strategies to suit different disciplines.

____ I can describe how individual ability differences influence study success.

____ I know how learning disabilities complicate learning and studying.

Preview

Hitting the books can be a frustrating experience unless you know how to make the best use of your time. In this chapter you will explore strategies that make your study time effective and efficient. You will also see how memory techniques apply to forgetting problems in everyday life. You will examine strategies for studying different disciplines and learn about ability differences that can facilitate or interfere with learning.

Chapter Outline

Images of College Success: Yo-Yo Ma

Why Study?
- Where to Study
- When to Study

Improving Your Memory
- How Memory Works
- How to Memorize

Study Strategies for Complex Ideas
- The Humanities
- Natural Science and Math
- Social Science
- Foreign Language

Factors That Influence Study Success
- Academic Strengths and Weaknesses
- Gender and Learning
- Learning Differences

Self-Assessments
- 6.1 Early Bird or Night Owl?
- 6.2 Am I Ready to Learn and Remember?
- 6.3 What Is My Frame of Mind?
- 6.4 Could I Have a Learning Disability?

On-Target Tips
- After Class Is Over
- Abstract Art
- Deep Study Strategies for the Humanities
- Becoming Better at Science and Math
- Thriving in Social Science
- Learning Languages
- Breaking the Silence

Images of College Success
Yo-Yo Ma

Yo-Yo Ma was born into a musical family in 1955. His father was a musicologist, violinist, and composer, and his mother was a mezzo-soprano. They introduced their young son to the violin but he was reluctant to learn. His sister was already playing that instrument. He wanted "something bigger" to play. At four Ma was far too small to manage a cello, so his father attached an endpin to a viola. Sitting on a stack of telephone books with the makeshift cello between his knees, Ma began his musical education.

His father's approach emphasized short periods of concentrated work in-

Yo-Yo Ma was already a celebrated musician when he entered Harvard, but he says that his college education helped him to make a more informed decision about his career.

stead of extended practice hours. Ma memorized two measures of Bach each day so by the age of five he knew three Bach cello suites by heart. At age seven, Yo-Yo Ma played his cello on national television and by age eight, he made a successful debut at Carnegie Hall. From this auspicious beginning, his musical career flourished.

He won the Avery Fisher prize for excellence, along with countless other accolades for his musical prowess. Orchestra conductors especially praise Ma's technical eloquence and personal charm because these qualities bring out the best performances from their orchestra.

With such extraordinary musical ability, a college education might have seemed unnecessary. However, Ma regarded his pursuit of a degree from Harvard as the wisest choice he ever made. He said his undergraduate degree helped him to make an informed decision about pursuing a musical career. It also put him in position to choose other directions if he desired.

A recent project for PBS gave Ma an unusual creative opportunity that took five years to complete. In "Yo-Yo Ma: Inspired by Bach," Ma shared his love of composer Johann Sebastian Bach in collaboration with filmmakers, ice dancers, and even kabuki theater performers. The three-week series helped Ma explore the richness of imagination. His education introduced him to all the possibilities available, making him ultimately feel more secure about committing to a career as a musician and artistic collaborator.

Why Study?

Some lucky people can memorize everything in sight. Others almost effortlessly develop sophisticated insights about their coursework. However, to do well in college most of us need concentrated time with the notes we have made from readings and classes.

Studying accomplishes many objectives. It makes it easier to recall the core material of the course. It helps you develop richer insights. It also facilitates good work habits that will carry over into your career.

The amount of time students report doing assignments or studying is related to many aspects of college success (Astin, 1993). Students who study more hours say they are more satisfied with college than students who study less. Also, students who study more report that college improves their cognitive skills and emotional life. But studying *more* is only one way to improve. Studying *more effectively* can also help. Among other benefits, sensible study methods save you time so you have more of it for social life and other interests.

Where to Study

The phone rings. Your downstairs neighbor is throwing a noisy party. The television in the living room is blaring a *Seinfeld* rerun. And your relentless appetite demands a hot fudge sundae. At times the world is so full of distractions that it seems impossible to find the right time and place to study. But your success as a student depends on your ability to conquer these distractions and stick to a good study routine.

You may find that you work best if you can arrange to study consistently in the same place. Your study area should be a comfortable temperature and be well-lit.

Minimize noise. Many people study best when the stereo, radio, or television is turned off. Some people like to have music on in the background to mask other sounds and give a sense of control over the environment. If you can't control the noise around you, try using headphones and soft instrumental music to minimize the distraction.

You may want to study in areas of the library designed to promote concentration. Colleges also usually try to maintain other quiet spaces on campus. Studying on campus may be especially useful for commuting students who have difficulty finding quiet places to study at home. If you commute, you can also think of your transit time as a possible study period. Use driving as an opportunity to review audiotapes of complicated lectures or carpool with someone in your class so you can review together. Riding on a bus or train, especially if the commute is a long one, can give you blocks of study time. If you live on campus, you should be able to find other dedicated space for study. Residence halls usually set aside quiet rooms away from noisy roommates.

Find private space to study. Some students can concentrate in strange postures and in strange places, but most find that sitting at a desk improves their concentration. Desks provide storage for study materials and help you stay organized. If you don't have a desk, find a big box that can contain all your supplies and books. You may be able to set up a simple filing system in the box.

What if you have to share study space at home with others, especially if the others are children? Assign desk drawers to everyone who will be sharing the

For a man to attain an eminent degree in learning costs him time, watching, hunger, nakedness, dizziness in the head, weakness in the stomach, and other inconveniences.

Miguel de Cervantes
Spanish author, 17th century

Temptations come, as a general rule, when they are sought.

Margaret Oliphant
English novelist, 19th century

> *There are some things which cannot be learned quickly, and time, which is all we have, must be paid heavily for their acquiring.*
>
> **Ernest Hemingway**
> **American author, 20th century**

Some students can study effectively in uncomfortable postures and distracting environments, but many students prefer to study at a desk or a table. Have you figured out the environment where you study best?

space. Then together figure out how best to share the space. Hang a bulletin board near your work space to display good work. This practice can motivate everyone to try harder. If you have to take over the kitchen or dining room table, be sure to tidy up after each study session unless you make other arrangements about the space with the family.

Use your desk *only* for studying. When you drift asleep at your desk, you learn to associate your desk with napping, a cue most students cannot afford. When you choose to nap or find yourself daydreaming a lot, go elsewhere to restore your concentration. Other ways to avoid dozing off include (Frank, 1996)

On Target Tips

After Class Is Over

What can you do after class to consolidate your learning? You can

- *Rewrite and reorganize your notes.* This not only allows you to create a neater, edited set of ideas for study, but also provides an immediate rehearsal to help you consolidate the information.
- *Highlight the most important ideas.* Underline or color-code the ideas that stand out as the most likely to appear on a test. Write notes in the margins that will make the material more meaningful to you.
- *Write a summary paragraph of the main ideas.* What were the main points covered in class? How did this class fit with the overall objectives of the course?
- *Identify any ideas that are still confusing.* Make notes about what remains unclear so you can look up the answers in your reading. You can also ask other students or the instructor.

- **Set an alarm.** Buy a wristwatch that can signal you at reasonable intervals to keep you on task.
- **Rely on friends or family to keep you awake.** Study with others so you can monitor your drowsiness. Ask a parent or partner to check on you.
- **Take a five-minute fresh air break.** A brisk walk can clear your mind so you can focus better when you return to your studies.
- **Avoid getting too comfortable.** This is just an invitation to doze at the first sign of boredom.
- **Stay involved in your reading.** The more invested you are, the less tempting it is to succumb to sleepy feelings.
- **Get enough sleep to begin with.** You can manage a late night every once in awhile but a steady diet of all-nighters guarantees that you will be fighting off the drive to doze.

When to Study

Try to allocate at least several hours outside of class for every hour you spend in class. Outstanding students often put in even more time. Although some study strategies can make you a better learner, there is no denying the need to study long hours for academic success. What are some ideas about how to use those hours wisely?

Review After Class One of the best study strategies is to review your notes immediately after class. This lets you rehearse new ideas and identify unclear ideas so you can clarify them with your instructor or in your reading. See "After Class Is Over" for tips on how to review.

Review Before Class Reviewing your class notes before the next class, along with your notes on reading assignments, adds another rehearsal session that prepares you to participate in the next class more effectively. You also will remember the concepts better. Good students often get to class about ten minutes early to review their notes.

Schedule Regular Cumulative Review Sessions Devote some time to seeing the big picture in each of your courses. Look at how each lecture fits the broader course objective. If you regularly review your notes during the term, you will need less review time right before exams.

Listen to Your Body Pay attention to your natural rhythms. If you are a night person, review sessions may be most effective after supper and late into the evening. If you are a morning person, you need to study earlier in the day to maximize your attention and concentration. Complete Self-Assessment 6.1 to evaluate your high- and low-energy periods.

Staying Out of the Pits

The Cramming Syndrome

Although cramming may produce occasional success in tests, it is a bad strategy for learning in many ways:

- *Cramming produces only short-term learning.* You probably won't remember what you stuffed inside your brain at the last minute.

- *Cramming may not be practical.* You may end up having to cram for more than one subject at a time. Professors may find it convenient to schedule exams just before school adjourns for a midterm vacation. This can result in a clustering of assignments and tests. If you wait to cram in all of your subject areas, the sheer quantity of what you have to learn may defeat you.

- *Cramming is hard on your health.* Pulling all-nighters, losing sleep, and plying yourself with caffeine or other attention-expanding drugs can harm your health, making you more vulnerable to colds and other illnesses.

Cramming is a bad idea. You could end up confused, distracted, overtired, and fragile in your learning. You may even be unable to stay awake through the exam. Have you been successful in reducing your need to cram for tests?

Self-Assessment 6-1

Early Bird or Night Owl?

Which is most characteristic of your approach?

___ I roll out of bed eager to face the day.	___ I drag myself out of bed, sorry the day has started.
___ I manage to get up without an alarm.	___ I regularly use the snooze button on my alarm clock.
___ I face complaints from my friends about being too chipper early in the morning.	___ I face complaints from my friends about being too crabby in the morning.
___ I tend to run out of steam in the middle of the afternoon.	___ I tend to start hitting my stride in the middle of the afternoon.
___ I prefer intense activity before noon.	___ I prefer intense activity after noon.
___ I cannot function without getting a minimum amount of sleep.	___ I can function on little or no sleep.
___ I leave parties early.	___ I leave parties late.

If you marked most items in the first column, you are an early bird. Try to schedule most of your classes in the morning. Consider catnapping in the afternoon to restore your energy. If you marked most items in the second column, you are a night owl. Avoid morning classes when you can. Be on guard to make sure that you don't get too run down.

Improving Your Memory

There are two general ways to put information into memory (Minninger, 1984): Memorize using rote rehearsal or remember through understanding. For example, if you are trying to learn a new procedure on your computer, you can just memorize the sequence of things you have to do to accomplish the job or strive to learn what each step accomplishes in relation to your goal. As you can imagine, the first approach leads to superficial learning. Rote learning tends not to last. The next time you have to repeat the procedure on the computer, you probably will have to relearn it. Learning through understanding initially may be more work, but the learning sticks.

Memorizing is a necessary skill in college. Some tests may depend entirely on your ability to memorize. Naming the levels of the phylogenetic scale in zoology or recognizing the musical instruments in a symphony requires memorization. Let's explore how memory works before we look at methods for improving memory.

How Memory Works

Two important memory systems involved in academic learning have different time frames: *short-term memory* and *long-term memory*.

Short-Term Memory Short-term memory ("working memory") enables us to get some work done without cluttering up our minds. For example, when you have to look up a new phone number, that number doesn't automatically go into your long-term memory storage for important numbers. Short-term memory lets us retain it briefly, about 30 seconds or so, just long enough to get the number dialed. Then it vanishes. If the number belongs to someone you met at a party last night and want to get to know better, you will need to rehearse the number, repeating it over and over to place it in long-term memory.

As helpful as short-term memory is to get basic tasks accomplished, it has some drawbacks. It has limited capacity. Short-term memory can hold approximately seven "chunks" of information before the system becomes overtaxed and information is dumped out of awareness (Miller, 1956). You may be able to trick short-term memory into holding more detail through a process called "chunking": making each memory chunk represent more than one piece of information. This is the basis for the *mnemonics*, or memory aids, discussed below.

Short-term memory is very fragile. Unless you rehearse information in short-term memory, it will be gone. If you are interrupted during rehearsal (suppose someone asks you a question after you have looked up a phone number) your short-term memory will be disrupted and you will probably lose the information.

Long-Term Memory Ideally, your learning strategies should be geared toward building your long-term memory for important and meaningful information. Your goal should be to learn course information so that it is viable not just for test time but well beyond the end of the course.

Feeling *Good*

The Night Before an Exam?

It might be hard to imagine, but some students manage to feel good the night before a test. If you have studied and reviewed adequately, you will need to study fewer hours the night before a test. This will give you more confidence, reduce your anxiety, and make you feel better than if you have to cram.

A great many people have asked how I get so much work done and still keep looking so dissipated.

**Robert Benchley
American humorist and writer,
20th century**

> *Patience and tenacity of purpose are worth more than twice their weight in cleverness.*
>
> **Thomas Henry Huxley**
> **English biologist, 19th century**

There appear to be no limits to the information we can store in long-term memory. You have already stored a mountain of facts and impressions in your long-term memory from your education and life experience. What is the meaning of *prerequisite*? When did the Great Depression begin? What was the best movie you ever saw? How do you ride a skateboard? Each memory exists in your long-term memory store and ideally you can *retrieve* it as you need it.

Long-term memories are organized around concepts and built through association. For example, if you are a fan of old movies, you may devote a lot of memory storage to retaining odd facts about directors, movie locations, and favorite actors. If you are *not* a sports fan, then you will feel bewildered when your sports-focused friends discuss obscure statistics related to the Superbowl. People easily store a lot of information in long-term memory on the topics that interest them most.

The more you know about a topic, the easier it is to learn more because you have more ways to make associations between new ideas and what you already know. If you don't know much about a subject, then your task is harder. You will be building your concept base from the ground up. This is why some course materials are harder to learn than others. You have to work harder to make associations.

How well your memory works depends not just on what you store, but on how efficiently you can retrieve the information (Schacter, 1996). Many long-term memories endure. For example, you may be able to recall the name of your first-grade teacher even though you haven't thought of him in a long time. We can remember vivid information without much practice.

Unfortunately, no matter how hard you study, you are bound to forget some things you learn. Experts cite two reasons why we forget: *interference* and *decay*. Interference can crowd out target memories, making them difficult to retrieve. This outcome is easy to understand when you are taking a full academic load. The sheer volume of what you are trying to learn may cause interference among the subjects, especially when courses use similar terms.

Memory decay makes memories hard to retrieve. Decay is the disintegration of memory when the ideas are not kept active through use. If you fail to review regularly or do not practice retrieving the information, you may find it impossible to recall the information at test time or at other times when you want it.

How to Memorize

There are various strategies to help new information take root in your mind.

Adopt the Right Attitude Memorizing new material is a challenge, but a positive attitude helps. Make a serious effort to develop interest in the subject you must study. Think about the potential personal or professional value the course may provide, even if you have to use your imagination a bit. Then study to meet specific learning objectives.

Look for connections that make learning personally meaningful (Matlin, 1998). This will make it easier to learn and recall unfamiliar or abstract ideas. For example, in history you may have to learn about periods that feel quite remote to you. Think about how these periods might have involved your own ancestors. For example, would your great grandmother have been a flapper during the Roaring '20s, or would she have led a different life?

> *God gave us memory so that we might have roses in December.*
>
> **Sir James M. Barrie**
> **Author of *Peter Pan*, 1904**

Make her the focal point of your learning about this era. If you didn't know about her, imagine her.

Pay Close Attention Don't allow yourself to be distracted when you are processing information about things you must do or remember. Some absent-mindedness is caused by failing to take in the information in the first place rather than forgetting.

Organize the Material Several organizational strategies can make memorizing easier to do.

Concentrate on one thing at a time. You may have to study multiple subjects in one session. If so, try to focus your attention on the subject at hand. Study the more difficult subjects first because you need more energy for the materials that are harder. Reward yourself for studying the more difficult subject by studying the subject you enjoy more last.

Create concept hierarchies. Organize concepts in a tree diagram to give yourself additional cues for remembering the ideas. For example, suppose you are studying important events in American history in the 1950s. Construct a map that captures the important details of the period to make it easier to remember. See Figure 6.1 for an example or refer to Chapter 5 for some other models.

Use or create mnemonics. Mnemonics are strategies that provide additional associations to help you learn. They involve linking something you want to remember to images, letters, or words that you already know or that are easy to recall because of how you've constructed the mnemonic. They can be visual or text-based, logical or goofy, and complex or simple and still be effective in promoting recall.

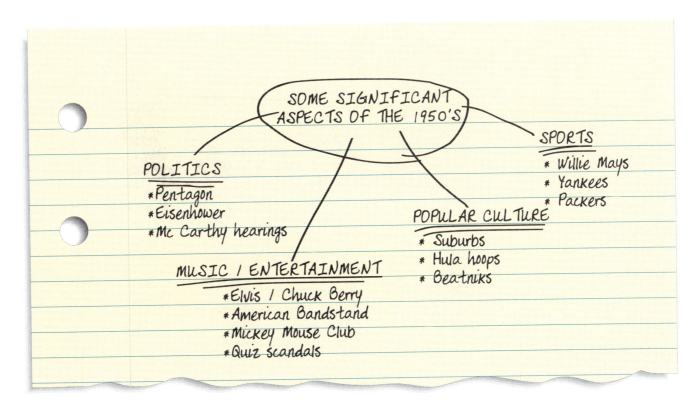

Figure 6.1   Concept maps branch out like trees to organize important information.

- **Rhymes and songs.** Nearly every child learns when Columbus came to America through rhyme: "Columbus sailed the ocean blue/In fourteen hundred ninety-two." The rhyme leaves an indelible impression. Eventually you do not have to repeat the rhyme to remember the date.

  A similar example can be found in health education in learning first aid: "When the face is red, raise the head. When the face is pale, raise the tail." Remembering the rhyme allows you make a swift decision about appropriate treatment.

  Melodies can also produce enduring memories. A generation of children learned how to spell *encyclopedia* by singing its spelling along with Jiminy Cricket on the Mickey Mouse Club in the early days of television. Many children learn their phone numbers or addresses when parents sing the information to them using a familiar melody. One inventive anatomy student learned different brain functions when she transformed the lyrics of an old rock song called "Maniac" to suit her purposes. (Of course, she renamed the song "Brainiac.")

- **Acronyms.** Acronyms are special words (or sentences) that you construct using the first letter from each word in the list you wish to memorize. The acronym cues you not only to the items on the list but also to their proper order. Table 6.1 shows some common acronyms from college courses.

- **Method of loci.** Another list mnemonic is associating the parts of a list with a physical sequence of activities or a specific location that

Table 6-1
Thanks for the Memory: Some Common Acronyms

DISCIPLINE	MNEMONIC	MEANING
Business	SWOT	Strengths, weaknesses, opportunities, threats (a technique for analyzing problems)
Physics	ROY G. BIV	Red, orange, yellow, green, blue, violet (visible colors in the light spectrum)
Anatomy & Physiology	On	olfactory
	old	optic
	Olympus'	ocular-motor
	towering	trochlear
	tops,	trigeminal
	a	abducent
	Finn	facial
	and	auditory
	German	glossopharyngeal
	viewed	vagus
	some	spinal
	hops	hypoglossal (the names of the cranial nerves)
Geography	HOMES	Huron, Ontario, Michigan, Erie, Superior (the Great Lakes)
Music	Every	E
	good	G
	boy	B
	does	D
	fine	F (the lines of the treble clef)
Astronomy	My	Mercury
	very	Venus
	elegant	Earth
	mother	Mars
	just	Jupiter
	served	Saturn
	us	Uranus
	nine	Neptune
	pickles	Pluto (nine planets in order from the sun)

you know well. For example, you can remember a long and difficult speech by thinking about walking through your home and associating a piece of the speech with being in each of the rooms. Another example of the method of loci can be found in "There's Blood in the Basement."

- **Visualization.** Using your imagination to come up with provocative images can provide memory cues. Making visualizations ridiculous is the best way to make them memorable (Lorayne & Lucas, 1996). Substitute or combine objects, exaggerate their features, make them disproportionate, or involve action in the image to make it distinctive. For example, you could remember elected representatives by

Amazing but True College Stories

There's Blood in the Basement!

When Wendy went to the recreation area in the basement of the residence hall to grab a soda, she was startled by what she saw. Her best friend, Debbie, was running from one corner of the large room to the other, pausing to rest occasionally, but talking to herself softly the entire time.

"Are you nuts?" Wendy asked. "What are you doing?"

"It's simple," Debbie said. "I have a physiology exam tomorrow. Right now I'm a red blood cell. The basement represents the body. I'm circulating. For example, this chair right here represents the right ventricle. Tomorrow when I have to describe this process on the exam, I'll just remember where I was when I was a blood cell!"

combining symbols that represent them in some outrageous way. Wisconsin Senators Feingold and Kohl become easy to remember if you picture the senate filled with coal dipped in 14 K (fine) gold.

- **Draw or diagram.** You do not have to be artistic to draw pictures, make arrows, or create stars in the margins of books or notes. Adding images can make it easier to recall details. Draw pictures of the comparisons that your instructor uses to clarify concepts. For example, if your psychology instructor describes Freud's view of the unconscious as similar to an iceberg, draw a large iceberg in the background of your notes. Drawings are especially helpful for visual learners.

Develop Retrieval Strategies Following are some strategies to improve your recall:

Strive for overlearning. Rehearse concepts not just to the point of confident retrieval, but *over*confidence. When you are comfortable that you know your stuff, study just a bit longer to overlearn the material. Overlearning improves the integration and the endurance of your learning.

Question yourself. By asking yourself questions about what you have read or what you have recorded about class activities, you expand the number of associations you make with the target information, which makes the ideas easier to recall, and you add to your rehearsal time. For example, the following questions may help you create additional links to the course concepts:

- Have I ever seen this concept before?
- Do I like or dislike the ideas?
- What are some practical examples of the concept?
- Are there other ways to explain the concept?

Not only will this practice improve your memory for course concepts, but it should improve your ability to think critically about them.

Minimize interference. If you are taking two similar subjects, space them apart when you study. This will reduce the amount of interference between the two sets of ideas.

Use props. Create a set of flash cards and carry them with you. Rehearse while you are waiting in grocery store lines, at laundromats, and at doctors' offices. Consider creating audiotapes of the ideas you want to memorize and review those while driving or doing chores.

Another strategy is to construct a "cram card" to help you retain difficult items, such as formulas, for tests (Frank, 1967). Whenever you can't commit important information to long-term memory through regular study and rehearsal, write down its essentials on a small card. Don't overload it with detail. Study the card up to the point when your instructor says to put materials away. Then put away the card but rehearse the information until you can write it down in the margins of your test booklet. Your short-term memory can help you succeed in remembering important information when your long-term memory has not been successful. Be sure to put the card away before the test begins. It could easily be mistaken for a crib note.

Remember the recency effect. Because of the recency effect, you are most likely to remember the last thing you learned. If you have to study multiple subjects in preparing for tests, try to schedule your final study session in a subject as the last thing you do before that test.

Exploit situational cues. If you can arrange it, sit in the seat you normally sit in for class when you take an exam. Being in the same place may help you dredge up some elusive memories. You may be able to recreate your memory of how an instructor described a fuzzy concept more readily from your original vantage point.

Avoid tip-of-the-tongue forgetting. Scott was distressed when he returned from his botany test. He told his brother that he studied hard, but studied wrong. "It was so frustrating," Scott said. "I thought I knew the concepts, but on many of the questions, I got this weird feeling. I could remember where they were on the page of my textbook. For example, '*photosynthesis*, p. 49, left column, upper third of the page.' I could see it clearly. But that's *all* I could remember. Next time, I'll have to study differently."

Scott's dilemma is a common one. Being able to remember where concepts appeared on the textbook page but failing to remember the concept's meaning is called partial memory. Or you may be able to remember that a concept you are trying to retrieve starts with "p" but the rest of the word eludes you. Both partial memory and this "tip-of-the-tongue" phenomenon suggest that your study strategies need more work to help you remember course concepts.

When you partially recall important information, you may be able to retrieve the whole of what you stored in memory if you temporarily change the direction of your thinking. Focusing away from the problem gives your mental circuits more time to warm up. Often this strategy will cause a term or name to surface.

Evaluate Your Progress How skilled are you in using your memory to retain information? Complete Self-Assessment 6.2 to identify the strategies you use and the ones that show promise for improving your memory.

Another strategy for evaluating your progress involves examining your test results to determine whether your strategies worked. You may need to study for longer periods of time or seek new, more efficient methods for remembering materials.

Study Strategies for Complex Ideas

Especially if you are majoring in an area that will train you for a specific profession, you may not have been thrilled to learn that you probably have to take a lot of liberal arts courses. However, each discipline represents a specialized way of thinking about human experience that should help you develop a richer perspective on life and a greater variety of ways to view and handle problems.

Courses differ in how much they make you think. Beginning courses in most disciplines are more likely to emphasize memorization and comprehension. Although memorizing is hard work, some courses require a lot more than memorizing information to be successful.

Self-Assessment 6-2

Am I Ready to Learn and Remember?

Review the elements of effective study strategies below and, for each of them, decide whether this characteristic is something you already do well or is a strategy you need to learn.

	STRENGTH	COULD BE IMPROVED
I purposefully schedule when I will study certain subjects to take advantage of my best energy levels.	_____	_____
I select study environments that have few distractions.	_____	_____
I review course input regularly to distribute my learning over time.	_____	_____
I try to find some angle in my assignments that will increase my interest in wanting to learn.	_____	_____
I question what I read to ensure my understanding and increase my personal involvement.	_____	_____
I look for ways to add meaning to course ideas during review sessions.	_____	_____
I rehearse the key ideas to the point of overlearning.	_____	_____
I use mnemonic strategies for memorization. List several	_____	_____

specific strategies you use: _____

_____

	STRENGTH	COULD BE IMPROVED
When I feel frustrated by partial recall, I divert my attention to recover more details.	_____	_____
I schedule an intensive review session before a test.	_____	_____
I avoid cramming whenever I can.	_____	_____
I use feedback on tests to evaluate whether I need to change my study strategies.	_____	_____

Look over your answers. Could the areas you need to improve be the difference between a mediocre performance and honor-quality work? What would you need to do to improve? How could you reward yourself for adopting more effective strategies?

If you prefer memorizing information to other kinds of academic work, you are in good company. Interviews by Marcia Baxter Magolda (1992) revealed that most beginning students prefer well-structured, simple learning tasks. Memorizing basic facts feels like a manageable challenge.

As your courses increase in difficulty, you often will move beyond memorization and comprehension. More sophisticated demands focus on the other skills that Benjamin Bloom and his colleagues (1956) call *higher-order* thinking skills. They include *application* (generalizing information to new situations), *analysis* (identifying the factors that explain an idea or event), *synthesis* (developing new combinations of ideas), and *evaluation* (making judgments about the quality of ideas). Practicing these skills during study can help you learn the material as you sharpen your higher-order thinking skills. In the next section, we will offer some strategies for pursuing higher-order thinking skills to improve your study in different disciplines.

When courses become more challenging, you will have to spend more time thinking abstractly or theoretically. Making the shift from thinking about well-structured, concrete learning tasks to unstructured, abstract challenges is not always easy. See "Abstract Art" for some tips on ways to make this shift. These strategies will improve your ability to study and learn complex ideas.

You have already noticed that you have to adjust your study strategies to the disciplines you are studying. Each discipline presents rules or laws that you must master, but it is usually not enough just to memorize the new concepts and terminology of the discipline. Most courses offer the opportunity to grapple with complex, discipline-specific ideas that require deeper thinking. Each discipline also may have special challenges associated with developing mastery. Following are some discipline-specific discussions to help your study strategies.

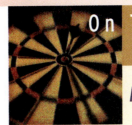

Abstract Art

Practicing the skills associated with abstract thinking may make it easier to perform related skills in your college courses:

- **Play strategic games.** Whether you are killing aliens on a CD-ROM or capturing someone's queen in an intense game of chess, strategic games help you develop reasoning skills.
- **Practice empathizing.** When you watch a movie, adopt the point of view of a minor character in the film. Try to relate to the events from that perspective. Discuss your insights with others to maximize learning from others' point of view.
- **Ask what-if questions.** A hypothesis is an unproven statement that, if it were true, would explain why certain things are true. When you come up with alternative explanations for something, you are practicing the art of making hypotheses and preparing the way for finding answers. You can improve your abstract thinking powers and give your imagination a workout by challenging yourself and others with frequent what-if questions.
- **Get into a good argument.** Look for opportunities to debate your opinions. Search for evidence, organize your ideas, and look for flaws in your opponents' positions to sharpen your reasoning skills.

The Humanities

Humanities courses develop your understanding of human experience. Most humanities courses emphasize exploring your subjective experience as you read great works of literature, examine specific periods in history, or evaluate the great ideas of philosophers.

The Rules Each humanities course typically is built around a particular framework, or set of concepts or theories, that will help you develop a new

Some leisure activities, such as playing chess, can help build your ability to think in abstract terms. How might your current leisure pursuits help build your ability to think abstractly?

On Target Tips

Deep Study Strategies for the Humanities

Suppose your have enrolled in a film appreciation class. You have just read a chapter about the works of American filmmaker Steven Spielberg. The following (or similar) questions during your review session will help you probe the material more deeply (based on Bloom, 1956):

Memorization	What are the names of Spielberg's past films? When did his first film debut?
Comprehension	Name the ways his films could be regarded as successful. What themes does he regularly present in his films?
Application	What other filmmakers tend to borrow from Spielberg's methods? Speculate about how a different director might have directed the film *E.T.*
Analysis	Why are his films so financially successful? What role has technology played in his productions?
Synthesis	Create a story line that would be intriguing to Spielberg. How might his films be different if he'd been born 20 years earlier?
Evaluation	In what ways do his critics fault his body of work? Rank order Spielberg's films from best to worst.

Notice that by using your imagination to think about your assignments, you also make new connections to the assigned material. The more connections you make, the easier it will be for you to recall the information that you need to memorize. An additional advantage of this strategy is that you may anticipate the kinds of questions that you might be asked on essay questions.

The answers you get from literature depend on the questions you pose.

Margaret Atwood
Contemporary Canadian novelist

---

perspective or richer appreciation for the human condition. For example, learning about literature will expose you to various frameworks of literary criticism, such as psychoanalytic or feminist criticism. Each framework is built on a distinct set of values and assumptions. Applying the frameworks to literature will probably lead you to different kinds of conclusions. A psychoanalytic framework encourages you to look at unconscious motivations; a feminist framework sensitizes you to social forces that create different options for women and men. Humanities instructors expect that your insights derived from intensive study demonstrate that you understand the frameworks. You know and can apply these frameworks to expand your personal insight.

The Risks Students may fear that their personal interpretations will get them in trouble in humanities courses. They assume that there may be only one possibility and they are afraid that they will look foolish if what they express is "wrong." However, the objective of most humanities courses is to encourage breadth of thinking, not to boil down the experience to a narrower view. Take the risk of sharing your insights. You may end up offering some ideas that your class members may never have heard. "Deep Study Strategies for the Humanities" illustrates one approach you can take for humanities assignments based on Bloom's taxonomy.

Natural Science and Math

Natural science explains the natural phenomena of the world, including everything from how fast an apple falls from a tree to the mysteries of the cell. Mathematics provides the tools to measure observations and assess change.

The Rules Natural science and math are loaded with theorems, laws, and formulas that you probably will need to memorize, but comprehension should be your primary objective. Most of the activities that you undertake in science and math give you practice in application, applying the rules to produce a specific outcome or solution. Obviously, the more you practice applying the principles or formulas, the more enduring your learning will be.

The Risks Natural science and math often have an unappealing reputation. The stereotype is that only science and math "geeks" do well in these courses. It will help if you deflate your images about science a little. For example, you regularly act like a scientist does when you figure out how things work, although you may not be as systematic or careful in your observations as scientists are. With some practice, you, too, can do real science. See "Becoming Better at Science and Math."

Social Science

The social sciences apply scientific methods to understand human experience. Thus, they are often a hybrid of the sciences and humanities.

The Rules The social sciences produce laws and theories to explain the behavior of individuals and groups. Concepts in the social sciences often serve as shorthand for complex patterns of behavior. For example, "social stratification," a sociology concept, refers to how people in a society can be classified into groups according to how much money they make, what types of jobs they have, how much power they wield, and so forth. Much of what you need to memorize in social science courses has to do with acquiring the conceptual language of social scientists, like the term *stratification*.

The Risks Learning in the social sciences can be challenging because what you are expected to learn may conflict with what you previously believed. For example, someone may have convinced you previously that it is dangerous to awaken a sleepwalker. In your psychology class, you discover that this knowledge is inaccurate, and that it is more dangerous to allow a sleepwalker freedom to walk into trouble. You have to reject some things you thought were true to make room for new ideas derived from social science research.

Trudy is feeling really frustrated. "I don't get it," she says. "I asked my psychology teacher why I can't get along with my sister and she says, 'It depends on lots of things.' That isn't the way shrinks answer questions on Oprah!" Another complication in social sciences involves multiple theories to explain the same thing. Social science is considered to be a "soft" science because it has to explain many deeply complex problems that involve extenuating circumstances. It can be frustrating when you look to social science for a simple answer and end up with five explanations.

What are some methods of efficient learning in the social sciences? See "Thriving in Social Science" for some advice.

Foreign Language

Many colleges require students to study a foreign language. This practice helps students step outside their own culture to develop a broader perspective.

The Rules Foreign language study is loaded with rules. Proper grammar, word tenses, and even designating the "feminine" and "masculine" all represent rules that you must learn to be successful in acquiring a new language.

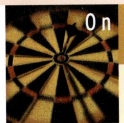

On Target Tips

Becoming Better at Science and Math

What are some strategies for improving your ability to learn science and math?

- *Talk about what you already believe.* Sometimes pre-existing notions can interfere with learning new ideas in science (Treagust & others, 1996). If you state what you really know or think about a scientific event, it may be easier for you to see where your explanation may not be adequate. Scientific explanations may offer a clear improvement.

- *Collaborate with others.* Despite the stereotype of the lone scientist working away on a discovery, most do not work in isolation. Collaboration is a good model to follow for beginners as well. By talking through problems out loud with other students, you can improve your scientific problem-solving.

- *Change representation strategies.* If you are trying to solve a problem, convert it to pictures or symbols. If the problem is presented in pictures or symbols, translate those to words. Science and math often feel too abstract for some students. By changing the format of the problem, you may get a clue about how to work with the ideas involved.

- *Know why you are studying.* Keep the larger picture in mind. What will you accomplish by learning the skills involved in any given assignment?

- *If you get confused, find another class section and sit in.* Sometimes it helps to sit through a class twice, which may be possible if your instructor teaches multiple sessions.

- *Be persistent and check your work.* Some problems don't yield a fast answer. Keep working, keep seeking, keep persisting until you gain the insight you need to crack the problem. Be sure to check your answers so you don't lose credit because of careless execution.

On Target Tips

Thriving in Social Science

- **Expect complexity.** You are less likely to be disappointed in the limits of social science if you understand that not all your questions will have clean answers. The most interesting topics are complex and may not have simple answers.

- **Use your own experience.** Most of the topics you will study correspond to things you have experienced. When you compare your experiences, you can bring additional associations to the concepts that will make them easier to learn, but don't restrict yourself to understanding only what you have personally experienced.

- **Stay open to alternative explanations.** Recognize that your experience may not be typical of the systematic observations that emerge in science. You will need to practice staying objective as you evaluate evidence, which may include re-evaluating your personal experience.

A special kind of beauty exists which is born in language, of language, and for language.

**Gaston Bachelard
French scientist,
20th century**

The rules can also extend to the norms and practices of the culture in which the language is practiced.

The Risks Many foreign languages have new sounds that may not be natural to your native tongue. Some students fear revealing that their "ears" for language may not be sensitive to these sounds. The amount of time you have to spend drilling can also be daunting.

Overcoming the risks and being successful in foreign language classes involve understanding and memorizing as much as you can. See "Learning Languages" for some successful strategies.

Factors That Influence Study Success

People differ in their ability to learn. Not everyone has the musical aptitude of Yo-Yo Ma, yet there are probably areas of learning in which he feels inferior. Some people seem to glide through courses getting top grades. Others struggle. In this section we will explore these capacities.

Academic Strengths and Weaknesses

Psychologist Howard Gardner (1983) believes that patterns of academic strengths and weaknesses reveal special areas of intelligence. He identified seven "frames of mind": verbal skills, math skills, spatial skills, movement skills, musical skills, insights about the self, and insights about others. For example, Yo-Yo Ma's musical skills represent heightened abilities in that frame of mind, just as tennis pro Martina Hingis demonstrates impressive movement skills.

Most traditional education does not fully exploit all seven frames of mind. Liberal arts courses tend to emphasize verbal and math skills to the exclusion of other frames of mind. Students who are strongest in verbal and math abilities have an advantage academically, but this doesn't rule out success for other students. It just means that they have to work harder. Their natural intellectual strengths simply may be in other areas not tapped as much by college.

Frames of mind may also predict the college majors students are drawn toward. Students with strengths in music are likely to be drawn to careers in music performance or education. Students with good verbal skills fare well in majors that emphasize language processing, reading, or writing. Students who show a ready grasp of math may feel pulled toward careers in engineering or research. Expertise in movement encourages majoring in physical education, physical therapy, or dance. Excellence in spatial abilities is the foundation of careers in design, technology, and architecture. Those with distinctive capacities for insight and human relations may be outstanding in human services careers.

As you think about your own academic ability profile, Gardner's framework may offer some direction. Complete Self-Assessment 6.3 to see how it might apply to you.

Gender and Learning

At the beginning of her American politics course, Gina almost always feels uncomfortable. The instructor regularly covers the material by having small group discussions. Gina reads all the assignments before class but never knows what to say when it is her turn to talk. She had not expected that she would have to talk in her college classes. She thought she would learn just by listening.

About halfway through the course, she notices that the small group discussions are getting easier. She is beginning to see how political ideas can be applied to her life. She sometimes gets so involved in the discussions, she stops noticing how nervous she is about talking. She is pleased that when she talks, many other students nod and smile.

Gender socialization may influence how women approach their studies as well as how they participate in the classroom (Gilligan, 1990; Paludi, 1998). Like Gina, some women initially may be more comfortable remaining silent. They define their learning task as passively recording the information conveyed by the instructor. They have little drive to share a personal perspective, often not feeling worthy of participating. They do not challenge the instructor's authority. They are happiest in classes where they can take notes from the experts, memorize the information, and report what they learned in test formats that do not require the expression of their own perspective. Although this pattern has been reported as more typical of women, men also may be passive bystanders in the classroom.

As they accumulate experiences in college, many quiet students begin to change. With practice, they move out of silence and discover their own voices. They recognize that their own ideas have value in group discussions and begin to look forward to opportunities to share what they think. With greater confidence, they begin to be more critical about the ideas they hear, regardless of the source. If you recognize silence as your style in class, turn to "Breaking the Silence" for some ideas about accelerating this process.

Not everyone agrees that learning patterns can be neatly sorted out by gender. Shyness may be even more important in explaining silence. However, many instructors recognize that silence does not necessarily mean students are uninvolved in the course. They often structure their class activities to empower learners to participate fully in class. Many instructors

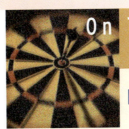

On Target Tips

Learning Languages

- **Use color-coded materials.** Color-coded flash cards may give you some additional cues about the kinds of words you are trying to learn. For example, use blue cards for verbs, yellow for nouns, and so on.

- **Construct outrageous images.** Construct an image from the sounds of the language that will help you recall the vocabulary. For example, if you want to learn the word for "dinner" in Portuguese ("jantar"), picture John eating a plate full of tar at the dinner table.

- **Don't get behind.** Keep up, because the continuing work of the class will pile up if you get behind.

- **Distribute your practice sessions.** Although it is a good idea to use shorter but frequent study sessions to memorize college material, it is *essential* to do so when learning a foreign language. Regular practice sessions make your learning last longer.

- **Immerse yourself.** Try to find some natural exposure to the language you are studying. Develop a penpal relationship or watch television programs that feature the language you are studying.

Some students find that silence is the most comfortable way to learn new ideas. As they gain more experience in the classroom, they are likely to trust their own ideas and show greater willingness to express them to their classmates. Do you find silence a comfortable place to be?

Self-Assessment 6-3

What Is My Frame of Mind?

Gardner describes seven different areas of cognitive ability. Complete the following to develop your own profile of strengths and weaknesses. Check the appropriate column.

	STRENGTH	WEAKNESS	NEITHER STRENGTH NOR WEAKNESS
Verbal skills	_____	_____	_____
Evidence: _____			
Math skills	_____	_____	_____
Evidence: _____			
Spatial skills	_____	_____	_____
Evidence: _____			
Movement skills	_____	_____	_____
Evidence: _____			
Musical skills	_____	_____	_____
Evidence: _____			
Insights about the self	_____	_____	_____
Evidence: _____			
Insights about others	_____	_____	_____
Evidence: _____			

As you examine the pattern of strengths and weaknesses, consider whether these patterns help explain your degree of academic success so far in the term. You also might want to consider whether the pattern you produced fits well with your intended major. Are there other areas you should consider to take advantage of learning that may come more easily to you?

especially enjoy watching the formerly quiet student discover a distinctive personal voice.

Learning Differences

Estimates vary, but perhaps nearly one in ten Americans experience academic complications caused by a learning disability or learning difference. They have difficulties processing the information they learn through reading or may have problems decoding what they hear. They may be unable to spell or manage numbers.

Despite their academic struggles, students with learning disabilities may be highly intelligent and successful people (Hallahan, Kaufman, & Lloyd, 1999). For example, some people with such learning differences have genius-level IQ scores. Famous people with learning disabilities include actors Tracy Gold and Tom Cruise, comedian Jay Leno, and writer–producer Stephen Cannell.

Dyslexia is a learning difference that interferes with the ability to read. People with dyslexia report that words and sentences are hard to decode. Because they have anxiety about performance and their slower rate of reading, students with dyslexia often feel singled out in classes for "not trying" or "failing to live up to their potential" despite they fact that they are trying hard to keep up.

If you have experienced similar criticisms about your performance even though you are trying hard, you may find it helpful to complete Self-Assessment 6.4, which identifies many characteristics of learning disabilities. This inventory is not definitive. It merely provides a rough outline of concerns that you can raise with your academic advisor to sort out whether more diagnostic testing is in order.

Many students think they might have learning disabilities when they really don't. They simply may not

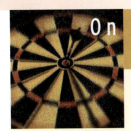

On Target Tips

Breaking the Silence

- *Formulate positions.* When controversial issues arise in class, force yourself to commit to a position in your notes. Try to do this before you hear the opinions of other people in the class. Come up with at least one reason why you believe what you do. If you change your mind after hearing the arguments others offer, make a note about why the shift is necessary.

- *Obligate yourself to talk outside of class.* Commit yourself to a study session with at least one student in the class, which can force you to talk about the ideas.

- *Obligate yourself to talk during class.* Make a promise to yourself that you will contribute to class discussion on a given day. Try to anticipate the nature of the discussion and prepare some ideas ahead of time so you won't have to do this "cold."

- *Say what you think in your own words.* Don't worry so much about whether you are using the specialized language of the discipline accurately.

Learning disabilities can be overcome, as shown by the successful careers of comedian Jay Leno, actress Tracy Gold, and actor Tom Cruise.

Surprised

Variations in Study Success

By now you have probably done some informal comparisons of your own study strategies with the ones that others use. You have probably discovered some people who work really hard but never seem to put together the right combination of strategies to be successful. That is, they work hard, but not smart.

On the other hand, you may hear some students brag about how little they work but still manage to do really well on exams. Should you believe them? Maybe. Some people are lucky in that their cognitive styles match the instructional design in a given course and they don't have to struggle as hard. Or maybe not. Sometimes people won't own up to how hard they must work to succeed.

What about you? The best strategy may be to think about each course as a puzzle you must solve. How can you adapt your study strategies for each new and interesting combination of you, the instructor, and the subject?

be putting in enough study time or their performance on tests is sabotaged by their anxious feelings. When you confer with your advisor about your academic struggles, prepare an honest evaluation of how much work you are putting in on your studies. Your problems may lie in bad strategies, not in learning disability.

If you have a learning difference, your academic outlook is not as bleak as you might think. Students who verify their learning differences through the evaluation of a qualified examiner may apply for special educational support through the *Education for All Handicapped Children Act of 1975*. In addition, the *Americans with Disability Act* encourages campuses to take measures to support the special needs of students with disabilities. Many instructors have also developed strategies to assist students to learn in their classes. For example, they may offer longer test periods for students with language processing problems. Table 6.2 offers some questions you might pursue with your instructor to help you stay competitive.

You can also compensate for learning differences in your study strategies. For example, students with dyslexia can use audiotaped versions of their textbooks. Or they can tape record lectures rather than reviewing and rehearsing written materials. Relying on an auditory channel reduces the need to use the skills that are more challenging. Students with spelling problems can use a spell-checker. Students with writing challenges can secure support from campus study skill centers. Or they can routinely engage friends to read their written work to catch errors in spelling and grammar.

Table 6-2
Talking with Your Instructors About Learning Disabilities

Questions you can ask your instructor to help you stay competitive if you have learning disabilities:

- Do you mind if I audiotape your lectures?
- Have you worked with learning disabled students before?
- What can you suggest for me to do that will help me stay current in the course?
- May I use a spelling device to help me during testing?
- May I arrange for extended time to finish exams? Can we arrange for someone to monitor me?
- Can you recommend a tutor if I run into difficulties in your course?
- When would be a good time for me to confer with you to clarify things I've learned in class?
- Would you like to have more information about my learning disability?

Self-Assessment 6-4

Could I Have a Learning Disability?

You may have a learning disability if you have difficulties in the following areas:

Misunderstand simple printed materials ____

Have a lot of trouble working with basic math problems ____

Have difficulty writing and speaking ____

Approach studying in a haphazard manner ____

Get easily distracted ____

Confuse *left* and *right* or other spatial words ____

Arrive late a lot (such as frequent late arrival to class) ____

Struggle with categories and comparisons ____

Have trouble with fine motor skills or finger control ____

Feel awkward in gross motor (body) movements ____

Misinterpret subtle nonverbal cues ____

Have difficulty following instructions ____

Reverse letters in words or words in sentences ____

Hear teachers complain that you "are not living up to your potential" ____

If you feel frustrated in these areas, you may want to explore the possibility of a learning difference. First, confer with your advisor about the nature of your difficulties. She or he can recommend changes in your study strategy or refer you to a specialist on campus who can help you with diagnostic testing. On some campuses, this evaluation can be expensive, but you are likely to get recommendations about compensating strategies that make the investment worthwhile.

Summary Tips For Mastering College

Developing Study Skills

Why Study?

1. Prepare to spend substantial amounts of time using study strategies that work to help you learn. Most students benefit from a personalized approach that takes into account their learning strengths and weaknesses.
2. Pick a place that is quiet and well lit, with minimum distractions for efficient study. You can adapt to adverse study conditions with some planning and a good pair or earplugs or headphones.
3. The secret of efficient study is creating multiple opportunities for review. Review after class, before class, and at other regular intervals to prevent the pressures of having to cram.

Improving Your Memory

1. Short-term memory and long-term memory play different roles in the memory process.
2. Effective memorization strategies involve careful preparation of materials to be learned. The more associations you can make to the material, the easier it will be to remember the ideas.
3. Efficient retrieval of what you have learned depends on how well you have rehearsed the materials. Improve retrieval by reducing interference, overcoming partial memories, and using situational cues to promote recall.
4. Pay attention in class.
5. Review your test results to provide feedback on the effectiveness of your memorizing strategies. You may detect patterns in your results that you can address more effectively on the next test.

Study Strategies for the Disciplines

1. To study complex ideas effectively, develop questions that will help you probe the subject matter more deeply. Bloom's taxonomy provides a framework that can help you generate questions (see Chapter 8).
2. Humanities classes promote the development of a personal perspective. Master the terminology, surrender the search for the "right" answer, and take the risk of expressing yourself to enhance your success.
3. Successful study in natural science and math classes requires conquering your fears and practicing skills until they are mastered. Collaborate with others, use figures and diagrams, and solve similar problems to develop appropriate analytic and problem-solving skills.
4. Social science will help you learn new terminology to explain patterns of behavior. You will be challenged to modify many of the things you have learned through experience to become more objective.
5. Foreign language classes require massive effort in memorizing. Distribute your study sessions over time and be careful not to fall behind.

Factors That Influence Study Success

1. People show different strengths and weaknesses in the learning skills. Academic programs don't always develop all those learning specialties.
2. Some students, perhaps especially women, may see their role in learning initially as quite passive. Passive learners can practice taking positions, first privately, then publicly, to break out of their silence.
3. Students who study hard but struggle with academic success should consider whether learning disabilities could be interfering with their study effectiveness. Consider specialized testing to confirm the diagnosis and suggest special strategies to help you compensate if your advisor believes that you have a learning disability.

College Success Checklist

Have your views changed about any of the following items since you filled out this checklist at the beginning of the chapter? Place a check mark beside any item for which you feel good about your current practice. Also check any item for which you now have new ideas about how to improve.

____ I know the benefits of good study habits.

____ I choose appropriate places and times to study.

____ I review regularly to learn course information better.

____ I organize materials to make them easier to learn and remember.

____ I use strategies to improve my memory related to coursework.

____ I recognize when I'm being asked to think abstractly.

____ I adapt my study strategies to suit different disciplines.

____ I can describe how individual ability differences influence study success.

____ I know how learning disabilities complicate learning and studying.

In the space below, list the items that you still need to work on the most. This list may help you complete the goal-setting exercise in the Learning Portfolio.

Review Questions

1 What should you do to secure adequate study space and time?

2 What are some good strategies for memorizing academic concepts?

3 How does using higher-order thinking skills enhance study success?

4 How do the disciplines encourage different kinds of study?

5 How do individual differences in cognitive ability influence study success?

Learning Portfolio

Learning by Reflecting... Journal Entries

Analysis of Forgetting
Review your own academic history. Chances are good that you have experienced forgetting in more than one situation. Try to identify a classroom situation and the outcomes in which you

- Experienced tip-of-the-tongue phenomenon

- Suffered interference in your retrieval

- Experienced decay in retrieving something you once knew well

- Crammed but performed poorly on a test

Reducing Your Disciplinary Risks
Many people experience fears related to disciplines they are required to study to complete their education in the liberal arts. Select the discipline with which you are least comfortable and describe the origins of your concern. What might you do to change your comfort level with this discipline

Leaving Silence
People differ in the comfort they feel in expressing opinions in the classroom. Think about your own style. What factors account for whether you participate in class activities or are silent? List some ideas here. Expand in your journal.

_____
_____
_____
_____
_____
_____

Learning by Doing... Action Projects

Debating the Difference
Students with learning disabilities are at a disadvantage in some testing procedures. Current laws suggest that accommodations should be made for them to help them stay competitive. For example, they may be allowed a longer answering period or schedule the test at an another time. Critics of this approach suggest that this offers students with learning problems an unfair advantage. Join a group assigned to debate one side of this argument. Generate an outline that captures the key points of your position.

Deep Study
Pick a topic area from a subject you are currently studying. Develop a question that represents a lower-order level of Bloom's taxonomy. For example, a multiple-choice question that you can answer through rote memory is a good example. Identify a tentative answer to the question. Then develop a higher-order question on the same topic. How much harder do you have to work to come up with a good answer to a higher-order question?

Adopting a New Frame of Mind
Fans of Howard Gardner's work propose that schools and colleges should be redesigned to focus on the seven frames of mind he articulated. How would your liberal arts requirements change if greater value were placed on developing all seven frames of mind? Create a short speech in which you describe one consequence of this shift in priorities.

Brainstorm ideas here.

_____
_____
_____
_____
_____
_____

Learning by Thinking Critically... Critiques

Spaced Versus Massed Practice
In the opening profile you learned about the strategies Yo-Yo Ma's parents used to help him develop his early proficiency on the cello. Critical to his success was practicing the cello in short but frequent sessions. The principle of regular spaced practice is recommended by study specialists as a preferred way of learning new skills. Can you think of any situations in which massed practice is better?

Justifying Your Cognitive Complexity
Evaluate the kinds of thinking required in your current courses. On a scale of 1 to 10, where 1 means very concrete skills and 10 means very abstract, give each course a rating that reflects the cognitive complexity of the course. How do these ratings relate to how well you like the course?

Expanding Study Time
Suppose that you have been asked to address the next incoming class of students about the importance of systematic study. How would you attempt to persuade them of the need to develop a sensible study plan? What arguments would you give?

List some main points here.
_____
_____
_____
_____
_____
_____
_____
_____

Learning by Thinking Creatively... Personal Vision

What's in a Name?
Locate one list in any of the content areas you are studying this semester. Develop a mnemonic device for remembering the list. Record it here.

New Horizons in Learning
Science fiction buffs are fond of plots that allow people to learn rapidly through some artificial means. If you had the option to expand what you know and what you could retrieve by taking a pill or having a microchip installed, do you think this would be a good idea? Brainstorm about the potential advantages and problems of this kind of augmentation.

A Memory Like a Sieve
Think about a metaphor that captures the essence of your own memorization skills. If possible, draw or find an image that illustrates the concept you are trying to portray. Then share your metaphors with a group. How are these concepts different? How are they similar?

Learning by Planning... Goal Setting

Review the results of the Self-Assessments you completed in this chapter. Also review the College Success Checklist. What can you conclude about things you need to do to improve your skills?

What goal should you select from this chapter for making positive changes that will help you master the college experience? (*Hint: Is your goal challenging, reasonable, and specific?*)

_____
_____
_____
_____
_____

What strategies will you use to achieve your goal? (*Hint: Can you organize your strategy into a series of smaller goals?*)

_____
_____
_____
_____
_____
_____
_____
_____
_____
_____
_____

What obstacles may be in your way as you attempt to make these positive changes?

_____
_____
_____
_____
_____

What additional resources might help you succeed in achieving your goal?

_____
_____
_____
_____

By what date do you want to accomplish your goal?

_____

How will you know you have succeeded?

_____
_____
_____
_____

Resources for Mastering the College Experience

Study Skills

How to Study (1994, 3rd ed.) by Ron Fry. Hawthorne, NH: Career Press.
A classic, comprehensive approach to more systematic and successful studying.

Last Minute Study Tips (1996) by Ron Fry. Franklin Lakes, NJ: Career Press.
Studying strategies organized according to amount of time before an examination begins.

Learning Skills for College and Career (1997, 2nd ed.) by Paul Hettich. Pacific Grove, CA: Brooks/Cole.
Links increased study efficiency with success in career preparation.

Memory

Total Recall (1984) by Joan Minninger. New York: Pocket Books.
Study insights from a memory enhancement consultant to many major corporations.

Your Memory: How It Works and How to Improve It (1988) by K. L. Higbee. Englewood Cliffs, NJ: Prentice Hall.
Incorporating memory principles into many aspects of your personal life.

Individual Differences

Women's Ways of Knowing (1986) by M. F. Belenky, B. M. Clinchy, N. R. Goldberger, and J. M. Tarule. New York: Basic Books.
A classic research study of how women change over time in their involvement in college.

Educating Ourselves (1995) by Rachel Dobkin and Shana Sippy. New York: Workman Publishing.
Organized around the practical concept of "reality 101." Emphasizes peer support in college.

Creating Minds (1993) by Howard Gardner. New York: Basic Books.
Examines the lives of seven outstanding talents matching the seven frames of mind in his theory of intelligences.

You Mean I'm Not Lazy, Stupid, or Crazy? A Self-Help Book for Adults with ADD (1993). New York: Fireside Publishers.
A variety of compensating strategies for the adult learner who is unusually distractible.

Association for Children and Adults with Learning Disabilities (ACLD), 4156 Library Road, Pittsburgh, PA 15234; 412-341-1515
An organization publishing free information and a newsletter. Also makes referrals for additional services.

Internet Resources

http://www.gasou.edu/psychweb/mtsite/memory.html.
To explore memory theory and technique.

http://www.vt.edu:120021/studentinfo/ucc/studydis.html.
To analyze distraction patterns.

http://www-hl.syr.edu/about/libart.html.
To read more about liberal arts education.

http:www.stedwards.edu/aps/lassi.htm
On-line learning and study strategies inventory. St. Edward's University.

http://www.d.umn.edu/student/loon/acad/strat/self_test.html
Diagnoses how you may be getting in your own way.

http://128.32.89.153/CalRENHP.html
Help in all aspects of study skills.

http://www.cortland.edu/www_root/000000/asap/STUDYREAD.HTML
Reading and study skills strategies that work across different areas of study. SUNY-Cortland.

Succeeding on Tests

CHAPTER 7

✓ College Success Checklist

Place a check mark beside the items that apply to you. Leave the items blank that do not apply to you.

____ I pace myself effectively to get ready for a test.

____ I figure out ahead of time what will be on the test and try to predict the test questions.

____ I control my nervous feelings about my test performance.

____ I size up the test to know what I need to do and read all directions carefully before I start.

____ I know effective strategies for scoring well on multiple choice tests.

____ I know how to do well on essay questions.

____ I regularly complete tests in the allotted time.

____ I know how to analyze test results to improve my learning and future test performances.

____ I know the consequences of academic dishonesty at my college.

Preview

Nowhere will you get more extensive experience with testing and feedback than in college. In this chapter you will examine why testing occupies so much of your experience in college and explore how to prepare for a test, including overcoming test anxiety. You will look at strategies to improve test performance and learn methods for reviewing your test results to improve your learning. You will also study grading issues and ethical concerns related to testing.

Chapter Outline

Images of College Success: Albert Einstein

"Why Do I Have to Take All of These Tests?"

Preparing for the Test
Sensible Study Strategies
Last-Minute Strategies
It's Test Day
In Case of Emergency
Controlling the Butterflies

Taking the Test
General Strategies
Multiple Choice
True-False
Fill-in-the-Blank
Short Answer
Essay Questions

Reviewing the Test

About Grades
College Versus High School Grades
Grading Systems

Integrity in Taking Tests
How Widespread Is Cheating?
Why Do Students Cheat?
Why Shouldn't Students Cheat?

Self-Assessments
7.1 Do I Have Test Anxiety?
7.2 How Well Do I Test?
7.3 How Honest Am I?

On-Target Tips
How *Not* to Cram
Will This Be on the Test?
Learning to Relax
Scoring Essay Brownie Points
Should I Challenge My Grade?

Images of College Success
Albert Einstein

When he was a small child, no one could have predicted the extraordinary future of Albert Einstein. He was slow in learning to talk and painfully shy. Although he loved science and mathematics, he struggled with the style of his formal education. His teachers at the Luitpold Gymnasium in Munich, Germany, taught by constant drilling, which Einstein found boring. He often skipped classes or was ill-prepared, resulting in punishment for his disobedience and scorn from his classmates. Although his teachers thought he was dull, Einstein simply hated the persistent drilling he faced in school. When his father's business failed and the family moved away to Italy, Einstein purposefully failed enough tests that he was asked to leave his school. One teacher told Einstein that he was glad to see him go because the teachers thought he encouraged other students to be disrespectful. In this situation, failing his tests enabled Einstein to be with his parents in Milan.

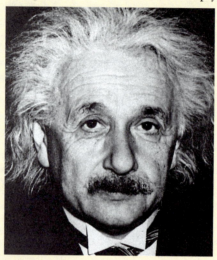

What can we learn from **Albert Einstein's** experiences in testing?

When his family later suggested that he needed to prepare for a career, Einstein applied to a technical school in Switzerland. To be admitted, he had to pass rigorous entrance examinations. Although his scores on his math and science exams clearly showed promise, he was a dismal failure in zoology, botany, and language. A remedial year at a more creative school, where his questioning was encouraged rather than discouraged, allowed him to catch up. He passed his entrance exams on his second attempt and went on to revolutionize the field of physics. Ironically, the Luitpold Gymnasium, an institution once offended by Albert Einstein's uncooperative and dull academic performance, was renamed in honor of him before he died (Levenger, 1949).

Succeeding on Tests

No matter what course of study you pursue, you are going to be evaluated. Before we examine the strategies you can use to succeed on tests, let's first explore why testing is such a prominent feature of the college experience.

"Why Do I Have to Take All of These Tests?"

Believe it or not, tests can benefit you. They can help you to

- **Pace your reading.** College reading assignments can feel overwhelming, so it is easy to get behind. Tests throughout the term push you to do the work on time.
- **Consolidate your learning.** Tests encourage you to study the course material more intensely. Your effort in preparing for tests can produce insights you might not have made on your own. Also, studying for tests may help you to retain the ideas longer.
- **Improve your thinking.** Tests sharpen your critical thinking skills. Whether you are figuring out which multiple choice alternative to eliminate or how to structure a solid essay, tests give you practice in careful observation, analysis, and judgment.
- **Get feedback.** Test results tell you whether your study strategies have worked. Good results confirm that you are on the right track. A string of poor scores suggests that you have not learned enough.
- **Achieve special status.** As demonstrated in the introductory story about Albert Einstein, test results can confer special status. For example, good results might qualify you for a scholarship or allow you to skip preliminary courses and move on to more advanced ones.

Preparing for the Test

You know the instructors are going to test you. What can you do to show them you've got the right stuff?

Sensible Study Strategies

Preparing for tests takes both long-term and short-term planning. Following are some good long-term strategies.

Pace Yourself It bears repeating. Don't count on cramming! Eleventh-hour learning is fragile. It may crumble under pressure. The strategies offered in "How *Not* to Cram" will help you pace yourself so you won't have to go through a last-minute rush to learn.

Commit to a Study Group (See also Chapter 2.) Study with others. It will motivate you to do your reading and help you to identify trouble spots. Ask other students who seem to understand the course—at least as well as you do if not better—to join you in the group. This screening process helps to ensure that the group will be productive and not slowed down by students who don't reliably do their work. To improve test success, study group members can:

Difficulties, opposition, criticism—these things are meant to be overcome, and there is a special joy in facing them and in coming out on top.

Vijaya Lakshmi Pandit
Indian Diplomat, 20th century

Learning is such a very painful business.

May Sarton
Contemporary American writer

On Target Tips

How *Not* to Cram

- *Concentrate on the big picture.* Keep a master calendar for the term. Put all of your scheduled tests on it. Post the calendar in your study area.

- *Design your test preparation across courses.* Plan how you will read, study, and review assigned materials and class notes according to the test demands in all your courses. Wherever possible, minimize interference between courses by distributing your study sessions over time.

- *Keep up with your reading.* If you keep up with your reading, class experiences will reinforce your learning. This should make it easier for you to learn. Avoid trying to do massive catch-up reading the night before the test because there probably will be too much ground to cover, understand, and remember.

- *Reward yourself for staying on target.* A shiny "A" would be a powerful reward for strong test preparation habits. However, that reward may be too far off to help you sustain better test preparation. Reward yourself on a regular basis for sticking to your study plan. For example, after you have studied hard each evening, watch a tape of a favorite TV show or have a pleasant talk with someone.

- *Schedule a concentrated review session.* If you have kept up, a solid review session the night before your test should be adequate.

> *Vitality shows in not only the ability to persist, but the ability to start over.*
>
> **F. Scott Fitzgerald**
> **American writer,**
> **early 20th century**

- **Compare perspectives.** Others may have developed different ideas that can help you grasp concepts better.

- **Share hunches.** Exchange ideas about what you think the instructor will emphasize and ignore.

- **Rotate special assignments.** For example, one member outlines a chapter and shares it with others. Next week, another member does the same.

- **Use flash cards and other memory supports.** Quiz each other until you feel competent to recall key ideas at testing time.

- **Create practice questions.** Compare group member strategies about how to address the material on which you will be tested.

- **State your understanding out loud and challenge fuzzy explanations.** Group members can advise you if you aren't explaining things clearly so you will still have time to revise your ideas.

Protect Your Health If you can stay healthy throughout the term, you will have fewer problems in managing your study schedule and fewer distractions at test time. You won't do your best when you are studying or taking a test if you are fighting off the urge to nap, feeling bad from a hangover, or coming down with a cold.

Take the Right Attitude Examinations can be emotional events. Nearly everyone feels some apprehension in getting ready. Some people feel overwhelmed and suffer test anxiety. We will address this problem later in the chapter. Others view testing like doing battle. They cast the instructor as a villain who is out to expose them. The student gets distracted into "outfoxing" the instructor rather than learning the material. Facing the test with the confidence that comes from good planning and systematic study is the best way to overcome negative attitudes and emotions.

What can you do on a short-term basis to prepare for a specific test?

Know What to Expect Test conditions vary. In large lecture classes, security issues may be intense. For example, you may be required to sit in alternate seats to reduce the risk of cheating. Proctors may roam the aisles and retrieve all materials after the test. Your instructor may not even be present, so you might want to get all of your questions answered before the day of the test. On the other hand, in smaller classes with the instructor present you may be able to clarify issues as they come up.

Get Some Idea of What's Going to Be on the Test Most instructors describe the kinds of tests they are planning during the class or in the syllabus. Some even make sample tests from prior semesters available. Many welcome questions about how to prepare. "Will This Be on the Test?" suggests questions that you can ask your instructor to clarify the nature of the exam.

You may know some students who have completed the course before you. Interview them about what tests were like. Find out what they did to succeed or what strategies didn't work. Don't be afraid to do research on your instructor's test construction practices.

Size Up the Teacher You have probably met some students who have an uncanny ability to guess what will be on a test. How do they do it? They size up the instructor by identifying what concepts have been stressed enthusiastically during class lectures and discussions. Instructors often use specific cues to communicate what they have said is important and *testable* (Appleby, 1997). They may be signaling test material when they

- Repeat or emphasize certain concepts
- Illustrate key ideas with examples
- Stop pacing back and forth behind the lectern
- Intensify eye contact
- Use gestures in more dramatic ways
- Change the tone of their voices
- Say "in conclusion. . ." or "to summarize. . ."
- Pause to allow you time to write your notes
- Write on the board or point to ideas on an overhead transparency
- Highlight ideas in their introductory remarks or conclusion

On Target Tips

Will This Be on the Test?

Some instructors don't offer many clues about the tests they give. If you have one of these instructors, you might ask these questions:

- How long will the test be?
- What types of questions will be on it?
- Are there any particular aspects of the work we have been doing that you will emphasize?
- What topics *won't* be on the test?
- Are there penalties for wrong guesses?
- Will this material also be covered on a cumulative exam at the end of term?

Match Your Study to the Test Format Know the format of the test ahead of time. You can practice making answers appropriate to that format. Heavy memorizing works for many kinds of tests. Other types of tests may require less memorizing and more thinking.

Know how the instructor will distribute points on the test. This knowledge may help you decide where to spend your time if it is clear you won't be able to finish the test. Find out whether there are penalties for guessing.

Objective Tests Memorizing is a good strategy for answering simple objective test questions. These include tests with multiple choice, matching, true–false, and fill-in-the-blank items. Helpful memorizing strategies (see also Chapter 6) include the following:

- Reorganize your notes.
- Use flash cards to rehearse critical ideas.

If you take any large classes, you probably will use a scantron form that allows the instructor to grade your responses electronically.

> *You have to accept whatever comes and the only important thing is that you meet it with the best you have to give.*
>
> **Eleanor Roosevelt**
> **American humanitarian and lecturer, 20th century**

- Make a course glossary on index cards.
- Review your text's study guide.
- Anything else that rehearses concepts.

At the college level, however, instructors are likely to ask objective questions that may require more than just responses from rote memory. For example, you may have to apply what you have learned to a new situation. Or you may have to use reasoning to identify the alternative that makes the most sense when a concept is being tested in a way that differs from how it was expressed in your reading. Rather than relying only on memory, a wiser strategy is to use organizational charts and diagrams to promote a deeper understanding.

Essay Tests Some instructors ask essay questions to evaluate not only what you have learned but how you think. In this case you can make up practice essay questions and write or map out answers to them. Ask or make some guesses about the kinds of questions that will be on the test.

Digesting a whole term's worth of material for an essay can be a challenge. If you know the specific topics ahead of time, scan the notes you have made and highlight all related ideas in a specific color. This will allow you to concentrate on those ideas as you think about questions or practice answers. If you don't know the essay topics ahead of time, go back over your course and reading notes. Write a paragraph for each entry, such as a text chapter or course lecture, into your notes that summarizes the key ideas in the passage.

Procedural Tests Some types of tests ask you to demonstrate specific procedures such as applying a formula to solve a math problem, demonstrating an interviewing technique in nursing, or solving for an unknown in chemistry. To prepare for procedural tests, go through the procedure several times until you are comfortable with it. If test time will be limited, build time limits into your practice.

Protect Your Study Time Jennifer is in the middle of her review session in the library when Mindy sits down at her table. They are both in the same biology class, but go about their work in very different ways. Jennifer regularly attends class, carefully takes notes, and plans out her study sessions. Mindy misses class a lot and relies on help from her classmates. "I just want to borrow your notes for the last two weeks so I can xerox them," says Mindy. "Okay?"

Jennifer thinks for a moment. Handing over the notes will reward Mindy for interrupting and relying on bad habits. Turning Mindy down may make Jenny feel guilty. But each request makes her more and more angry. "Mindy," she says, "we've got to talk."

Especially if you share a residence with classmates, they may request your help at the last minute. You may happily accept. Helping others can make you feel good and also can help you rehearse material. Or you may need your solo time to master the material. If giving help does not appeal to you, explain that you have planned out your study strategy and need every minute to concentrate.

What if a loved one makes demands on your time that interfere with your study schedule? It helps to explain to partners or family members, including children, that you need extra help from them before a test to make it as easy as possible to study. Promise them that you will spend time with them after the test. Then keep your promise.

If you practice good long-term and short-term strategies, your work is much easier as the test gets closer. Table 7.1 summarizes strategies for pacing yourself for the least stressful test preparation.

Table 7-1
A Timetable for Sensible Study Strategies

After each assignment	Write a summary paragraph of what you learned and how it relates to the course objectives.
After each class	Review your notes to consolidate your learning.

During the last class before the test	Find out about the test:
	    What will be and won't be on the test
	    The format of the test
	    The contribution of the test to your grade
	Clarify any confused ideas from past classes.

After the last class before the test	Plan your final review session.

The night before the test	Organize your notes for systematic review.
	Study the test material exclusively—or last—to reduce interference.
	Practice the kind of thinking the test will require:
	    Rehearsal and recital for objective tests
	    Critical analysis for subjective tests
	Identify any fuzzy areas and confer with classmates to straighten out your confusion.
	Get a good night's sleep.

The day of the test	Organize your supplies. Eat a good breakfast/lunch/dinner. Review your notes, chapter summaries, course glossary.
The hour before the test	Review your notes. Go to the classroom early and get settled. Practice relaxing and positive thinking.

Last-Minute Strategies

It's a bad idea to depend on cramming, but sometimes it can't be helped. You may have too many courses to manage any other way in some. Instead of going unprepared, what are some ideas for last-minute, concentrated study?

- **Clear the decks.** Dedicate your last study session before the test only to that test. Studying anything else can interfere with the test at hand.

- **Skim for main ideas.** Scan each paragraph in relevant readings for the key ideas. Topic sentences that capture the central idea of each paragraph are usually the first or the last sentences in the paragraph. But do skim the entire assignment to improve your chances of remembering the material.

- **Divide and conquer.** Once you have skimmed the entire body of study materials, size up how much you have to learn in relation to your remaining time. Divide the information into reasonable subdivisions and make your best guess about which subdivision will have the largest payoff. Master each subdivision in turn with whatever time you have left. Even if you don't get to the lower-priority units, your test performance may not suffer much.

> *Sixty minutes of thinking of any kind is bound to lead to confusion and unhappiness.*
>
> **James Thurber**
> **American cartoonist,**
> **20th century**

- **Set the stage.** Study in good light away from the lure of your bed. Take regular breaks and exercise mildly to stay alert through your session. Caffeine in moderation and regular snacks may also help.
- **Use study aids.** Some textbooks include summaries. Use them if you cannot master the entire chapter. Use professional summaries of great works if you cannot complete full reading. If you rent a film version of a great work, be aware that films sometimes depart from the author's original creation in ways that may reveal that you have taken a shortcut.
- **Learn from your mistakes.** When you enter a test feeling underprepared, you have undermined your ability to be successful. Even if you luck out and do well, this strategy is unlikely to serve your learning over the long term. Think about what factors left you in such desperate study circumstances. Commit yourself to doing all you can not to get stuck in a situation where you have to cram.

It's Test Day

It's here already. Whether you are filled with dread or eager to show what you know, the following strategies give you the best chance of doing well:

- **Get a good night's sleep.** If you are well-rested, you have a better shot at sounding smart.
- **Bring supplies for your spirit.** A bottle of water or cup of coffee may keep up your spirits (and your caffeine level). Instructors usually specify what comforts you can bring to class. Avoid causing distractions, such as unwrapping noisy candy wrappers. (Other students are likely to be as nervous and distractible as you are.) If you get stress headaches, don't forget to pack your aspirin.
- **Bring required academic supplies—and spares.** You may need to bring a blue book (a standard lined essay book for hand-written responses). Also, bring a sharpened pencil or pen and a backup, a calculator, scratch paper, or whatever other supplies the instructor allows. Make sure you have a watch or can see a classroom clock so you can pace your work.
- **Organize your resources.** In some cases, instructors may let you bring a summary of notes to jog your memory during the test. They even may let you have open access to your books and notes (a sure sign that the test will be harder). Write your summaries clearly so that you don't lose time trying to decode your own writing. Attach some tabs, use marked index cards, or highlight your resources in other ways that will make them easy to navigate under pressure.

  If you struggle with writing and spelling, bring a dictionary or a spell-checker if they are permitted. Many instructors will let you use them because it shows your desire to do good work. Some instructors will refuse because of concerns about security.

In Case of Emergency

What happens if you cannot make it to the test? Most instructors have strict regulations about taking scheduled tests on time to ensure fair treatment for all stu-

"Hello, you've reached the office of Professor Arte. If your excuse for not turning your paper in on time is that your computer broke down, press '1.' If your excuse is that you had psychological problems, press '2.' If your excuse is that your grandmother died, press '3.' If your excuse is . . ."

dents. However, sick children, car accidents, and deaths in the family can interfere with your plans to be present for a test.

If you can't report at the scheduled time, call your instructor *before* the test. Explain your situation. Ask whether you can take a make-up exam. Being courteous encourages your instructor's cooperation. Instructors may ask you to document your absence (such as a doctor's excuse) before they will give you a make-up test. Do all you can to take tests promptly to avoid this kind of complication.

Controlling the Butterflies

Just moments before your instructor hands out the exam, you may feel as if you are in the first car of a roller coaster about to hurtle down the first drop. Your heart pounds. You are sweating. The butterflies just won't go away.

What Is Test Anxiety? A few butterflies are okay. A little anxiety even can be a good sign. It signals you to prepare for the test and can motivate you to do your very best.

Too many butterflies can harm you. Anxiety can cripple your test performance. Nervousness and worry activate the emergency systems in your body. Your pulse increases. Your heart beats faster. Your hands perspire. In other stressful circumstances, these responses prepare you to flee or to fight. They help you survive. But in the quiet of the classroom, they interfere with your ability to focus on the test.

Text-anxious students sabotage their own efforts because they focus on themselves in negative ways (Kaplan & Saccuzzo, 1993). Preoccupied with the certainty of their own failure, they cannot free up the energy to perform well. This reaction increases the chances of failure. Test-anxious students interpret even neutral events as further proof of their own inadequacy. For example, if a

Anxiety is the interest paid on trouble before it's due.

**William R. Inge
American playwright,
20th century**

On Target Tips

Learning to Relax

You can bring your test anxiety under control by following these strategies:

1. **List each aspect of the test situation that makes you feel nervous.** For example, you might list the following events:
   - You sit down to review one week before the exam.
   - You get in your car to go to the exam.
   - Your instructor hands back an exam that you think you did badly on.
   - You see the instructor carrying a stack of exams into the class.
   - You read the exam instructions.
   - You read on the calendar that a test is scheduled.
2. **Place each aspect of the test situation in order of intensity from least to most anxiety-provoking.** Least anxiety-provoking might be reading about when the test is scheduled. Most anxiety-provoking might be having your instructor hand back the exam.
3. **Imagine the least anxiety-provoking situation on the list and relax.** Breathe deeply. Concentrate on driving muscle tension out of parts of your body. Work on even deeper levels of relaxation until your body feels calm, warm, and heavy.
4. **Imagine the next situation that represents slightly greater anxiety and relax.** Find the relaxation procedure that works most efficiently for you and practice until your body feels free of tension.
5. **Work your way through the rest of the anxiety situations by practicing relaxation in each imagined situation.** You may need to repeat this procedure many times until you can imagine the most anxiety-provoking situations without feeling anxious or disturbed.

---

person monitoring the test looks troubled, the test-anxious student may assume that her own behavior somehow caused the troubled look. Test anxious students also are more likely to experience stress-related physical symptoms, such as an upset stomach or a stiff neck, that further hinder performance.

Reducing Test Anxiety Two things can be done:
- Improve study skills to build competence and confidence
- Cope with the anxiety

If you get a lot of anxiety about tests, you may need to use both strategies (Zeidner, 1995). If you only learn to cope with anxiety without improving your study skills, this can make you feel calmer and more in control, without improving your performance. On the other hand, if you improve your study skills, but cannot master your anxious feelings, the results may be eroded. What are some specific things you can do to master test anxiety?

- **Replace anxiety with relaxed feelings.** One simple strategy is to neutralize your anxious feelings by relaxing. Although it is a simple idea, it is hard to carry out in practice. "Learning to Relax" outlines the steps for tackling test anxiety.

- **Positive self-talk.** Test-anxious students often make their anxieties worse by predicting their own failure. Instead of tormenting yourself with criticism and dire predictions, substitute positive statements, such as "I will overcome this challenge" or "I feel confident I will do well." By practicing a more positive outlook, you build your confidence and overcome your anxiety.

- **Support groups.** Most campuses offer support groups for test anxiety. These groups emphasize study strategies, anxiety management techniques, and moral support. They may be free.

- **Regular exercise.** Many students find relief from their anxieties by building a regular exercise program into their busy schedules. Exercise is a great stress reliever. It also promotes deeper, more restful sleep.

- **Avoiding drug use.** Monitor your caffeine intake. Too much can compound agitated feelings. But this is a minor problem compared to those that result from using harder drugs to ward off anxiety or stay alert. See "Just Say 'Whoa'" on the cost of drug abuse.

Self-Assessment 7.1 will help you determine whether you need help with test anxiety.

Self-Assessment 7-1

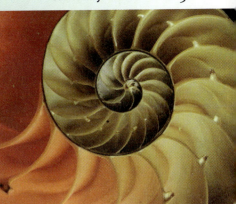

Do I Have Test Anxiety?

Check the category that best describes the way you feel when you are taking a test:

	NEVER	OCCASIONALLY	REGULARLY
I feel physically ill just before a test.	___	___	___
I fail to complete a test because I fret about what will happen when I fail.	___	___	___
I cannot seem to organize my time to prepare well for an exam.	___	___	___
I know I could do better if I could ignore how nervous I feel during the test.	___	___	___
I struggle with stomach pain and bathroom urges just before a test.	___	___	___
My mind has gone completely blank during the middle of an exam.	___	___	___
I fear that I will end up turning in the worst performance on the test in the entire class.	___	___	___
I have difficulty getting a good night's sleep before a test.	___	___	___
I'm very concerned about what my instructor will think of me if I don't do well on a test.	___	___	___
I get distracted during the test more than my peers seem to.	___	___	___
I start to panic when other students finish their exams while I'm still working.	___	___	___
I know the material better than my exam score indicates.	___	___	___
I know I won't be able to have the kind of future I want unless I can get a better grip on my testing fears.	___	___	___

These items give you a general idea about whether test anxiety is interfering with your test performance. If you marked any items "regularly" or marked several "occasionally" and "regularly" responses, you might benefit from a more in-depth assessment of your test anxiety. Contact the center on your campus that assists students in developing more effective study skills. After evaluating the nature of your difficulty, these study skills specialists can make specific recommendations to help you master your anxiety.

Staying Out of the Pits

Just Say "Whoa"

Gary stared at his test paper and realized that what he had written didn't make sense. But he couldn't stay focused long enough to fix it. His hands were starting to shake. He looked at the clock and prayed for the hour to be over soon.

Under the pressures of trying to meet the demands of multiple courses, some students turn to drugs to sustain a higher level of energy and attention. Stimulants can stave off sleep, but at a cost. You may feel out of control when the drug kicks in. You may "crash" after using stimulants. This will just put you further behind and maintain the incentive to keep using the drugs. It's a losing proposition. Don't even start.

Taking the Test

The test is just moments away. You take your seat. The class quiets down as the instructor hands it out. What can you do while you are taking the test to maximize your performance?

General Strategies

Some good general strategies during the test are to

- **Relax.** Take a deep breath. Try to relax. The calmer you stay during a test, the better you will do. Take relaxing breaths at the start and continue breathing calmly throughout the test. Concentrate on breathing slowly from your diaphragm. When you do this right, your stomach will move out as you breathe in and in as you breathe out.

- **Look at the entire test.** Examine the structure. Count the pages. Think about how you should divide your time, given your strengths and weaknesses. If the test includes different types of questions (such as multiple choice and short essay), begin with the type you do best on to build your confidence. As you plan how to allot your time, leave more time for parts that require more effort or that make up more of your total score. Plan some time at the end to review your work.

- **Read the instructions . . . twice!** You will be very upset if you discover near the end of the exam time that you were supposed to answer only certain questions rather than all the questions on the test. Read the instructions carefully first. Then read them again.

- **When you are stuck, mark the problem and move on.** You will be taking most exams under time pressure, so you cannot afford to spend much time probing the depths of your memory. If time is left over after you have finished the parts of the exam that you were able to answer with confidence, return to the parts you skipped.

- **Concentrate despite distractions.** If you start daydreaming, mark the item that got you off task and move ahead. Come back to it later. Avoid getting caught up in any competition with other students who complete the test early. Do the test at your pace and don't worry about who gets done first.

- **Ask for clarification.** When you are confused, ask your instructor or proctor for help. Most instructors try to clarify a question if they can without giving away the answer. An instructor may even decide that the question does not work and will throw it out. Your classmates also may appreciate your speaking up.

- **Learn from the test.** The test itself may jog your memory. One area of the test might hold clues that could help you with other areas.

- **Proofread your work.** Whether it is a series of math problems or an extended discussion of Japanese haiku, review your work.

Under pressure, it is easy to misspell, miscalculate, and even make errors on things you know well. Clear editing marks on your test paper demonstrate that you were being as careful as possible about your work.

Multiple Choice

You will probably face many tests that are mainly multiple choice: stem questions or incomplete statements followed by possible answers from which to choose. Figure 7.1 provides an example. To improve your scoring on multiple choice questions,

- **Read the test items carefully and completely.** Cover up the alternatives and read the stem without distractions. See whether you can answer the question in your head before you look at the alternatives. Then read *all* the alternatives before you identify the best one. This is especially important when your instructor includes "all of the above" or "A and C only" types of choices.

- **Strike out wrong answers.** When the correct answer is hard to identify, eliminate the wrong choices so you can concentrate only on real contenders.

- **Mark answers clearly and consistently.** Use the same method of marking your choices throughout the test. This may be important if questions arise later about an unclear mark. If your test is machine scored, avoid having extra marks on the answer sheet. They can be costly.

- **Change your answers cautiously.** Make sure you have a good reason before you change an answer. For example, change your answer if you
  - Mismarked your exam
  - Initially misread the question
  - Clearly know you are moving to the correct alternative.

  If you are not certain, it is best not to change. Your first impulse may be better.

- **Guess!!** Some tests subtract points for incorrect answers. In this case, answer only the questions that you know for certain. However,

Figure 7.1

Multiple Choice Format

The best way to succeed on multiple choice tests is:	[question stem]
A. read the question carefully	[alternative]
B. check on the weather	[distracter]
C. look for language cues to throw out choices	
D. cry like a baby	
E. A & C	[answer]

Figure 7.2

Using Grammar Clues to Find Multiple Choice Answers

What grammar clues can help you determine the correct answer in this multiple choice question?

Don't change your multiple choice answers unless you can find an:

A. error in how you marked your test booklet

B. typo in the sentence stem

C. justification from peeking at your lecture notes

D. clues from cloud formations out the classroom window

most multiple choice tests give credit for correct answers without extra penalty for wrong answers. In this situation, guess. If the question has four alternatives, you have a 25% chance of being correct.

- **Look for cues.** When the item involves completing a sentence, look for answers that read well with the sentence stem (see Figure 7.2). Sometimes instructors don't pay close attention to how the wrong alternatives read. If a choice does not work grammatically with the stem, it is probably not the right choice. In complex questions, the longest alternative may be the best one. The instructor may simply require more words to express a complex answer.

- **Do not spend time thinking about how the question could have been better written.** You may be tempted to answer a different question than the one the instructor has created because you think it would be a better question. You may be right, but it's a waste of time. Do the best you can with the question as it is written. Select the best alternative even if it is not written exactly as you would like.

True-False

True–false questions ask you to make judgments about whether propositions about the course content are valid or truthful. For example, consider this item: *"True or False:* It is always a bad idea to change your answer." This would be a good true–false question to assess your understanding of the last section on multiple choice questions. (The answer is *false*.)

To maximize your performance on true–false items,

- **Go with your hunch.** When you don't know the answer on a true–false question, you have a 50% chance of being right when you guess. Choose the alternative with the intuitive edge.

- **Don't look for answer patterns.** Instructors generally strive to make the order of true–false answers random. This means there is no

Final page of the Medical Boards

particular pattern to the "T" answers or "F" answers. Selecting "F" on question 35 should have no bearing on how you answer question 34 or 36. Focus your energies on the questions themselves rather than on trying to detect nonexistent patterns.

- **Honor exceptions to the rule.** If you can think of exceptions to the statement, even one exception, then the statement is probably false. In the earlier example, if you can think of even one circumstance in which changing your answer is a good idea, then the statement is not valid across all situations and should be marked "false."
- **Analyze qualifying terms.** Words that specify conditions, such as *always*, *never*, and *usually*, usually identify an item that is false. Those terms suggest an unlikely or unwarranted generalization. Notice in our example, "It is always a bad idea to change your answer," the word *always* makes the statement invalid because there are some situations when changing your answer makes sense.

> *Do not on any account attempt to write on both sides of the paper at once.*
>
> **W. C. Sellar**
> **British writer, 20th century**

Fill-in-the-Blank

Like multiple choice questions, fill-in-the-blank questions test how well you recall information. An example of a fill-in-the-blank format is *"Instructors try hard to make a _____ pattern of answers on true–false tests."* (The answer is *random*.) You probably either know or don't know the answers on these kinds of questions.

Short Answer

Short answer questions demonstrate how well you can explain concepts briefly. For example, a short essay question about the last section might be *"Describe some strategies for doing well on true–false questions."*

To maximize your score on short answer questions, write clear, logical, and brief answers. Writing a lot more than asked or including information not asked for suggests that you do not understand the concepts. When you skip a short essay question because it stumps you, look for cues in the rest of the test that may help you go back and answer it later.

Essay Questions

Essay questions evaluate the scope of your knowledge and your ability to think and to write. For example, an essay question derived from this chapter might be, "Compare and contrast multiple choice and essay question strategies as ways of measuring your learning." Notice how much more demanding this kind of question is than multiple choice.

To do well on essay questions,

- **Anticipate what kinds of essay questions may be asked.** If you were in your teacher's shoes, what kinds of questions would you ask? Thinking about the course in terms of potential questions encourages you to stand back from the detail and consider the larger themes. If you practice predicting and answering questions, that will probably improve your test performance even if your predictions aren't on target.
- **Read the question carefully.** It won't help to write a brilliant answer if you are not answering the question. Circle the key concepts as you read to make them stand out and keep you focused.

- **Analyze the question.** Essay questions often require higher-order thinking skills. Table 7.2 gives key words often contained in essay questions. (The categories in the table represent different types of thinking discussed in Bloom's taxonomy, discussed in Chapters 6 and 8.) These key words provide hints about the kinds of thinking you should do to be successful. If the question asks you to create an argument, then you will be wasting time if you only define and explain terms. Underline the verbs that hint at the kind of thinking the question requires. Gear your responses to that kind of thinking.
- **Map your ideas.** Outline or map a general structure for your response before you begin to write. This overview will help you write a more coherent, persuasive answer. Write the outline down in the margins or at the beginning of the essay. This will show the

Table 7-2
Decoding Essay Questions

Look carefully at the verbs your instructor has used in the essay question. This table organizes these verbs into categories based on Bloom's taxonomy and alerts you to the kind of thinking the instructor expects to see in your answer:

SOME QUESTIONS EMPHASIZE *MEMORY* OF IMPORTANT INFORMATION ABOUT A TOPIC. LOOK FOR THESE KEY WORDS.

define	describe	label	locate	recite	list
recognize	name	state	select	identify	number

SOME QUESTIONS EMPHASIZE *COMPREHENSION*, OR YOUR UNDERSTANDING OF CONCEPTS. LOOK FOR THESE KEY WORDS.

change	transform	interpret	express	illustrate	paraphrase
restate	match	convert	perceive	explain	give examples
discuss	predict	defend	generalize	summarize	distinguish

SOME QUESTIONS EMPHASIZE *APPLICATION*, OR EXTENDING THE CONCEPTS IN NEW DIRECTIONS. LOOK FOR THESE KEY WORDS.

apply	change	choose	solve	show	sketch
modify	classify	produce	use	paint	dramatize
discover	prepare	generalize	fix	adapt	demonstrate

SOME QUESTIONS EMPHASIZE *ANALYSIS*, OR BREAKING IDEAS APART OR RELATING THEM TO OTHER IDEAS. LOOK FOR THESE KEY WORDS.

analyze	classify	survey	distinguish	subdivide	categorize
infer	select	separate	compare	contrast	differentiate
relate	connect	link	account for	explain	

SOME QUESTIONS EMPHASIZE *SYNTHESIS*, OR ORGANIZING CONCEPTS TO PRODUCE SOMETHING NEW. LOOK FOR THESE KEY WORDS.

combine	plan	invent	compose	revise	design
construct	create	develop	produce	originate	hypothesize

SOME QUESTIONS EMPHASIZE *EVALUATION*, OR MAKING WELL-REASONED JUDGMENTS. LOOK FOR THESE KEY WORDS.

compare	critique	support	summarize	judge	consider
evaluate	criticize	weigh	evaluate	appraise	recommend

instructor your command of the question. It may demonstrate what you know if you run out of time on the test.

- **Reflect the question in your opening sentence.** Do not waste time rewriting the question. Instead, use an opening sentence that directly reflects the question. For example, suppose that your literature instructor writes, "*Compare Emily Dickinson's earlier and later poetry.*" You could answer, "*Emily Dickinson's later poetry can be compared to her earlier work in many ways.*" Notice how the subject of the question is reflected in the opening sentence of the answer and sets the stage for the information to follow.

- **Write like a reporter.** Journalists describe key ideas in their opening paragraph and continue with appropriate detail. The same approach works in an essay. First, identify the scope of what you intend to say, then fill in the details. If you cover the crucial ideas early in your answer, you may get partial credit even if you run out of time and can't complete the essay.

    Write precisely. Even if the question touches on other areas that you enjoy and want to write about, don't get seduced into wasting time off task. Be especially careful to spell key terms correctly.

- **Don't bluff.** Your first sentence or two usually signals whether your answer will be solid. Your instructor may not be entertained by attempts to camouflage how little you know. Avoid padding your answer. The longer you write, and the more you ramble, the more you may expose what you don't know.

- **Write legibly.** Reading scrawl does not sit well with instructors. As a result, they may not give you the benefit of the doubt when the grading decision can go either way. Instructors may simply reject handwriting they cannot read.

    Your handwriting may worsen under the stress of testing. If it becomes very bad, unless you can learn to print fast, the best solution may be to slow down. Slower writing is usually easier to control.

    Some students intentionally write illegibly on essay questions when they don't know the answer. They hope that the instructor will glance over the hard-to-read sentences. This rarely works. Unclear writing draws the instructor's attention.

    Some other strategies that foster your instructor's good will are described in "Scoring Essay Brownie Points."

- **Be careful in your use of humor.** Sometimes when students feel stuck for an answer, they produce a light-hearted response to ease their own frustrations. This strategy helps you blow off steam, but you run a risk of sounding disrespectful. Unless you have clear cues from your instructors that they would appreciate your creative efforts, don't substitute humor for effective answers.

Self-Assessment 7.2 evaluates your test-taking practices.

On Target Tips

Scoring Essay Brownie Points

You can maximize your score on essay questions by making your answers easy to read and follow:

- Use dark ink or pencil.
- Carefully cross out parts that you no longer want evaluated.
- Avoid drawing numerous arrows to redirect your instructor's attention.
- Write on just one side of the paper.
- Use organizing notations, headings, or subpoints to clarify the order of your thoughts.
- Leave space between answers so your instructor can give you feedback or you can add ideas that you think up later.

To talk without thinking is to shoot without aiming.

English proverb

Self-Assessment 7-2

How Well Do I Test?

Review the characteristics of effective test-taking below.

RATE HOW YOU USUALLY PERFORM IN THESE AREAS

	Always	Usually	Sometimes	Never
As part of my general test-taking strategy				
I stay relaxed during the exam.	____	____	____	____
I look at the entire test before I start.	____	____	____	____
I read the instructions carefully.	____	____	____	____
I concentrate even when distracted.	____	____	____	____
I ask the instructor for help when confused.	____	____	____	____
I move on when I get stuck.	____	____	____	____
I look for clues in other parts of the test.	____	____	____	____
I proofread my work.	____	____	____	____
In multiple choice questions				
I read the test items carefully and completely.	____	____	____	____
When I'm uncertain which answer is right, I take steps to rule out the alternatives that are wrong.	____	____	____	____
I mark the correct answer clearly and consistently.	____	____	____	____
I change my answers only when I am certain I should do so.	____	____	____	____
I guess when I don't know.	____	____	____	____
When stumped, I look for cues in the question's structure.	____	____	____	____
On true-false items				
I go with my hunches.	____	____	____	____
I avoid looking for patterns on the answer sheet.	____	____	____	____
I analyze qualifying terms (such as *always*, *never*).	____	____	____	____
I try to find exceptions to the rule.	____	____	____	____
On fill-in-the-blank questions				
I do not loiter when stumped.	____	____	____	____
In short essay questions				
I write brief, logical answers.	____	____	____	____
In essay questions				
I underline the verbs in the question to help figure out what kind of thinking I need to do.	____	____	____	____
I think and outline before I write.	____	____	____	____
I reflect the question in my opening sentence.	____	____	____	____
I write main ideas first and fill in details and examples later.	____	____	____	____
I do not bluff when I do not know.	____	____	____	____
I write for readability.	____	____	____	____
I am careful in my use of humor.	____	____	____	____

Now go back over the list and circle the test management skills that you marked "rarely" or "never." What would you have to do to incorporate these skills into your test-taking approach?

Reviewing the Test

When you get your test back, you may be tickled by a high grade or deflated by a low one, but your job isn't over yet. Some reviewing will help you do better on the next test, including reviewing to consolidate your learning, reviewing to analyze what worked and what didn't work in your study strategy, and reviewing to confirm grading accuracy.

Review all items, not just ones on which you made mistakes. Review and rehearse one more time the material that your instructor thinks you need to learn in the course. This can help you in the long run, especially if you have a cumulative exam at the end of the term. Even without a comprehensive final, test review consolidates your learning.

Your test review should tell you whether your study strategy worked. Did you spend enough time studying for the test? Did you practice the right kinds of thinking to match the particular demands of this teacher? How can you use your study time more efficiently for the next test? Confer with the instructor about better ways to prepare.

Also check the grading. Instructors easily can make errors in applying test keys or counting up point totals. Also identify questions that were not clearly written. Even if your critique of a question does not persuade an instructor to change your grade, your review may give you insight into how the instructor constructs tests, which can help you on the next one.

What if your instructor doesn't allow extensive time for review of your exam during class—or worse, doesn't return the exams at all but only posts the grades? Visit your instructor during office hours and ask for the chance to review your work. This visit also allows you to clarify any questions you have about your instructor's testing or grading practices.

Instructors are unlikely to change a grade without good reason (Moses, 1990). Most construct tests carefully and grade them as fairly as possible. However, if you believe the instructor misunderstood you or made an actual error in calculating your score that affects your grade, by all means ask for a grade change. Remember, though, that instructors can't give you extra points if it gives you an unfair advantage over others in the class.

Students view grades as a key to the future, so it is not surprising that you want to fight for the grade you deserve. Some strategies for getting maximum consideration from your instructor are shown in "Should I Challenge My Grade?"

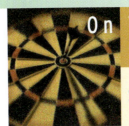

On Target Tips

Should I Challenge My Grade?

What are some strategies that might get the instructor to reconsider my grade?

- *Ask for time after class to present your case.* Most instructors will not spend class time on the challenges of one student.
- *Develop your argument.* Point to evidence, such as an interpretation in the book that conflicts with something said in lecture, to support your request.
- *Explain your interpretation.* If you misinterpreted a question, describe your interpretation. Instructors will sometimes grant partial credit for a well-argued but off-base interpretation.
- *Avoid labeling a question as "bad."* Placing blame on the instructor will probably not encourage a helpful response.
- *Be gracious, whether you win or lose.* Most instructors remember and admire students who effectively advocate for themselves.

About Grades

Ben is really looking forward to getting his test results. He studied hard and thought carefully about his answers. When his instructor returns the test, he is shocked by the "D" at the top of the page. Have you ever been confident about what you knew but got a bad test score? Tests only sample your learning. And, as with Ben, sometimes the sample does not reflect what you have really learned.

Surprised

No Pain, No Gain

A national survey compared high school and college grades (Astin, 1993). As you can see in the graph, grades drifted downward from high school to college. This means that you have to study harder to maintain the same grade point average in college.

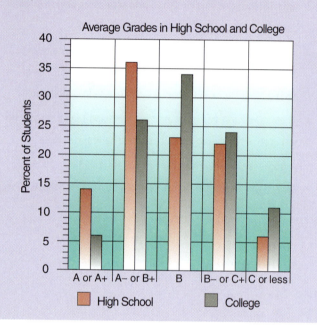

Grades do not change what you learned for the test, but grades can affect your motivation to study in the future. For example, good grades make you feel proud. They encourage you to stick with the study strategies that worked. Bad grades prompt you to make changes if you are going to be successful. Bad grades also can be a blow to your self-esteem.

College Versus High School Grades

Many students are surprised by the differences in high school and college grading. Most students regularly take more tests and quizzes in high school than in college. But most students also say that tests in college are harder (see "Surprised? No Pain, No Gain"). The moral? For grades like ones you got in high school, you have to study harder in college. Otherwise, your grades will probably decline.

Grading Systems

What types of grading systems do most colleges use?

Traditional Grades Most schools use the traditional A–F grading system. Many also include plus (+) and minus (−) judgments to make even finer distinctions in quality of work. Schools that use the traditional system convert grades into a *grade-point average*, or GPA. In this system, A = 4 points, B = 3 points, C = 2 points, and D = 1 point. The point values of grades in all your courses are added up. Then they are averaged to create your GPA.

For example,

American history	C	2 points
College algebra	A	4 points
Intro to business	A	4 points
Sociology	B	3 points

GPA = 13 points divided by 4 courses = 3.25

A higher GPA improves your chances of getting a good job after college and getting into graduate school.

A GPA has special meaning at some colleges. For example, GPAs over 3.5 may qualify you for the *Dean's List*, the roster of students recognized for academic excellence based on the grades they earn. Some academic honor societies, such as *Phi Beta Kappa* and *Phi Kappa Phi*, invite students to join on the basis of the GPA.

If your GPA falls below 2.0, you may be placed on academic restrictions or probation. On some campuses, this may limit the number of courses you can take in the next term and slow down your progress in your major. If your GPA remains low, you can flunk out.

Instructors sometimes assign test or course grades by using a curve. The overall results of the test for the class are tied to the strongest performance in the class. Other students' scores are judged in relation to that score. For example, suppose that on a test with 100 points the highest score was 85. An instructor who is grading on a curve might give As to all scores of 76–85, Bs to scores of 66–75, and so on. Instructors may turn to this practice when a test turns out to be much harder than originally intended. However, not all instructors use a curve. Even when most of the class performs poorly, some instructors don't curve the grades.

Pass-Fail Systems Some schools determine progress on a pass–fail basis. They don't give grades A through F, only pass (P) and fail (F) grades. When this is the only grading system a college uses, students often get extensive feedback about what they have achieved. Instead of a grade-point average, students graduate with other indicators of the quality of their work, such as a *narrative transcript*. In this document, their instructors describe their academic work and how well they achieved their goals.

Some colleges use both A–F and pass–fail grading. For example, students might get A–F grades in most of their courses, but be allowed to take a certain number of credits outside their majors on a pass–fail basis. This dual system allows students to take some courses that they otherwise might avoid because of a potential mediocre grade.

"GETTING AN 'A' OR A STAR IS ALL RIGHT, BUT I'D LIKE SOME SORT OF PROFIT-SHARING PLAN AROUND HERE."

Integrity in Taking Tests

Integrity matters. Each test that you take gives you an opportunity to be honest or cheat.

How Widespread Is Cheating?

Unfortunately, cheating is widespread in college. A comprehensive survey of 6,000 college students showed how big the problem is (Davis & others, 1992). More than 90% said that it was wrong to cheat. However, 75% said that they had cheated in college or high school, or both.

Most students won't report other students' cheating. In one survey, three-fourths of the students witnessed cheating by others but only one in a hundred informed the instructor (Jendrek, 1992). Many of the students ignored the situation even though they were angered or upset by the cheating. One-third of the students said they weren't bothered by the cheating.

Why Do Students Cheat?

Cheating in college has many causes (Keith-Spiegel, 1992). Students who cheat often feel pressure to succeed. They feel overwhelmed by the demands of so many deadlines and cannot see any other way. Cheating gives them better grades with less effort.

Many students and instructors simply expect that people will cheat when they have the opportunity. They reason that because most students cheat, it's okay for them to cheat, too. Instructors sometimes make it easy to cheat by not monitoring tests closely.

Students who cheat often do not get caught and may not be punished when they are. Most students recognize that cheating involves some risk. However, they report that they have seen students cheat and get away with

Few things help an individual more than to place responsibility upon him, and to let him know you trust him.

**Booker T. Washington
American educator,
19th century**

Character is destiny.
Heraclitis
Greek philosopher, 500 B.C.

it. Many instructors don't feel confident in challenging students who cheat, so they overlook suspicious acts. Inaction by the instructor encourages others to cheat.

Some students who cheat may not recognize when they are cheating. Some students "work together" and share answers either before or during a test. They believe that there is nothing wrong with sharing answers as long as both parties agree to collaborate. These students don't recognize that how you arrive at answers is just as important as the answers themselves.

Why Shouldn't Students Cheat?

Would you want to be cared for by a physician who cheated her way to a degree? Obviously not. When the outcome of education involves life and death decisions, it is clear that we want to be cared for by someone whose knowledge and skills are sound.

Even if you are not preparing to become a physician, you will benefit from direct and accurate measurements of what you know. For example, your survival in more difficult, advanced courses may depend on your learning from an earlier course. By cheating, you increase the likelihood of future academic problems.

In their mission statements, most colleges pledge to foster moral and ethical behavior. Some colleges have a stringent honor code. These principles, usually described in the student handbook, recognize that students will have plenty of opportunities to take advantage of circumstances and cheat. When you exercise integrity, however, you demonstrate not just to your instructor but to your classmates that you are a trustworthy, moral person.

Cheating can have ugly consequences. Even if they get away with cheating, some students struggle with a nagging conscience. The relief they initially feel in escaping a bad grade can be replaced by self-doubt, dissatisfaction, and guilt. These students suffer because they have fallen short of their own ideals. However, once you cheat and get away with it, you may be tempted to do it again the next time you aren't as prepared as you should be.

When cheaters do get caught, they face multiple risks. Being accused of cheating in front of others is humiliating. Being found guilty of cheating means you may have to explain this judgment to your friends or parents. Worse, some instructors will turn you over to a student court for punishment, spreading your humiliation even further. Penalties for cheating differ. Your instructor may give you a "0" on the exam or an automatic "F" in the course. On campuses that practice a strict honor code, one episode of cheating leads to expulsion.

On some occasions, cheating students have gotten some surprising consequences. Randy was appalled to discover that when his only episode of cheating surfaced, all of his instructors refused to write reference letters for him. This outcome ruined his plans for grad school. To examine your own beliefs about cheating, complete Self-Assessment 7.3.

Self-Assessment 7-3

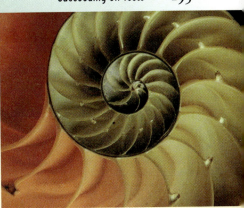

How Honest Am I?

Answer the questions below as honestly as you can.

Do you think it is wrong to cheat? _____ **Justify your answer.** _____
_____

Under what circumstances do you think most students might be inclined to cheat?

    When it is unlikely that they would be caught _____

    When they feel desperate to get a better grade _____

    When there is a lot riding on this particular grade _____

    If they haven't managed their time well enough to study effectively for this challenge _____

    When they might be teased by their peers if they refused to cheat _____

    Other: _____

Rank order the factors that discourage you from cheating:

    I would lose my self-respect. _____

    I would be frightened of getting caught. _____

    I want my test results to accurately reflect my learning. _____

    I consider it my honor to uphold academic integrity. _____

    I don't want to give in to group pressures to do unethical things to get by. _____

    Other: _____

If someone is caught cheating, which consequence do you think is the most appropriate?

    Expulsion from school _____

    Failure in the course where the cheating occurred _____

    Failure of the assignment on which the cheating occurred _____

    Review by the school's honor board _____

    Public censure _____

    Repeat the assignment without cheating _____

    Depends on the cheater's history _____

As you review your responses to this Self-Assessment, think carefully about the role of integrity in your own development. Developing competent study patterns will reduce the temptation you may feel to cheat in college. Even if your test scores are not as high as they might be if you cheated and got away with it, the result will be an accurate reflection of your learning and your character.

Summary Tips For Mastering College

Succeeding on Tests

Preparing for the Test

1. Pace yourself to be at your best for testing challenges. This means plotting out your tests on a master calendar and studying regularly.
2. Think strategically about how to organize yourself. Not all tests emphasize memorization. Find out about the test. Digest your notes appropriately for the kind of test you will be taking.
3. Bring the right support materials. A hot cup of coffee, a dictionary, an extra blue book, and other permitted materials may be just the right supplies to get you through.
4. Alert your instructor when you must miss an exam. Make your best pitch about alternative arrangements. Be prepared to document your excuse.
5. Actively address test anxiety that interferes with your performance. You can try some strategies on your own or join a support group to learn new skills and manage anxiety.

Taking the Test

1. Try to stay relaxed through the exam. Breathe deeply.
2. Use strategies to stay on target. Proofread your paper. Look to the structure of the test for hints about how to answer.
3. Read multiple choice alternatives carefully. Some question formats will trap you if you fail to read all the way through.
4. Use language cues to decode true–false questions. Look for grammatical consistency, length alternatives, and exceptions to the rule to identify the answer.
5. Write brief responses to short essay questions and move on. Adding too much information can alert your instructor to the possibility that your knowledge is wobbly.
6. Think and map your answer before you write essays. By carefully considering your options, you will write a more thorough and logical answer.

Reviewing the Test

1. Examine your test results thoroughly. This gives you one more chance to learn the important material and correct your errors.
2. Review your test to see whether your study strategy worked. If not, you can change directions for the next challenge.
3. Determine whether your instructor calculated your score properly. Mistakes are easy to make. You can advocate for a change if you find a problem.

About Grades

1. Make more effort in college than you did in high school. This will help you earn the same or even better grades.
2. Work toward a GPA that will open opportunities in your future. Many future options may depend on how well you did in college.

Integrity in Taking Tests

1. Adopt standards about test-taking that reflect academic integrity. This practice will help others trust your judgment and admire your character.
2. Avoid cheating because it can bring humiliating and punishing consequences.

College Success Checklist

Have your views changed about any of the following items since you filled out this checklist at the beginning of the chapter? Place a check mark beside any item for which you feel good about your current practice. Also check any for which you have new ideas about how to improve.

____ I pace myself effectively to get ready for a test.

____ I figure out ahead of time what will be on the test and try to predict the test questions.

____ I control my nervous feelings about my test performance.

____ I size up the test to know what I need to do and read all directions carefully before I start.

____ I know effective strategies for scoring well on multiple choice tests.

____ I know how to do well on essay questions.

____ I regularly complete tests in the allotted time.

____ I know how to analyze test results to improve my learning and future test performances.

____ I know the consequences of academic dishonesty at my college.

In the space below, list the items that you still need to work on the most. This list may help you complete the goal-setting exercise in the Learning Portfolio.

Review Questions

1 What is valuable about testing?

2 How should you prepare for a test?

3 What can you do about test anxiety?

4 What should you do on the day of the test?

5 How do strategies differ for different test formats?

6 What are the three purposes of reviewing test results?

7 What are the advantages of not cheating?

Learning Portfolio

Learning by Reflecting... Journal Entries

Then and Now

Think about the grades you made in high school. How much time did you put into studies to achieve your high school grades? Now contrast your high school pattern to the work you are investing in your college grade-point average. Are you managing the same levels of achievement? Have you had to increase your effort just to hold your ground? Are you now studying harder than you ever have? Is that effort resulting in the achievement you are aiming for?

Evaluating Your Exam Luck

Remember two kinds of evaluation experiences. In one, you got a good grade you did not deserve because you got lucky with how the instructor constructed the test. In the other, you got a bad grade that did not really reflect what you had learned.

- What were your reactions on receiving your evaluation?

- Which pattern is more typical of your exam luck?

- What actions, if any, did you take to feel comfortable with the outcome?

Reflections on Cheating

You have probably experienced a situation in which you easily could have cheated but you resisted the opportunity.

- Describe what would have made the cheating easy to accomplish.

- Identify the feelings and values that were involved in the resolution of this problem.

- Were you satisfied with the resolution?

Learning by Doing... Action Projects

Construct Your Own Exam

Construct a sample test for the next real test you will face. If you were the teacher, what would be the most important concepts to test for? How would you go about assessing them?

Researching Success

Do a survey in one of your classes where a test has just been returned. Find out how other students prepared. On average, how many hours did your classmates study?

How did the hours of study correlate with the degree of success on the test?

What pointers do classmates have for more effective preparation?

Learning to Relax

Find a partner who is willing to help you develop some healthy strategies for managing test anxiety. Take some time to develop a hierarchy of the things that make each of you nervous about test situations. Compare your hierarchies. How are they alike? How different? Then practice relaxing as you move through your lists from least to most anxiety-provoking situations. Each of you should take a turn relaxing while the other reads relaxation instructions. Evaluate how effective this strategy might be for you if you practiced it over the course of the semester.

Learning by Thinking Critically... Critiques

Grades: Carrots or Sticks?
Many students thrive in graded systems. They like the clear-cut messages they get when their efforts are rewarded by good grades. However, other students find grades less rewarding. They think competition for grades undercuts meaningful learning and feel stressed out by the process. Collaborate with a group of students and discuss the advantages and disadvantages of using grades to evaluate student achievement.

Decoding Essay Instructions
Find some examples of essay questions, preferably ones that you may have had to respond to on tests already this term. Circle the verbs that represent the kind of thinking the instructor has asked you to do in completing the essay. Speculate about what kind of question is being asked. What is the thinking emphasis of each question on the test?

memory

application

synthesis

comprehension

analysis

evaluation

Judging Exam Quality
Look at an exam that you have completed this term. As unemotionally as you can, evaluate how effective the exam was in representing your knowledge. In what ways was the exam design effective? In what ways could the exam be improved to be a better measure of learning?

Learning by Thinking Creatively... Personal Vision

Promoting Better Test Preparation
Create a 60-second public service announcement about the hazards of cramming that could be aired over the campus radio station during midterms or final exams.

Finding Your Quiet Place
Envision your favorite peaceful place. Where would it be? What would you be doing there? The purpose of being able to imagine this calming refuge is to help you ward off anxiety during testing. What would you need to do to make this image one you can visit during stress to restore your peace?

Everybody's Einstein
The chapter began with an account of how Albert Einstein failed in some of his earlier educational experiences. Is there any parallel between Einstein's frustrating experiences in school and the experiences you have had? Assuming that you achieve great academic and career success, decide what building you would like to have named after you, or identify some other honor that would be even more satisfying. Explain your choice.

Learning by Planning... Goal Setting

Review the results of the Self-Assessments you completed in this chapter. Also review the College Success Checklist. What can you conclude about things you need to do to improve your skills?

What goal do you want to select from this chapter for making positive changes that will help you master the college experience? *(Hint: Is your goal challenging, reasonable, and specific?)*

___

What strategies will you use to achieve your goal? *(Hint: Can you organize your strategy into a series of smaller goals?)*

___

What obstacles may be in your way as you attempt to make these positive changes?

___

What additional resources might help you succeed in achieving your goal?

___

By what date do you want to accomplish your goal?

___

How will you know you have succeeded?

___

Resources for Mastering the College Experience

The Everything Study Book (1996) by **Steven Frank. Holbrook MA: Adams Corp.**
A manual for obtaining superior grades without spending all your time in the library. Illustrates with humorous profiles of ineffective strategies.

Up Your Grades (1997) by **A. H. Tufariello. Lincolnwood, IL: VGM Career Horizons.**
TBriefly describes many strategies for maximizing success on exams, includes how to persuade instructors to give you the higher of two possible grades.

Last Minute Study Tips (1996) by **Ron Fry. Franklin Lakes, NJ: Career Press.**
Covers more in his text than just last-minute tips. A careful timeline showing how preparations change in your study depending on how much time is left until the test.

The Anxiety and Phobia Workbook (1995) by **Edmund J. Bourke. Oakland, CA: New Harbinger Publications.**
A comprehensive, sympathetic guide to managing fear and anxiety. Not specifically directed toward college, but applicable to test anxieties.

Internet Resources

http://www.csbsju.edu/advising/help/testskil.html.
Learn test-taking skills.

http://www.chre.vt.edu/cdfs/learningStrategies/HTML_Pages/Test_Anxiety.htm
How to conquer anxiety at test time.

http://www.gse.ucla.edu/mm/cc/info/prep/tests/tips.html
Ways to prepare for success on tests; UCLA.

http://www.lssu.edu/LC/test.htm
Hints about figuring out a teacher's style of testing.

http://webster.commnet.edu/HP/pages/lac/tests.htm
Thorough review of how to prepare for different kinds of tests; Capital Community-Technical College.

Thinking

CHAPTER 8

✓ College Success Checklist

Place a check mark beside the items that apply to you. Leave the items blank that do not apply to you.

____ I know how college can improve my thinking skills.

____ I can explain the various levels of thinking that are required in college assignments.

____ I can describe the differences between critical and uncritical thinking.

____ I know how to ask good questions.

____ I can create persuasive arguments.

____ I use strategies to be an effective problem-solver.

____ I understand and practice appropriate decision-making strategies.

____ I know the advantages and disadvantages of responding creatively.

____ I use holistic strategies to enhance my thinking.

____ I recognize that my attitudes affect the quality of my thinking.

Preview

The chapter covers an important academic goal in college: becoming a better thinker. You will learn how thinking demands differ in complexity in college assignments and disciplines. And you will read about thinking critically, thinking creatively, and thinking holistically.

Chapter Outline

Images of College Success: Temple Grandin

Critical Thinking
　Bloom's Taxonomy
　Some Keys to Good Critical Thinking

Creative Thinking
　Individual Creativity
　Csikszentmihalyi's Ideas on Creativity
　Breaking Mental Locks

Holistic Thinking
　Right-Brained Thinking
　The Medicine Wheel
　Mindfulness

Self-Assessments
　8.1　Where Do I Bloom?
　8.2　The Critical Difference
　8.3　How Systematically Do I Solve Problems?
　8.4　My Creative Profile

On-Target Tips
　Decoding Assignments
　Coming Up with Alternatives
　I Have a Question
　Making Good Decisions
　Making Sound Judgments

Images of College Success
Temple Grandin

"I think in pictures," says Temple Grandin, a professor at Colorado State University. "Words are like a second language to me. I translate both spoken and written words into full-color movies, complete with sound, which run like a VCR tape in my head.... In my job as an equipment designer for the livestock industry, visual thinking is a tremendous advantage" (Grandin, 1995, p. 19).

Grandin's designs for solving problems in managing livestock have helped to make her an international celebrity. However, this woman's accomplishments are all the more remarkable because she has a rare form of autism called Asperger's syndrome. Among other problems, the condition causes her to behave in eccentric ways with repetitive actions, abrupt shifts in conversation, and limited social skills. In her book, *Thinking in Pictures*, Grandin describes the immense problems of acceptance she has faced as a result. She believes that she doesn't possess the basic brain wiring that most people have to read and react to social behavior. She often compares her existence with the emotionless character Data on *Star Trek*. For example, she never could understand or relate to what was going on between Romeo and Juliet.

However, Grandin's intellectual gifts are dazzling. She solves problems in livestock management by assuming a "cow's eye view." Her careful observations, well-developed spatial and critical thinking skills, and knowledge of animal behavior have produced many creative solutions that have advanced the humane treatment of animals.

Temple Grandin's social skill deficits have not been an obstacle in her success in resolving problems in livestock management.

Critical Thinking

You are likely to hear that "critical thinking" is a goal in many of your courses. Although there are many definitions of "critical thinking," it generally refers to thoughtful, systematic, and careful examination of ideas (Meltzoff, 1998). When you think critically, you improve your ability to learn and retain new learning. When you think more systematically about what you are learning, you also may change and refine your beliefs. Or you may be better able to defend what you already believe. Critical thinking generally reflects the higher-order thinking skills described in Bloom's taxonomy, also mentioned in chapter 2.

Bloom's Taxonomy

One of the earliest educators to examine the nature of thinking skills was Benjamin Bloom, who, with his colleagues (1956), developed a *taxonomy*, or hierarchy, of thinking skills that describes the thinking skills college work requires. Table 8.1 defines and summarizes Bloom's six levels of critical thinking. Bloom defines two skills—memorization and comprehension—as lower-order skills and four—application, analysis, synthesis, and evaluation—as higher-order skills.

Beginning courses tend to emphasize lower-order thinking skills. However, to go beyond rote memory and simple comprehension, you have to draw upon

> *It is such good fortune for people in power that people do not think.*
>
> **Adolf Hitler**
> **German dictator, 20th century**

On Target Tips

Decoding Assignments

When your instructors want you to...	They might ask you to...
Memorize	Recite lists
	Complete objective tests
	Recognize familiar terms
Comprehend	State the ideas in your own words
	Translate the author's meaning
	Outline key ideas
Apply	Explore a case study
	Solve a problem
	Provide examples to support your idea
Analyze	Complete an essay question
	Sort ideas into proper categories
	Identify assumptions and values
Synthesize	Create and defend a position
	Make a unique creation
	Improve on an existing design
Evaluate	Criticize a position
	Judge quality using criteria
	Cite advantages and disadvantages

higher-order thinking skills. Understanding Bloom's taxonomy can help you see the kinds of thinking your instructors want from you by giving you clues about how to think at the right level of complexity (see Figure 8.1). "Decoding Assignments" summarizes how the six levels of thinking are targeted by different kinds of college assignments. You can also incorporate the spirit of the taxonomy into your own approach to study. If you work with a subject on a higher level, not only memorizing content, your retention is likely to be stronger. Let's examine each of the important domains in Bloom's taxonomy.

Memorization Many people overlook the role of memory in thinking. Memory determines the pool of facts and ideas (the content) from which you can reason and draw conclusions. To think effectively you need information to think about. Courses differ in how much memorization is required, but each is based on a body of knowledge that you are expected to master. Strategies to improve memorization generally ask you to identify specific facts and rehearse them until you can recall them easily.

Comprehension Comprehension means understanding of a new concept and correct interpretation of ideas. To show comprehension in an art appreciation class, you might be asked to give the hallmarks of impressionist painting. In a nursing course, you might be asked to explain the highest priorities in a nursing care plan. To improve your comprehension, monitor how well you understand what you are learning. For example, as you encounter a new idea in a course, imagine that you have to explain it to a friend who is not in the class. If you can't do this easily or if you are not sure

Table 8-1
Thinking Skills in Bloom's Taxonomy

LEVEL	DESCRIPTION	RELATED SKILLS
Memorization	Learn course concepts and facts; produce a solid knowledge base	Recognize, recall, recite, name, define, describe
Comprehension	Show understanding of course concepts and facts	Restate, explain, interpret, discuss, summarize, defend
Application	Extend course concepts and facts in new directions	Classify, apply, produce, discover, modify, prepare
Analysis	Break ideas apart and relate to other ideas	Compare, contrast, connect, relate, categorize, analyze
Synthesis	Create new organizations of ideas	Design, organize, construct, compose, revise, develop
Evaluation	Make well-reasoned judgments and decisions	Recommend, judge, critique, decide, evaluate, support

The Characteristics of Good Critical Thinkers

Critical Thinkers...

Practice honesty with themselves, acknowledging what they don't know, recognizing their limitations and being watchful of their own errors.

Regard problems and controversial issues as exciting challenges.

Strive for understanding, keeping curiosity alive, remaining patient with complexity, and being ready to invest time to overcome confusion.

Base judgments on evidence rather than personal preferences, deferring judgment whenever evidence is insufficient and revising judgment when new evidence reveals error.

Show interest in other people's ideas and willingness to read and listen attentively, even when they tend to disagree with the other person.

Recognize that extreme views (whether conservative or liberal) are seldom correct, so they avoid them, practice fair-mindedness and a balanced view.

Practice restraint, controlling their feelings rather than being controlled by them, and thinking before acting.

Uncritical Thinkers...

Pretend they know more than they do, ignoring their limitations, and assuming their views are error-free.

Regard problems and controversial issues as nuisances or ego threats.

Show impatience with complexity and thus would rather remain confused than make the effort to understand.

Base judgments on first impressions and gut reactions, showing no concern about the amount or quality of evidence, and clinging steadfastly to earlier views.

Preoccupy themselves with their own opinion, so they are unwilling to pay attention to others' views. At the first sign of disagreement, they tend to think, "How can I refute this?"

Ignore the need for balance and give preference to views that support their established views.

Tend to follow their feelings and act impulsively.

Figure 8.1

your comprehension is correct, seek more information until you are confident that you correctly interpret the key ideas.

Application Application encourages you to stretch by seeing how what you learned in one situation might apply in other. For example, you might apply certain principles of education to the operation of your college day care center or to modifying the rules of a competitive game in physical education. Creating applications can be used to comprehend and retain ideas. If you can apply an idea to your own life, you often can master it more completely.

Amazing but True College Stories

Things I Learned Freshman Year

By Robert Benchley, 1921

- Charlemagne either died or was born or did something with the Holy Roman Empire in 800.
- By placing one paper bag inside another paper bag you can carry home a milk shake in it.
- There is a double *l* in the middle of *parallel*.
- Powder rubbed on the chin will take the place of a shave if the room isn't very light.
- French nouns ending in *-aison* are feminine.
- Almost everything you need to know about a subject is in the encyclopedia.
- A tasty sandwich can be made by spreading peanut butter on raisin bread.
- A floating body displaces its own weight in the liquid in which it floats.
- A sock with a hole in the toe can be worn inside out with comparative comfort.
- The chances are against filling an inside straight.
- There is a law in economics called *The Law of Diminishing Returns*, which means that after a certain margin is reached returns begin to diminish. This may not be correctly stated but there *is* a law by that name.
- You begin tuning a mandolin with A and tune the other strings from that.

It isn't so astonishing, the number of things that I can remember, as the number of things I can remember that aren't so.

Mark Twain
American writer and humorist, 19th and 20th centuries

Application is at the heart of solving problems, which we will explore below.

Analysis When you analyze an idea, you take it apart and study how its parts are related. For example, you might ask what socioeconomic factors shape attitudes toward rap music. Or you might compare and contrast two works of art by Picasso during different phases of his life. "Compare and contrast" is a popular essay strategy used in many disciplines to evaluate analytic thinking. Analysis skills contribute to your effectiveness in reasoning and asking questions.

Synthesis To synthesize means to integrate ideas. For example, when you combine new course ideas with knowledge you already possess, you may synthesize a new perspective. You might compose a song with others in a class on jazz or create a plan to enhance political activism in your home community. Synthesis builds upon other skills. To synthesize ideas, you not only must comprehend them, but also analyze their interconnections.

Evaluation To evaluate is to form a conclusion or judgment. Evaluating often involves applying standards or criteria. For example, you may be asked to determine which of several speeches is most persuasive or judge whether gun control laws are effective in reducing violence. The ability to evaluate well often depends on the other thinking skills. Evaluation is the key to making decisions and offering criticism.

You may recognize that some kinds of thinking in Bloom's taxonomy are easier for you than others. Complete Self-Assessment 8.1, "Where Do I Bloom?" to study your profile as a thinker.

Some Keys to Good Critical Thinking

Different disciplines tend to view critical thinking in distinctive ways. For example, the natural sciences often emphasize problem-solving skills. The humanities often focus on critical analysis. One goal of a liberal arts education is to help you develop critical thinking skills by sampling the various ways of thinking refined in different disciplines and incorporating the approaches to help you live a more well-rounded life (Beyer, 1997).

Regardless of differences in emphasis, there is some agreement about what good critical thinkers do, as described in Figure 8.1. Self-Assessment 8.2, "The Critical Difference," will help you identify your own critical thinking profile. Next we explore some aspects of good critical thinking in more detail.

Solving Problems Temple Grandin demonstrated elegant problem-solving skills when she figured out how to manage livestock by looking at problems from a cow's point of view. After careful examination of all

Self-Assessment 8-1

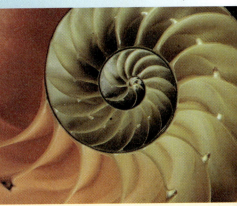

Where Do I Bloom?

Rank order the levels of Bloom's taxonomy in relation to your own abilities. For example, the ability you rank as number 1 should be the skill that you think you are best at. Then describe your evidence for ranking the skill at the right.

RANK ORDER THESE SKILLS:	WHICH OF THESE DO YOU DO MOST EASILY?
Memorization	Memorize facts and new ideas
Comprehension	Understand and interpret most new course concepts
Application	Transfer course ideas to apply to new situations
Analysis	Probe concepts to understand them better
Synthesis	Use course concepts to come up with new insights
Evaluation	Show critical judgment about quality of course ideas

#1: Evidence:

#2: Evidence:

#3: Evidence:

#4: Evidence:

#5: Evidence:

#6: Evidence:

How challenging was it for you to rate your abilities in different kinds of thinking? You already may have developed some clear preferences. Will you have many opportunities to practice these skills in your chosen major? If there are some kinds of thinking that you don't like to do, where can you get some practice to overcome your negative feelings?

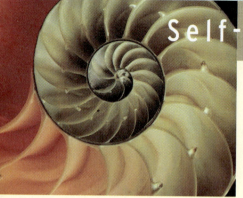

Self-Assessment 8-2

The Critical Difference

Review the general approach you take to most intellectual challenges. Check the category that most closely corresponds with your usual pattern of critical thinking.

	ALWAYS	USUALLY	SOMETIMES	RARELY
I like to talk about topics when I have solid background.	___	___	___	___
I do not pretend to know more than I really do.	___	___	___	___
I feel energized by differences in opinion.	___	___	___	___
I get more enthusiastic as ideas get more complicated.	___	___	___	___
I regularly need to revisit what I think to correct errors.	___	___	___	___
I like to look more deeply into things to get greater insight.	___	___	___	___
I'm not afraid to change my mind.	___	___	___	___
I prefer evidence over intuition as a way to persuade others.	___	___	___	___
I am able to spot flaws in arguments.	___	___	___	___

If you marked most of the columns "always" or "usually," you demonstrate the characteristics of a good critical thinker. Those marked "sometimes" show some room for improvement. Work on items marked "rarely" to maximize your ability to think critically.

Creativity is inventing, experimenting, growing, taking risks, breaking rules, making mistakes, and having fun.

Mary Lou Cook
American environmentalist,
20th century

the contributing factors, she discovered that applying some form of pressure made cows less agitated when herded from one area to another. She redesigned entry ramps to provide pressure, experimenting with different design strategies, until she successfully produced a design that reduced agitation in the herds. Her ideas were so successful that the livestock industry widely adopted them for more humane care.

But her problem-solving didn't stopped there. She adapted the same techniques that calmed livestock to her own struggles to stay calm when she felt overstimulated by social activity. She developed a "human squeeze box," similar to the device that she designed to help calm livestock, which provides gentle pressure on her when she climbs into it. She uses this device regularly to restore her feelings of control.

As you can see, problem-solving relies on many skills in Bloom's taxonomy. Grandin comprehended the relationship between pressure and calmness after analyzing the relevant factors. She applied different strategies in designing the best configuration, ultimately synthesizing a strategy that worked best for cows and for humans. She also evaluated the success of her results. Although not all the problems we face have the broad implications of the ones resolved by Grandin, the process she completed reflects the basic steps of a good problem-solving strategy.

The IDEAL Method Many people find it helpful to solve problems by using a specific problem-solving *protocol* or system. One systematic approach to problem-solving is the five-step IDEAL method (Bransford & Stein, 1984):

1. *Identify the problem.* First recognize that a problem exists. For example, suppose Bernita discovers on the first day of her art appreciation class that her instructor already started when she arrived. The instructor looks distinctly displeased as Bernita takes a seat in the back of the class. When she looks at her watch, Bernita discovers that she was two minutes late. Obviously she didn't want to annoy her instructor by arriving late to class each day, so she had a problem.

2. *Define the problem.* In defining a problem, be as specific and as comprehensive as you can. Outline the contributing factors. What contributed to Bernita's late arrival to art class? Was her watch faulty? Was she slowed down by carrying too many books? Did she merely walk too slowly between classes? Probably it was the distance between the art class and the English class that Bernita had on the other side of the campus in the prior period. Even if she walked at top speed, she couldn't get to the art class on time.

3. *Explore alternative approaches.* Systematically gathering and exploring alternative solutions helps you isolate the best approach. Assuming that arriving late to class makes her uncomfortable enough to take action, what are some reasonable alternatives Bernita might consider? She can drop either class, transfer into another section that prevents the conflict, or ask the art instructor to wait until she gets there . . . well, maybe not. Or perhaps she can talk to both instructors and explain her situation. "Coming Up with Alternatives" suggests ways to generate solutions.

4. *Act on the best strategies.* Take specific action to resolve the problem. Possibly include more than one strategy. Bernita decided to explain to her art instructor why she would be a few minutes late

Surprised

Inventions that Were Ridiculed

Identifying problems often involves asking questions in creative ways (Goleman, Kaufman, & Ray, 1993). Bill Bowerman (inventor of Nike shoes) asked, "What happens if I pour rubber over an iron?" Fred Smith (founder of Federal Express) asked, "Why can't there be reliable overnight mail service?" Godfrey Hounsfield (inventor of the CAT scan) asked, "Why can't we see in three dimensions what is inside the human body without cutting it open?" Masaru Ibuka (honorary chairman of Sony) asked, "Why don't we remove the recording function and speaker and put headphones on the recorder?"

Many of these questions were ridiculed at first. Other shoe companies thought Bowerman's waffle shoe was a "really stupid idea." Fred Smith proposed the idea of Federal Express during his days as a student at Yale and got a C on the paper. Godfrey Hounsfield was told that the CAT scan was impractical. And Masaru Ibuku was told "A recorder without speakers—you must be crazy!"

A problem well stated is a problem half-solved.

**Charles Kettering
American engineer, 20th century**

On Target Tips

Coming Up with Alternatives

These approaches may help you generate new ideas for resolving problems:

- Examine how you feel about the situation.
- Seek specialists' input about a solution.
- Collect opinions about possible approaches.
- Do research on what experts would do.
- Subdivide the problem into smaller pieces.
- Think through the consequences of leaving the problem alone.
- Work backward from the preferred outcome.

to class, added that she would do her best to get there on time, and asked for her instructor's support. The instructor verified that Bernita would be late only by two minutes and asked that she sit near the door to minimize disruptions. She also thanked Bernita for her courtesy.

5. *Look back to evaluate the effects.* When you have chosen a solution, the final step is to evaluate whether it works. You might be thrilled with how well it works and feel free to move on to your next challenge. Or you might discover it was not effective. In this instance, Bernita's problem-solving was successful. Her solution not only saved her from the trouble and expense of dropping the class, but gave her a better personal connection with her instructor.

To evaluate how systematic you are in problem-solving, complete Self-Assessment 8.3. Look for ways to improve your system.

Characteristics of Good Problem-Solvers Good problem-solvers have certain qualities (Whimbey & Lochhead, 1991). They

- **Observe carefully.** They try to identify all relevant factors in a problem from the outset. Superficial observation misses factors that hold keys to ultimate solutions. Careful observation involves analysis, identifying the relationships among the elements of the problem.

- **Use systematic strategies.** They try not to jump to conclusions. Some problems may have several solution methods. Good problem-solvers evaluate the strengths and weaknesses of the different methods. They can explain why they chose a certain method.

- **Are positive and persistent.** They aren't beaten by frustration. They search for ways to make the struggle invigorating rather than frustrating.

- **Show concern for accuracy.** They pay attention to detail. They know how easy it is for small errors to happen in moments of inattention. They take care not to leave out crucial information. They proofread statements and recheck calculations before submitting their work for review.

Reasoning Good critical thinkers also demonstrate their ability to create and defend intellectual positions (Beyer, 1998). You can improve your reasoning skills in the following ways.

Ask Questions Sometimes students feel discouraged about asking questions in college. They may have acquired passive learning habits in earlier years of school. Yet when you were little, you were probably constantly asking questions. If you don't ask questions often, your questioning skills may be in hiding.

You see, but you do not observe.

**Sherlock Holmes
Fictional detective created by Arthur Conan Doyle, 19th century**

Self-Assessment 8-3

How Systematically Do I Solve Problems?

Think about the problems you have faced in your academic and personal life in the last month. Review how regularly you went through each of the stages of the IDEAL model.

	USUALLY	NOT USUALLY	EXPLAIN
Identification: I accurately identify when something needs attention.	___	___	_____
Definition: I describe problems comprehensively, including the factors that might influence the problem.	___	___	_____
Evaluation: I figure out different approaches to take and decide on the best alternative.	___	___	_____
Action: I effectively put my plans into action.	___	___	_____
Looking back: I purposefully examine how effective my chosen solutions are in solving problems.	___	___	_____

As you examine the results of your review, which aspects of problem-solving are your strengths? What elements do you need to practice to become more systematic in your problem-solving? What ideas do you have for incorporating these skills in your problem-solving style?

The problem may be fear of embarrassment. You may think of good questions to ask but worry about what others will think of you. Perhaps the instructor will think your question comes from left field. Or maybe other students will think you are showing off what you know. The problem with worrying so much about what others think is that you sacrifice your opportunity to stretch as an intellectual. It is *your* education. If you don't take risks, you won't get the maximum benefit in developing your mind.

Get your curiosity out in the open. If you recapture your enthusiasm for asking questions, your college years will be more interesting and more fun. A special kind of thrill occurs when your mind works well. "I Have a Question" gives some tips on how to ask good questions.

Be Willing to Argue You may have some negative feelings about the word *argument* based on the tension that you have felt when in conflict with a friend or loved one. In college contexts, *argument* refers to developing a well-reasoned

> *To swallow and follow, whether old doctrine or new propaganda, is a weakness still dominating the human mind.*
>
> **Charlotte Gilman Perkins**
> **American social critic, early 20th century**

position about some unsettled question. You may have to present a position in a term paper, in a speech, or in answer to a complex question in class. Reasoning is studied as a formal science in logic classes, but you will certainly have opportunities to create and defend arguments in many other formal and informal situations.

Distinguish Forms of Argument Two types of argument include *inductive reasoning* and *deductive reasoning*. Inductive reasoning involves generalizing from specific instances to broad principles (see Figure 8.2). For example, perhaps you really enjoy your first college foreign language class. Based on that experience, you might reason inductively that *all* language classes in college are great. Notice that your conclusion or rule—your *induction*—might be incorrect because your next course may turn out to be disappointing. You will learn to reason inductively to reach good and probable generalizations in a variety of college courses.

In contrast, deductive reasoning works from general situations or rules to specific predictions or applications. Deductive reasoning parallels the hypothesis-testing procedures used in the sciences. For example, your chemistry professor may ask you to identify an unknown substance. By applying specific strategies of analysis

Figure 8.2

Using Induction and Deduction

From specific observations	→	to general principles	=	INDUCTIVE REASONING
Maria has red hair and a bad temper.	--→	Most redheads probably have bad tempers.		
Waking up on the past three Mondays was a hard thing to do.	--→	Waking up on Mondays will probably always be a hard thing to do.		
T.S. Eliot's "The Wasteland" is a masterpiece.	--→	The rest of Eliot's poetry will be impressive.		

From broad generalizations, observations	→	to specific conclusions	=	DEDUCTIVE REASONING
Butlers tend to have evil minds.	--→	The butler must have been the murderer!		
All cats have scratchy tongues.	--→	This is a cat. It must have a scratchy tongue.		
My roommate Ted seems really cranky.	--→	He must have flunked his math test.		

Questions posed to you by instructors can show how you are thinking. Many instructors expect you to ask questions to indicate your interest and improve your grasp of course concepts.

or by trial and error, you narrow the possibilities until you deduce its true identity.

Check Your Assumptions It is easy to reach wrong conclusions from wrong assumptions. For example, satirist Jonathan Swift caused a stir in the 18th century when he proposed one solution for two serious problems facing British society: too many orphaned children and not enough food. Swift proposed that both problems could be solved if the orphans were eaten! Those who *assumed* Swift was putting forward a serious position were outraged. Those who carefully examined Swift's real purpose and *assumed* he meant to bring serious attention to these social problems were amused by his wit and sensitized to the problem. It helps to identify your assumptions because they shape how you interpret evidence.

Know the Language Being good at reasoning depends on being able to interpret the specialized language used in proposing or defending arguments.

Take Time Before Concluding Sometimes we short-circuit effective reasoning. It is easy to get excited about a bright idea and simply stop the hard analytic work involved in thinking the problem through to the end. A premature judgment may work out, but this tends to make us even less exacting next time we analyze a problem. Careful reasoners resist impulsive judgments.

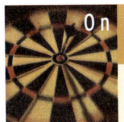

On Target Tips

I Have a Question

You can improve your analytic skills by learning to ask questions that will help you break open the ideas you are studying (Browne & Keeley, 1990). Here are some questions that may help you strengthen these important skills.

- What are the issues and the conclusion?
- What are the reasons?
- What words or phrases are ambiguous?
- Are there value conflicts?
- What assumptions are being made?
- What is the evidence?
- Are there other ways to explain the results?
- Are there flaws in the reasoning?
- Is any information missing?
- Do the conclusions fit the reasons?
- How do the results fit with my own values?

Staying Out of the Pits

Understanding the Language of Arguments

Understanding specific phrases or terms can be helpful when you are constructing or defending arguments. What do the following terms or comments mean?

- *"That begs the question."* This statement means that a prior comment has wandered off the topic. To beg the question means to avoid dealing with the topic at hand in a meaningful fashion.

- *"It's a moot point."* This expression means that there is no point in continuing to discuss a certain question. The issue is judged to be dead . . . but it may not be!

- *"Use logic, not emotion."* Many arguments play on our emotions. In some situations, an emotional argument can be very persuasive. However, in college settings, arguments based on logical reason usually get a more positive response. Review your position to see whether the power of your argument derives from passion or from reason.

- *"Argumentum ad hominem."* Sometimes unpleasant people create solid arguments. You should not reject an argument simply because you may not like the person who poses the argument. Rejecting an argument on that basis is called an argumentum ad hominem, meaning argument against the person.

- *Infer versus imply.* People don't always say what they mean. Listeners then must fill in the missing pieces as they interpret the message they hear. Listeners can *infer* meaning based on their assumptions and values and understanding of the context. On the other hand, the speaker may *imply* additional information without directly stating it. For example, in his management class Dr. Roth *stated* that the percentage of unemployed people is low. He *implied* (but did not directly state) that the economy is in good shape. As a listener, you could *infer* that he pays attention to financial news or that he probably reads the *Wall Street Journal* regularly, based on what he discussed in class.

They thoroughly review the argument to make sure they have addressed all questions.

Know Your Own Bias We all have strong preferences and prejudices that may prevent us from evaluating an argument fairly. By knowing your own prejudices, you can increase the likelihood of coming up with more effective arguments. For example, if you know that you feel strong sympathies for single parents, you can take this bias in account when you evaluate government policies that affect their lives. Good reasoners guard against their own "soft spots" to increase their objectivity.

Making Decisions Some decisions, such as what kind of cereal to have in the morning, may be trivial. Other decisions have far-reaching consequences. For example, you decided where to go to college. To make that decision, you may have used some systematic criteria. Perhaps you wanted a college that is close to home, has low tuition costs, and offers specific majors. Or you may have decided to go to the campus that was the most appealing to you when you visited. How satisfied you are now with your college experience may reflect how carefully you considered your basic concerns.

Making decisions involves not only higher-order thinking skills, but integrating those skills with your own values and your knowledge about yourself. Good decisions solve problems and make your life better. Bad ones often make a mess.

To improve the quality of your decisions, see "Making Good Decisions."

Offering Criticism Dr. Reedy shuts off the videotape of President Clinton's State of the Union address, turns to the class, and says, "What do you think?" Jeff dreads moments like this because the question feels so open-ended. He's never sure what instructors want when they ask questions like that.

Classes that give you opportunities to express opinions or criticisms can feel intimidating. However, some strategies can make these opportunities less daunting. First, decide whether you like what you are judging. Your general reaction can set the stage for more detailed analysis later on. Then you can use specific criteria to form detailed judgments. "Making Sound Judgments" suggests some typical criteria for evaluating ideas. You may need to develop your own set of relevant criteria for your analysis. When you are criticizing, include both positive and negative comments. (Some people believe that criticism involves only spotting flaws.)

Creative Thinking

The need for creativity is great in college. In many situations creativity will be expected, appreciated, and rewarded. For example, humanities teachers appreciate students' creative insights about artistic works. The sciences thrive on original ways of explaining the world and its mysteries. The arts depend on unique personal expressions.

Creative thinking also plays an important role outside classes. Campus celebrations usually have a creative flair. Competitions among student groups may showcase dazzling talents. College abounds with opportunities to discover and express your uniqueness.

Individual Creativity

Creative thinking tends to be fueled by the following characteristics (Perkins, 1984):

- **Concerns for aesthetic standards.** Creative thinkers enjoy applying standards of beauty in their work. They look for elegance in explanations or respond positively to simplicity or efficiency as aesthetically pleasing. This principle also applies to how creative people submit assignments in college. Their work often reflects their distinctive view. For example, Cassandra has a take-home essay test in psychology in which she is asked to explore different kinds of human motivation. She illustrates her insights with cartoons that increase her own interest in the work. Her instructor is impressed and asks to keep the illustrations for use in future teaching.

- **The art and motivation of solving problems.** Creative thinkers enjoy solving problems and developing different perspectives. The art of creativity is often in the way people see things. When 20th-century British biologist Alexander Fleming came back from a vacation and found that the bacteria in one of his petri dishes had died, he did not regard it as a trivial failure. Rather, he recognized that something important had occurred, even though it was not at all what he was looking for. While investigating the "accident" in the petri dish, Fleming discovered penicillin.

    As a student, enjoy solving problems and be motivated to pursue different perspectives. Creative students consider multiple approaches in completing assignments and strive to produce a distinctive product.

- **Flexibility and playfulness in thinking.** Creative thinkers are flexible and play with problems, which gives rise to a paradox. Although creativity takes hard work, the work goes more smoothly if you take it lightly. In a way, humor greases the wheels of

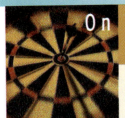

On Target Tips

Making Good Decisions

As your life becomes more complicated, how can you improve your personal decisions?

- *Gather as much information as possible.* The more information you have, the easier the issue will be to analyze.

- *Outline criteria that can help you analyze the problem.* Identify the most compelling aspects of the decision you must make. Outlining criteria helps to structure your decision.

- *Predict what will happen if you fail to take action.* Some problems (but not many) will go away with time. What are the risks of putting off a decision?

- *Think about all of the consequences.* Sometimes a decision produces a good short-term outcome but makes problems worse in the long run. Think about the possible good and bad that can result from your decision. Listing advantages and disadvantages on paper can make these elements more tangible.

- *Talk it over.* Get someone to listen to your strategy. An outsider often can be more objective in identifying flaws in your plan.

- *Sleep on it.* Letting your decision percolate overnight may help you recognize some weaknesses in your approach.

- *Avoid emotional decisions.* Making up your mind when you are too upset or excited can lead to trouble. Try not to take action when you are under duress.

- *Minimize regrets.* You may be able to see some risk for regret in the decision you form. Before taking action, think carefully about how much regret you can bear about a bad decision.

Too often we . . . enjoy the comfort of opinion without the discomfort of thought.

**John F. Kennedy
U.S. President,
mid-20th century**

> *A hunch is creativity trying to tell you something.*
> **Frank Capra**
> **American film director,**
> **20th century**

Paul MacCready is one of America's most prolific inventors. His best-known invention is the Gossamer Condor, the first human-powered plane to travel a mile. MacCready's task was to design something stable and very light that would fly. This had to be done in a way different from any other airplane. MacCready's accomplishment won him a $100,000 prize and a place in the Smithsonian Institute next to the Wright Brothers' plane. MacCready says that asking the right questions and seeing things in a fresh way are critical for creativity.

creativity (Goleman, Kaufmann, & Ray, 1992). When you are joking around, you are more likely to consider any possibility. Having fun helps to disarm the inner censor that often condemns your ideas as off-base. Playfulness itself is a creative state. As a clown named Wavy Gravy put it, "If you can't laugh about it, it just isn't funny anymore."

- **Willingness to risk.** Creative people make more mistakes than their less imaginative counterparts. It's not that they're less proficient, but that they come up with more ideas, more possibilities. They win some, they lose some. For example, Picasso created more than 20,000 paintings; not all of them were masterpieces. Creative thinkers learn to cope with unsuccessful projects and see failure as an important opportunity to learn.

- **Objective evaluation of work.** Despite the stereotype that creative people are eccentric and highly subjective, most creative thinkers strive to evaluate their work objectively. They may use an established set of criteria to make this judgment or rely on the judgments of trusted others. In this manner, they can determine whether further creative thinking will improve on their work.

- **Inner motivation.** Creative people are often motivated by the joy of creating. They tend to be less inspired by grades, money, or favorable feedback from others. Creative students

On Target Tips

Making Sound Judgments

Many instructors ask their students to make evaluations in class. When you have to evaluate the quality of a presentation, proposal, position, or other intellectual effort, the following criteria may give you a good place to start in forming your opinions:

To what degree is the work . . .

effective?	sufficient?
efficient?	adequate?
reasonable?	logical?
aesthetically pleasing?	sensitive?
practical?	accurate?
bullet-proof	stimulating?
justifiable?	comprehensive?
understandable?	relevant?

Be prepared to back up your judgment with examples or other evidence.

Self-Assessment 8-4

My Creative Profile

Review your creative track record. Do these descriptions fit you and your work? Check the place on the continuum that corresponds to your judgment and add an example that illustrates your own behavior.

	NOT AT ALL LIKE ME	VERY MUCH LIKE ME
I try to produce work that is aesthetically pleasing.	___	___

Example: _____

I enjoy experimenting with different approaches to solve problems.	___	___

Example: _____

I like to engage in speculation rather than follow a rigid set of expectations.	___	___

Example: _____

I enjoy taking risks.	___	___

Example: _____

I can learn from failure.	___	___

Example: _____

I try to evaluate the quality of work I produce.	___	___

Example: _____

I enjoy working on creative projects for the sheer joy of creating.	___	___

Example: _____

analyze the aspects of their work that can produce joyful feelings so they can recreate those conditions. They also develop their own individual criteria for success.

To evaluate your own creative history, complete Self-Assessment 8.4, "My Creative Profile."

Csikszentmihalyi's Ideas on Creativity

Mihaly Csikszentmihalyi (pronounced ME-high CHICK-sent-me-high-ee) (1995) interviewed 90 leading figures in art, business, government, education,

Don't be afraid to go on a wild goose chase. That's what wild geese are for.

Anonymous

Mihaly Csikszentmihalyi conducted an extensive study of the lives of some of the world's most creative people. He believes that the first step toward being a creative person is to cultivate your curiosity and interest.

The horse is here to stay, but the automobile is only a novelty—a fad.

President of the Michigan Savings Bank advising Henry Ford not to invest in Ford Motor Company

Heavier-than-air flying machines are impossible.

Lord Kelvin, British scientist, 1895

Video won't be able to hold on to any market it captures after the first six months. People will soon get tired of staring at a plywood box every night.

Daryl Zanuck, head of 20th Century Fox movie studios, commenting on television in 1946

and science to learn how creativity works. He discovered that creative people regularly experience a state he calls *flow*, a heightened state of pleasure we experience when we are engaged in mental and physical challenges that absorb us. Csikszentmihalyi (1997) believes everyone is capable of achieving flow. Based on his interviews with some of the most creative people in the world, the first step toward a more creative life is cultivating your curiosity and interest. How can you do this?

- **Try to be surprised by something every day.** Maybe it is something you see, hear, or read about. Become absorbed in a lecture or a book. Be open to what the world is telling you. Life is a stream of experiences. Swim widely and deeply in it and your life will be richer.

- **Try to surprise at least one person every day.** In a lot of things you do, you have to be predictable and patterned. Do something different for a change. Ask a question you normally would not ask. Invite someone to go to a show or a museum you have never visited. Buy a bagel for someone who shares your commute.

- **Write down each day what surprised you and how you surprised others.** Most creative people keep a diary, notes, or lab records to ensure that their experiences are not fleeting or forgettable. Start with a specific task. Each evening record the most surprising event that occurred that day and your most surprising action. After a few days, reread your notes and reflect on the past experiences. After a few weeks, you might see a pattern of interest emerging in your notes, one that may suggest an area you might explore in greater depth.

- **When something sparks your interest, follow it.** Usually when something captures your attention, it is short-lived—an idea, a song, a flower. Too often we are too busy to explore the idea, song, or flower further. Or we think these areas are none of our business because we are not experts in them. Yet the world is our business. We can't know which part of it is best suited to our interests until we make a serious effort to learn as much about as many aspects of it as possible.

- **Wake up in the morning with a specific goal to look forward to.** Creative people wake up eager to start the day. Why? Not necessarily because they are cheerful, enthusiastic types but because they know that there is something meaningful to accomplish each day and they can't wait to get started.

- **Take charge of your schedule.** Figure out which time of the day is your most creative time. Some of us are more creative late at night, others early in the morning. Carve out some time for yourself when your creative energy is greatest.

Breaking Mental Locks

Many people think they can't lead creative lives. Despite childhoods that may have been filled with creative and imaginative play, most of us learn to surrender our sense of play and curiosity, which harms our capacity for creativity. Robert Van Oech (1990) lists a whole sequence of mental locks that prevents

  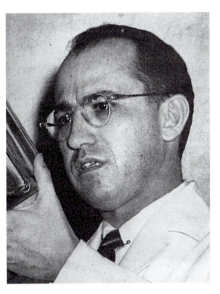

U.S. Poet Laureate Mark Strand says that in his most creative moments he loses a sense of time and becomes absorbed in what he is doing. In this state, he feels he is dismantling meaning and remaking it. Strand comments that he can't stay in this absorbed frame of mind for an entire day. It comes and goes. His attention coils and uncoils. His focus sharpens and softens. When an idea clicks, he focuses intensely, transforming the idea into a vivid verbal image that communicates its essence to the reader.

Nina Holton, a leading contemporary sculptor, turns playfully wild germs of ideas into stunning sculptures. She says that sculpture is a combination of wonderful, unique ideas and a lot of hard work. She comments that when she is introduced to people they often say, "It must be so exciting and wonderful being a sculptor." Holton loves her work, but says that most people see only its creative side, not the hard work.

Jonas Salk, who invented the polio vaccine, says that his best ideas come to him at night when he suddenly wakes up. After about five minutes of visualizing problems he had thought about the day before, he begins to see an unfolding, as if a poem, painting, story, or concept is about to take form. Salk also believes that many creative ideas are generated through conversations with others who have open, curious minds and positive attitudes. Salk's penchant for seeing emergent possibilities often brought him in conflict with people who had orthodox opinions.

us from pursuing more creative responses (see Table 8.2). By having a more flexible attitude, you set the direction for developing more creative responses.

Holistic Thinking

One purpose of a good liberal arts education is to develop the capacity to see things in a comprehensive or *holistic* manner. As your college transcript grows, your experience in various classes will improve your ability to grapple with complex topics in increasingly sophisticated ways.

You may find opportunities to carry over ideas you learn in one discipline to your learning in another. This is sometimes called *transfer of learning*. For example, you may be able to use theories from psychology to analyze communication strategies in a public speaking course. Actively look for opportunities to exercise what you have learned in new situations. It will make your learning stronger and make you more well-rounded in your thinking. Let's explore some ways to become a more holistic thinker.

Right-Brained Thinking

You may have heard or read that thinking is related to how the hemispheres of the brain function (Halonen & Santrock, 1999). For example, Americans

Table 8-2
Some "Mental Locks" That Reduce Your Creativity—and What to Do About Them

MENTAL LOCK	THE CREATIVE KEY
I have to have the right answer.	Sometimes the right answer isn't as much fun or as satisfying.
I must be logical.	But I need to get in touch with my emotional side.
I must follow the rules.	But breaking the rules can be really liberating!
I have to be practical.	But not in every situation.
Play is frivolous and time-wasting.	And I miss it! And I want those feelings back!
That's not my area.	But it could be!
I must avoid ambiguity.	But ambiguity can open new doors.
I can't appear to be foolish.	Until I remember that foolishness can be fun.
To err is wrong.	And I'm designed to derail from time to time.
I'm not creative.	But I could be!

commonly use *left-brained* and *right-brained* to describe which brain hemisphere is dominant in thinking. According to this approach, people with dominant left hemispheres tend to be logical, rational, and *linear*, meaning that they prefer tidy problems and systematic approaches. People with dominant right hemispheres are supposed to be intuitive, creative, and *holistic*, meaning that they thrive in more chaotic conditions and maintain a focus on the big picture when solving problems.

Although it is a popular way to distinguish thinking behavior, this simplified description, popularized by the media, misses the complexity of brain function. No complex creative act involves the action of only the right hemisphere. For example, reading, creating music or art, and inventing involve communication across the specialized centers of the brain. When you read a novel, both hemispheres are active. The left decodes word order and grammar while the right interprets the emotion the author intended to convey. Thus, nearly all complex behavior and certainly holistic thought and behavior involve more than just an active right brain.

But one good outcome of the right-brain/left-brain fascination is that it has made us more aware that people differ in their cognitive styles and talents. For example, Temple Grandin's inventions demonstrated her well-developed spatial skills. "Thinking in pictures" allows her to create more effectively than if she were limited to symbols or words. On the other hand, some people think and create better with words than pictures or symbols. For these people, math classes may be especially challenging unless the problems can be presented in stories that they can vividly imagine. And some people are especially good at working with symbols. They like abstract ideas and feel frustrated when presented with stories as a vehicle for learning. Regardless of where your own strengths lie, your college education will give you the opportunity to develop stronger big-picture skills and a more holistic perspective.

Pop psychology attributes Madonna's music talents to her right-brain activity and William Gibson's (futurist who predicted the internet's arrival) sci-fi writing talents to his left-brain logic. These stereotypes are exaggerated. Madonna's creative singing talents and Gibson's logical writing talents are due to activity in both brain hemispheres.

The Medicine Wheel

One strategy that promotes holistic thinking involves the medicine wheel of the Lakota (Native American) tradition. The medicine wheel envisions life as a circle with north, south, east, and west quadrants. If you conscientiously regard issues or problems from the center of the wheel, the quadrants will remind you of different meaningful aspects of life and help you become a comprehensive, holistic thinker (Frederick, 1991). (See Figure 8.3.)

The north dimension of the wheel is associated with the head. It represents intellectual or cognitive powers, such as reason and wisdom. The south dimension is associated with the body and represents feelings and reactions. The east quadrant represents life-giving forces, as well as ethical and spiritual awareness. This includes ethical and spiritual matters. Finally, the west quadrant emphasizes the alteration of physical matter as it deteriorates, dies, or becomes transformed. In addition to the insight that can be gained by the systematic consideration of the quadrants, the circle itself emphasizes the interconnectedness of the ideas.

How can you apply the medicine wheel to assist you in coursework? Suppose your history instructor asks you to discuss the effects of prohibition on society. Your systematic use of the wheel can lead you to take various perspectives, including

- The physical (west) aspects of the problem, such as the decline in production of alcohol in legitimate markets or the effects of reduced alcohol flow on the physical health of the citizens

- The spiritual (east) aspects of the problem, such as the growth in temperance movements and the support of prohibition by various religious groups

Figure 8.3 **The Medicine Wheel.** The medicine wheel provides a problem-solving heuristic to promote holistic ways of thinking.

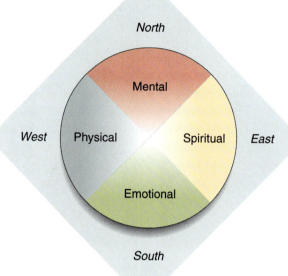

- The emotional (south) aspects of the problem, such as the strain that resulted in homes where alcoholics felt deprived of alcohol, or the exhilaration of those who championed the successful movement
- The mental (north) aspects of the problem, such as the reasoning that persuaded legislators to turn prohibition into a law or the justifications people gave for buying alcohol through the black market.

Although you might not decide to include every insight about prohibition that you obtain by using this approach, this type of systematic consideration provides more options from which to choose.

Mindfulness

Psychologist Ellen Langer (1989, 1997) proposed another holistic thinking strategy. She coined the term *mindfulness* to capture a particular mindset that is responsive to new information. She believes many people are victimized by bad thinking habits (mindlessness) that lead to rigid categorical thinking, a condition she called "hardening of the categories."

Langer demonstrated the power of mindfulness in an interesting way. She and her colleague Judith Rodin (1977) recruited residents of a home for the elderly to participate in an experiment. They randomly assigned residents to one of two groups. Staff members encouraged the members of the first group to exercise more personal responsibility. For example, those people decided who could visit them and what movies they wanted to see. The members of the second group did not get the same opportunities to exercise personal control. Langer compared the activities of the two groups and came to a surprising conclusion. Not only did the group exercising personal choice report being happier, they also lived longer. Eighteen months after the experiment began, only half as many in the personal responsibility group had died. The respon-

Everything is complicated; if that were not so, life and poetry and everything else would be a bore.

**Wallace Stevens
American poet, 20th century**

sibility created a new mindset about their usefulness and contributed to their longer lifespan.

Several behaviors you can use to think more mindfully in college and beyond are as follows (Langer, 1989, 1997):

- **Create new categories.** We often dismiss things by categorizing them in a global way. For example, you might dismiss a "bad" instructor as not worthy of attention. However, if you apply finer distinctions about various aspects of teaching, your perceptions will be richer. For example, perhaps the instructor's delivery is plodding but his choice of words is rich. Or his ideas are delivered without enthusiasm but his precise examples always make things easier to understand. Finer discriminations can make us less judgmental and more tolerant.
- **Welcome new information.** We tend to disregard information that does not fit with what we already know. This will be an especially important tendency to overcome as you begin to do research. Staying open to new information maximizes your pool of ideas. You may begin with one idea of what you want to prove, but find that another possibility is actually more exciting.
- **Consider more than one point of view.** People use different labels to explain the same occurrence. For example, you might view a classmate's behavior as "high-achieving," but the classmate himself may feel "driven." Using a variety of labels (and explanations) gives us greater flexibility in understanding an event.
- **Take control over context.** The Birdman of Alcatraz overcame a narrowed context. When an injured bird found its way into his prison cell, the Birdman nursed it to health. This act began a love of learning about birds that helped him to transcend confinement. When you feel like your own options have been constrained, reexamine your circumstances to see whether you have overlooked some aspect of the situation that could make it more palatable or more rewarding.
- **Enjoy the process.** It is easy to become so single-minded about achieving a goal that you forget to pay attention to the process of achieving it. Remember that the process is just as important as the outcome. At times you may feel like the task before you is too large to finish. By taking a large project and breaking it into smaller, achievable deadlines and goals, you may be able to feel a greater sense of competence. You will also stay mindful of the learning that occurs along the way.

The brain is wider than the sky.

**Emily Dickinson
American poet, 19th century**

Ellen Langer, a professor at Harvard University, has contributed to our understanding of how important it is to think in mindful ways. Langer (1997) closed her most recent book by emphasizing how important it is to ask good questions. As she commented, "How can we know if we don't ask?" By paying attention to our questions, we can increase the power of our mindful learning.

I didn't want to be thought of as mindless so I changed the name of what I was studying from mindlessness to mindfulness.

**Ellen Langer, contemporary
American psychologist**

Summary Tips For Mastering College

Thinking

Levels of Thinking: Bloom's Taxonomy

1. Recognize that different learning situations call for different levels of thinking. Some courses focus on memorizing; others challenge you to do more complex forms of thinking.
2. Higher-level strategies can be used to master course ideas. The more actively involved you are with course ideas, the easier it will be to learn and retain important information.
3. Study assignment instructions to figure out what kind of thinking is required. Most instructors offer cues in verbs about what kind of effort will be most successful.
4. Expect thinking requirements to get more complex over time. Beginning coursework will give you practice in basic thinking skills and lay a foundation for more complex demands later.

Critical Thinking

1. Don't expect your instructors all to mean the same thing when they use the term *critical thinking*. Disciplines vary in how they promote careful and thorough consideration of the ideas in their courses.
2. Develop a systematic approach to problem-solving in and outside class. More careful problem-solving strategies lead to more satisfying long-term solutions.
3. Get comfortable with asking questions and creating arguments. It's all right to reveal what you don't know. Asking questions demonstrates your interest and enthusiasm in your learning. Expect that you will have to develop arguments and learn to defend them.
4. Consider issues carefully before committing to a decision. Quick solutions often lead to regret and more problems to solve.
5. Be prepared to offer a critical opinion. Use criteria to make your judgment more sophisticated.

Creative Thinking

1. Seek opportunities to practice creative thinking. In coursework, extracurricular activity, and even personal relationships you can often express yourself uniquely.
2. Don't think of yourself as uncreative. Listening for fresh ideas can help you break out of past self-doubts about your own creative potential.
3. Practice overcoming mental locks. Identify and exploit your strengths but continue to try out new areas of creativity and interest.

Holistic Thinking

1. Right-brained thinkers supposedly do a better job of holistic thinking. Seeing the big picture is far more complex and interesting than right- and left-brain clichés suggest.
2. Use insights from the medicine wheel to improve the quality of your thinking. Holistic strategies can improve your ability to make sound predictions and recognize important issues.
3. Guard against "hardening of the categories." Mindful attention to your thinking will make you more flexible and less inclined to narrow thinking.

College Success Checklist

Have your views changed about any of the following items since you filled out this checklist at the beginning of the chapter? Place a check mark beside any item for which you feel good about your current practice. Also check any for which you now have new ideas about how to improve.

____ I know how college can improve my thinking skills.

____ I can explain the various levels of thinking that are required in college assignments.

____ I can describe the differences between critical and uncritical thinking.

____ I know how to ask good questions.

____ I can create persuasive arguments.

____ I use strategies to be an effective problem-solver.

____ I understand and practice appropriate decision-making strategies.

____ I know the advantages and disadvantages of responding creatively.

____ I use holistic strategies to enhance my thinking.

____ I recognize that my attitudes affect the quality of my thinking.

In the space below, list the items that you still need to work on the most. This list may help you complete the goal-setting exercise in the Learning Portfolio.

Review Questions

1 What is Bloom's taxonomy and why does it matter?

2 How can you improve your ability to ask good questions?

3 What are some good problem-solving tactics?

4 How can you improve your creativity?

5 What is holistic thinking and how does it apply to college work?

6 What are the benefits of practicing mindfulness in college?

Learning Portfolio

Learning by Reflecting... Journal Entries

No Regrets

Think about a decision you made that was very satisfying to you. What about the process you went through helped to ensure that it was right? What aspects of this process can you practice regularly in making sound decisions? Make notes here to expand in your journal.

_____
_____
_____
_____
_____
_____
_____

The Medicine Wheel and You

The Lakota medicine wheel can help you combat a tendency to indulge in biased thinking. Examine the four quadrants of the wheel. Try to identify the quadrant you are most naturally drawn to when you are solving problems and describe why this might be so. How could using the wheel help you overcome your biases?

Going with the Flow

By the time they reach college many people have formed some firm ideas about whether they are creative. Do you consider yourself creative? In what respects? Explain your judgment. If you don't feel creative, describe what advantages you could gain by practicing some strategies to improve your "flow."

Learning by Doing... Action Projects

Giving Them What They Want

Examine the instructions for a class assignment. Circle all of the verbs in the instructions that give you some direction about how to perform the task. Then compare the verbs to the list of thinking skills in Table 8.1. How would you categorize the complexity of thinking required according to Bloom's taxonomy?

A Question a Day

Sometimes it is hard to overcome the impression that if you ask questions, other people will think you don't know what's going on. Good questions show just the opposite—that you are alert, you are thinking, and you are invested. For at least one week, make a point to ask a good question in each of your classes. If the class is not one where questions are typically discussed during class, ask your instructor after class or e-mail your question. Then analyze how you feel about being more actively involved through questions.

Rhymes and Reasons

Review your notes from two different classes. Color code reasoning examples that could be classified as inductions and those that would be deductions. How do the two classes compare in the kinds of reasoning being promoted?

Learning by Thinking Critically... Critiques

More Mindful Management
Collaborate with a group to describe how mindlessness might creep into your study habits and test preparation strategies. Create a list of recommendations that could help students become more mindful and more successful in these areas.

The Great Debate
Think about an issue or controversy that arose in one of your classes that stirred your feelings. Perhaps it is a political concern or a strong reaction you had to a poem or painting. Briefly map your position about this issue, including key ideas that support your position. Now assume you have been assigned to argue the opposite side in a debate. Map this position as well.

Did careful articulation of the opposing side do anything to weaken your commitment to the original position?

The Limits of the IDEAL Method
You learned about the IDEAL method of problem-solving by Bransford and Stein earlier in this chapter. This five-stage method is useful in developing solutions for a variety of problems, but can you think about some situations in which this approach might not be necessary or effective?

_____
_____
_____
_____
_____
_____

Learning by Thinking Creatively... Personal Vision

"I Wonder..."
A simple exercise to increase your creative thinking follows. Each day for a week, take a few minutes to ask yourself a question that begins with, "I wonder...." Ask this question about a particular aspect of your life. It is important not to censor yourself, no matter how impractical or outlandish the question sounds. After you have some practice doing this, go public with your questions by posing them to your friends. Focus on something that you sincerely are curious about and that matters to others. Listen carefully to your friends' responses. You probably will discover that your questions have some assumptions that deserve to be challenged or fine-tuned (Goleman, Kaufman, & Ray, 1993).

Critical Thinking Collage
Select an issue of a familiar magazine. Cut out all the words you can find that correspond to the skills of reasoning and problem-solving and make a collage that captures the kind of thinking the magazine promotes. What can you conclude about the complexity of thinking the publishers expect from their readers?

Playing "What If?"
One critical feature of developing a more creative lifestyle is staying open to new alternatives. Participate in a group attempting to solve a problem but commit yourself to helping the group explore new ideas. How many different ways can you help the group break open a boundary in their discussion by starting your contribution with what-if questions?

Learning by Planning... Goal Setting

Review the Self-Assessments you completed in this chapter. Also review the College Success Checklist. What can you conclude about things you need to do to improve your skills?

What goal do you want to select from this chapter for making positive changes that will help you master the college experience? (*Hint: Is your goal challenging, reasonable, and specific?*)

_____
_____
_____
_____
_____

What strategies will you use to achieve your goal? (*Hint: Can you organize your strategy into a series of smaller goals?*)

_____
_____
_____
_____
_____
_____
_____
_____
_____
_____

What obstacles may be in your way as you attempt to make these positive changes?

_____
_____
_____
_____
_____

What additional resources might help you succeed in achieving your goal?

_____
_____
_____
_____
_____

By what date do you want to accomplish your goal?

_____

How will you know you have succeeded?

_____
_____
_____
_____
_____

Resources for Mastering the College Experience

Critical Thinking

Thinking Critically about Critical Thinking (1996) by Diane Halpern. Mahwah, NJ: Erlbaum.
This book includes lots of exercises to stimulate your critical thinking.

Beyond Feelings: A Guide to Critical Thinking (1990) by Vincent Ryan Ruggiero. Mountain View, CA: Mayfield.
Encourages control of emotion in effective critical thinking.

Asking the Right Questions: A Guide to Critical Thinking (1990) by M. Neil Browne and Stuart M. Keeley. Englewood Cliffs, NJ: Prentice Hall.
Explores standard questions for examining the quality of evidence in arguments. Also explores biases that block effective thinking.

Six Sure Ways to Solve Problems, No Matter What (1994) by William J. Diehm. Nashville, TN: Broadman & Holman.
Uses the analogy of a windowpane to explore what keeps us from solving problems. Proposes problem-solving strategies.

How We Know What Isn't So: The Fallibility of Human Reason in Everyday Life (1991) by Thomas Gilovich. New York: Free Press.
A fascinating exploration of blinders in everyday reasoning.

The Power of Logical Thinking (1993) by Marilyn Vos Savant. New York: St. Martin's.
A question-and-answer format like the author's national column. Logical analyses of everyday problems.

Critical Thinking about Research: Psychology and Related Fields (1998) by Julian Meltzoff. Washington, DC: American Psychological Association.
Contains lots of examples of flawed thinking about research issues in various fields.

Creative Thinking

A Whack on the Side of the Head: How You Can Be More Creative (1990) by Robert von Oech. New York: Warner Books.
A clever, illustrated book on blocks to creative thinking and principles to help overcome creative inhibitions.

The Creative Spirit (1993) by Daniel Goleman, Paul Kaufmann, and Michael Ray. New York: Plume.
Stimulating examples of creativity at work. Can help you to let go of your doubts and unleash your imaginative mind.

Creativity (1995) by Mihaly Csikszentmihalyi. New York: HarperCollins.
A prescription for becoming more creative. Many examples of how famous people come up with creative insights.

Critical and Creative Thinking: The Case of Love and War (1993) by Carole Wade and Carol Tavris. New York: HarperCollins.
An appealing book on how to improve thinking skills in the context of intimacy concerns.

Holistic Thinking

The Power of Mindful Learning (1997) by Ellen Langer. Reading, MA: Addison-Wesley.
Engagingly explores how to break out of robotic responses that do not do justice to the complex challenges we face.

Internet Resources

http://www.sonoma.edu/cthink/university/univlibrary/library.nclk
Learn more about critical thinking.

http://www.math.utah.edu/~alfeld/math/polya.html
Learn more about problem-solving.

http://www.hi.syr.edu/abaout/Libart.html
Learn more about liberal arts education.

http://www.twsu.edu/~coewww/mi.html
Describes the theory of multiple intelligences; profiles Howard Gardner.

http://www.cyberspace.com/~building/trm_sternberg.html
Summarizes key features of Sternberg's challenge to traditional measures of intelligence.

http://www.hcc.hawaii.edu/hccinfo/facdev/Questioning.html
How to form questions that develop deeper study strategies.

http://www.sjsu.edu/depts/itl/
Resources and theories on solving problems through critical thinking.

http://www.math.utah.edu/~alfeld/math/polya.html
A protocol for conquering problems; takes you through a set of questions. University of Utah.

Writing and Speaking

CHAPTER 9

✓ *College Success Checklist*

Place a check mark beside the items that apply to you. Leave the items blank that do not apply to you.

____ I know the role that writing and speaking skills play in college and careers.

____ I prepare writing projects well in advance and pace myself to submit a polished version on time.

____ I pursue criticism from other people to improve my writing skills.

____ I can overcome the problems that interfere with good writing.

____ I know how to avoid problems with plagiarism.

____ I seek out opportunities to speak in groups.

____ I know what makes a speech effective.

____ I ask people to give me feedback on my speeches so I can improve.

____ I can control my nervousness about speaking.

Preview

An exciting aspect of college is the opportunity to develop poise and polish in how you express yourself. In this chapter you will examine how college assignments develop your ability to speak and write effectively. You will also read about some strategies for overcoming common problems in communication assignments.

Chapter Outline

Images of College Success: Amy Tan

Self-Expression, College, and Careers

Writing
- Learning to Write and Writing to Learn
- Expressive Writing
- Formal Writing
- Habits of Effective Writers
- Writing Problems

Speaking
- Speaking Your Mind
- Good Speaking
- Overcoming Problems

Self-Assessments
- 9.1 What Are My Writing Strengths and Weaknesses?
- 9.2 What Are My Speaking Strengths and Weaknesses?

On-Target Tips
- Organizational Behavior
- The Saving Grace
- Anti-Theft Protection
- Surviving the Home Stretch

Images of College Success
Amy Tan

When she won her first essay contest at age 8, Amy Tan knew she wanted to write fiction. However, her mother wanted her to follow a different dream. In the late 1940s Tan's parents had emigrated from China to Oakland, California. They were eager for their only daughter to have the advantages of their adopted homeland but to honor her Chinese heritage. After her father's unexpected death from a brain tumor, Tan's mother enthusiastically supported her decision to major in pre-med at Linfield College in Oregon. But the lure of the liberal arts proved too strong. Despite her mother's protests that her father would have been disappointed in her decision, she chose English as a major. Tan completed her education at San Jose City College and San Jose State University.

Writing was not easy for Tan. Living with her pessimistic mother had undermined her ability to express herself. She was even advised by a former employer to go into accounting because her writing skills were so poor. Despite these obstacles, she began doing freelance writing. This developed into a successful career in business writing, including projects with companies such as IBM. As Tan acquired more and more clients, she struggled with working 90-hour weeks and a growing sense of feeling unfulfilled. She joined a writer's group and began to write fiction. Tan published her insights as a series of interrelated stories about the struggle between Chinese mothers and Chinese-American daughters. Published in 17 languages, including Chinese, *The Joy Luck Club* has sold more than three million copies and became a successful film. Tan not only achieved her childhood dream of writing fiction professionally but often speaks to enthusiastic audiences on book promotion tours.

Amy Tan delved deep into her relationship with her mother to launch a successful writing and speaking career.

Self-Expression, College, and Careers

Imagine where you might be 10 years from now. If you enter the world of business or a profession, part of your work will probably be communicating with others regularly. If you choose your college opportunities carefully, you will learn to express yourself in writing and speaking with precision, poise, and polish.

Communication projects sharpen skills that employers value (Appleby, 1994). Writing projects help you learn to develop effective memos, proposals, and reports. They improve your attention to detail through practice in editing and proofreading. They also encourage the kind of creativity that might secure jobs in advertising, publishing, and marketing. Classroom speaking provides practice for employment that involves interviewing, supervising, persuading, negotiating, selling, and other aspects of working with the public.

Most colleges provide many opportunities for you to express yourself. Courses that introduce you to communication skills probably will give you the chance to speak or write mainly about your own experiences. Writing and speaking assignments are likely to be more complex in other disciplines. With practice you can improve your communication skills dramatically by graduation. How much you get to develop those skills depends largely on your own ingenuity in seizing opportunities to do so.

Writing

Over time, writing projects improve not only your writing skills but also your confidence as a writer.

Learning to Write and Writing to Learn

Writing-to-learn strategies help you become accustomed to college-level writing (Maimon & others, 1989). For example, after you have read a biology assignment on theories in evolution, writing a position statement about evolution helps you learn the details. By summarizing key ideas and adding your own perspective, you gain practice in writing and you make your learning more meaningful.

In free writing assignments, you simply write whatever you think about the subject. These assignments are generally unstructured but time-limited. A free writing assignment might be "Write about *King Richard III* for five minutes." The experience helps you uncover new ideas, questions, and connections. In general, these writing assignments will not be collected because the main objective of free writing is to help you uncover your own thinking.

One-minute assessments are in-class writing assignments. They give you experience with writing in a discipline. They also give you the chance to say what you did and did not understand from class (Angelo & Cross, 1993). Typically, you write for one minute in class to capture main ideas or pose questions you still have. Instructors collect and review the results to identify topics to review or questions to answer in the next class. They probably won't give you any feedback on how to improve your writing, but the assignments do let the instructor know your needs or opinions.

> *Good communication is as stimulating as black coffee, and just as hard to sleep after.*
>
> **Anne Morrow Lindbergh**
> **American poet, 20th century**

> *Writing is no trouble; you just jot down ideas as they occur to you. The jotting is simplicity itself—it is the occurring which is difficult.*
>
> **Stephen Leacock**
> **Canadian author, 20th century**

How can I know what I think till I see what I say?

**Isaac Bashevis Singer
Polish-American writer,
20th century**

You don't need to wait for instructors to assign a writing-to-learn project to benefit from its uses. Use free writing as a powerful supplement to your regular study and review practices. Pick out the hardest concept to understand or a concept that you think the instructor might ask about in an essay question. Use that as the basis for free-writing practice.

Expressive Writing

In an expressive writing assignment, you reveal your emotions as well as your thoughts. This is a subjective style of writing.

Letter or memo writing can help you make a transition to more challenging forms of college writing. For example, after reading a short story by Mark Twain, you may be asked to write a letter to Twain explaining aspects of the work that are meaningful to you or that make you curious about his motivation to write the story. Writing informally to a specific audience, you may be asked to explain some key idea. This will reveal how well you understand the ideas.

Especially when a subject connects with your personal life, journal writing lets you explore the personal significance of the material. For example, when you take courses that require field work, a journal will help you capture what is most important about the experience. Journal writing is usually not graded in a traditional way. However, you may receive feedback about the seriousness or insightfulness of your effort.

In creative writing assignments, you can explore your inventive side. These include poetry, short stories, and other creative forms in which you discover and refine expressive skills. In beginning courses, the grading and feedback will probably be more encouraging than critical.

Formal Writing

Formal writing emphasizes expressing yourself to a professional audience using an objective point of view, a precise writing style, and evidence to support your conclusions (Kennedy, 1998).

Writing essays trains you in developing a formal argument. For example, in an art history class you might be asked to contrast the work of two impressionist painters. Essays demonstrate your ability to think analytically about a subject. Typically, you state a problem or question at the beginning of the essay, along with a *thesis statement* that conveys your general answer. You then support the thesis with evidence, such as research or the opinions of experts. References to research or expert opinions are called *citations*.

A longer, more fully developed essay also is called a thesis. This often is written as part of completing the special requirements of a major. It is usually a one-time requirement completed in senior year. For example, honors programs may require an extensive position paper in the major, called an honors thesis. In graduate school, masters or doctoral work usually includes a thesis.

In science classes, you may work independently or collaborate on a lab report that describes a scientific procedure you completed. Lab reports are often highly structured, based on a preassigned set of headings. For example, a botany instructor might ask you to experiment with how different nutrient levels affect plant growth. The write-up of the experiment might have four sections: introduction, methods, results, and discussion. In the *introduction*, you present the nature of the scientific problem. Under *methods* you describe the procedure used to investigate the problem. Under *results* you present your findings. Under *discussion* you speculate about the significance of the results or recommend ways to improve the procedure.

Writing is easy: all you do is sit staring at the blank sheet of paper until the drops of blood form on your forehead.

**Gene Fowler
American biographer,
20th century**

In social sciences, business, and nursing classes, you may be asked to summarize group work in a project report. The format varies depending on the project but the goal is efficient reporting of the group's problem-solving effort. For example, nursing students might collaborate to make recommendations for improving the quality of care under staffing limitations. In projects like this, you may need to define the problem clearly, speculate about the origins of the problem, propose some solutions, and predict any positive or negative consequences that might follow from the solution.

Habits of Effective Writers

Regardless of the writing task, writers must develop effective strategies for various stages of the work.

Getting Ready   Curiously, not all of the activity involved in preparing to write is logical. Some students report that they go through some specific writing rituals to bring them good luck. For example, Jim does not feel confident about his writing unless he is using his "lucky" pen, a scratched-up, medium point Papermate he has had since tenth grade. Alicia must have her beagle resting his head in her lap before she can be creative! Ernest Hemingway sharpened a certain number of pencils before he wrote each morning. As long as they don't take too much time, such rituals are not harmful. As your abilities and confidence grow, you probably will not need to cling to such lucky charms to bring out your best. Here are other ways to prepare:

- **Stake out the right territory and time.** Establish a place to write where you keep your writing resources and works in progress (Table 9.1). Most writers say that they need uninterrupted time to think about their writing. Find a quiet place where you won't be interrupted. Hang a "Do Not Disturb" sign on your door to reduce distraction.
- **Plan a reasonable writing schedule.** Starting a paper the night before it is due is not a sound strategy. Set some intermediate goals for completing the task so that the assignment will not seem so forbidding. Table 9.2 is a sample timetable for more thoughtful work.

Research is to see what everybody has seen, and to think what nobody else has thought.

**Albert Szent-Gyorgi
Hungarian biochemist,
20th century**

Table 9-1
The Well-Equipped Reference Shelf

These resources will help you find facts, abide by conventions, and answer questions as you revise your work.

TYPE	FUNCTION
Dictionary	Word definitions, pronunciation, and spelling
Thesaurus	Word synonyms
Atlas	Geographic facts
Style manual	Grammar and writing conventions
	American Psychological Association
	Modern Language Association
Book of quotations	Proverbs and memorable quotations organized by topic, author, or key phrases

Writing—the art of applying the seat of the pants to the seat of the chair.

**Mary Heaton Vorse
American writer, 20th century**

Table 9-2
A Sample Timetable for a Writing Deadline

Time	Tasks
1-2 months before deadline	Select your topic.
	Map your ideas.
	Develop your writing plan.
	Begin to develop a thesis statement.
	Start your research.
Two weeks before deadline	Develop individual sections of your paper.
	Revise with vigor.
	Complete your research.
	Finalize your thesis statement.
The week before deadline	Polish the individual sections of the paper.
	Create an interesting title.
	Check your references for accuracy.
	Get some feedback from a friend.
The night before deadline	Combine the parts of the paper.
	Print the final draft.
	Proofread your paper.
	Assemble the paper.
The morning of the deadline	Proofread your paper one more time.

Getting Started There are generally two schools of thought on how to begin a writing project. One school suggests that you think through your intentions carefully, make maps or outlines of your writing objectives, and then begin writing when your prewriting activities are complete. The other school suggests you just start writing. Roughing out your ideas on paper gives you material that you can then reorganize and improve.

Selecting a Topic Most instructors select the writing topic for you, at least in a general way. However, you still may have to narrow the topic yourself. What are some alternatives for narrowing down the possibilities?

Re-examine the directions for the assignment and all relevant information. Make sure that you understand the goal of the assignment. Ask questions to clarify any aspect of the assignment that is unclear. Compare your ideas with your classmates' perceptions. Ask yourself, "How does this project fit in with the big picture of the course?"

Course readings often include examples or illustrations that can help you find a relevant topic. Think about the various sources you might draw upon to get you started. Look at the list of sources in the footnotes or recommended readings in your textbook. Explore the encyclopedia, cruise the Internet, or review your lecture notes to spark your imagination.

Brainstorm ideas. Write down key features of the assignment at the top of a blank page. Then add any meaningful associations you have with the assignment. As you continue to develop clusters of ideas, a focus may emerge. Or explore your personal experience. Try to think about aspects of the assignment that naturally connect to your own life. For example, Amy Tan's troubled relationship with her own mother became the basis for her remarkable novels.

As you explore possible topics, it's a good idea to avoid ones that are too large, too obscure, too emotional, or too complicated for you to work with in the allotted time. Do not write in areas where you have little knowledge. Do research or redesign the project until you have the needed knowledge.

Good students see the value of an ongoing focus for their college papers (Hansen & Hansen, 1997). They develop a research stream that begins with the first paper they write and builds with each new project. They don't have to start from scratch with each new assignment. For example, Paulo enjoys thinking about environmental issues. He looks for opportunities in his writing assignments to read what he enjoys. He writes about literature with ecological themes, evaluates ecology-related legislation in social science classes, and explores environmental crises in natural science term papers. As a result, Paulo knows his material very well and builds a collection of focused writing that may serve his job-hunting future better than a hodgepodge of unrelated essays.

Crafting a Thesis Most formal writing projects involve drafting a thesis statement or statement of purpose that becomes the backbone of your work. The thesis statement sets the tone for your work and states its main idea. Following are some sample thesis statements from formal writing in different disciplines:

- **Economics:** Supply-side economic theory adequately explains today's business environment.
- **Astronomy:** The appearance of a comet often has been interpreted as a significant mystical event.
- **Sociology:** Affirmative action programs should be retained to promote advantages for those with less privileged backgrounds.

Think of the thesis as your working argument. Your task is to persuade your audience that your argument is sound and well-documented. Once you identify your thesis, stay focused on it. Many students write the thesis on a separate card and keep it in front of them as they write the paper to avoid losing time on irrelevant tangents. You may need to revise your thesis as you learn more about your topic.

Developing Your Ideas Effective writers make a point to use the most appropriate content in their work. They use the concepts, frameworks, or theories that are relevant to the course. These may represent ideas drawn from the course text, lecture notes, or related readings and research. But the point of any formal writing assignment is to demonstrate your learning of these course-related ideas.

Good writers find and carefully show persuasive evidence. They use various forms of evidence but stick with evidence that is appropriate to the project and the discipline. For example, you can include statistics in a political science essay because numerical evidence communicates information about voting trends. However, citing statistical evidence in an expressive essay about literary criticism in a humanities class probably won't fly.

Become familiar with your library's resources so you can locate information quickly. Plan to read more materials than you ultimately will refer to in your work. You may not always have a clear idea about what will help you until you have done some research. Not every resource you read will have a strong connection to what you actually write. Choose those that help you develop your argument and abandon those with a weaker connection. Quality of evidence, not quantity, will impress your reader.

Remember to review your textbook for relevant sources. Consult its list of references. Also use books from prior courses. You may have the book you need already sitting on your shelf.

> *Everybody is ignorant, only on different topics.*
>
> **Will Rogers**
> **American humorist and writer, 20th century**

On Target Tips

Organizational Behavior

Effective writers use a variety of organizing strategies to produce good work. To develop a strong internal organization in your writing projects,

- *Work from an outline or map.* A formal structure of your intentions can keep you on task. You can modify your map if your writing goes in other meaningful directions.

- *Challenge whether each idea is necessary for your argument.* When you have completed a paragraph, compare it to your thesis statement. If it supports your purpose, keep it. If it somehow falls short, throw the paragraph out and start over again.

- *Make clear transitions between paragraphs.* Some papers feel disjointed because the writer has failed to make solid connections between key ideas. Organize the paragraphs in the order that makes maximum impact and link the paragraphs to develop continuity. Phrases, such as "In contrast to . . . ," "Additional insight comes from . . . ," and "A third perspective . . ." make strong transitions.

As you develop your ideas, discuss sources that raise counterarguments to your argument. When you anticipate criticisms that the reader might have and defend against them in your writing, your overall argument is stronger.

Write down complete reference information for each source. It's aggravating to assemble a reference list and discover you forgot to write down the year a book was published or the page number for key information.

Organizing Your Argument Formal papers usually have three parts: introduction, body, and conclusion. The introduction lays a foundation for the rest of the piece. Good writers establish the context or the purpose for writing, even when the instructor is the audience. They state their intentions early and anticipate the kinds of information readers might want to know to help them understand the motive in writing. Throughout the paper, keep in mind what your audience already knows and what they need to know.

The body of the paper should include your opinions and the evidence that supports your argument. Each paragraph in the body should develop a separate idea. Each paragraph must follow logically from the one before, and all paragraphs must relate to the thesis of the paper.

The end of your paper should summarize your argument. Make sure that your conclusions fit with the thesis statement you established in the beginning of the paper. You can say more about its implications for action or further study. For other strategies to improve your writing, see "Organizational Behavior."

Creating the Right Tone Effective writers also project the right tone. For example, project reports are objective and precise, whereas essays are more likely to be exploratory and imaginative. Some formats allow for a casual tone; others require a more formal professional tone.

Following the Rules Effective writers are careful about following the rules or *conventions* of good writing. Conventions include standards in grammar and spelling. In general, these are essential elements of a successful paper. This book adheres to most of the conventions of the American Psychological Association (APA), which is often the standard for writing in the natural and social science disciplines. Another common set of guidelines is published by the Modern Language Association (MLA).

Instructors vary in how much they care about whether you follow the guidelines. Some simply reject papers that include substantial problems with spelling, grammar, and sentence structure. Others overlook these matters if the ideas are good. Some are sticklers about learning and implementing APA or MLA format. They may provide a style sheet that states how the paper must be written. Others may not specify guidelines but expect you to observe the principles of good writing that you have learned in composition class.

Avoid the common problems that easily surface in but tend to weaken the quality of formal writing. Even seasoned writers have questions about punctua-

---

We are as much informed of a writer's genius by what he selects as by what he originates.

Ralph Waldo Emerson
American essayist,
19th century

tion or grammar in their writing. Have a reference manual handy during polishing and proofing.

Drafting and Revising Some instructors will look at drafts of your work to help you get comfortable with revising. Some helpful drafting and revising hints include:

- **Write fast or talk it out.** Spontaneous writing may help you uncover your best thoughts. Some people find it easier to write a first draft by pretending they are talking to an imaginary audience. Once you have some ideas to work with, you can always correct and revise.
- **Leave time for revising.** Effective writing is rarely a one-draft process. As you plan your schedule, allow time for rewriting and revising to take advantage of new ideas. A good piece of writing usually does take several drafts.
- **Chop unnecessary verbiage.** Most first- and even second-draft writing contains nonessential elements and long-winded sentences. For example, phrases such as "It is well known that" or "There are many things that" are unnecessary. Using a lot of adjectives and adverbs also slows down your writing. Review your writing carefully to pare it down. Frustrated by being unable to persuade his students about the importance of revising, one writing teacher posted this sign on his office door:

"I think about you all the time and admire you for all your many qualities.
   I probably even love you. I could go on and on...."
First draft.

"How do I love thee? Let me count the ways."
   –Elizabeth Barrett Browning, 10th century poet
Final draft.

Consulting The stereotype is that writers lead a solitary life. However, most writers benefit from the reviews of others who know good writing. When your draft is close to completion, get feedback from others who write well. Ask them to point out places where you are not clear or identify points that need

Blot out, correct, insert, refine
Enlarge, diminish, underline,
Be mindful, when invention fails,
To scratch your head, and bite your nails.

Jonathan Swift
English satirist,
18th century

PEANUTS reprinted by permission of United Feature Syndicate, Inc.

On Target Tips

The Saving Grace

Using a word processor can help your writing, but some precautions are in order.

- *Save your writing as you go.* Nothing is more frustrating than having the power go down after you have been working on your computer for hours. In this situation you will lose everything that has not been saved. Develop a habit of frequently saving what you write. For example, save your work every time you complete a section or a page of writing. Turn on the automatic save function of your computer so you won't have to think about doing it manually.

- *Make a backup copy—just in case.* Computer viruses can play havoc with your hard drive. By making a backup copy on a floppy disk, you will still have your complete work in case your hard drive crashes. Label your disks so you don't have to waste time searching every disk you own to find your paper.

- *Avoid eating and drinking around your computer.* A spilled soda can foul up your computer and lead to expensive repairs. Move away from your computer when you eat and drink.

- *Have a backup plan.* Even the most reliable computer can go down when you need it most. If you have duplicated your work on a floppy disk, make sure you know where you can find a compatible system to use in a pinch. Your campus computer center may provide some backup machines.

I love criticism just so long as it's unqualified praise.

**Noel Coward
English playwright,
20th century**

further development. For example, Amy Tan still uses her writing support group to help her in refining her work despite her successful publishing record. Find a writing partner and exchange services. Your campus may have a writing center where experts will help you improve your writing.

Finishing Touches Your writing is an extension of you. Your final product not only reveals your ability to construct an argument, but also communicates your pride about your own work. Smudge-free, easy-to-read writing also tends to please the grader.

Many assignments that you write may not require a title. Some writers wait until the project is almost completed before creating a title that captures the appeal of the work.

Most instructors expect you to type your paper. Use a word processor to make the best use of your writing time. You can revise easily when your paper is on computer. Although word processors can save time, they can also frustrate if you overlook some simple precautions. See "The Saving Grace."

Proofreading can be tricky. You may be so close to what you have created that it is hard to spot errors. For example, Bret likes to get a good night's sleep before he proofreads and prints his final draft. By returning to the paper after a good sleep, he feels more confident about catching the subtle errors that he might miss when he is tired.

Proofreading your paper aloud may help you catch more errors. Also, some experts recommend reading your paper sentence by sentence from back to front (Axelrod & Cooper, 1993). Altering your usual method of reading may heighten your awareness of weak sentence structure. When you are satisfied that you have caught all errors, proofread one more time.

Word processors can save you time on your writing projects. They are especially helpful for rewriting and revising. If you don't own a computer, find out when you can use your school's computers.

Self-Assessment 9-1

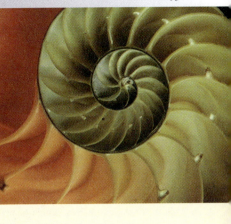

What Are My Writing Strengths and Weaknesses?

Once you have completed at least one formal college writing assignment, examine your work using the guidelines below (after Alverno College, 1995). The feedback or grade you received from your instructor may provide some clues about areas that you need to improve.

	COMPLETELY	PARTIALLY	BARELY OR NOT AT ALL
I followed the instructions	___	___	___

	EFFECTIVELY	PARTIALLY	BARELY OR NOT AT ALL
I established *appropriate context* and kept this focus throughout.	___	___	___
I crafted the *style* of the paper and selected *words* carefully to suit the purpose.	___	___	___
I showed conscientious use of appropriate *conventions*, including spelling and grammar.	___	___	___
I *structured* the paper, including an introduction, main body, and conclusion.	___	___	___
I included *evidence* to support my thesis.	___	___	___
I added *content* that reflected learning specific to the course.	___	___	___

Review the conclusions you have reached about your writing style. What do you need to do to write better papers?

Include a cover page that shows the title of the paper, your name, your instructor's name, the course, and the date unless your instructor requests a different format. Be sure to number the pages. Ask your instructors for other format preferences, including whether they like fancy covers. Many look on plastic folders or binders as a waste of money. On the other hand, some think a cover gives a more professional look. It is probably best to ask.

When the paper is finished, good writers perform one more task. They assess the quality of their work. Complete Self-Assessment 9.1 to explore review skills that will lead to better papers. If you evaluate the quality of your work early enough, you still may have time to revise it and earn a better grade.

Turn projects in on time or negotiate an exception with an instructor *before the deadline*. Even if you have written the best paper in the history of the class, many instructors penalize late submissions. Some even refuse to accept late papers.

Learn from Feedback Instructors vary in the methods they use to evaluate papers. Some simply assign a grade that captures the overall quality of your work. Others provide detailed feedback. When you get feedback, read it

I have only made this letter rather long because I have not had time to make it shorter.

Blaise Pascal
French mathematician,
17th century

Staying Out of the Pits

Good Intentions Won't Do It

Katie knows that she needs to get started on her term paper due the next day, but she can't concentrate. She decides to do some laundry first. She notices that the laundry area needs straightening. "Looks like the washer could use a wipe-down," she thinks. Before she knows it, two hours slip away. The laundry room is squeaky clean but all she has to show for her term paper are good intentions. At least she will have a clean t-shirt when she has to explain to her instructor where her paper is.

> Writing is just having a sheet of paper, a pen and not a shadow of an idea of what you're going to say.
>
> **Françoise Sagan**
> **French writer,**
> **20th century**

carefully so you can learn something that will help in future assignments.

A river of red ink can be hard to take. Read extensive criticisms quickly, then take some time to recover before you try to learn from the feedback. Let your disappointment happen. Maybe even mope a little. Then return with the intention of learning what to do to improve your writing. Remember, we often learn more from mistakes than from successes.

Ask for feedback if you do not understand the grade. Many instructors believe students are willing to settle for a summary judgment—a grade—with little or no justification. However, when you don't understand how a grade was derived, ask. Specific feedback on your strengths and weaknesses is essential to becoming a good writer.

Keep track of your growth as a writer by making a cumulative record of how your papers are improving. Review this record now and then, especially when you are disappointed by an evaluation. Many students retain their papers so they can review their progress. In some college programs, you may be asked to construct a portfolio of your work to track your growing skill.

Writing Problems

Even the best writers sometimes run into problems. Common problems include procrastination, writer's block, plagiarism, and difficulty developing a distinctive voice.

Procrastination Like many writers, you may struggle with getting started on time. Sometimes delay is caused by distraction. Other more pressing projects may be taking the time you should be spending writing. You suddenly find yourself with a deadline pressing down on you. Or you may have a habit of submitting assignments that you dashed off at the last minute. Submitting a rough draft may make your instructor think that you weren't taking the task seriously. To combat writing procrastination, plan a reasonable schedule that breaks the tasks of research and writing into manageable parts. Then stick to it. Reward yourself for completing each phase.

Writer's Block Sometimes you have nothing to say. Don't panic. All writers experience occasions when words do not come easily and inspiration fails. One good response, oddly, is to write about your writer's block. Write about how it feels to be empty and the nature of your blocks. You may gain insight into your resistance and ideas that will get you going.

Another good step is asking for a conference with your instructor. By talking about the assignment, you may find a new twist that unleashes your creativity. Ask whether your instructor has saved any model student papers of similar assignments. Observing how others tackled related problems, you may be able to spark some ideas of your own.

You can also try a creativity-generating computer program that provides a systematic approach to helping you plumb your ideas. *Inspiration* and *IdeaFisher* are popular programs.

Plagiarism *Plagiarism* means presenting someone else's words or ideas as your own. Plagiarism is a serious academic offense. Experienced instructors have read a lot of student papers and can be adept at noticing plagiarism, whether it is intentional or careless. Instructors may have different ideas about what actions constitute plagiarism. Many frown on being given a paper you wrote for a different class in response to an assignment in their course.

How can you avoid plagiarism? "Anti-Theft Protection" gives some ideas.

Finding a Distinctive Voice Most instructors give high marks to writing that is logical and uncluttered. However, there is also room for originality. Consider what it must be like for the instructor to grade one essay after another that strives merely to meet a narrow set of criteria. Like most other people, instructors generally appreciate variety, creativity, and even some humor.

You can be creative in various ways. Consider a different slant for the project. Find out what approaches students typically take. Do something different. Create an engaging title. Use a thesaurus to expand your word choice. Add interesting quotations.

Speaking

Although both speaking and writing give you an opportunity to express yourself, speaking differs from writing in some significant ways. In most writing tasks, you can refine your work until it says exactly what you want. However, in most speaking experiences, even though you can practice to a fine point, the reality of live performance adds a whole new challenge.

Speaking Your Mind

Opportunities to improve your speaking include both impromptu moments and formal occasions to demonstrate what you know and believe.

Informal Opportunities Do not underestimate the value of putting yourself in situations where you must talk informally about your learning. If you participate in tutoring sessions, whether you are receiving or giving help, you will review the material and rehearse your ideas in ways that will help you learn to converse about course concepts.

Classes provide an excellent opportunity to practice the arts of listening and questioning. Although the class size may be intimidating and some instructors discourage questions, you have the right to ask them. Questions can serve many functions. You can clarify murky ideas, get additional examples, or confirm new ideas of your own related to the topic.

Although many instructors reassure you that "there is no such thing as a stupid question," there are *unwelcome* questions. These include questions that detract from the momentum of the class, focus more on self concerns than on the needs of the class, or demonstrate that the questioner has failed to pay attention.

On Target Tips

Anti-Theft Protection

How can you minimize the likelihood that you will be involved in plagiarism?

- *Paraphrase when you do research.* As you take notes from resources, translate the ideas of others into your own words. Compare what you have written to the original source to make sure that your paraphrase captures the spirit of the ideas written, not the actual words and phrases themselves.

- *Give proper credit.* When you directly quote or refer to the ideas of another writer, provide source information in the format required.

- *Make your own observations stand out in your notes.* Put your own ideas in the margin or print them so that they look physically different from the material you got from other authors. Then you can include these observations in your writing without fear of committing plagiarism.

- *Use quotations sparingly.* Rely on the words of expert resources only when their writing is so elegant that your paraphrase will not do it justice. Using many or long quotations is a sign that you are uncomfortable expressing your own ideas.

- *Don't help others plagiarize.* Lending out your papers when you know the borrower plans to submit your work (or something based closely on your work) implicates you in plagiarism problems. If the borrower's submission is questioned, you may find yourself in the unpleasant situation of explaining why you lent your paper for an unethical purpose.

- *Guard against others plagiarizing your work.* If you use a community-based computer, do not store your work on the computer's hard drive. Others who use the computer can easily download your writing and submit it as their own without your knowledge or permission.

Amazing but True College Stories

A Robin's Eye View

Robin was so discouraged by the hard work she had put in on her paper about the Civil War. She liked the topic but found she had trouble writing about it for some reason. As the term paper deadline crept closer, she turned to the Internet for some samples of writing that might inspire her. She found a term paper resource on the net and found a great sample, but as she read the paper, she knew she could never write with the crispness and authority that this author did. Although she knew it was wrong, she retyped the paper and submitted it as her own. She was startled when she got the paper back that it had an "F" and "See me after class!" in large red letters. The instructor explained, "This was a pretty good paper—an A— I think—when it was first written. I ought to know. I wrote it. I don't know how you managed to find this but let's talk about your future in this course."

A #2 pencil and a dream can take you anywhere.

Joyce A. Myers
American businesswoman,
20th century

The best impromptu speeches are the ones written well in advance.

Ruth Gordon
American actor and writer,
20th century

This includes asking questions about topics already sufficiently covered or questions completely unrelated to the topic. If you are unsure of the value of your question, reduce your risk by asking it before or after the class.

Formal Presentations Most of the opportunities you will have to refine your speaking skills are assignments to make a speech. In beginning courses, speeches may last only five to ten minutes. In advanced courses they may be longer. You may be asked to deliver a speech to persuade, inform, or entertain. At the same time, you almost certainly will be expected to demonstrate knowledge of ideas from the course.

Some speeches are extemporaneous. In this situation, you get a few moments to prepare your opinion on a course-related topic. Mercifully, such speeches tend to be short. Because you do not have time to conduct research, your audience will expect to hear your opinions and feelings rather than a documented and tightly reasoned perspective.

In some courses, especially those in business management, education, or human services, you may report on a particular client or practical activity. Case presentations involve reviewing pertinent records and applying course ideas. For example, in an education class you may report the progress of a child you are tutoring or in a business class you may discuss the status of a new business practice implemented at a fast food restaurant.

Another popular type of formal speaking is the panel discussion. A committee of students shares the responsibility for addressing a complex topic. For example, a class in women's studies might explore the growth of feminist literature in different historical periods. Each panel member might represent feminist literature in a particular period. Panel presentations are more successful when the members meet ahead of time to coordinate their ideas and plan transitions between their individual presentations.

Debates are a stimulating alternative to individual speeches. Unless debate techniques are themselves the focus of the course, most classroom debates are not highly formal. The main idea is simply to air different sides of a controversy. You may be able to volunteer for the side that appeals to you most. Whatever side you argue, successful debaters rely more on reason than emotions to create the most persuasive case.

You may have an opportunity to introduce a speaker, whether it is a guest speaker on campus or another student who will present a formal speech. Before you introduce the speaker, find out what details he or she would like you to mention. Learn how to pronounce the speaker's name and learn the title of the speech. Good introductions are brief because most of the audience came to hear the speaker, not the introducer.

Some courses in the arts and humanities provide opportunities to speak through dramatic reading of poetry, book passages, or scenes from plays. Although you don't have to supply the raw material, reading the words of others to an audience can give you practice in many important aspects of public speaking, including pacing, voice quality, verbal fluency, and connecting to the audience.

Being a Good Audience Member You can learn a lot about speaking by being a frequent, vigorous audience member for other good speakers. College campuses often host dynamic speakers who will show you how it's done. In addition, you can get experience in the spotlight by asking questions at the end of the speech. If that option feels overwhelming at first, approach the speaker with your questions or comments when the speech is over. Most speakers want to know their impact on your thinking.

Good Speaking

Formal speeches must first be written. Therefore, much of what we said about preparing good papers also pertains to preparing good speeches. What are some additional strategies that can help you make good speeches?

Following Directions Be sure to follow directions carefully. It can be embarrassing to misunderstand the purpose, be unprepared when your time to speak arrives, or run too short or too long.

To reduce your risk in public speaking assignments, confer with your instructor about your intentions. Submit a topic sentence or an outline or map of the speech beforehand and ask for comments. If you need to reschedule your presentation, give the instructor maximum notice so that alternative activities can be scheduled. If you fail to show up at the designated time, you may forfeit your opportunity.

Selecting a Topic In most cases, you will give the best speeches about material you know well. For example, reminiscences and personal stories often provide a good foundation. However, some personal topics can pose a threat to your composure during the speech because you may unravel as you make an emotional disclosure. For example, if you have a sibling with addiction problems, talking about alcohol and drug issues might be too emotional for you to handle.

Choosing a Title If your speech requires a title, select one that entices the audience to listen. Adapt song or movie titles to create a lively title. You might be able to borrow a phrase from a familiar poem or slogan. For example, "A Mime is a Terrible Thing to Waste" is a more creative title than "An Exploration of the Art of Mime."

Rehearsing Rehearsal time is often the difference between a good speech and a great one. Know your speech well enough that you need your notecards only for cues about what you intend to say. Otherwise, you may be tempted to read what you have written, which disconnects you from the audience. Practice working with the overhead projector, the flip chart, or the computer ahead of time.

Opening the Speech Relate a personal experience or a joke. You can introduce an interesting news item, quotation, or an event that the audience will remember. Regardless of your beginning tactic, your opening should conclude with a statement of your objective and a description of where you intend to go.

Effective speakers know their own intentions and order of ideas well enough that they do not need to rely heavily on their notes or a memorized script. They give the impression of connecting with the audience by talking with them rather than reciting from memory or reading directly from a prepared text.

> *My father gave me these hints on speechmaking: "Be sincere . . . be brief . . . be seated."*
> **James Roosevelt**
> **American philanthropist,**
> **20th century**

> *A poor speaker quits when he is tired. A good speaker quits when the audience is tired.*
> **Anonymous**

THE FAR SIDE By GARY LARSON

Identify your purpose and scope early in your speech. Do this even if your audience is just other students in your class, rather than assuming your audience knows why you are speaking. Keep in mind what your audience knows already and what they need to know.

Effective speakers address the audience on its level. For example, if your college recruits you to talk to high school students about college life, your vocabulary and examples might be different than if you give the same kind of speech to their parents. Good speakers also try to understand the values of their audience so they appeal to them more effectively.

Some speaking opportunities are formal, others more casual. But even speeches in a casual style benefit from the polish that comes from practice. Minimize the number of pauses, "ums" and "ahs," or other interruptions that invite your audience to stop listening. Strive to make eye contact with audience members and pace your speech to draw maximum attention. Stand straight, breathe in a controlled manner, and harness other nervous mannerisms that might distract from your message. Effective speakers also project their voices to reach people at the back of the room. They put life in their voices to keep peoples' attention.

Building the Speech Class speeches should reflect your learning from the course. You can draw ideas from the textbook, class notes, or other readings that relate to the discipline you are studying. However, if you give a speech that shows no evidence that you have learned from the course, your grade will probably suffer.

Nothing can harm good ideas more than bad grammar and sentence structure. You may head off potential harm by first giving your speech to a friend and asking for specific feedback on the grammar and language.

An anonymous speech instructor once recommended the perfect structure for public presentations: "Tell 'em what you are going to tell 'em, tell 'em, then tell 'em what you told 'em." Although this approach might sound boring, it is important to repeat the key ideas of a speech. As in good writing, the main point of the speech serves as the backbone and each portion of the speech must support it. Many speakers like to hand out a printed outline of the speech so the audience can follow it better.

As you construct the body of your talk, pay attention to the kinds of support that appeal most to the audience. You do not have to overwhelm your audience with statistics and stories to make your point. Choose your evidence carefully to create both emotional and logical appeal.

Speakers can use a variety of means to make their ideas believable, including stories, video clips, quotations, statistics, charts, and graphs. Every element should play a meaningful role in the development of the speaker's position. In addition, each point should follow logically from the previous point.

If you have an important point to make, don't try to be subtle or clever. Use a pile driver. Hit the point once. Then come back and hit it again. Then hit it a third time—a tremendous whack!

**Winston Churchill
British prime minister,
20th century**

If you use an overhead projector, make the lettering large and easy to read. (To test the size of your lettering, put the overhead on the floor and stand over it. If you can read it from this position, the font is probably large enough.) Prepare typed overheads (handwritten overheads suggest a lack of pride in your work). If you use audio or videotapes to support your presentation, be sure to wind the tape to the appropriate starting point ahead of time. If you plan to use a computerized presentation, check the lighting conditions ahead of time to be sure it will be visible.

Closing the Speech When you conclude your speech, return to the key themes that began it. Summarize the territory you have covered and identify any actions you expect the audience to take as a result of your speech. If you have given a long speech, reorient the audience to your objectives. Smile and prepare to receive your applause.

Handling Audience Response Most college audiences will be sympathetic. After all, your peers are likely to be in your shoes before the term is over. This usually provides a uniquely supportive environment in which to learn to give a speech. If you assume that your audience is supportive, you may feel less apprehensive about giving the speech.

Many instructors include a question-and-answer period following a student's speech. Such activity encourages you to think on your feet and to learn how to manage unexpected events. See "Surviving the Home Stretch" for how to manage the question-and-answer period.

Evaluate Your Work Good speakers monitor the quality of their speaking throughout rehearsal as well as during and after the actual performance. Complete Self-Assessment 9.2 to examine your speaking strengths and weaknesses.

Overcoming Problems

Three common obstacles to successful speaking are speaking phobia, delivery problems, and embarrassing moments.

Speaking Phobia It should be no surprise that having to speak in public is consistently ranked as one of the greatest fears of adult Americans. Many people deny

On Target Tips

Surviving the Home Stretch

When your classmates ask questions that stump you, some strategies for coping with the strain are as follows:

- **Ask for a restatement of the question.** This can give you some additional cues to help you answer the question or provide extra time to think through your response.

- **Say "I don't know."** Sometimes it is a good strategy to admit that the questioner poses a new and confusing area for you. Then move on. No one expects a speaker to have all the answers.

- **Ask the questioner for an opinion.** Many people who ask questions have their own ideas about what constitutes a satisfying answer. Your willingness to share the stage will be seen as gracious and the gesture gives you more time to respond.

FRANCIE reprinted by permission of United Feature Syndicate, Inc.

Self-Assessment 9-2

What Are My Speaking Strengths and Weaknesses?

You may already have had a speaking assignment in college. Even if you haven't, you probably have developed a sense of where your strengths and weaknesses are in presentations. Review these criteria, based on *Alverno College Writing and Speaking Criteria* (1995), to determine how effective you are as a public speaker:

	ROUTINELY	OFTEN	RARELY
I *connect with the audience* by talking directly to them rather than reading my notes or delivering a memorized script.	___	___	___
I state my *purpose* and keep this focus throughout.	___	___	___
I craft the *style* of the speech and select *words* carefully to suit the purpose.	___	___	___
I effectively *deliver* the speech, using eye contact, supportive gestures, and effective voice control.	___	___	___
I follow appropriate *conventions*, including grammar.	___	___	___
I *organize* the speech well, including an introduction, main body, and conclusion.	___	___	___
I include evidence that *supports* and *develops* my ideas.	___	___	___
I use *media* effectively to help the audience grasp key ideas.	___	___	___
I include *content* that reflects my learning from the course.	___	___	___

What conclusions have you reached about your public speaking skills? What do you need to do to improve these skills?

---

themselves the pleasure of specific courses or even a college education just so they won't have to speak in front of a class. Speaking phobia is an irrational fear that results from a preoccupation with what others are thinking about your performance. Speech phobics worry that the audience will think they are incompetent. They may worry so much that they cannot concentrate on their preparation. What can you do to minimize the negative effects of speech phobia?

Connect Focus on the most supportive faces in the audience. Some old, and not very good, advice suggests gazing just over the heads of the audience members to avoid eye contact. The problem with this suggestion is that you won't feel connected to your audience and may misinterpret their interested silence as hostile. Instead, scan the audience for positive responses. Remember that they want you to succeed. Find the most responsive faces and give your attention to them. This will help you connect with and stay connected to the audience.

> *There is nothing so bad and so dangerous in life as fear.*
>
> **Jawaharlal Nehru**
> **Indian prime minister,**
> **20th century**

Elizabeth hated to speak in public until she found a strategy that diminished her fears. She saw an old movie, *Auntie Mame*, on television and thought the leading character was not only outrageous, but fearless. She decided that when she had to speak, she would pretend to be Auntie Mame.

Many speakers manage their fears by acting like successful speakers. By adopting that role, they pretend their way into successful presentations. Try it. If the speech is not effective, you can blame your bad acting. If it succeeds, you can abandon your role and claim your success.

Trying to reduce your anxiety with tranquilizers or other drugs is not a good idea. Altering your feelings chemically may also reduce your capacity to respond to unexpected events or to answer questions.

Delivery Problems Many students experience distracting physical symptoms when they speak to a group. Choking, tearing up, and other obvious signs of nervousness can undermine your effectiveness. However, there are strategies that you can practice to put yourself more at ease.

Use a tape or video recorder to rehearse. Notice any mannerisms or gestures that may turn off or distract your audience. Practice reducing these problems until you are satisfied you can perform smoothly.

One common result of fear is the need to use the bathroom. Take care of this pressure just before the class, and you are less likely to be distracted by it during your talk. Stretch and breathe deeply to give your body other signals about your intention to control your nervousness. A glass of water can relieve parched lips and also give you an excuse to pause and compose yourself.

If a situation develops in which you no longer feel in control of your speech, you should probably own up to the problem. If you lose your place, admit the problem to the audience and stop to regain control. You can prevent losing your place if you use well-organized, easy-to-read notecards. Number the cards so that you can restore the order if you drop the stack.

If you lose your composure because you feel overwhelmed by emotion, tell the audience that this topic is hard for you. They'll appreciate your candor and support you. However, it is not a good idea to tell your audience that you are nervous. If you announce that your hands are shaking or your knees are knocking, chances are good your audience will attend to your hands or knees and not your ideas.

Embarrassing Moments What is the worst thing that could happen when you speak in public? For some students, it is failing in a public appearance. They feel certain that they will not be able to recover from the humiliation. Recovery may be a little painful but there are things you can do to bounce back.

All great speakers have bad performances. When you accept your own limitations in a given speech, you create a baseline from which you can grow. Recognize your potential to learn from experiences that do not go well. Then commit yourself to better preparation and performance in the future.

You may be able to negotiate a second chance with your instructor. Sometimes your speech can be videotaped in the college media facilities so the instructor can review it at a convenient time. Whether this second chance improves your grade or not, you will benefit from turning in a performance in which you have greater pride.

Surprised

By Fast Relief

If you have rehearsed properly, you know the ideas in your speech better than anyone else in the room, even the instructor. So once your speech gets under way, it doesn't take long—maybe a minute or two—until your nervousness subsides and you can begin talking with the audience. It may seem strange that your worries go away so quickly when you fretted for so long before starting the speech. Keep in mind that it is hard for people to sustain extreme emotional states for long. Once you stop thinking about your nervousness, you can begin to enjoy the fun side of public speaking.

It is no sin to attempt and fail. The only sin is not to make the attempt.

SuEllen Fried
American social activist,
20th century

Summary Tips For Mastering College

Writing and Speaking

Self-Expression, College, and Career

1. Writing and speaking in college will make you a better job candidate after graduation.
2. Some colleges may not provide many opportunities for writing and speaking. Seek as many opportunities as you can to help improve your expressive skills.

Writing

1. Prepare to write in different formats. Some kinds of projects may seem easier than others, but all of them will give you important practice.
2. Follow project directions. Read the directions at least twice and ask questions to clarify directions.
3. Create a reasonable writing plan that allows you time to revise. Very few students can succeed by submitting a first draft.
4. Select topics that help you show what you have learned. Be vigilant about incorporating course concepts and ideas into your work.
5. Maximize your efficiency by working from a map or outline. An on-target thesis statement and a map or outline can help you organize effectively.
6. Conduct research to strengthen your argument. Give credit when you include the words or ideas of others to avoid plagiarism.
7. Write to a specific audience with a specific purpose in mind. By staying focused on your target, you will choose the right level of sophistication and abide by the proper conventions.
8. Use a word processor. Computers help you revise, edit, and polish your work.
9. Overcome the obstacles. Write about your troubles, keep making connections to the problem, and talk with others to learn new strategies.
10. Grow from feedback. Use it to learn how you can improve your skills.

Speaking

1. Seek opportunities to speak in class and in public. Ask questions in class, talk about your learning with others, and make formal presentations to improve your skills.
2. Choose topics you know something about. Avoid topics that are too intellectually or emotionally challenging.
3. Connect with the audience. Use visual aids, comprehensible language, and smooth delivery to keep your audience on your side.
4. Concentrate on the key ideas. Tell your audience what you intend to tell them, tell them, and tell them what you told them.
5. Invest in solid rehearsal time. Few speakers are successful when they wing a presentation. If possible, try to rehearse in the room where you will give the speech. Practice with any technology you will use.
6. Be prepared to answer audience questions. Admit that you don't know the answer if you don't or ask the audience for their opinions.
7. Take steps to counteract fears about speaking. Rehearsal, role-play, and imagining success can help you master your fears. Don't imagine the worst or take substances to conquer fears; these approaches are likely to backfire.

College Success Checklist

Have your views changed about any of the following items since you filled out this checklist at the beginning of the chapter? Place a check mark beside any item for which you feel good about your current practice. Also check any for which you now have new ideas about how to improve.

____ I know the role that writing and speaking skills play in college and careers.

____ I prepare writing projects well in advance and pace myself to submit a polished version on time.

____ I pursue criticism from other people to improve my writing skills.

____ I can overcome the problems that interfere with good writing.

____ I know how to avoid problems with plagiarism.

____ I seek out opportunities to speak in groups.

____ I know what makes a speech effective.

____ I ask people to give me feedback on my speeches so I can improve.

____ I can control my nervousness about speaking.

In the space below, list the items that you still need to work on the most. This list may help you complete the goal-setting exercise in the Learning Portfolio.

Review Questions

1 Why are writing and speaking skills important for life after graduation?

2 What strategies lead to effective writing?

3 What are some common problems that prevent effective writing?

4 What are the common characteristics of good speakers?

5 What can you do to manage speaking anxiety?

Learning Portfolio

Learning by Reflecting... Journal Entries

Nothing to Do but Read

Suppose you were stuck on an island with books as your only form of entertainment. With what type of writing would you most like to be marooned? List some of your favorite authors below and expand on the following in your journal.

- What aspects of this category of writing appeal to you?
- Do you think you could produce writing like this?
- What aspects of this writing style could influence the way you write for projects at college?

_____
_____
_____
_____
_____
_____

The View from the Audience

Recall a time that you observed someone making a bad speech.

- At what point did you recognize the speech would be unsatisfying?
- Did the speaker make any attempts to correct the failing outcome during the speech?
- How did you feel watching the speech flop?
- What advice could you have offered the speaker to turn the speech around?

Exploiting Your Life

Amy Tan explored a turbulent theme in her own personal life—the challenging relationship between mother and daughter—that resonated with her audience. Make a list of important events in your own life that might become a resource for future expressive writing projects.

1. _____
2. _____
3. _____
4. _____
5. _____

Learning by Doing... Action Projects

Lucky Charms

In a group discussion, explore the significance of the rituals people perform before they start writing. Describe the range of these activities and identify any "magic" practices that you may be using to facilitate your writing. Speculate what would have to happen before you could abandon your magic practices. Prepare for the discussion by writing down any rituals of your own.

_____
_____
_____
_____
_____

Evaluating History

Find a videotape of a famous speech. For example, your college may own a video of Martin Luther King's "I Have a Dream" speech or other famous speeches. Watch the speech and evaluate its effectiveness using criteria found in this chapter. What feedback would you give the speaker? Why was the speech so well regarded?

Tips from the Masters

Choose someone you know who seems comfortable speaking in public. This could be a good teacher, a peer, or someone else who deals with the public in professional life. Interview that person to find out the strategies they used to become comfortable with public speaking. Borrow some strategies to improve your own comfort level.

Writing to Learn

Select the discipline-based course that you find most challenging this term. Identify some complex issues that are difficult to understand and practice writing to learn. Draft a position statement, summarize the key ideas, and describe your personal perspective. Then evaluate "Writing to Learn" as a technique for better comprehension. How well does it work for you?

Learning by Thinking Critically... Critiques

Compare and Contrast
Discuss the general advantages and disadvantages of speeches, debates, and panel presentations. Which type suits you best? Why?

The Cost of Plagiarism
Identify reasons why students may plagiarize. Once you have developed a list of reasons, speculate about what the consequences of plagiarism may be, whether the student is caught or not.

Promoting Feedback
Suppose you have received a grade but little feedback about why you received that grade on a writing or speaking project. Evaluate the quality of your performance using the criteria suggested in the appropriate Self-Assessment from this chapter. Then schedule an appointment with your instructor to see whether your critical insights are correct.

In Other Words
Paraphrase the following sayings to practice your analyzing and expressing skills:

"A watched pot never boils."
_____
_____

"Don't cry over spilt milk."
_____
_____

"He who laughs last laughs best."
_____
_____

"Absence makes the heart grow fonder."
_____
_____

"A stitch in time saves nine."
_____
_____

Learning by Thinking Creatively... Personal Vision

Entitlement
Go back over some papers or speeches you have written and revise the titles to make them more creative. Work with others to generate improved titles.

A Vision of Peace
Describe how you think you would look and feel if you were able to deliver a perfect speech. Identify the obstacles you experience in real life that keep you from achieving this vision. What can you do about each obstacle?

Creating a New Role
Elizabeth picked the perfect role model to help her overcome her speaking fears. By pretending to be Auntie Mame, she was able to master her fears until she could own her own success as a speaker. Whom would you select as a good role model for speaking? What characteristics do you particularly admire? How challenging would this role-playing strategy be to adopt if you need help in managing your fears?

_____
_____
_____
_____
_____
_____
_____
_____
_____

Learning by Planning... Goal Setting

Review the results of the Self-Assessments you completed in this chapter. Also review the College Success Checklist. What can you conclude about things you need to do to improve your skills?

What goal should you select from this chapter for making positive changes that will help you master the college experience? (*Hint: Is your goal challenging, reasonable, and specific?*)

_____
_____
_____
_____
_____

What strategies will you use to achieve your goal? (*Hint: Can you organize your strategy into a series of smaller goals?*)

_____
_____
_____
_____
_____
_____
_____
_____
_____
_____

What obstacles may be in your way as you attempt to make these positive changes?

_____
_____
_____
_____
_____

What additional resources might help you succeed in achieving your goal?

_____
_____
_____
_____

By what date do you want to accomplish your goal?

_____

How will you know you have succeeded?

_____
_____
_____
_____

Resources for Mastering the College Experience

Style Manuals

MLA Handbook for Writers of Research Papers (1995), 4th ed. New York: Modern Language Association.
Standards for writing expressive work, including standards for footnotes.

Publication Manual of the American Psychological Association (1994), 4th ed. Washington, DC: American Psychological Association.
Standards for writing scientific reports, including laboratory reports and theoretical reviews.

Writing Guides

Writing with Style: Conversations on the Art of Writing (1975) by John K. Trimble. Englewood Cliffs, NJ: Prentice Hall.
A short, fun-to-read paperback. Guidelines on writing concise, clear prose.

How to Write Term Papers and Reports (1997, 2nd ed.) by L. S. Baugh. Lincolnwood, IL: VGM Career Horizons.
Tips on every stage of writing and presenting. Includes strategies on selecting topics and word processing.

12 Easy Steps to Term Papers (1996) by Nell W. Meriwether. Lincolnwood, IL: NTC Publishing Group.
Includes visual aids that make the steps of writing more understandable.

For Writers Only (1994) by S. Burnham. New York: Ballantine.
A pleasant text on basic problems in effective writing. Advice on writer's block.

The College Writer's Reference (1996) by Toby Fulwiler, A. K. Hayakawa, and C. Kupper. Upper Saddle River, NJ: Prentice Hall.
A brief handbook by distinguished writing scholars. Addresses special challenges of different kinds of writing.

The Transitive Vampire (1984) by Karen E. Gordon. New York: New York Times Books.
A highly enjoyable handbook for beginning writers.

How to Write Themes and Term Papers (1989) by B. L. Ellis. Hauppauge, NY: Barrons.
Shows how academic standards differ across disciplines and influence writing conventions.

Electronic Creativity Resources

IdeaFisher, Fisher Idea Systems, Inc., 2222 Martin St. #10, Irvine, CA 92715; 800-289-4332.
Problem-solving strategy that increases creative connections. Promotes more creative approaches to research topics, title development, or other communication projects.

Inspiration, Inspiration Software, Inc., 7412 SW Beaverton Hillsdale Highway, Suite 102, Portland, OR 97225-2167; 800-877-4292; http://www.inspiration.com.
A computer program that helps you to develop conceptual maps by organizing your ideas in outlines and diagrams.

Internet Sites for Writing Assistance

http://www.erin.utoronto.ca/academic/writing/essay.htm
For developing more effective essays.

http://www-english.tamu.edu/wcenter/handouts.html
For improving writing skills in general.

http://world.std.com/~emagic/mindmap.html
To generate and organize ideas in writing.

http://www.psych-web.com/resource/apacrib.htm
For clarifying questions about APA style.

http://www-dept.usm.edu/~engdept/mla/rules.html
For help in interpreting MLA conventions.

http://www.starlingtech.com/quotes
To find just the right quote.

http://www.nhmccd.cc.tx.us/~ljc/lit/ritetips.html
For help in writing about literature.

http://www.azstarnet.com/~poewar/writer/pg/essay.html
To stimulate your creative instincts.

http://www.indiana.edu/~cheminfo/ca_swa.html
To improve your scientific writing.

http://www.inkspot.com/genres/biz.html
For learning to write effectively about business.

Speaking

Strategies of Argument (1996, 2nd ed.) by S. Hirschberg. Boston: Allyn & Bacon.
Explores how arguments vary across disciplines and how to tailor arguments in specific disciplines.

ASAP: The Fastest Way to Create a Memorable Speech (1992) by William Mooney and Donald J. Noone. Hauppauge, NY: Barrons.
Short guidelines by a management consultant and a soap opera veteran on how to construct speeches quickly, even on the way to the podium.

Public Speaking: A Cultural Perspective (1995) by Clella Jaffe. Belmont, CA: Wadsworth.
A provocative cross-cultural textbook on making speeches in oral, literate, and electronic communities.

I Can See You Naked (1992) by Ron Hoff. Kansas City, MO: Andrews & McMeel.
Disputes the old remedy of envisioning your audience without clothes. Explains why it doesn't work. Gives other ways to combat fear of speaking.

Mastering Public Speaking (1995) by George L. Grice and John F. Skinner. Needham Heights, MA: Allyn & Bacon.
A comprehensive textbook using contemporary speakers and examples.

How to Make Presentations That Teach and Transform (1992) by Robert J. Garmston and Bruce M. Wellman. Alexandria, VA: Association for Supervision and Curriculum Development.
A short text focusing on educational presentations. Especially valuable for education majors.

Successful Presentations for Dummies (1996) by Malcolm Kushner. Foster City, CA: IDG Books International.
A refreshing, humorous approach to all aspects of speaking. Pointers for beginning and experienced speakers.

Internet Site for Speaking Assistance

http://www.writingshop.com
Workshops to improve your writing; gives feedback on your own writing samples.

http://world.std.com/~emagic/mindmap.html
Develops your brainstorming skills for topics and approaches.

http://www.abacon.com/pubspeak/
Five models to help you prepare and deliver your best ideas.

http://www.coun.uvic.ca/learn/pubspk.html
Learning Skills Program offers a public speaking group to develop skills and conquer speaking anxiety.

http://www.lm.com/~chipp/spkrref.htm
The Speaker's Companion Page offers comprehensive resource lists for all aspects of public speaking.

http://www.toastmasters.org/
Home page for the famous Toastmasters International, a volunteer group promoting effective speaking.

http://www.ljlseminars.com/monthtip.htm
An international professional speaker offers tips on effective speaking.

http://www.npadnews.com/selfhyp.htm
Lean how to use self-hypnosis to conquer speaking fears.

http://www.concentric.net/~Sp-saa/
Learn how common speaking fears are by visiting the Social Phobia home page.

CHAPTER 10

Communicating and Developing Positive Relationships

✓ College Success Checklist

Place a check mark beside the items that apply to you. Leave the items blank that do not apply to you.

____ I am an active listener when I communicate with others.

____ I know what the barriers to communication are and how to overcome them.

____ I understand the nature of nonverbal communication.

____ I can describe how females and males communicate differently.

____ I appropriately use self-disclosure in close relationships.

____ I express myself assertively.

____ I know how to negotiate effectively.

____ I have a good relationship with my parents.

____ *For students with roommates:* I know what it takes to get along with roommates.

____ *For students with partners/families:* I do a good job of balancing my academic life and my life with my partner or family.

____ I know what strategies to use to make new friends.

____ If I experience heartbreak, I know some good strategies for coping with it.

____ I know some safety guidelines for avoiding settings in which rape occurs.

Preview

In this chapter, we will explore some of the most important aspects of the college experience. Communicating effectively with others can make a big difference in whether first-year college students are happy and enjoy college. We will examine the best strategies for resolving conflicts. And we will describe ways to communicate more effectively in relationships with parents, roommates, friends, and dates or partners.

Chapter Outline

Images of College Success:
Oprah Winfrey

Communicating Effectively
Developing Good Listening Skills
Barriers to Effective Verbal Communication
"You" Messages and "I" Messages
Communicating Nonverbally
Gendered Communication

Resolving Conflict with Others
Being Assertive
Negotiating Effectively

Relationships
With Parents
With Partners
With Children
With Roommates
Loneliness and Friends
Dating

Self-Assessments
10.1 Do You Blow Up, Get Down and Dirty, Cave In, or Speak Up?

On-Target Tips
Developing Active Listening Skills
How to Become More Assertive
Getting Along with a Roommate
Coping with Heartbreak

Images of College Success
Oprah Winfrey

Oprah Winfrey hosts one of the most watched TV shows in America. She also received an Oscar for her role in *The Color Purple*, in which she played a proud, assertive woman. Oprah was born on a Mississippi farm. She spent her early years there and was reared by her grandmother. When Oprah was six, she was sent to live with her mother in a Milwaukee ghetto. Beginning at the age of nine, she was sexually abused by a series of men she trusted. She began committing delinquent acts as a young adolescent. Then her father had Oprah come live with him in Nashville.

Oprah Winfrey is a master communicator with outstanding speaking and listening skills. Despite earning millions, she is strongly motivated to seek new avenues for her energy and talent. Oprah also gives considerable time to helping young girls improve their lives.

At that point, her life improved dramatically. As a high school senior, while raising money for charity, Oprah visited a local radio station and talked her way into a part-time job broadcasting the news. On a scholarship at Tennessee State University, she started a major in speech and drama. At age 19 she switched from radio to local television, broadcasting the evening news. Still, she continued college until a Baltimore TV station lured her away in her senior year. A few years later, she moved to Chicago and a local talk show that eventually became The Oprah Winfrey Show.

The millions of dollars Oprah has earned have not lessened her motivation to achieve. She continues to seek new ways to use her tremendous energy and talent productively. As Oprah says, "I have been blessed, but I create the blessings."

Success has not spoiled her. Oprah spends many nights lecturing, often for free, at churches, shelters, and youth organizations. She established the Little Sisters program in a poverty-stricken area of Chicago. She continues to spend some of her Saturdays working with young girls to improve their lives.

Oprah was a multi-millionaire when she finally finished college. In 1987, invited to speak at TSU's commencement, she insisted on finishing the last bit of coursework for her degree. Then, because her father had always urged her to finish college, she endowed ten scholarships in his name.

Communicating Effectively

Oprah Winfrey's communication skills are admirable. She listens attentively, shows interest, and asks appropriate questions. She also knows how to get people to open up, talk, and feel good about themselves. It is hard to do much in this life without communicating. We communicate in every social context. We communicate in the warmth of an intimate exchange, the heat of an intense conflict, even the chill of a faded relationship. Let's explore some of the characteristics of good communication.

What you are speaks so loudly I cannot hear what you say.

Ralph Waldo Emerson
American poet, essayist, 19th century

Developing Good Listening Skills

You can hear what another person is saying without really listening. As one college student put it, "My friends *listen*, but my parents only *hear* me talk."

Listening is a critical skill for making and keeping relationships. If you are a good listener, others will be drawn to you. Bad listeners hog conversations. They talk *to* rather than *with* someone. Good listeners *actively* listen. They don't just passively absorb information. "Developing Active Listening Skills" provides some good tips.

Barriers to Effective Verbal Communication

Mike says, "I blew it again. When I went home last weekend, I vowed I wouldn't let my older brother get to me. We were only with each other for about 10 minutes when he started in on me. I couldn't take his criticism any more. I started yelling at him and calling him names."

All too often, as in Mike's situation with his brother, we want to communicate better with others. However, we easily can fall prey to communication barriers.

Barriers to communicating effectively include (Gordon, 1970)

- **Criticizing** (making negative evaluations), as in "It's your fault. You should have studied."
- **Name-calling and labeling** (putting down the other person), as in "What a dope you are for not planning better."
- **Advising** (talking down to the other person while giving a solution to a problem), as in "That's so easy to solve. Why don't you just . . . ?"
- **Ordering** (commanding the other person to do what you want), as in "Get off the phone, right now!"

PEANUTS reprinted by permission of United Feature Syndicate, Inc.

On Target Tips

Developing Active Listening Skills

- **Pay careful attention to the person who is talking.** This shows the person you are interested in what he or she has to say. Maintain good eye contact and lean forward slightly when another person is saying something to you, at least in the American culture.

- **Paraphrase.** This means to state in your own words what someone just said. You can start your paraphrase with words like, "Let me see, what I hear you saying is . . ." or "Do you mean . . . ?" Paraphrase when someone says something that is important.

- **Synthesize themes and patterns.** The conversation landscape can become strewn with bits and pieces of information that are not tied together in meaningful ways. A good active listener puts together a summary of the main themes and feelings the speaker has expressed over a reasonably long conversation. The following sentence stems can help get you started in synthesizing the themes of a conversation:
  - "One theme you seem to be coming back to is . . ."
  - "Let's go over the ground we have been covering so far . . ."

- **Give feedback in a competent manner.** Verbal or nonverbal feedback gives the speaker an idea of how much progress he or she is making in getting a point across. Good listeners give feedback quickly, honestly, clearly, and informatively.

The reason we have two ears and only one mouth is so we can listen more and talk less.

Zeno of Citum
Greek philosopher,
3rd century B.C.

- **Threatening** (trying to control the other person), as in "If you don't listen to me, I'm going to make your life miserable."
- **Moralizing** (preaching to the other person what he or she should do), as in "You know you shouldn't have gone there tonight. You ought to be sorry."
- **Diverting** (pushing the other person's problems aside), as in "You think you have it bad. Let me tell you about my midterms."
- **Logical arguing** (trying to convince the other person with logical facts without considering the person's underlying feelings), as in "Look at the reasons why you failed. Here they are. . . . So, you have to admit I'm right." It's okay to use logic to try to persuade someone, but if you lose sight of the person's feelings, no matter how right you are, the other person won't be persuaded.

"You" Messages and "I" Messages

One type of communication deserves special mention. How often have you been involved in a conversation when someone says,

"Why are *you* being so critical?"

"*You* did not keep your promise."

"*You* are really crude."

These are examples of "you" messages, although, despite its label, "you" communication does not always include the word "you." "You" is implied when someone says,

"That was a really dumb thing to say" (which means "What *you* said was dumb")

"Stay out of my business" (which means "*You* are being too nosy")

It is easy to fall into the communication trap of using too many "you" messages and not enough "I" messages. "You" messages communicate that the speaker is qualified to judge the listener. Such language can make the listener defensive. In contrast, "I" messages are less provocative. They reflect your own true feelings better than judgmental "you" statements.

Communication experts recommend replacing "you" messages with "I" messages:

"*I'm* angry that *I* get criticized so much around here."

"*I* don't like it when promises get broken."

"*I'm* embarrassed by those remarks."

"I" messages like these help to move conversation in a more constructive direction. "You" messages bog down conversation with judgments of the other person, whereas "I" statements express your feelings without judging the other person.

Communicating Nonverbally

Does the way you fold your arms, cast your eyes, move your mouth, cross your legs, and touch someone communicate messages to other people? Communication experts believe it does. We might

- Lift an eyebrow for disbelief
- Clasp our arms to isolate or protect ourselves
- Shrug our shoulders for indifference
- Wink one eye for intimacy
- Tap our fingers for impatience
- Slap our forehead for forgetfulness

Many communication experts believe that most interpersonal communication is nonverbal. Even if you are sitting in a corner silently and reading a book, your nonverbal behavior communicates something; perhaps it communicates that you want to be left alone. It might also communicate that you are intellectually oriented. Consider another situation. A student staring out the window communicates something just as strongly as if the student shouted, "I'm bored!" Given the expressiveness of nonverbal behavior, it may be impossible not to communicate. You will have a hard time trying to mask or control your nonverbal messages. True feelings usually express themselves, no matter how hard we try to conceal them. So a good strategy is to recognize that your nonverbal behavior communicates how you truly feel.

Bodies never lie.

Agnes De Mille
American dancer and writer,
20th century

Facial Expressions and Eye Communication Our faces not only disclose specific emotions, they also telegraph what really matters to us. A smile, a frown, a puzzled look all communicate. In the United States, when we like someone, we increase eye contact. When we dislike them, we avoid eye contact. If you want people to know you like them, smile and maintain eye contact with them.

Touch Touch can communicate sexuality, consolation, and support. Touch is a primary form of sexual interaction, from holding hands to sexual intercourse. Touch also is used to console, as when we put our arms around someone, hold their hands, or hug them. We often don't realize how important touch is when are communicating with someone. Use touch appropriately and courteously as part of your communication. Be aware that in some ethnic traditions touching is used more often than in others as part of positive interpersonal communication. Also remember that you have the right not to be touched if you do not want to be.

Space Each of us has a personal space that at times we don't want invaded by others. We usually don't want a stranger to get too close to us or roommates to put their belongings in our space. You are entitled to some personal space and should courteously respect others'. Personal space also differs across cultures. For example, in many Middle Eastern and Latino cultures people prefer to stand close when talking.

Silence In our fast-paced culture we often act as if there is something wrong with anyone who remains silent for more than a second or two after something is said to them. However, by being silent a good listener can

- Observe the speaker's eyes, facial expressions, posture, and gestures for communication
- Think about what the other person is communicating

- Wonder what the other person is feeling
- Consider what the most appropriate response is

Of course, silence can be overdone and is sometimes inappropriate. It is rarely wise to listen for an excessive length of time without making some verbal response. Interpersonal communication should be a dialogue, not a monologue.

Gendered Communication

Do women and men learn to talk in different ways? Communication expert Deborah Tannen (1990, 1998) thinks so.

Rapport Talk and Report Talk Tannen distinguishes between *rapport talk* and *report talk*.

- **Rapport talk** is the language of conversation. Rapport talk establishes connections and negotiates relationships. Tannen says that females like to engage in rapport talk more than males do.
- **Report talk** is the language of public speaking and talk designed to give information. Tannen says that males enjoy report talk more than females do.

Is either sex right or wrong? Gender expert Carol Tavris (1992) says neither sex has all the answers. Couples can regard each other as a source of charming anecdotes and a repository of a different kind of expertise. They can exchange help, knowledge, talents, stories, and experiences. Partners do not need to be the same. They should show respect for differences when they are present.

Self-Disclosure One of Oprah Winfrey's strongest communication skills is her easy style of self-disclosure. It helps people to feel connected and open up themselves.

Some people are especially reluctant to engage in *self-disclosure*, which means communicating intimate details about themselves to someone else.

How might the communication and relationship orientation of these college students differ in these contexts: male/female and female/female?

CATHY © 1993 Cathy Guisewite. Reprinted with permission of UNIVERSAL PRESS SYNDICATE. All Rights Reserved.

Self-disclosure has a special power in close relationships. Early on, we usually don't engage in self-disclosure as much as when a relationship has endured the test of time and trust develops. It is *risky* when we tell someone about

- A private thought
- An embarrassing impulse
- A romantic feeling
- An unvarnished truth we previously concealed

In some instances, mental health problems develop because of poor self-disclosure skills (Park & Stiles, 1998). People may be too unwilling or too fearful, or simply do not have the ability to disclose psychologically painful information to friends or family. Self-disclosing such information requires that we trust the listener. When we don't discuss our problems with someone, tension can build up and overwhelm us. On the other hand, some people self-disclose too much. They give monologues rather than participating in dialogues.

Appropriate self-disclosure is difficult for many people, especially males. If you want to disclose more about yourself to someone, how do you start? Don't rush to unveil all of your darkest life moments, especially to someone you do not know very well. Self-disclosure usually proceeds gradually, with one person revealing a minimally private thought to a friend or partner. Then the friend or partner reciprocates with a minor revelation of their own. Eventually, you both may reach a point in the relationship at which you feel safe to reveal more painful or embarrassing truths.

Each of us has different levels of intimacy needs. Some people feel a lot more comfortable opening up and divulging private information than others do. Each person needs to evaluate his or her own comfort level.

Resolving Conflict with Others

Conflicts are inevitable in our everyday interactions with people, especially in an intense college environment. Developing skills to resolve these conflicts can

Some things are better left unsaid. But so many unsaid things can be a burden.

Virginia Axline
American psychotherapist and author, 20th century

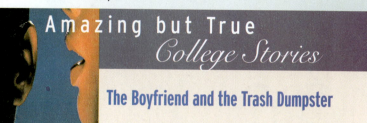

Amazing but True College Stories

The Boyfriend and the Trash Dumpster

First-year student Jeanette decided to visit her boyfriend at his apartment without notice. She entered without knocking and found him in bed with another woman. She lost it and pulled a recreation of Angela Bassett in the movie *Waiting to Exhale*. She grabbed every piece of clothing she had bought for him, the TV she bought him, and a number of other items. Jeanette took them and threw them in the trash dumpster, minus the TV, which she kept for herself. She returned to his apartment and began embarrassing him in front of his roommates. What do you think? Did her boyfriend get what he deserved? Was Jeanette too aggressive or was she just being assertive?

make your life calmer and more enjoyable. Strategies for reducing interpersonal conflict include being assertive and negotiating effectively.

Being Assertive

Assertive expression has become a communication ideal. The Bill of Assertive Rights is presented in Figure 10.1. However, not everyone acts assertively.

Styles of Dealing with Conflict We can deal with conflict in our lives in four main ways: aggressively, manipulatively, passively, and assertively. That is, when faced with conflict you can blow up, get down and dirty, cave in, or speak up.

- **Acting aggressively.** People who respond aggressively to conflict run roughshod over others. They communicate in demanding, abrasive, and hostile ways. Aggressive people often are insensitive to the rights and feelings of others.

- **Acting manipulatively.** Manipulative people try to get what they want by making other people feel sorry for them or feel guilty. They don't take responsibility for meeting their own needs. Instead, manipulative people play the role of the victim or martyr to get others to do things for them. They work indirectly to get their needs met.

Figure 10.1

Bill of Assertive Rights

1. You have the right to be the judge of your own behavior, thoughts, and emotions, and to take responsibilty for their initiation and consequences.

2. You have the right NOT to offer reasons or excuses to justify your own behavior, and the right to judge whether stating a reason is necessary in a given situation.

3. You have the right to judge whether or not to be reponsible for finding solutions to other people's problems.

4. You have the right to change your mind.

5. You have the right to be wrong.

6. You have the right to make mistakes, and to be responsible for your mistakes.

7. You have the right to say, "I don't know."

8. You have the right to be independent of the good will of others before choosing how to behave with them.

9. You have the right to say, "I don't care."

10. You have the right to say, "No."

- **Acting passively.** Passive people act in nonassertive, submissive ways. They let others run roughshod over them. Passive people don't express their feelings. They don't let others know what they want or need.

- **Acting assertively.** Assertiveness is an attitude and a way of acting. Be assertive in any situation in which you need to express your feelings, need to ask for what you want, or want to say "no" to something you don't want.

  When you act assertively, you act in your own best interests. You stand up for your legitimate rights. You express your views openly and directly. In the view of assertiveness experts Robert Alberti and Michael Emmons (1995), assertiveness builds equal relationships.

Of the four styles of dealing with conflict, acting assertively is clearly the most appropriate. To determine your dominant style, take Self-Assessment 10.1.

The strategies advocated by behavioral expert Edmund Bourne (1995) are described in "How to Become More Assertive."

Feeling Good

By Being Assertive

It doesn't feel good to be passive and let others run roughshod over you. Maybe you have a roommate who borrows your clothes all the time. You might have an older brother or sister who tries to manipulate you. Possibly you have a romantic partner who is more aggressive than you like. Or maybe you have a classmate who talks down to you. Do you stand up for your rights in these situations? When you first start being assertive toward such people, you may feel a little funny doing it. Before long, with some success you will feel good about standing up for your rights.

Negotiating Effectively

Everybody negotiates. You negotiate when you apply for a job, dispute a grade with a teacher, buy a car, ask your landlord to paint your apartment, or try to get your roommate or partner to do something.

Anytime you want something from someone who has conflicting interests, you are in a negotiating situation.

Some negotiation strategies are better than others. Negotiating effectively helps you to get what you want from others without alienating them. Negotiation experts often describe three main ways of solving problems with others: win–lose, lose–lose, and win–win.

- **Win-lose strategy.** In this type of negotiating, one party gets what he or she wants and the other comes up short. This either–or strategy often goes like this: "Either I get my way or you get your way." For example, a couple has limited money. They totally disagree on how to spend it. Most of the time a win–lose strategy is not wise. Why? Because the loser may harbor long-term ill feelings.

- **Lose-lose strategy.** Neither side is satisfied with the outcome in this strategy. This usually unfolds when both parties initially try a win–lose strategy that does not work. As a result of the struggle, both end up losers.

- **Win-win strategy.** The goal in this strategy is to find a solution that satisfies both parties. They avoid trying to win at each other's expense. They believe that by working together it is possible to find a solution that leaves everyone satisfied with the outcome.

Some compromises approach this win–win ideal. You and the seller settle on a price for a used car. The price is between what the seller was asking and you were willing to pay. Neither of you got exactly what you wanted, but the

Be fair with others, but then keep after them until they are fair with you.

Alan Alda
American actor, 20th century

Self-Assessment 10-1

Do You Blow Up, Get Down and Dirty, Cave In, or Speak Up?

Think about each of the following situations. How have you typically handled it or a similar circumstance? Is your approach aggressive, manipulative, passive, or assertive? Check which style you use in each situation.

	ASSERTIVE	AGGRESSIVE	MANIPULATIVE	PASSIVE
You are being kept on the phone by a salesperson trying to sell you something you don't want.	___	___	___	___
You want to break off a relationship that is no longer working for you.	___	___	___	___
You are sitting in a movie and the people behind you are talking.	___	___	___	___
Your doctor keeps you waiting more than 20 minutes.	___	___	___	___
You are standing in line and someone moves in front of you.	___	___	___	___
Your friend has owed you money for a long time and it is money you could use.	___	___	___	___
You receive food at a restaurant that is over- or undercooked.	___	___	___	___
You want to ask a major favor of your friend, romantic partner, or roommate.	___	___	___	___
Your friends ask you to do something that you don't feel like doing.	___	___	___	___
You are in a large lecture. The instructor is speaking too softly and you know other students are having trouble hearing what is being said.	___	___	___	___
You want to start a conversation at a gathering, but you don't know anyone there.	___	___	___	___
You are sitting next to someone who is smoking, and the smoke bothers you.	___	___	___	___
You are talking to someone about something that is important to you, but they don't seem to be listening.	___	___	___	___
You are speaking and someone interrupts you.	___	___	___	___
You receive an unjust criticism from someone.	___	___	___	___

Total up the number of your aggressive, manipulative, passive, and assertive marks. Whichever style has the most marks is your dominant personal style of interacting with others in conflict situations. If you did not mark the assertive category 10 or more times, you would benefit from working on your assertiveness.

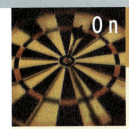

On Target Tips

How to Become More Assertive

- *Evaluate your rights.* Determine your rights in the situation at hand. Hang onto The Bill of Assertive Rights (Figure 10.1) and refer to it when conflicts with others appear.

- *Designate a time for discussing what you want.* Find a mutually convenient time to discuss the problem with the other person involved. Omit this step when you need to be assertive on the spot.

- *State the problem to the person involved in terms of its consequences for you.* Clearly outline your point of view, even if it seems obvious to you. This allows the other person to get a better sense of your position. Describe the problem as objectively as you can without blaming or judging. For example, you might tell someone you live with, "I'm having a problem with your music playing so loud. I need to study for a test tomorrow and the stereo is so loud I can't concentrate."

- *Express your feelings about the particular situation.* When you express your feelings, even others who completely disagree with you can tell how strongly you feel about the circumstance. Remember to use "I" messages rather than "you" messages (see page 262).

- *Make your request.* This is an important aspect of being assertive. Simply ask for what you want (or don't want) in a direct, straightforward manner. Following are some guidelines for making assertive requests:

- *Use assertive nonverbal behavior.* Establish eye contact, square your shoulders. Remain calm and self-confident.

- *Keep your request simple.* One or two easy-to-understand sentences is adequate. For example, "We need to go see a counselor to get our problems straightened out."

- *Avoid asking for more than one thing at a time.*

- *Don't apologize for your request.* Request directly, as in "I want you to...." Don't say, "I know this is an imposition on you, but...." What if the other person responds with criticism, tries to make you feel guilty, or makes sarcastic remarks? Simply repeat your assertive request directly, strongly, and confidently.

- *State the consequences of gaining (or not gaining) the other person's cooperation.* With close friends or intimate partners, stating the positive consequences of their compliance can be an honest offer of mutual give-and-take rather than manipulation (for example, "If you give me time to finish this project, then we will have more time to do something special together").

outcome left each of you happy. Similarly, you and your companion each want to see a different movie. In order to spend the evening together, you might choose another movie that you both agree on.

The best solutions of all, though, are not compromises. Rather, they are solutions in which all parties get what they want. For example, Andrea and Carmen are roommates with different study habits. Andrea likes to study in the evening. This leaves most of her day free for other activities. Carmen thinks that evenings should be for relaxation and fun. They arrived at the following solution: Monday through Wednesday, Andrea studies at her boyfriend's. Carmen does anything she wants. Thursday and Sunday Carmen agrees to keep things quiet where she and Andrea live. On Friday and Saturday they both have fun together.

What the win–win strategy gives you is a creative way of finding the best solution for a problem among two or more parties. You can use it to resolve conflicts with others and make everyone involved feel better.

Surprised

You're Not a Kid Anymore

Jason says that the most surprising thing about college life is the sudden sense of freedom. You can go to sleep when you want. You can miss a class. You can just do as you please without your parents hounding you. There are no more, "Did you do your homework?" "Go to bed, you have a class in the morning," or any of a number of other things Jason's parents used to bug him about. What also surprises Jason is that when he goes home for the holidays, his parents still treat him as an adolescent.

Relationships

Relationships play a powerful role in college life. As you think about your relationships with the people in your life, such as family members, partners, roommates, friends, and dates, keep in mind that the communication, assertiveness, and negotiation strategies we just discussed will serve you well.

With Parents

For college students who still depend on their parents financially and in other ways, relationships can vary considerably. Some parents treat their first-year students as if they still are completely under their wing. Some college students remain too dependent on the security of their parents. They don't tackle enough new challenges on their own. Some parents have little contact and provide little support for first-year students. Some students break off communication with their parents.

No matter how much independence you want, it is a good idea not to break off communication with your parents. There will be a time when you need them, possibly for money, a place to live, or emotional support.

Maintaining communication with folks back home doesn't mean you have to write them a letter three times a week or call every night. You don't have to tell them everything you do. However, if they don't hear from you for a couple of weeks, they may fear that something really bad has happened to you. They regularly want to know how you are getting along and that you haven't fallen off the planet.

What is regular contact? If you're away from home, a phone conversation once a week should be adequate. One first-year student didn't want his roommates to kid him about calling home regularly, so he wrote a coded reminder on his calendar once a week. The reminder? "E.T.," which he associated with the movie and which signaled him to phone home. Also, if you and your parents use e-mail, you might want to communicate periodically in this manner. It's cheap, convenient, and easy.

If you are a traditional-aged first-year student, your parents probably are concerned about your increased independence. They may ask questions that seem intrusive. How much are you studying? How come you didn't get an "A" on your English test? What is your roommate like? Are you dating anyone? Have you been going to religious services? Try to listen politely to their questions. Realize that they have your best interests at heart. You don't have to tell them all of the details of your life. They usually will accept your answers if you tell them a few general things and contact them weekly.

With Partners

Students who are married or have a partner face special challenges. Following are some strategies for keeping relationships with a partner on the positive side while you are going to college (Sternberg, 1988):

- **Don't take your relationship for granted.** The seeds of a relationship's destruction are planted if you or your partner take each other for granted. Continue to nourish the relationship, giving it high priority along with your studies. You don't want to get a degree and lose your partner. Schedule time with your partner just as you schedule time for classes and study. Don't expect your partner to take over all of the household duties or pamper you.

- **Develop a positive identity.** Don't seek in your partner what you lack in yourself. Feel good about your pursuit of education. It will enhance your identity. When both partners have positive identities, their relationship benefits.

- **Share your college life with your partner.** Don't isolate your partner from what you are doing in college. Discuss your schedule, what you are learning, and what your day is like. Look for campus activities or events—such as lectures, sporting events, and plays—that you can attend with your partner. Stay balanced in your focus. Remember to ask about your partner's activities to avoid being too self-focused.

- **Be open with your partner.** It is sometimes easy to lie or hold back the truth when we communicate with a partner. The problem is that once omissions, distortions, and flat-out lies start, they tend to spread and ultimately can destroy a relationship. Eventually, the relationship becomes like a shell. When the partners talk, they say empty things because the relationship has lost its depth and trust.

- **See things from your partner's point of view.** It is easy to want to give less than we get. Ask yourself how your partner perceives you. This helps you to develop the empathy and understanding that are important in a satisfying, successful relationship.

With Children

If you are a student and a parent, you also face some special challenges. Following are some helpful strategies for parents who are going to college:

- **Be an authoritative parent.** University of California psychologist Diana Baumrind (1991) wanted to know whether one type of parenting style is linked with having a child who is well-adjusted and competent. She found that the best parenting style is *authoritative*, which involves being nurturing, engaging in verbal give-and-take with the child, and exercising some control, but not punitively. That is, the authoritative parent doesn't let children run wild and gives them feedback to help them develop self-control. By contrast, being permissive and uninvolved, or punitive and cold, are ineffective parenting styles. Children reared by these types of parents often have trouble controlling their behavior.

- **Use good communication skills.** If your children are old enough, talk with them about how important they are to you. Also discuss with them how important your education is to you. Be a good listener and each day set aside time for your child's interests.

- **Be a good time manager.** At times, you may feel overwhelmed with having to juggle a family and school. Planning can be an important asset in your effort to balance your academic and family time. Check into child care and community agencies that may provide services and activities for your children before and after school.

On Target Tips

Getting Along with a Roommate

Following are some suggestions for getting along better with a roommate:

- *Cut off problems early.* Problems crop up for most roommates. Whenever two people live together, problems appear. Don't let the problems fester. Detect them early and then resolve them.

- *Use good communication skills.* Earlier in the chapter you read about some good communication skills. These included being an active listener and avoiding barriers to communication. If you are having a roommate problem, review the strategies. Use them in communicating with your roommate.

- *Be responsible.* You may have gotten into the habit of not keeping your room clean before you came to college. Old habits are hard to break. Do your share of keeping the room clean. Make your bed. Pick up your clothes.

- *Show respect.* You can learn a lot about the importance of reciprocity in relationships by living with a roommate. To get along, you have to show respect for each other. It is not a good idea to come in at 2 A.M., flip the lights on, and wake up your roommate. It also is not a good idea to rev up the stereo when your roommate is trying to study.

- *Be assertive.* If you think that you are doing more than your fair share of the giving in your roommate relationship, start being more assertive. Stand up for your rights. Use the strategies for being assertive we outlined earlier in the chapter.

- **Don't forget to reserve some time for yourself.** It's not going to be easy, but be sure to block out at least some time each week for activities you enjoy or for relaxation. You might have a hobby, like to exercise, or enjoy going to movies. Build time for such activities into your weekly schedule.

With Roommates

Relationships with roommates can vary. You might become best friends. You might grow to hate each other. You might be indifferent and simply live in the same place.

In many cases, a first-year student's roommate is a total stranger. You are going to live in close quarters for nine months with someone you know little or nothing about. That's enough to cause some apprehension for anyone.

What are some good strategies for getting along with this total stranger who is now your roommate? "Getting Along with a Roommate" provides some helpful tips.

What if, after trying hard to reconcile problems, you still hate your roommate? You have differences that can't be resolved. Your roommate situation is lowering your grades. What recourse do you have?

If you live in a college dorm, you probably have an RA (resident advisor) with whom you can discuss your roommate problems. Take the initiative. Go to the RA and ask for advice about what to do. Try out the advice and give it a chance to work. Then, if things are still intolerable, go to the campus housing office. Be courteous but clearly state your roommate problems. Campus housing offices usually don't like to change roommates. However, if your problem is severe enough, they might accommodate you.

Loneliness and Friends

Loneliness can be a dark cloud over a person's everyday life. Be sure not to confuse loneliness with being alone. Time spent alone can be meaningful and satisfying. However, when we feel isolated and long to be with others, we need to do something to become more connected.

When traditional-aged college students leave the familiar world of their home town and family to go to college, loneliness is common (Perlman & Peplau, 1998). Many first-year college students feel anxious about meeting new people and developing new social lives. One student comments,

> My first year here at the university has been pretty lonely. I wasn't lonely at all in high school. I lived in a fairly small town. I knew everyone and they knew me. I was a member of several clubs and played on the basketball team. It's not that way here. It is a big place. I've felt like a stranger so many times. It has taken a while but I'm finally adapting better. In the past few months I've been making a special effort to meet people and get to know them. It has not been easy.

As the passage indicates, first-year students rarely carry their high school popularity and social standing into college. Especially when students attend college away from home, they face the challenge of forming new social relationships. In one study, two weeks after the college year began, 75% of the first-year students felt lonely at least part of the time since arriving on campus (Cutrona, 1982). Loneliness is not reserved for traditional-aged first-year students, though. Older first-year students can be lonely as well. The demands of school, work, and family may leave little time to feel replenished through contacts with friends.

How can you determine whether you are lonely? If you feel like you are not in tune with the people around you and you can't find companionship when you want it, you probably are lonely. If you have recently left an important relationship, you are likely to feel lonely until you rebuild your social network.

If you feel lonely, how can you become better connected with others? Following are some recommendations:

- Become involved in activities with others through college, work, community announcements, or religious organizations. Join and volunteer time with an organization you believe in. You probably will meet others who share your views. One social gathering can lead to new social contacts. This is especially true if you take the initiative to introduce yourself to others and start a conversation. Tell yourself that meeting new people and developing new social ties always entails risks. Also tell yourself that the benefits outweigh the risks. Consider joining a new group at dinner, sitting with new people in class, or finding a study or exercise partner.
- Recognize the warning signs of loneliness early on. Take action to head off deeper stages of loneliness. People often become bored or alienated before loneliness sinks in. Heading off loneliness by planning new activities is easier than struggling to get out of it.
- Draw a diagram of your social network and list how the people in the network meet or do not meet your social needs. Are there discrepancies? Take time to think about the people you see now and the people you would like to meet.
- Practice certain qualities when interacting with friends or potential friends. Be kind and considerate. Be honest and trustworthy. Share and be cooperative. Use active listening skills. Have a positive attitude. Be supportive. Comment on something special about the other person.
- If you cannot shed your loneliness and make friends on your own, contact the student counseling center at your college. A counselor will talk with you about ways to connect with others on your campus and reduce your loneliness. Also, see the Resources section

Staying Out of the Pits

The Arrival of Twins

Dating and love relationships can get first-year students into a lot of trouble. Tom has gotten himself into a big mess. Last month he found out that his ex-girlfriend is going to have twins—his twins. When he told his family about the twins, they disowned him, quit sending him money, and cut off communication with him. Tom has decided to help support the twins, although he is not going to marry their mother. He has enough money to finish the semester but he plans to drop out of college next semester to help pay for the care of the twins. To avoid problems like Tom's, what would you have done?

Where you used to be, there is a hole in the world, which I find myself constantly walking around in the daytime, and falling into at night.

**Edna St. Vincent Millay
American poet, 20th century**

On Target Tips

Coping with Heartbreak

Heartbreak can be a stressful experience. If someone breaks off a relationship with you,

- *Don't isolate yourself.* Talk with a friend or a counselor about the breakup. Be open and honest about the relationship and your feelings.

- *Recognize that your self-esteem depends on more than the soured relationship.* When someone breaks up with you, your self-esteem often suffers. When this happens, examine different aspects of yourself. Think about your positive features and strengths.

- *Stop self-defeating thoughts.* When someone breaks off a relationship with you, it is easy to think self-defeating thoughts like "I'm worthless," "I can't go on with school," "I deserved what I got," and so on. Replace the self-defeating thoughts with positive self-statements like "I'm a worthy person" or "This is a challenge but I'm going to cope with it and go on."

- *Don't jump into another romantic relationship right away.* Give yourself time to cope with the emotional trauma of the lost love. However, do motivate yourself and take suggestions from well-meaning friends to get out and meet new people.

at the end of this chapter to find readings that focus on ways to reduce loneliness.

Dating

Dating can involve wonderful, happy times. It also can be a source of unhappiness, anxiety, and turmoil, including sexual assault.

The Dating Scene Some first-year students date a lot, others very little or not at all. Some students view dating as a way to find a spouse. Others see it as an important part of fitting into the social scene. Some students date for romantic reasons, others for friendship or companionship.

Dating can detract from or enhance your college success. It's clearly not a good idea to get so head-over-heels in passionate love that all you can think about is your romantic partner. If that happens to you, you probably will not spend enough time studying. On the other hand, some people who date someone regularly or live with a partner feel more settled down and freer to work.

It is not unusual for traditional-aged first-year students to have high school boyfriend or girlfriend back home. Also, many commuter students have a romantic partner who does not go to college or goes to college somewhere else. You do not necessarily have to give up this romantic relationship. However, it is important to evaluate how much time you are spending thinking about a distant romance at the expense of concentrating on your academic work and exploring relationships on your campus.

Too many first-year students get caught up in wanting to date an ideal person rather than a real person. They search for the stereotyped jock, person with movie-star looks, or punk rocker. Some first-year students also look at every date as a potential girlfriend or boyfriend, someone they eventually might marry. College counselors say that such students probably will be better adjusted and happier if they broaden their perspective on dating. Don't look at every date as a potential Mr. or Mrs. Perfect. Dates can be potential friends as well as romantic partners.

Heartbreak The collapse of a romantic relationship can be traumatic (Knox & others, 1997). It can trigger depression, obsessive thoughts, an inability to focus on school, and self-blame. It's hard to think clearly when someone breaks off a relationship. If someone breaks off a relationship with you, what are some ways to cope?

Rape and Unwanted Sexual Acts Rape is sexual intercourse that is forced on a person who does not give consent. A special concern in college is date or acquaintance rape. One-third to one-half of college men admit that they have forced sexual activity on women (Koss & Boeschen, 1998).

Rape is a traumatic experience for victims. They initially feel shocked and numb. The person's recovery benefits from the support of parents and friends.

Professional counseling also can help. Figure 10.2 presents some safety strategies for avoiding settings in which rape most often occurs.

Some people engage in unwanted sexual acts when not physically forced to do so. Why would they do this? They might be

- Turned on by their partner's actions and later regret it
- Fearful that the relationship will end if they don't have sex
- Intoxicated
- Feeling obligated because of the time and money spent by a partner

In sum, monitor your sexual feelings and make good sexual decisions. As in other aspects of communication and relationships, being aware of people's motives and acting assertively rather than aggressively, manipulatively, or passively are good strategies.

Figure 10.2

Strategies for Avoiding Settings in Which Rape Most Often Occurs

THINGS TO DO:

Go places with other people.

If you go alone, tell someone your plans.

Walk briskly, with purpose.

Stay in well-lighted, populated areas.

Limit your drug and alcohol intake since these can make you vulnerable.

Excercise good judgment about whom you give private information.

Have your keys ready when going to your car or residence.

Lock all doors and windows in your car and residence.

Do not open doors for strangers.

Carry a whistle or other alarm.

If someone is following you or you feel threatened, go to a public place, call the police, run, scream, or blow a whistle.

THINGS TO REMEMBER:

No one has the right to rape you.

Rape is a criminal act of violence for power.

Date or acquaintance rape is rape.

Any rape is a sexual assault.

Rape is not the fault of the person who is raped.

Summary Tips For Mastering College

Communicating Effectively and Developing Positive Relationships

Communicating Effectively

1. Develop good active listening skills. Bad listeners hog conversations. Talk with someone, not to someone. Pay careful attention to the person who is talking. Paraphrase. Synthesize the themes and patterns you hear. Give feedback.
2. Avoid barriers to effective communication such as criticizing, talking down to the person, and ordering.
3. Understand the role of nonverbal behavior in communication.
4. Know that females and males often communicate differently.
5. Engage in appropriate self-disclosure.

Resolving Conflict with Others

1. Know your interaction style. The assertive style works best. Avoid communicating with others by being passive, manipulative, or aggressive.
2. To become more assertive, evaluate your rights. Designate a time for discussing what you want. State the problem to the person involved in terms of its consequences for you. Express your feelings about the particular situation. Make your request in a direct, straightforward manner.
3. There are three main ways to negotiate: win–lose, lose–lose, and win–win. Practice using the win–win strategy.

Developing Positive Relationships

1. Develop and maintain good relationships with your parents. Although you are becoming more independent, don't break ties with them. You will need them at some point. Keep in regular contact.
2. Develop a good relationship with your roommate, if you have one. Resolve problems early. Use good communication skills when talking with a roommate. Be responsible. Show respect. Use an assertive interaction style. If roommate problems become overwhelming, contact the resident advisor, or ultimately the housing office.
3. If you have a partner or family, work on developing a healthy balance between your academic life and your life with your partner/family.
4. Know that loneliness is a common problem of first-year students. Recognize the warning signs of loneliness early on. Practice the strategies necessary for making and maintaining friendships. If you can't shed your loneliness on your own, contact the counseling service at your college.
5. Develop positive dating experiences or a positive relationship with a partner. Don't let dating detract from your college success.
6. The collapse of a romantic relationship can be traumatic and undermine college success. If someone breaks off a relationship with you, don't isolate yourself. Be aware that there is more to your self-esteem than the soured relationship.
7. Be aware of the problem of acquaintance rape. Know the safety guidelines for avoiding settings in which rape occurs.

✓ College Success Checklist

Have your views changed since you completed this checklist at the beginning of the chapter? Place a check mark beside any item for which you feel good about your current practice. Also check any item for which you have new ideas about how to improve.

____ I am an active listener when I communicate with others.

____ I know what the barriers to communication are and how to overcome them.

____ I understand the nature of nonverbal communication.

____ I can describe how females and males communicate differently.

____ I appropriately use self-disclosure in close relationships.

____ I express myself assertively.

____ I know how to negotiate effectively.

____ I have a good relationship with my parents.

____ *For students with roommates:* I know what it takes to get along with roommates.

____ *For students with partners/families:* I do a good job of balancing my academic life and my life with my partner or family.

____ I know what strategies to use to make new friends.

____ If I experience heartbreak, I know some good strategies for coping with it.

____ I know some safety guidelines for avoiding settings in which rape occurs.

In the space below, list items that you still need to work on the most. This list may help you complete the goal-setting exercise in the Learning Portfolio.

Review Questions

1 What are some ways to develop good active listening skills?

2 What are some barriers to effective verbal communication?

3 How do people communicate nonverbally?

4 How do women and men communicate differently?

5 What are good strategies for resolving conflict with others?

6 How can you communicate more effectively with your parents?

7 What are some effective strategies for students with a partner or family?

8 What are some ways that roommates can get along better?

9 What are some strategies for reducing loneliness and making friends?

Learning Portfolio

Learning by Reflecting... Journal Entries

Lovability

By examining your personal qualities that contribute to a close relationship, you should be able to understand them better and improve them.

List some qualities that you think make you a lovable person. These might include your ability to care for others, your sensitivity, your sense of humor, or your trustworthiness.

What are some ways you could become more lovable? These might include being less defensive, improving your self-esteem, taking better care of your appearance, and complimenting other people more.

How Much Do I Want to Reveal of Myself?

How much self-disclosure, honesty, and openness do you want in intimate relationships? Reflect on how much you would share with your best friend and with a romantic partner about the following:

Sexual fantasies

Secrets

Angry feelings

Times when I feel inadequate

Times when the relationship bores me

My need for emotional support

Reflecting on Conflicts with Others

Think about the conflicts you have had with others that you do not feel good about. What are some ways that you could have behaved more assertively to achieve a more satisfactory outcome?

Learning by Doing... Action Projects

Observing Interaction Styles

Good observation is an important skill. In the next few days, observe the people you interact with—your roommate, partner, classmates, friends, teachers, people in an interest group you attend, and so on. How would you describe their interaction style: aggressive, passive, manipulative, or assertive? How do you think they would classify your interaction style? Write your conclusions in your Learning Portfolio.

Evaluating Romance

Get together with several other students and discuss the most important aspects of a dating relationship. Is sex the most important aspect? What role does intimacy (self-disclosure) play? Does the other person need to share your interests for the relationship to work? Are most people's dating expectations too high?

Exploring Self-Help Books

There are hundreds of self-help books on love and relationships. A lot of them have catchy titles such as *Men Who Hate Women, and the Women Who Love Them; Women Men Love, Women Men Leave;* and *What Every Woman Should Know About Men.* Instead of books like these, examine the books listed in Resources for Mastering the College Experience under "Developing Positive Relationships." Go to a bookstore and look through these books. Pick out one that interests you and spend some time with it. What did you learn about relationships from the book?

Learning by Thinking Critically... Critiques

Evaluating a Person's Speech Characteristics

In trying to communicate more effectively, it can help to monitor the other person's tone and style of speaking. For example, if a person speaks in a monotone voice, it might mean that the person is bored. What are some probable meanings of the following speech characteristics:

Slow speech, low pitch
_____
_____

Loud voice, high pitch
_____
_____

Abrupt speech
_____
_____

Concise speech/loud tone
_____
_____

What Does Touch Communicate?

Touch can be an important form of communication. What are some different ways touch can communicate information? How might the same touch be interpreted differently depending on the identity of a person being touched—a friend, a romantic partner, a teacher, a person of a different age, or a stranger, for example?

What Is Love?

For centuries, philosophers, songwriters, and poets have been intrigued by love. But what is love? What are its components? Must love include passion, affection, altruism (having a selfless orientation and being motivated to help others), and friendship? Do components such as passion and affection change over time in a love relationship? For example, is passion more important in the early part of a relationship and affection more important as the relationship endures?

Learning by Thinking Creatively... Personal Vision

Creating a Quotation

We have included a number of short quotations throughout this book, such as "What you are speaks so loudly I cannot hear what you say" and "Bodies never lie." Write a quotation of your own about communicating effectively and developing positive relationships.
_____
_____
_____
_____

Writing a Poem

There is no shortage of poems about love. Try your hand at poetry. Write a poem about love.

Listen and Laugh

Gathering accurate information is important in the early part of creative thinking. The more good information you have, the better chance you have of devising a creative solution. When the creative challenge involves other people, the art of careful listening is even more important.

Other important ingredients of creativity are playfulness and humor. Although creativity takes hard work, the work goes more smoothly if you take it lightly. Having fun helps you to disarm the inner censor that all too quickly condemns your ideas as being too bizarre or off base.

Get together with a group of students and brainstorm about some creative ways to resolve conflicts with a roommate, partner, friend, or family. In the group work, focus on becoming a better listener and on letting your playful self emerge.

Learning by Planning... Goal Setting

Review the results of the Self-Assessments you completed in this chapter. Also review the College Success Checklist. What can you conclude about things you need to do to improve your skills?

What goal do you want to select from this chapter? *(Hint: Is your goal challenging, reasonable, and specific?)*
_____
_____
_____
_____
_____

What strategies will you use to achieve your goal? *(Hint: Can you organize your strategy into a series of smaller goals?)*
_____
_____
_____
_____
_____
_____
_____
_____
_____
_____
_____

What obstacles may be in your way as you attempt to make these positive changes?
_____
_____
_____
_____
_____

What additional resources might help you succeed in achieving your goal?
_____
_____
_____
_____

By what date do you want to accomplish your goal?
_____

How will you know you have succeeded?
_____
_____
_____
_____

Resources for Mastering the College Experience

Communicating Effectively

Gendered Communication (1996) by Julia Wood (Ed.). Mountain View, CA: Mayfield.
Leading experts' views on gendered patterns in family communication, friendships, and love, on campus, and in the workplace.

The Hidden Dimension (1966) by E. T. Hall. New York: Doubleday.
How to understand people better by analyzing how they use personal space, by the author who initiated the interest in personal space and its meanings.

Looking Out/Looking In (1999, 9th ed.) by Ronald Adler & Neil Towne. Ft. Worth, TX: Harcourt Brace.
Communication topics such as hearing versus listening, nonverbal communication, and keys to effective communication.

The Talk Book (1988) by Gerald Goodman and Glenn Esterly. New York: Ballantine.
Valuable suggestions for how to talk effectively with others. Good strategies for self-disclosure.

You Just Don't Understand (1990) by Deborah Tannen. New York: Ballantine.
How women and men communicate—or, all too often, miscommunicate. How to adapt communication styles to get along better with each other.

Resolving Conflict with Others

Your Perfect Right (1995, 7th ed.) by Robert Alberti and Michael Emmons. San Luis Obispo, CA: Impact.
The most widely recommended assertiveness training book. Takes you step by step through ways to improve your self-expression. Many examples and exercises.

Win–Win Negotiating (1988) by Fred Jandt. New York: Wiley.
How to turn conflict into agreement. How conflict is inevitable but not always bad, and resolvable if everyone involved makes an honest effort.

Developing Positive Relationships

The Art of Living Single (1988) by Michael Broder. New York: Avon.
Strategies for coping with life as a single adult, including how to appreciate time spent alone and how to make better use of time in social situations when you enter them by yourself.

The Dance of Intimacy (1989) by Harriet Lerner. New York: HarperCollins.
An excellent portrait of a woman's current self and relationships. How women can move from being stuck in destructive or directionless relationships to intimate connections and a solid sense of self.

Getting the Love You Want (1988) by Harville Hendrix. New York: Henry Holt.
An outstanding guide for couples giving concrete ways to improve close relationships. In essence, a 10-week course in couple therapy: how to communicate clearly and sensitively, eliminate self-defeating patterns, and focus your attention on your partner's needs.

Intimate Connections (1985) by David Burns. New York: William Morrow.
Starts from the premise that lonely people need to change their patterns of perception in order to overcome loneliness. Tells you how to make social connections and develop close relationships with others. Contains checklists, daily mood logs, and self-assessments.

Shyness (1987) by Phillip Zimbardo. Reading, MA: Addison-Wesley.
How shy people got that way. Ways to build self-esteem and, most importantly, social skills you need to develop to move into the social worlds of others.

Internet Resources

http://www.personal.psu.edu/faculty/n/x/nxd10/family3.htm
Ideas on relationships, from dating to coping with the demands of relatives.

http://www.nau.edu/~fronske/defense.html
How to protect yourself against attack.

http://www.psychtests.com/assert.html
On-line test to identify aspects of assertiveness that you may need to work on.

http://www.apa.org/pubinfo/anger.html
How to manage anger. American Psychological Association.

Living in a Diverse World

CHAPTER 11

✓ College Success Checklist

Place a check mark beside the items that apply to you. Leave the items blank that do not apply to you.

____ I value diversity among people.

____ I treat people as individuals first rather than as members of a cultural or ethnic group.

____ I don't think I am sexist; for example, I always show respect to females and males.

____ I am satisfied with my gender role orientation.

____ I know what women need to do to improve their lives.

____ I know what men need to do to improve their lives.

____ I do not engage in sexually harassing tactics.

____ I am comfortable with my sexual orientation.

____ I can articulate the issues returning students face in achieving success in college.

____ I know how to communicate comfortably with a student who has a disability.

____ I know what strategies I can use to improve my relationships with others of a different background.

Preview

We live in a world of increasing diversity. In this chapter, we will explore this diversity, focusing on culture, ethnicity, gender, sexual orientation, and age. We also will examine strategies for interacting more effectively with people from other backgrounds.

Chapter Outline

Images of College Success: Ana Bolado de Espino

Diversity in Culture and Ethnicity
 Collectivism, Individualism, and Diversity Within Groups
 Ethnic Identity and Diversity on Campus

Diversity in Gender
 Gender Controversy
 Androgyny
 Improving the Lives of Women and Men

Diversity in Sexual Orientation

Diversity in Age

Strategies for Improving Relations with Diverse Others
 Assess Your Attitudes
 Work on Taking the Perspective of Others
 Seek Intimate Contact
 Respect Differences and Don't Overlook Similarities
 Seek More Knowledge
 Treat People as Individuals Instead of Stereotyping Them
 Show Enthusiasm
 Resolve Conflicts

Self-Assessments
 11.1 Are You Androgynous?

On-Target Tips
 Communicating More Effectively with People from Individualist and Collectivist Cultures
 International S.O.S.
 Gender-Based Strategies for Self-Improvement
 Returning Student Strategies
 Communicating Across Ability Levels

Images of College Success
Ana Bolado de Espino

Ana Bolado de Espino came to Dallas, Texas, from Mexico in 1980. She did not speak a word of English when she arrived in the United States. She did have a dream. Ana wanted to become a medical doctor. She worked as a maid, scrubbing floors and doing laundry for 15 years to earn enough money to get through college. Divorced, she raised two children while attending college and working.

She feared that she would never make it to med school. She also hit a major snag. As a young teen, her daughter began to hang out with a gang, ran away, and became pregnant. Ana thought about dropping out of college to spend more time with her daughter. Her daughter told her to stay in college. Since then, the daughter, now 15, has started to turn her life around.

Ana was 38 years old when she obtained her college degree with a GPA of almost 4.00. She worked as an outreach AIDS counselor for a year after graduating from college. Recently she was accepted into medical school (Schwartz, 1996).

Diversity in Culture and Ethnicity

We should be accustomed to thinking of America as a country with many different cultures. Our population is diverse and comes from many different places. Some college campuses are among America's most diverse settings, although smaller colleges tend to be more homogeneous, with most students and faculty sharing a predominant ethnic or religious heritage. Larger campuses tend to be more diverse; most have international students and American students from many ethnic backgrounds. Faculty and staff also are mixed in cultural background.

Despite the opportunities to mix, people often associate with their "own kind." Think about where you eat lunch. Commuters often hang out with other commuters. Fraternity and sorority members sit off by themselves. Faculty and students tend not to mix. Our fear of the unknown may keep us close to those whose background we share. This can prevent us from taking advantage of the rich opportunities on campus to meet and learn about people who are different from us. Let's explore some factors that can help us understand diversity better.

Collectivism, Individualism, and Diversity Within Groups

Cross-cultural expert Harry Triandis (1994) believes that cultures can be classified as individualist or collectivist. The United States is an individualist culture. It gives priority to personal goals rather than group goals, emphasizes the self, and advocates independence. Like most Eastern countries, Japan and China are collectivist cultures. They emphasize being connected to a group and maintaining harmonious relationships.

How can individualists and collectivists communicate more effectively with each other? See "Communicating More Effectively with People from Individualist and Collectivist Cultures" for suggestions from an expert on East–West communication, Richard Brislin (1993).

People from certain backgrounds tend to favor certain communication patterns. African Americans often limit direct eye contact when they communicate. Latinos may stand close and touch when they communicate. Native Americans tend to speak softly and slowly. White Americans emphasize efficiency and directness when they talk. Asian Americans may avoid direct talk as a sign of respect.

Of course, within any group there can be great diversity. Some Latinos came to the United States from South America, others from Mexico, and others from Cuba and other countries. Many Latinos are Catholic, some are not. The same diversity is true of Asian Americans, African Americans, and all other ethnic groups. Failure to recognize the extent of individual variation can lead to numerous misunderstandings with people from different cultural groups.

Ethnic Identity and Diversity on Campus

How important are ethnic considerations for you? If you are white, you may think about your heritage in terms of your European roots. You may know precisely where your ancestors came from and why they made their way to the United States. Possibly you have roots to England on both sides of your family; or one side may be German, the other Austrian; both might be Italian; and so on. Your European roots may be a source of great pride to you. Or your specific ethnic heritage may have been lost over the generations or be too diverse to keep track of any longer.

We need every human gift and cannot afford to neglect any gift because of artificial barriers of sex or race or class or national origin.

Margaret Mead
American anthropologist, 20th century

How unpleasing to the eye if all the flowers and plants, the leaves and blossoms, the fruits, the branches, and the trees were all the same shape and color. Diversity of hues, form, and shape enriches and adorns the garden.

'Abdu'l-Bahá
Persian Baha'i religious leader, 19th–20th century

On Target Tips

Communicating More Effectively with People from Individualist and Collectivist Cultures

If you are individualist, the following are ways to communicate more effectively with a collectivist:

- Learn to pay more attention to group memberships.
- Place more emphasis on cooperation than competition.
- If you have to criticize, do so carefully and only in private situations. Never criticize someone in public.
- Cultivate long-term relationships. Be patient. People in collectivist cultures value dealing with "old friends."

If you are a collectivist, the following are ways to communicate more effectively with an individualist:

- Compliment the person more than you are used to doing in your culture.
- Avoid feeling threatened if the individualist acts competitively; don't take the individualist's competitiveness as a personal offense.
- Talk about your accomplishments. You don't have to be as modest when you are among individualists. At the same time, it's not a good idea to boast.
- Recognize that individualists don't value allegiance to the group as much as you do.

I am here and you will know that I am the best and will hear me. The color of my skin or the kink of my hair or the spread of my mouth has nothing to do with what you are listening to.

Leontyne Price
African-American opera star,
20th century

America's citizens with European roots historically experienced advantages over other ethnic groups. When Africans were imported to America as slaves, they were described as property and treated inhumanely. In the first half of the 20th century, most African Americans still lived in the South and were largely segregated from white Americans by law. Segregation was practiced in almost all public places. Even now, a much higher percentage of African Americans than whites still live below the poverty line.

A number of diversity issues and concerns are present on college campuses. Ethnic conflict is common on many campuses, according to a survey of students at 390 colleges and universities (Hurtado, Dey, & Trevino, 1994). More than half of the African Americans and almost one-fourth of the Asian Americans said that they felt excluded from college activities. Only 6% of Anglo Americans said that they felt excluded. In spite of diversity initiatives, we still have a long way to go in reducing discrimination and prejudice.

Many of us sincerely think that we are not prejudiced. However, experts on prejudice believe that every person harbors some prejudices (Sears, Peplau, & Taylor, 1997). Why? Because we naturally tend to do several things that promote stereotyping and prejudice. For example, we tend to identify with others who are like us. We tend to be *ethnocentric*, favoring the groups we belong to and tending to think of them as superior. We also tend to fear people who are different from us.

To explore prejudice on campus, think about these stereotypes: the blonde cheerleader; the computer nerd; the absent-minded professor; the rigid, snarly librarian; the female basketball star; and the class clown.

Notice that with only a simple label we can conjure up an image and expectations about what these people are like. Now imagine that you get to know these people. You discover that

- The blonde cheerleader has a 4.0 average.
- The computer nerd plays in a hot new jazz band at a local club on weekends.
- The absent-minded professor never misses a class or arrives late.
- The rigid, snarly librarian gives freely of her time to local charities to help improve the lives of children.
- The female basketball star is dating a man in his second year of law school.
- The class clown recently organized a campuswide initiative to decrease the pollution coming from a nearby chemical plant.

Clearly, stereotypes lead us to view others in limited and limiting ways. There's so much more to people than the social roles they play or the groups to which they belong.

Prejudice is ugly and socially damaging. Many people believe that college campuses should demonstrate leadership in reducing its presence. Recently, various diversity initiatives have been enacted to work toward this goal: on-campus celebrations of ethnic minority group achievements, festivals that highlight different traditions or beliefs, required coursework to promote the explorations of traditions other than one's own, and inclusion of examples from a broader range of human experience in required readings.

Why are college faculties enacting such broad-based initiatives? Because they are aware that prejudice has wreaked destruction so many times throughout history. As one of many examples, more than 6 million Jews were murdered by the Nazis in the 1940s. This mass killing was justified because Hitler said the European racial stock needed to be "purified." Only a fraction of the world's Jews remain in Europe today. In our own country, the population of North American Indians dropped from an estimated 3 million in the 17th century to about 600,000 today as a result of the European acts of genocide against this continent's original inhabitants.

Some conservative thinkers charge that too much concern for diversity may undermine the quality of college education. They fear that the curriculum may have been diverted from "proven" classic studies to the pursuit of ideas that may be less valuable in the long run. In particular, they believe that some important Western traditions are being sacrificed in the current push for diversity. Critics also argue that diversity initiatives could have a boomerang effect. That is, conflicts generated by diversity initiatives might polarize people even more.

An equally important concern has been expressed regarding academic freedom. "Political correctness" agendas are alleged to discourage certain kinds of expression as insensitive or uncivil. Many critics of diversity believe that careful screening of language to prevent offenses could reduce the free expression of ideas and muffle intellectual inquiry.

Surprised
By How a Stereotype Does Not Hold True

The stereotype of Asian-American students is that they all are very bright superachievers. Many, but not all, Asian-American students do well in college. College adjustment is easier for Asian Americans who come from well-educated professional families that have immigrated to the United States from India, Hong Kong, South Korea, the Philippines, and Vietnam, just as it is easier for Euro-Americans and African Americans from the educated middle class. However, this stereotype does not fit many Indochinese refugees who fled Vietnam, Laos, and Cambodia in the late 1970s. Many of these immigrants came from poverty in their homeland. They arrived in the United States with few skills and little education. They speak little English and have had problems finding decent jobs. Adjusting to school and college is more difficult for them than for their Asian counterparts who come from well-educated professional families.

An increasing number of college students are from what Anglo Americans call ethnic minority groups. It is important to keep in mind that each ethnic group is diverse. Not taking this diversity and individual variation into account leads to stereotyping. A good strategy is to think of other students as individuals, not as members of a majority or minority group.

On Target Tips

International S.O.S.

- *Be patient.* Give yourself time to adapt to your new life. Things may not be easy at the beginning. Over time, you will develop greater comfort with U.S. culture.
- *Create or join a support system.* Most campuses have international student clubs where you can meet and get to know other international students.
- *Make new friends.* Get the most out of your international experience by reaching out to others to learn about their cultures.
- *Share your culture.* Look for opportunities to share your background so your teachers and classmates can learn about your culture.

International Students Most colleges have students from a wide range of countries. These students bring with them customs, values, and behaviors that may be quite different from those of American students (Lin & Yi, 1997). If you are an American-born student, consider getting to know one or more international students. It will expand your education.

If you are an international student, even if you were well-adjusted at home, adapting to college in America may bring some confusion and problems. You now have to cope with a whole new set of customs and values. In some cases, you have to learn a new language and new rules for social conduct. "International S.O.S." provides some helpful tips.

Diversity in Gender

Gender refers to our social and cultural experiences as a female or a male. We live in a changing gendered world and these changes have affected campus life. For example, first-year student Gina is the first woman in her family ever to attend college. Her grandmother did not go because it was not an option. Neither did her mother, who still believed that her place was in the home. However, her mother supported Gina's desire for a different kind of life. Women now attend college and seek careers outside the home in greater numbers than ever before in history. In 1966, 57% of first-year college students agreed that a married woman should be confined to the home and family; in 1996, that figure had dropped to 24% (Astin & others, 1997).

Gender Controversy

Not long ago, virtually all boys were expected to grow up to be "masculine" and girls to be "feminine." The gender blueprints seemed clear-cut. The well-adjusted male should be independent, assertive, and dominant. The well-adjusted female should be dependent, nurturing, and submissive.

> *Prejudice is the reasoning of fools.*
>
> **Voltaire**
> **Philosopher and essayist,**
> **18th century**

If you are a student from the United States, respect the differences between yourself and international students. Value diversity. If you are from another country, create a support system and get involved in campus life. Be patient in adjusting to this new culture.

These beliefs and stereotypes led to *sexism*, the negative treatment of females because of their sex. Some examples of sexism are

- Thinking that women are not as smart as men
- Not being equally comfortable with a woman or man as a boss
- Thinking that a woman's only place is in the home

Today's society is generally more flexible, but this produces confusion and uncertainty for many people. Although women have gained greater influence in a number of professional spheres, many still experience invisible ceilings that limit their access to the most powerful positions. In contrast, women who choose more traditional roles sometimes think that they are criticized unfairly by other women for "selling out."

Some men are confused by the changes in gender expectations. They struggle to grasp what life is really like for women. Some women are angry at men in general for their historic abuse of privilege. Some men, especially white men, are angry themselves. They don't like losing privilege in the job market because of policies that put women on a more equal footing.

The test for whether or not you can hold a job should not be the arrangement of your chromosomes.

**Bella Abzug
Congresswoman from New York,
1970s**

Androgyny

Beginning in the 1970s, the concept of *androgyny* emerged. The basic idea of androgyny is that the most competent males *and* females have *both* positive masculine and feminine characteristics (Bem, 1977). That is, a competent male is both self-assertive *and* nurturing. So is a competent female. To examine your own gender role orientation, take Self-Assessment 11.1.

Androgyny is an improvement over the old masculine/feminine dichotomy because it promotes greater flexibility for females and males. However, the concept of androgyny still has its critics. Some critics say that we need to think more about the context in which gendered behavior occurs (Paludi, 1995). The idea of androgyny is that, regardless of the context, androgynous behavior is best, not masculine behavior or feminine behavior. However, in achievement contexts, "masculine" traits of self-assertiveness and dominance have served both men and women well. In close relationships, the "feminine" traits of nurturance and sensitivity to others often improve the lives of both women and men. Other critics say that there is too much talk about gender (Pleck, 1983). Instead, they say that we should transcend gender by thinking of people as people rather than as masculine, feminine, or androgynous.

Improving the Lives of Women and Men

Both women and men may find themselves constrained by gender expectations. College experiences offer opportunities to examine and re-evaluate those expectations.

Improving Women's Lives Gender expert Jean Baker Miller (1986) examined women's lives. She concluded that a large part of what women do is active participation in the development of others. Women foster the improvement of others along many lines. They help others emotionally, intellectually, and socially. For example, Ana Bolado de Espino supported her daughter while pursuing her dream of going to medical school and her daughter supported her. Miller argues that women need to retain their relationship skills but become more self-motivated as well. This self-motivation includes focusing more on themselves and their own needs. Another gender expert, Harriet Lerner (1989), echoes these

"So according to the stereotype, you can put two and two together, but I can read the handwriting on the wall."

Self-Assessment 11-1

Are You Androgynous?

The items below are from a widely used measure of androgyny, the Bem Sex-Role Orientation. To find out whether you are mainly masculine, feminine, or androgynous, rate yourself on each item from 1 (never or almost never true) to 7 (always or almost always true).

1.	Self-reliant	1	2	3	4	5	6	7
2.	Yielding	1	2	3	4	5	6	7
3.	Helpful	1	2	3	4	5	6	7
4.	Defends own beliefs	1	2	3	4	5	6	7
5.	Cheerful	1	2	3	4	5	6	7
6.	Moody	1	2	3	4	5	6	7
7.	Independent	1	2	3	4	5	6	7
8.	Shy	1	2	3	4	5	6	7
9.	Conscientious	1	2	3	4	5	6	7
10.	Athletic	1	2	3	4	5	6	7
11.	Affectionate	1	2	3	4	5	6	7
12.	Theatrical	1	2	3	4	5	6	7
13.	Assertive	1	2	3	4	5	6	7
14.	Flatterable	1	2	3	4	5	6	7
15.	Happy	1	2	3	4	5	6	7
16.	Strong personality	1	2	3	4	5	6	7
17.	Loyal	1	2	3	4	5	6	7
18.	Unpredictable	1	2	3	4	5	6	7
19.	Forceful	1	2	3	4	5	6	7
20.	Feminine	1	2	3	4	5	6	7
21.	Reliable	1	2	3	4	5	6	7
22.	Analytical	1	2	3	4	5	6	7
23.	Sympathetic	1	2	3	4	5	6	7
24.	Jealous	1	2	3	4	5	6	7
25.	Has leadership abilities	1	2	3	4	5	6	7
26.	Sensitive to the needs of others	1	2	3	4	5	6	7
27.	Truthful	1	2	3	4	5	6	7
28.	Willing to take risks	1	2	3	4	5	6	7
29.	Understanding	1	2	3	4	5	6	7
30.	Secretive	1	2	3	4	5	6	7
31.	Makes decisions easily	1	2	3	4	5	6	7
32.	Compassionate	1	2	3	4	5	6	7

#								
33.	Sincere	1	2	3	4	5	6	7
34.	Self-sufficient	1	2	3	4	5	6	7
35.	Eager to soothe hurt feelings	1	2	3	4	5	6	7
36.	Conceited	1	2	3	4	5	6	7
37.	Dominant	1	2	3	4	5	6	7
38.	Soft-spoken	1	2	3	4	5	6	7
39.	Likable	1	2	3	4	5	6	7
40.	Masculine	1	2	3	4	5	6	7
41.	Warm	1	2	3	4	5	6	7
42.	Solemn	1	2	3	4	5	6	7
43.	Willing to take a stand	1	2	3	4	5	6	7
44.	Tender	1	2	3	4	5	6	7
45.	Friendly	1	2	3	4	5	6	7
46.	Aggressive	1	2	3	4	5	6	7
47.	Gullible	1	2	3	4	5	6	7
48.	Inefficient	1	2	3	4	5	6	7
49.	Acts as a leader	1	2	3	4	5	6	7
50.	Childlike	1	2	3	4	5	6	7
51.	Adaptable	1	2	3	4	5	6	7
52.	Individualistic	1	2	3	4	5	6	7
53.	Does not use harsh language	1	2	3	4	5	6	7
54.	Unsystematic	1	2	3	4	5	6	7
55.	Competitive	1	2	3	4	5	6	7
56.	Loves children	1	2	3	4	5	6	7
57.	Tactful	1	2	3	4	5	6	7
58.	Ambitious	1	2	3	4	5	6	7
59.	Gentle	1	2	3	4	5	6	7
60.	Conventional	1	2	3	4	5	6	7

Scoring:

Add up your ratings for items 1, 4, 7, 10, 13, 16, 19, 22, 25, 28, 31, 34, 37, 40, 43, 46, 49, 55, and 58. Divide the total by 20. That is your masculinity score.

Add up your ratings for items 2, 5, 8, 11, 14, 17, 20, 23, 26, 29, 32, 35, 38, 41, 44, 47, 50, 53, 56, and 59. Divide the total by 20. That is your femininity score.

If your masculinity score is above 4.9 (the approximate median for the masculinity scale) and your femininity score is above 4.9 (the approximate femininity median) then you would be classified as androgynous on Bem's scale.

Staying Out of the Pits

Robert's Downward Spiral

Robert is a football player in his first year of college. He grew up in a large inner-city area where crime and drugs were common. He never knew his father and his mother left home when he was six. He lived with his grandmother until he started college this fall.

Robert was a star player in high school. So far his first year in college has been frustrating. He no longer is a star and is thinking about dropping out of college. He went to all of his classes the first two months. Now he can't motivate himself to go. He has started hanging out with some guys his age who didn't go to college. They got him to take some cocaine last week.

Students like Robert desperately need to get counseling support to stop the downward spiral. A mentor also can make a big difference.

> *To be meek, patient, tactful, modest, honorable, brave, is not to be either manly or womanly, it is to be humane.*
>
> **Jane Harrison**
> **English classic scholar,**
> **early 20th century**

> *If you are going to generalize about women, you will find yourself up to here in exceptions.*
>
> **Dolores Hitchens**
> **American mystery writer,**
> **20th century**

beliefs. She states that competent women can stay emotionally connected with others ("YOU-ness"). They also need to focus on improving themselves (their "I-ness").

Yet another expert, Carol Tavris (1992), wrote in *The Mismeasure of Woman* that no matter how hard women try, they can't measure up. They are criticized for being too female or not female enough. However, Tavris argues, women are judged by how well they fit into a man's world. That man's world tends to fixate on the beauty of a woman's body. Tavris said that we need more emphasis on a woman's *soul* as the key indicator of competence and worth.

The message to women is this. Women are certainly not inferior to men. Start evaluating yourself in terms of female competencies, not male competencies. For example, women (and our entire society) need to place a higher value on relationship skills. Women do not need to stop caring for others to be leaders. Developing positive relationships with others and developing yourself are both important. The goal for both sexes should be to add positive qualities.

Improving women's lives also requires reducing and eventually eliminating sexual harassment. Sexual harassment in colleges and the workplace is a major barrier to women's progress. It is estimated that two million women currently enrolled in college will experience some form of sexual harassment in their student lives (Paludi, 1998).

Sexual harassment includes

- **Gender harassment.** Sexist remarks and behavior that insult and degrade women, a problem apart from harassment for sex.
- **Seductive behavior.** Unwanted, inappropriate, and offensive advances.
- **Sexual bribery.** Harassment for sex, with the threat of punishment for refusal. For example, a woman might be fired or demoted by her boss if she doesn't go along with the sexual demand.

Every college is required by law to take action against sexual harassment. Many colleges and communities have resources to protect women from sexual harassment. If you are sexually harassed, report it to your school's administration. The Resources section at the end of the chapter includes some valuable material on sexual harassment and what to do about it.

Improving Men's Lives Some men believe that men today have become soft and vulnerable, letting women dictate their lives. One such man is Robert Bly (1990), author of *Iron John*. Iron John is a mythological creature with a deep masculine identity. He is spontaneous, sexual, and aggressive. He has untamed impulses and thoughtful self-discipline. Will Bly's proposal of a return to the virile, forceful man of yesterday make today's world a better place to live? Many critics say that Bly's strategy only creates more turmoil between the sexes and will not promote male/female coexistence.

If heightened masculinity isn't the answer for males, what is? Gender expert Herb Goldberg (1980) says that a precipitous gulf separates the sexes: Women sense and articulate feelings; men tend not to because of their masculine conditioning. Men's defensive armor causes them to maintain self-destructive patterns. Men become effective work machines but they suffer emotionally. As a result, men live about eight years less than women, have higher hospitalization rates, and have more behavior problems. Goldberg believes that men are killing themselves when they strive to be "true" men like Iron John. That is a heavy price to pay for masculine "privilege" and power.

How can men escape the dilemma? How can they live more physically and psychologically satisfying lives? Goldberg argues that men need to become better attuned to their emotional makeup and relationships with others. He believes that men can retain their self-assertiveness while building better relationships and becoming more attuned to feelings.

For more recommendations on how women and men can lead more competent lives, see "Gender-Based Strategies for Self-Improvement."

Diversity in Sexual Orientation

Until the end of the 19th century, people were described as either heterosexual or homosexual. Today, many experts on sexuality view sexual orientation as a continuum ranging from exclusive heterosexuality to exclusive homosexuality (Doyle & Paludi, 1998).

A large majority of people are heterosexual. Although for many years it was estimated that about 10% are homosexuals (that is, they are attracted to people of the same sex), more recent surveys put the figure at about 2–5% (Michael & others, 1994). About 1% are bisexual (attracted to both males and females).

Sexual orientation is not necessarily a fixed decision that is made once in life forever. For example, it is not unusual for a person to experiment with homosexual behavior in adolescence but not as an adult.

What are homosexuals like?

- Except for having a different sexual orientation, heterosexuals and homosexuals have many similarities in attitudes, behavior, and adjustment. Both heterosexual and homosexual students want to do well in school, have friends, get a job, and find someone to love.
- Although some people think they can always tell whether someone is gay or lesbian by their mannerisms, many masculine women are not lesbians and many effeminate men are not gay. You can't necessarily tell someone is homosexual by how they dress, wear their hair, or behave.
- Like heterosexuals, homosexuals come from diverse cultures, have diverse interests, and pursue diverse careers.
- Children raised by gay and lesbian parents are no more likely to become homosexual than children raised by heterosexual parents.
- Why people develop homosexual versus heterosexual orientation is not known, although sexual orientation probably is determined by a combination of genetic, hormonal, cognitive, and environmental factors.

In most ways college success for homosexual and bisexual college students is no different than for heterosexuals. However, their minority status does entail some difficulties. Too many heterosexual students still consider them as abnormal,

On Target Tips

Gender-Based Strategies for Self-Improvement

Women

- Don't use male standards to judge your competence.
- Retain strengths in building relationships and staying in touch with emotions. Be proud of them.
- Improve your self-motivation. Be more self-assertive. Focus on knowing your own needs and meeting them. Go beyond the idea that this is selfish. It is self-assertive.
- Don't put up with sexual harassment. Know what qualifies as sexual harassment. Report it when it happens.

Men

- Retain your strengths. Be self-motivated and achievement-oriented.
- Do a better job of understanding your emotions and self. Explore yourself. Ask yourself what kind of person you want to be. Think more about how you want others to perceive you.
- Work on your relationship skills. Give more consideration to the feelings of others. Make relationships a higher priority in your life.
- If you are aggressive and hostile, tone down your anger. Be self-assertive but not overly aggressive. That is, control yourself and your emotions. Work toward better understanding of your own emotions and the feelings of other people.

> *To me old age is always 15 years older than I am.*
>
> **Bernard Baruch**
> **American statesman and businessman,**
> **20th century**

> *Age only matters when you are aging. Now that I have reached a great age, I might as well be twenty.*
>
> **Pablo Picasso**
> **Spanish artist,**
> **20th century**

rather than simply different. Even the American Psychiatric Association once labeled homosexuality as abnormal behavior and a mental disorder. That is no longer the case, but the stigma is there, along with discrimination. Homosexual and bisexual students encounter physical abuse, hostile comments, and demeaning jokes. Heterosexuals may feel uncomfortable around them. For example, Jim said he felt uncomfortable when he found out that one of his fraternity brothers, Bob, was gay. When he found out, he increasingly avoided him. Several years later, Jim said that he regrets that he treated Bob the way he did. He realized that nothing prevented a heterosexual from being friends with a homosexual.

How can gays, lesbians, and bisexual students improve their lives in college? What positive role can heterosexuals play in this?

- Many campuses have organizations for gays, lesbians, and bisexuals. If you are a homosexual or bisexual student, you may want to get involved with these organizations. Some of them include not only the campus gay and lesbian population, but also their friends and family, as well as other students with questions, regardless of sexual orientation. These organizations provide a safe place for students to voice their thoughts and feelings about sexual orientation.

- If you are homosexual or bisexual and your campus does not have a related organization, you might consider starting one. This may require following whatever procedures your student activities office has established for starting a campus organization. If you feel uncomfortable on your own campus, consider joining a gay, lesbian, or bisexual organization on a nearby campus or in the local community.

- Some good books have been written by and for homosexual and bisexual people, covering many practical issues. See the list in the Resources at the end of this chapter.

- Be tolerant of the sexual orientation of others. If you are a heterosexual and harbor negative feelings toward homosexuals, consider taking a course on human sexuality. You will learn not only about homosexuality but about yourself as well. Researchers have found that college students who take a course in human sexuality develop more positive views of homosexual and bisexual people (Walters, 1994).

Be tolerant of others' sexual orientations that are different from yours.

Diversity in Age

At 56, Bill looks around the classroom at his community college in New Jersey. To his surprise, he is not the oldest student in the class. Ed Stitt, age 87, just started attending. His goal is to get his community college degree by his 90th birthday. Ed says that going to college keeps him from getting "old-timer's" disease and keeps his brain alive. When Gladys Clappison returned to college and entered the dorm at the University of Iowa, she was 82 years old (Moawad, 1993).

An increasing number of students start or finish college at an older age (Fleming & Morning, 1998). More than 1 of every 5 full-time students today is a returning student. About two-thirds of part-time students are returning students. Among them, some are working full-time, are married, have children or grandchildren; some are divorced, are retired, or changing careers. Some attended college earlier in their lives.

Increasing numbers of returning students are single parents, single women motivated to advance in their careers, people of color, and people from low-income backgrounds.

Students who enter or return to college at an older age may experience college life differently than recent high school graduates. Some older students have to balance their classwork with commitments to partners, children, jobs, and community responsibilities. They may have less flexibility about when they attend classes, they may need child care, and they may have special transportation needs. Some returning students lack confidence in their skills and abilities. They often undervalue their knowledge and experience.

Despite the hardships that returning students face, they bring certain strengths to the campus:

- Life experiences that can be applied to a wider range of issues and problems in academic settings.
- Multiple commitments that may stimulate them to be more skilled in managing their time.
- Greater maturity in work habits and more experience participating in discussions.
- Better perspective on minor setbacks. Failing a pop quiz is not as traumatizing to a returning student who has experienced greater disappointments and recovered from worse setbacks.

"Returning Student Strategies" provides some helpful tips (Weinberg, 1994).

On Target Tips

Returning Student Strategies

- ■ *Evaluate your support system.* A strong and varied support system can help you adapt to college. If you have a partner or family, their encouragement and understanding can help a lot. Your friends also can provide considerable support.

- ■ *Make new friends.* Seek out friends of different ages, but especially talk with other older students. You will find that many other older students juggle different responsibilities and are anxious about their classes too.

- ■ *Get involved in campus life.* The campus is not just for younger students. It also is your campus. Check out the organizations and groups at your college. Join one or more that interest you.

- ■ *Don't be afraid to ask for help.* Become aware of the services your college offers. The health and counseling services can help you with special concerns of older students. These include parenting and child care, divorce, and juggling roles. If you have any doubts about your academic skills, get some help from the study skill professionals on your campus.

Strategies for Improving Relations with Diverse Others

How can we get along better with people who are different from us? In addition to the ideas presented in this chapter, you may want to consider any

On Target Tips

Communicating Across Ability Levels

- Consider the person with a disability as a *person* first. Refer to him or her as a "person who is blind" rather than a "blind person" if you must refer to the disability.
- If the disability is not relevant to your conversation, don't mention it.
- Avoid terms that indicate victimization or dependence.
- Most students with a disability are not sick. Thus, using medical terms such as *patient* and *illness* are inappropriate.
- Students with a disability need to trust you and feel comfortable around you. Until they feel comfortable with you, they probably won't talk openly about themselves.
- If you have a roommate or friend who has a disability, learn as much about the condition as possible. Talk with them about their specific needs.

> *In case you are worried about what is going to become of the younger generation, it is going to grow up and start worrying about the younger generation.*
>
> **Roger Allen**
> **Contemporary American writer**

problems you have had in relating honestly with students who have a disability. "Communicating Across Ability Levels" provides some helpful tips.

Assess Your Attitudes

One of the first steps in improving relations with people who are different from you is to assess your attitudes. Most of us sincerely think that we are not prejudiced. Are there people you don't like because of the group they belong to? Honestly evaluate your attitudes toward people who

- Are from cultures different from your own
- Are from ethnic groups different from your own
- Are of the other sex
- Have a different sexual orientation
- Are of other ages
- Have a disability

Work on Taking the Perspective of Others

You can improve your attitude toward different others by clarifying your perspective. Ask yourself,

- "What is this different person feeling and thinking?"
- "What is she or he really like?"
- "What about their background and experiences make them different from me?"
- "What kinds of stress and obstacles are they facing?"
- "Is the fact that they are different reason enough for me not to like them or to be angry at them?"
- "How much do I really know about the other person? How can I learn more about them?"

Seek Intimate Contact

Martin Luther King once said, "I have a dream that my four little children will one day live in a nation where they will not be judged by the color of their skin but by the content of their character." How can we reach the world Martin Luther King envisioned, a world beyond prejudice and discrimination? Mere contact alone with people from other ethnic groups won't do it. However, a particular type of contact—intimate contact—often is effective in improving relations with different others (Brislin, 1993).

Intimate contact does not necessarily mean sexual relations. Rather, it means sharing one's worries, troubles, successes, failures, personal ambitions, and coping strategies. When we reveal information about ourselves, we are more likely to be perceived as individuals than stereotyped as members of a group. When we share personal information with people we used to regard as "them," we begin to see that they are more like "us" than we thought.

Respect Differences and Don't Overlook Similarities

Think how boring our lives would be if we were all the same. Respecting others with different traditions, backgrounds, and abilities improves communication and cooperation.

Unfortunately, too often we look at differences between "our" group and other groups as deficits on the part of the other group. The differences range from the type of music we like, to how we look, to what kind of clothes we wear, to how "intelligent" we are, to what values we cherish. Most of us are ethnocentric. Feel pride about your own group. It will help your self-esteem. However, don't let your in-group pride lead you to think that people from other groups are not as good as you are. Work on respecting differences between you and others. Don't fall into the ethnocentric trap of demeaning others.

When we perceive people as different from us, we often do so on the basis of one or two limited characteristics. Maybe it is skin color or sex, possibly age, or maybe a disability. How often, though, do you explore ways that you might be similar? Think about the many similarities between you and someone you regard as totally different because of skin color or national heritage. You might have similar personalities. Both of you might be shy and anxious, fearful of speaking in public. Both of you might feel overwhelmed by all the demands you need to juggle. If the person is attending your college, you have both chosen the same campus to pursue your education. You might have similar achievement standards, both hoping to make the Dean's List. You may share a keen interest in a certain sport or both be passionate about Ben and Jerry's ice cream. And so on. You probably have a lot more in common than you imagine with people you perceive as different.

Feeling *Good*

About Getting to Know People Who Are Different from You

You may be reluctant to interact with some people because they are different from you. Put away your fears, stereotypes, and prejudices. Think of them as individuals, which is how you want them to think of you. Make an effort to get to know people who are different than you. Be willing to share your worries, hopes, and daily lives with them. You will be enriched and so will they. You will feel better about them. They will feel better about you.

Seek More Knowledge

In many instances, the more you know about people who are different from you, the better you will be able to interact with them. Learn more about the customs, values, interests, and historical background of people who are different from you. Take a course on cultures around the world, for example.

Treat People as Individuals Instead of Stereotyping Them

In our culture, people want to be treated as individuals. You want to be someone who is unique and not like any other person. So do most other people. You will get along much better with different others if you keep in mind that they are individuals than if you think of them as members of a group. Talk with different others about their concerns, interests, worries, hopes, and daily lives.

Show Enthusiasm

Interaction with different others improves when the participants are *enthusiastic* about the interaction. Many students merely tolerate such interaction or avoid it entirely. Enthusiastic students look forward to the stimulation that diversity brings. Enthusiasm can help people overcome the discomfort that results from making mistakes or saying something wrong.

Resolve Conflicts

Conflicts with different others can arise no matter how well-intentioned people are. Learn more about ways to resolve conflicts. Too often we get into a mode of treating conflicts as win–lose situations. We want to win. We want them to lose. Don't look at conflict as a win–lose proposition. Instead, look at it as a win–win situation and a chance for creative cooperation.

Summary Tips For Mastering College

Diversity in Culture and Ethnicity

1. Value diversity among people. Think how boring the world would be if we all were the same. Know how collectivists and individualists can interact with each other more effectively.
2. Prejudice is ugly. Treat people as individuals, not as members of a cultural and ethnic group.
3. If you are an international student, give yourself time to adapt to this new culture. Develop a support system and get involved in campus life.

Diversity in Gender

1. Accept that we live in a changing gender world.
2. Avoid stereotyping males and females. Being sexist is not part of being a competent human.
3. Know your gender role orientation and be comfortable with it. If you aren't comfortable with it, change it.
4. Women can improve their lives by not using male standards to judge their competence, retaining their relationship skills, improving their self-motivation, and not putting up with sexual harassment.
5. Men can improve their lives by retaining their self-motivated strengths, improving their relationship skills, and understanding their emotions better.

Diversity in Sexual Orientation

1. Recognize that there is a continuum of sexual orientation from exclusively heterosexual to exclusively homosexual. Sexual orientation is not always a fixed decision. Homosexual and heterosexual people often are very similar.
2. Our society often has attached a stigma to being homosexual or bisexual. Gay, lesbian, and bisexual people may benefit from joining a campus organization involved with their concerns. Some heterosexuals need to be more tolerant of homosexuals and vice versa. Taking a course on human sexuality might achieve this goal.

Diversity in Age

1. Returning students should recognize that their knowledge and experience can make valuable contributions in college.
2. Strategies for returning students include evaluating their support system, making new friends, getting involved in campus life, and asking for help.

Strategies for Improving Relations with Diverse Others

1. Assess your attitudes and evaluate whether you are prejudiced.
2. Engage in perspective taking.
3. Seek intimate contact by sharing worries, successes, coping strategies, and your daily lives.
4. Respect differences and don't look at them as deficits.
5. Don't overlook similarities.
6. Seek more knowledge about people who are different from you.
7. Treat people as individuals instead of stereotyping them.
8. Be enthusiastic and motivated to interact with different others in positive ways.
9. Resolve conflicts by seeking creative opportunities to overcome differences.

College Success Checklist

Have your views changed since you completed this checklist at the beginning of the chapter? Place a check mark beside any item for which you feel good about your current practice. Also check any item for which you have new ideas about how to improve.

____ I value diversity among people.

____ I treat people as individuals first rather than as members of a cultural or ethnic group.

____ I don't think I am sexist; for example, I always show respect to females and males.

____ I am satisfied with my gender role orientation.

____ I know what women need to do to improve their lives.

____ I know what men need to do to improve their lives.

____ I do not engage in sexually harassing tactics.

____ I am comfortable with my sexual orientation.

____ I can articulate the issues returning students face in achieving success in college.

____ I know how to communicate comfortably with a student who has a disability.

____ I know what strategies I can use to improve my relationships with others of a different background.

In the space below, list items that you still need to work on the most. This list may help you complete the goal-setting exercise in the Learning Portfolio.

Review Questions

1 How can individualists and collectivists interact more effectively with each other?

2 What types of diversity initiatives have been implemented on college campuses?

3 How can international students adapt to college in the United States?

4 What is androgyny? What are some alternatives to androgyny?

5 How can women's lives be improved? How can men's lives be improved?

6 What are some characteristics of sexual orientation? What are some similarities between heterosexuals and homosexuals? How can gays, lesbians, and bisexuals effectively adjust to college?

7 What are some issues and concerns involving returning students?

8 What are some strategies for improving relations with diverse others?

Learning Portfolio

Learning by Reflecting... Journal Entries

Evaluate Your Attitudes Toward Different Others

No matter how well-intentioned we are, life circumstances produce some negative attitudes toward others. Think about people from cultural and ethnic backgrounds different from yours, people of the other sex, people with a sexual orientation different from yours, and people of different ages.

- Do you have any negative attitudes toward these people? If so, which ones?
- Did the negative attitude come from one bad encounter with someone you decided was representative of the group?
- Have you learned any prejudices by modeling the attitudes of others you admire?
- What will it take for you to eliminate your negative attitudes toward this group or person?

Improving Relations with Different Others

We described a number of ways that you can improve your relations with different others. Review these strategies and describe

- Which strategies you have used in the past
- Which strategies you have never used
- Which three strategies you think will help you develop better relations with different others

Your Own Experiences with Discrimination and Prejudice

What life experiences have you had with discrimination and prejudice? Describe them. The discrimination might have been directed at you, or perhaps you saw someone else experience it. What were the consequences? If the discrimination took place in school, did anyone do anything about it? The discrimination doesn't have to be about race or gender. You might have been discriminated against because of the part of the country you are from, the way you dress, the way you wear your hair, or for other reasons. When you were discriminated against, how did it make you feel?

Learning by Doing... Action Projects

Seeking Common Ground

Identify someone who comes from a different cultural and ethnic background from you. It might be a classmate, someone who lives in your neighborhood, or someone in an interest group you attend. Ask him or her to sit down and talk with you for 15 minutes. Tell them this involves a requirement for a college class you are taking. Your conversation objective: Establish how similar you are in as many ways as you can. Describe the identity of the person and discuss your similarities in your Learning Portfolio.

Shaping Gender in Childhood

Get together a group of students that includes both sexes. Have the members of the group express their views on how they would raise their child in terms of gender roles. Traditional? Androgynous? Would they play down gender? Write the views of the group in your Learning Portfolio.

Checking Out Campus Groups

What organizations exist on your campus for

- International students
  _____
  _____
- Students of color
  _____
  _____
- Homosexuals and bisexuals
  _____
  _____
- Returning students
  _____
  _____
- Students with disabilities
  _____
  _____

Go the campus activities office and obtain information about one or more of these groups.

Learning by Thinking Critically... Critiques

Seek Multiple Explanations

Good critical thinkers often seek multiple or alternative explanations of something. They avoid believing something is due to a single cause. For example, consider 19-year-old Tom, a Native American. He dropped out of college midway through his first year. Suppose you heard someone say, "Tom quit college because he wasn't smart enough to do college work."

- Is this statement a valid judgment or an unfortunate stereotype?
- Generate at least three other reasons Tom might have quit college.
- Speculate about how you can find out for certain which factors are responsible.

Examine Generalizations About Gender

In one of the short quotations in this chapter, author Dolores Hitchens commented that if you are going to generalize about women, you will find yourself up to here in exceptions. Consider the following statement in a recent magazine article: "Males are better than females at math."

- Is this an overgeneralization?
- Does it mean that all men are better than all women at math?
- If you are a man, have you known any women who are better than you at math?
- If you are a woman, have you known any men who are worse than you at math?
- Does it mean that the difference is due to biology?
- What can be done to provide females with better opportunities in math and science?

Identifying Biases

Many things we hear about culture, ethnicity, gender, sexual orientation, age, and disability are subjective and biased. Go through some newspapers and magazines. Find one or more articles about these topics. Critically evaluate the articles. Do they contain stereotyped statements about the group involved?

Learning by Thinking Creatively... Personal Vision

Collaborate to Improve the Lives of College Students with Disabilities

A common misconception about creativity is that artists always work alone. Creativity can come from groups and can be sparked by collaborating with others. Get several students together. Generate a novel way that your college can improve the lives of students with a disability. Try to include a student with a disability in your collaborative creative strategy session. Record some ideas here that you will take to the discussion.

_____
_____
_____
_____
_____
_____
_____

Create a Responsible Ad

Advertisements have not always been kind to people from ethnic minority groups, women, the elderly, and people with disabilities. They are often underrepresented in ads. They often are stereotyped when they are included. Create an ad that includes people from one or more of these groups and does not include stereotypes.

Brainstorm Across Generations

Get together a group of students of different ages. Try to include at least one student over 50. Brainstorm about solving problems and concerns of returning students. Are the brainstorming contributions of students of different ages similar or different?

Learning by Planning... Goal Setting

Review the results of the Self-Assessment you completed in this chapter. Also review the College Success Checklist. What can you conclude about things you need to do to improve your skills?

What goal do you want to select from this chapter for making positive changes that will help you master the college experience? (*Hint: Is your goal challenging, reasonable, and specific?*)

___

What strategies will you use to achieve your goal? (*Hint: Can you organize your strategy into a series of smaller goals?*)

___

What obstacles may be in your way as you attempt to make these positive changes?

___

What additional resources might help you succeed in achieving your goal?

___

By what date do you want to accomplish your goal?

___

How will you know you have succeeded?

___

Resources for Mastering the College Experience

Culture and Ethnicity

Racism on Campus (April 19, 1993) by Mel Elfin with Sarah Burke, U.S. News & World Report.
Includes interviews with many students about the nature of ethnic and racial realities at American colleges.

Psychology and Culture (1994) by Walter Lonner & Roy Malpass (Eds.). Boston: Allyn & Bacon.
Includes articles about people from many different cultures and ethnic groups. Discusses prejudice and the stress encountered when people enter a new culture.

Understanding Culture's Influence on Behavior (1993) by Richard Brislin. Ft. Worth, TX: Harcourt Brace.
Includes strategies for communicating more effectively with different others. By a leading authority on cross-cultural communication.

Gender

American Association of University Women, 111 Sixteenth Street, Washington, DC 20036.
Promotes education and equity for girls and women.

The Complete Handbook for College Women (1994) by Carol Weinberg. New York: NYU Press.
An excellent resource guide to college for women, including living in a diverse environment, ethnicity and culture, and disabilities. Author is director of residential living at Goucher College.

The Mismeasure of Woman (1992) by Carol Tavris. New York: Touchstone.
Proposes that women have been measured too much by men's standards, so women's strengths have been undervalued.

National Association for Women in Education, Suite 210, 1325 185th St. NW, Washington, DC 20036-6511; 202-659-9330.
Provides information and assistance in fighting sexual harassment.

National Women of Color Association, Department of Women's Studies, 336 North Hall, University of Wisconsin LaCrosse, LaCrosse, WI 54601; 608-785-8357.
An association of women from diverse ethnic groups. Publishes a newsletter and shares research information about women of color.

The New Male (1980) by Herb Goldberg. New York: Signet.
Important messages to men to improve their health, well-being, and relationships with others.

A New Psychology of Men (1995) by Ronald Levant and William Pollack (Eds.). New York: Basic Books.
Features many different facets of men's lives and positive strategies for coping more effectively with life as a man.

The Psychology of Women (1998) by Michelle Paludi. Upper Saddle River, NJ: Prentice-Hall.
Valuable insights about sexual harassment from a leading expert.

Sexual Orientation

National Lesbian, Gay, and Bisexual Student Caucus, 815 Fifteenth St. NW Suite 838, Washington, DC 20005; 202-347-USSA.
An advocacy group for homosexual and bisexual rights and issues.

Parents and Friends of Lesbians and Gays Federation (P-Flag), Box 77605, Washington, DC 20038; 202-638-4200.
A support group for parents and friends of homosexuals.

Permanent Partners (1988) by Betty Berzon. New York: Plume.
How lesbian and gay couples can make their relationships work.

Our Sexuality (1999, 7th ed.) by Robert Crooks and Karla Bauer. Pacific Grove, CA: Brooks Cole.
Includes details about the nature of homosexuality and bisexuality.

Age

The Adult Experience (1997) by Janet Belsky. Pacific Grove, CA: Brooks/Cole.
Explores many aspects of how we develop as adults, including socioemotional and lifestyle changes.

The Adult Learner on Campus (1992) by Jerold Apps. New York: Cambridge.
What it is like to be a nontraditional-aged student on campus.

New Horizons: The Education and Career Planning Guide for Adults (1985) by William Haponski and Charles McCabe. Princeton, NJ: Peterson's.
Evaluates the nature of education for nontraditional-aged students. Examines career strategies.

Internet Resources

http://www.public.iastate.edu/~savega/multicul.htm

http://latino.sscnet.ucla.edu/diversity1.html
Two sets of comprehensive links to other sites concerning multicultural issues.

http://www3.arcade.uiowa.edu/gw/comm/GenderMedia/tvfilm.html
Explores how gender is treated in the popular media. University of Iowa.

http://www.planetout.com
World-wide on-line community for gay, lesbian, and bisexual people.

http://www.ubp.com
The Universal Black Pages; resources, news, and lists of organizations for Black students.

http://www.latinolink.com
Latinolink; information, chat forums, and bulletin boards of interest to Latino and Hispanic students.

http://www.mit.edu:8001/afs/athena.mit.edu/user/i/r/irie/www/aar.html
Discusses issues related to Asian-American students.

http://galaxy.einet.net/GJ/disabilities.html
Comprehensive resource for students with disabilities.

Being Physically and Mentally Healthy

CHAPTER 12

✓ College Success Checklist

Place a check mark beside the items that apply to you. Leave the items blank that do not apply to you.

____ I live a healthful style of life.

____ I exercise regularly.

____ I get enough sleep.

____ I eat right.

____ I don't smoke.

____ I don't take drugs.

____ I make the right sexual decisions.

____ I cope effectively with stress.

____ I have high self-esteem.

____ I am emotionally intelligent.

____ I am not depressed.

____ I know how to talk with someone who is contemplating suicide.

____ I know how to seek help for mental health problems.

Preview

Your health is important for your college success. This includes both your physical health and your mental health. Making the right physical and mental health decisions will help you to master your college experiences.

Chapter Outline

Images of College Success: Arnold Schwarzenegger

Physical Health
- Know Your Health Style and Your Body
- Exercise
- Sleep
- Eat Right
- Don't Smoke
- Avoid Drugs
- Make the Right Sexual Decisions

Mental Health
- Cope with Stress
- Have High Self-Esteem
- Be Emotionally Intelligent
- Get Rid of Depression
- Understand Suicide
- Seek Help for Mental Health Problems

Self-Assessments
- 12.1 What Is Your Health Style?
- 12.2 Do You Abuse Drugs?
- 12.3 How Emotionally Intelligent Are You?
- 12.4 Is Depression a Part of Your Life?

On-Target Tips
- Motivating Yourself to Exercise
- How to Sleep Better
- Improving Your Self-Efficacy
- What to Do When Someone Is Contemplating Suicide

Images of College Success
Arnold Schwarzenegger

One of the world's most popular movie stars is Austrian-born body-builder Arnold Schwarzenegger. After graduating from high school in Austria, Arnold joined the Austrian army. At the age of 20 he became the youngest man to win the Mr. Universe contest.

He moved to the United States. With fellow body-builder Franco Columbo, Schwarzenegger founded a bricklaying business called Pumping Bricks. With money saved and borrowed, Arnold also started a mail-order business in fitness books and videocassettes.

Arnold Schwarzenegger

Arnold wanted to become better educated. At the age of 26, he attended college part-time. His regular study routine included time for working out and eating right. He stayed with his rigorous exercise program even through intense study periods. Arnold said that working out helped him to blow off steam and clear his mind. Then when he studied, he could concentrate better.

Seven years later he earned his bachelor's degree in business and international economics from the University of Wisconsin–Superior. Along the way, Arnold took English lessons, developed a rehabilitation-through-weight-training program at California prisons, and was national weight training coach for the Special Olympics. He said that until you help someone like the people with disabilities who participate in the Special Olympics, you have no idea how good it can make you feel.

In addition to parlaying his body-building prowess into movie stardom, Schwarzenegger has been chairman of the President's Council on Physical Fitness and Sports. How does Arnold keep in shape now that his body-building contest days are over? He works out for an hour each day with weights and does a cardiovascular activity such as rowing, running, or hiking.

Physical Health

> *Nothing can be changed until it is faced.*
>
> **James Baldwin**
> **American novelist, 20th century**

If you are like a lot of college students, you are not nearly as healthy as you could be. In a recent national survey, almost one of every two first-year college students said their health could be improved (Sax & others, 1995).

Good health requires good health habits. By making some lifestyle changes you may be able to live a much longer, healthier, happier life. In fact, as many as 7 of the 10 leading causes of death (such as heart disease, stroke, and cancer) can be reduced by lifestyle changes.

Most of us have knowledge about health that we could be applying more effectively to our own lives. Consider that, in one study, most college students said that they never would have a heart attack or a drinking problem, but that other college students would (Weinstein, 1984). The following lifestyle patterns have been linked with poor health in college students:

- Skipping breakfast or regular meals
- Relying on snacks as a main food source
- Overeating
- Smoking
- Abusing alcohol and drugs
- Avoiding exercise
- Not getting enough sleep

Young adults have some hidden health risks. Ironically, one risk stems from the fact that they often bounce back quickly from physical stress and abuse. This can lead them to push their bodies too far and neglect their health. The negative effects of abusing one's body do not always show up immediately. However, at some point later we may pay a stiff price.

Know Your Health Style and Your Body

To evaluate your health style, take Self-Assessment 12.1.

How did you fare on the health style test? Are you putting your health knowledge to work with good health habits? If you had low scores on the test, ask yourself some frank questions. Low scorers probably are not doing all they can to be healthy.

However well or poorly you scored, be sure to seek medical help promptly when you have a detectable problem. For example, seek medical attention without delay if you (Vickory & Fries, 1996)

- Develop a lump in your breast
- Have unexplained weight loss
- Experience a fever for more than a week
- Cough up blood
- Encounter persistent or severe headaches
- Have fainting spells
- Develop unexplained shortness of breath

In some circumstances, these symptoms can signal a cancer or other problems. In many cases, though, a thorough medical exam will confirm that nothing serious is wrong.

> *After 30, a body has a mind of its own.*
>
> **Bette Midler**
> **American actress, 20th century**

Self-Assessment 12-1

What Is Your Health Style?

The following brief test was developed by the Public Health Service. Its purpose is to help you gauge how well you are doing in your effort to stay healthy. The behaviors covered in the test are recommended for most people, although some of them may not apply to people with chronic diseases or disabilities, or to pregnant women.

Instructions: For each item, check one box:
- A = Almost always
- S = Sometimes
- N = Almost never

EXERCISE/FITNESS

	A	S	N
1. I maintain a desired weight, avoiding overweight and underweight.	3	1	0
2. I do vigorous exercises for 15 to 30 minutes at least three times a week (examples include running, swimming, brisk walking).	3	1	0
3. I do exercises that enhance my muscle tone for 15 to 30 minutes at least three times a week (examples include yoga and calisthenics).	2	1	0
4. I use part of my leisure time participating in individual, family, or team activities that increase my level of fitness (such as gardening, bowling, golf, and baseball).	2	1	0

■ Exercise/fitness score: _____

EATING HABITS

	A	S	N
1. I eat a variety of foods each day, such as fruits and vegetables, whole-grain breads and cereals, lean meats, dairy products, dry peas and beans, and nuts and seeds.	4	1	0
2. I limit the amount of fat, saturated fat, and cholesterol I eat (including fat in meats, eggs, butter, cream, shortenings, and organ meats such as liver).	2	1	0
3. I limit the amount of salt I eat by cooking with only small amounts, not adding salt at the table, and avoiding salty snacks.	2	1	0
4. I avoid eating too much sugar (especially frequent snacks of candy or soft drinks).	2	1	0

■ Eating habits score: _____

ALCOHOL AND DRUGS

	A	S	N
1. I avoid drinking alcoholic beverages *or* I drink no more than one or two drinks a day.	4	1	0
2. I avoid using alcohol or other drugs (especially illegal drugs) as a way of handling stressful situations or the problems in my life.	2	1	0
3. I am careful not to drink alcohol when taking certain medicines (for example, medicine for sleeping, pain, colds, and allergies), or when pregnant.	2	1	0
4. I read and follow the label directions when using prescribed and over-the-counter drugs.	2	1	0

■ Alcohol and drugs score: _____

CIGARETTE SMOKING	A	S	N
If you never smoke, enter a score of 10 for this section and go the next section on stress control.			
1. I smoke only low-tar and low-nicotine cigarettes *or* I smoke a pipe or cigars.	2 ☐	1 ☐	0 ☐

■ Smoking score: _____

STRESS CONTROL	A	S	N
1. I have a job or do other work that I enjoy.	2 ☐	1 ☐	0 ☐
2. I find it easy to relax and express my feelings freely.	2 ☐	1 ☐	0 ☐
3. I recognize early and prepare for events or situations likely to be stressful for me.	2 ☐	1 ☐	0 ☐
4. I have close friends, relatives, or others whom I can talk to about personal matters and call on for help when needed.	2 ☐	1 ☐	0 ☐
5. I participate in group activities (such as church and community organizations) or hobbies that I enjoy.	2 ☐	1 ☐	0 ☐

■ Stress control score: _____

SAFETY	A	S	N
1. I wear a seat belt while riding in a car.	2 ☐	1 ☐	0 ☐
2. I avoid driving while under the influence of alcohol and other drugs.	2 ☐	1 ☐	0 ☐
3. I obey traffic rules and the speed limit when driving.	2 ☐	1 ☐	0 ☐
4. I am careful when using potentially harmful products or substances (such as household cleaners, poisons, and electrical devices).	2 ☐	1 ☐	0 ☐
5. I avoid smoking in bed.	2 ☐	1 ☐	0 ☐

■ Safety score: _____

Total your score separately for each of the six health styles and then evaluate your scores as follows:

9–10   Your health style in this area is excellent. You not only are aware of the importance of this area to your health but also are practicing good health habits in the area.

6–8   Your health style in this area is good but you have room for improvement. Look at the items you answered with "Sometimes" or "Almost Never." What changes can you make in this area to improve your health style?

3–5   Your health is at risk in this area. Seek help for your health problems in this area.

0–2   Your health is at serious risk in this area. You need to change your health-compromising behaviors. Go to your health or counseling center for help with your problems.

On Target Tips

Motivating Yourself to Exercise

- ■ *Make exercise a high priority in your life.* Give exercise a regular place in your schedule. Don't let unimportant things interfere with your exercise routine. Don't make excuses. In a national survey of first-year college students, regular exercise was related positively to good health (Astin, 1993). Heavy TV viewing was linked with poor health.

- ■ *Chart your progress.* Record each of your exercise sessions in a systematic way. Use a notebook or a calendar, for example. This practice can help you to maintain the momentum you need to work out regularly.

- ■ *Make time for exercise.* It is easy to sabotage your own commitment to exercise with excuses. If your excuse is, "I don't have time," find time. Ask yourself, "Am I too busy to take care of my health? What do I lose if I lose my health?"

- ■ *Learn more about exercise.* The more you know about exercise, the more you are likely to continue it. Examine the Resources at the end of this chapter and read more about exercise.

Exercise

Exercise will do you good. It can be aerobic or anaerobic. *Aerobic exercise* is moderately intense, sustained exercise that stimulates your heart and lungs. Jogging, cycling, and swimming are aerobic. Many health experts recommend that you raise your heart rate to 60% of its maximum. Your maximum heart rate is calculated as 220 minus your age, times .6. Thus, if you are 20, aim for an exercise heart rate of 200 times .6, which is 120. If you are 45, strive for an exercise heart rate of 175 times .6, or 105. What exercise heart rate should you aim for?

$$(220 - \text{your age}) \times .6 = \underline{}$$

Anaerobic exercise involves quick or intense movement. This includes doing push-ups or running a 100-yard dash. In contrast, running a long distance is mainly aerobic. Aerobic exercise has significant cardiovascular benefits and burns fat (what you want for weight loss). Anaerobic exercise builds muscle tissue but does not help you lose weight. Many exercise activities are both aerobic and anaerobic. For example, tennis, basketball, and circuit training (circulating among different exercise machines and stations), have both aerobic and anaerobic benefits. Figure 12.1 shows some common exercise activities and whether they are mainly aerobic or anaerobic.

If you don't exercise, how can you motivate yourself to get going? "Motivating Yourself to Exercise" gives some tips.

Before you begin any exercise program, consult a doctor. Do this especially if you are overweight or have a history of health problems. Finding time for exercise is important to a healthful life.

Sleep

Most of us have occasional sleepless nights. Maybe we feel a lot of stress and can't sleep soundly. In this case, we don't deliberately lose sleep. However, many college students deliberately have a sleepless night now and then when they pull an all-nighter to cram for a test. In a national survey, more than 80% of first-year college students said they stayed up all night at least once during the year (Sax & others, 1995).

How Much Sleep Do You Need? The amount varies from person to person. Most students need at least seven hours of sleep to function competently (Maas, 1998).

Why Might You Be Having Sleep Problems? As many as 1 in 5 students have *insomnia*, a sleep disorder that involves an inability to sleep. Alcohol, nicotine,

Make exercise a high priority in your life. It is easy to get caught up in academic college life and neglect your physical health. Exercise has excellent physical and mental benefits.

Some Common Aerobic and Anaerobic Exercise Choices

AEROBIC	ANAEROBIC
Walking, Jogging, Biking, Swimming, Rowing, Aerobics, Cross-Country Skiing	Weight Lifting, Sprinting: (Running or Swimming) Calisthenics: (Push-ups, Sit-ups, Pull-ups)

Figure 12.1

and caffeine can interfere with your sleep. For example, drinking before you go to sleep keeps you from getting a full night of restful sleep. Stress also can cause sleep problems.

For more on good sleep, see "How to Sleep Better."

Eat Right

Among the best nutrition guidelines are the *Dietary Guidelines for Americans*, issued by the U.S. Department of Health and Human Services. They were first published in 1980 and have been revised every five years. The most recent guidelines support seven principles:

- **Eat a variety of foods.** Use the four basic food groups to evaluate your diet:
  - The milk group (cheese, yogurt, milk)
  - The fruit and vegetable group
  - The grain group (cereals, bread, noodles)
  - The meat group (includes far more than just red meat; also includes poultry, fish, and nuts)

  Healthy adults need to eat at least three servings of vegetables, two of fruit, and six of grain products every day. Megadose supplements of vitamins are no substitute for a healthful diet. Avoid them.

- **Maintain a healthy weight.** Some college students are overweight, others underweight. Preoccupation with dieting can lead to dangerous loss/gain cycles that are hard on your body. Strive to maintain a reasonable, manageable weight.

- **Follow a diet low in fat, saturated fat, and cholesterol.** Unfortunately, many of the best-tasting foods are the worst for you. Fat is big in fried foods (fried chicken, doughnuts), rich foods (ice cream, pastries), greasy foods (spare ribs, bacon), and many spreads (butter, mayonnaise). In contrast, yogurt is low in saturated fat. Cholesterol, a key contributor to heart disease, is found only in animal products, never in plant products.

  Fitness expert Covert Bailey (1991) says that if you throw a pound of butter in a swimming pool, it will float just like a cork. That fat in your body will float in the same way. The

On Target Tips

How to Sleep Better

- *Get into a regular daily routine.* This lets you go to sleep and wake up at approximately the same time each day.
- *Do something relaxing before you go to bed.* Maybe listen to some soft music.
- *Avoid discussing stressful problems before you go to bed.* This includes money or dating problems.
- *Make sure your sleeping area is good for sleeping.* It should have minimum light, minimum sound, and a comfortable temperature.
- *Engage in regular exercise.* However, don't exercise just before going to bed because exercise increases your energy and alertness.
- *Manage your time effectively.* You can get 7-8 hours of sleep every night.
- *Manage your stress.* Stress can rob you of sleep. Learn how to relax and cope with stress effectively.
- *Contact your college health center.* If the above strategies don't work, get some help from health professionals.

We are underexercised as a nation. We look instead of play. We ride instead of walk. Our existence deprives us of the minimum physical activity essential for healthful living.

**John F. Kennedy
U.S. president,
20th century**

fatter you are, the more you will float. Bailey says that he once had a friend who floated so well he could read a book while coasting along on top of the water in a swimming pool.

If you have more than 25% body fat, you will float easily. At 13% or lower, you will sink quickly. Healthy body fat percentages vary for women and men. The highest healthy body fat content is 22% for women, 15% for men. Unfortunately, the average woman has 32% body fat, the average man 23%.

- **Substitute a diet with plenty of vegetables, fruits, and grain products for unhealthful foods.** Replace fatty foods with more healthful sources of starch and fiber. This involves eating grain products, legumes (dried beans, peas), fruits, and vegetables.
- **Use sugar only in moderation.** In addition to table sugar, other common sugar products include brown sugar, syrups, honey, jams, jellies, ice cream, cookies, cakes, and most other desserts. Try eating fresh fruit for dessert instead of sugar-added food. Replace soft drinks with water.
- **Use salt and sodium in moderation.** Some people are sensitive to sodium and are at risk for hypertension (persistent high blood pressure). To reduce the sodium in your diet, eat less salt. Flavor your food with lemon, spices, herbs, or pepper.
- **If you drink alcoholic beverages, do so in moderation.** Moderate drinking means no more than one drink per day for women, two for men. Better yet, don't drink. Heavy drinking can cause a number of health problems. These include cirrhosis of the liver, high blood pressure, pancreas inflammation, stroke, and increased cancer risk. Even moderate daily drinking will impair your ability to study and concentrate. Never drink before you have to study or take a test.

Dieting and the "Freshman 15" The "freshman 15" refers to the approximately 15 pounds that many first-year students gain. The weight often shows up in your hips, thighs, and midsection. Why do first-year students gain this weight? During high school many students' eating habits are monitored by their parents and they eat more balanced meals. Once in college, students select their own diets. Too often their diets consist of chips, chips, and more chips, fast food, ice cream, late night pizza, and beer. Once the extra 15 pounds arrive, what do first-year students do? They diet.

Dieting is a way of life for many college students. Do diets work? Some work in the short run. Over the long haul, most fail.

Does exercise lead to weight loss? Yes! Exercise burns up calories while you are working out. It also raises your metabolic rate (the rate at which your body burns its fuel) for several hours after the workout.

What are some bad dieting strategies? Crash dieting and skipping meals keep you from getting adequate nutrients. Don't jump on every dieting fad that comes along. Poor diets can harm your kidneys and other internal organs. See the Resources at the end of the chapter for more about healthful dieting.

Anorexia Nervosa and Bulimia Nineteen-year-old Andrea gradually eliminated foods from her diet to the point at which she subsisted on jello and yogurt. She spent hours observing her body. She wrapped her hands around her waist to see whether it was getting any thinner. She fantasized about becoming a fashion model. Even when her weight dropped to 80 pounds, Andrea still felt fat. She continued to lose weight and was hospitalized. She was treated for *anorexia nervosa,* an eating disorder that involves the relentless pursuit of thinness through starvation. Anorexia nervosa can eventually lead to death.

Most anorexics are white adolescent or young adult females from well-educated middle- and upper-income families. They have a distorted body image, perceiving themselves as overweight even when they become skeletal. Numerous causes of anorexia nervosa have been proposed (Mussell & Mitchell, 1998). One is the current fashion image of thinness, reflected in the saying, "You can't be too rich or too thin." Many anorexics grow up in families with high achievement demands. Unable to meet these high expectations and control their grades, they turn to something they can control: their weight.

Bulimia is a disorder that involves binging and purging. Bulimics go on an eating binge. Then they purge by vomiting or using a laxative. Sometimes the binges alternate with fasting. However, they can alternate with normal eating. Anorexics can control their eating; bulimics cannot. Bulimia can produce gastric and chemical imbalances in the body, as well as long-term dental damage. Depression is common in bulimics. If you have anorexic or bulimic characteristics, go to your college health center for help.

Don't Smoke

Some frank, stark figures reveal why smoking is called suicide in slow motion:

- Smoking accounts for more than one-fifth of all deaths in the United States.
- Smoking causes 32% of coronary heart disease cases in the United States.
- Smoking causes 30% of all cancer deaths in the United States.
- Smoking causes 82% of all lung cancer deaths in the United States.
- Passive smoke causes as many as 8,000 lung cancer deaths a year in the United States.

More than 50 million Americans smoke cigarettes. In a recent large-scale national survey, daily smoking rates in 19- to 22-year-olds increased from 19% in 1993 to 23% in 1994 (Johnston, O'Malley, & Bachman, 1996). Smoking rates have been on the rise in high school students since 1992. That means smoking among college students is likely to increase in the future.

Most smokers want to quit. Can they? Unfortunately, the survey just mentioned offers some more bad news. About half of the smokers seriously had tried to quit smoking but had lost the battle. The immediate addictive, pleasurable effects of smoking are extremely difficult to overcome. There was some good news, though. About half of Americans who ever smoked have quit.

Eat, drink, and be merry, for tomorrow ye shall diet.

Lewis Henry
American writer,
20th century

Staying Out of the *Pits*

"Let's Get Wasted"

Art tells his friend, "It's been a bummer of a week. I blew two tests. I'm depressed. Let's get wasted." And they do. They drink a fifth of gin and pass out. Sound common? Sound harmless?

It's common. It often is not harmless. When students get wasted, they get arrested and go to jail, they have car wrecks, dorm rooms accidentally get set on fire, they flunk out of school, they damage property, and women get raped.

Avoid being friends with someone who likes to get wasted. Stay away from parties where getting wasted is the main objective. If you get tempted, keep in mind all of the things that can go wrong when you lose control and consciousness. Also, keep thinking about how you will feel the next day.

I'm glad I don't have to explain to a man from Mars why each day I set fire to dozens of little pieces of paper, and then put them in my mouth.

**Mignon McLauglin
American humorist and writer, 20th century**

If you are a smoker, how can you quit? Many different strategies have been tried to help people quit smoking. They include drug treatments, hypnosis, and behavior modification. Drug treatments include *nicotine gum*, a prescription drug that smokers chew when they get the urge. Another drug treatment is the *nicotine patch*, a nonprescription adhesive pad that delivers nicotine through the skin. The dosage is gradually reduced over a period of 8–12 weeks. Some smokers, usually light smokers, are able to quit cold turkey. The Resources at the end of the chapter include good information about ways to quit smoking.

Avoid Drugs

We are a drug-using society. Hardly a day goes by when most of us do not take a drug, although we don't always call it that. For example, many cola beverages contain the drug caffeine.

Why Do People Take Drugs? People are attracted to drugs because they help us to adapt to or escape from an ever-changing, stressful environment. Smoking, drinking, and taking drugs can reduce tension and frustration, relieve boredom and fatigue, and help us to ignore the world's harsh realities. Drugs can give us brief tranquility, joy, relaxation, kaleidoscopic perceptions, and surges of exhilaration. They sometimes have practical uses; for example, amphetamines can keep you awake all night to study for an exam. We also take drugs for social reasons. We hope they will make us feel more at ease and happier at parties, on dates, and in other anxious social contexts.

However, the use of drugs for personal pleasure and temporary adaptation can be dangerous. The use can lead to drug dependence, personal distress, and in some cases fatal diseases. What initially was intended for pleasure and adaptation can turn into pain and maladaptation. For example, on a short-term basis, a few drinks help some people to relax and forget about their problems. However, drinking can become an addiction that destroys relationships, careers, minds, and bodies. Ruptured lives and families, permanent liver damage, and depression are common outcomes of alcoholism.

The Increase of Drug Use in College Students Many college students takes drugs (including alcohol) more than they did in high school (Johnston, O'Malley, & Bachman, 1996). Among the reasons for the increased use of drugs among first-year college students are

- Greater freedom from parental supervision
- High levels of stress and anxiety associated with academic and financial concerns
- Peer use of drugs for recreational purposes

Alcohol Alcohol abuse is a special concern. Alcohol is the most widely used drug in our society. More than 13 million people in the United States call themselves alcoholics. Alcoholism is the third leading killer in the United States. Each year about 25,000 people are killed, and 1.5 million injured, by drunk drivers. More than 60% of homicides involve the use of alcohol by either the offender or the victim. About two-thirds of aggressive sexual acts toward women involve the use of alcohol by the offender.

Almost half of U.S. college students say they drink heavily (Johnston, O'Malley, & Bachman, 1996). The drinking takes its toll on them. In a recent national survey of drinking patterns on 140 campuses, almost half of the binge drinkers reported problems that included missing classes, injuries, troubles with police, and unprotected sex. See also Figure 12.2. Binge-drinking college students were 11 times more likely to fall behind in school, 10 times more likely to drive after drinking, and twice as likely to have unprotected sex than college students who did not binge drink. Self-Assessment 12.2 can help you judge whether you are a substance abuser.

If you have a substance abuse problem, what can you do about it?

- **Admit that you have a problem.** This is tough. Many students who have a substance abuse problem won't admit it. Admitting that you have a problem is the first major step in helping yourself.

Alcohol is a good preservative for everything but brains.

Mary Poole
American writer,
20th century

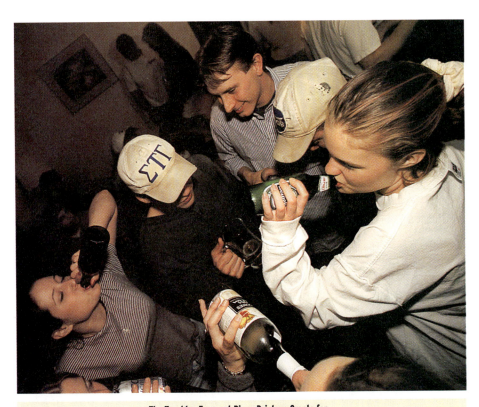

Figure 12.2 The Hazardous Consequences of Binge Drinking in College

The Troubles Frequent Binge Drinkers Create for...

Themselves[1]		and Others[2]	
(% of those surveyed who admitted having had the problem)		(% of those surveyed who had been affected)	
Missed a class	61	Had study or sleep interrupted	68
Forgot where they were or what they did	54	Had to care for drunken student	54
Engaged in unplanned sex	41	Were insulted or humiliated	34
Got hurt	23	Experienced unwanted sexual advances	26
Had unprotected sex	22	Had serious argument	20
Damaged property	22	Had property damaged	15
Got into trouble with campus or local police	11	Were pushed or assaulted	13
Had five or more alcohol-related problems in school year	47	Had at least one of above problems	87

[1]Frequent binge drinkers were defined as those who had had at least four or five drinks at one time on at least three occasions in the previous two weeks.
[2]These figures are from colleges where at least 50% of students are binge drinkers.

Self-Assessment 12-2

Do You Abuse Drugs?

Check *Yes* or *No*.

	YES	NO
I have gotten into financial problems because of using drugs.	___	___
Using alcohol or other drugs has made my college life unhappy at times.	___	___
Drinking alcohol or taking other drugs has been a factor in my losing a job.	___	___
Drinking alcohol or taking other drugs has interfered with my preparation for exams.	___	___
Drinking alcohol or taking drugs is jeopardizing my academic performance.	___	___
My ambition is not as strong since I've been drinking a lot or taking drugs.	___	___
Drinking or taking other drugs has caused me to have difficulty sleeping.	___	___
I have felt remorse after drinking or using other drugs.	___	___
I crave a drink or other drugs at a definite time of the day.	___	___
I want a drink or another drug the next morning.	___	___
I have had a complete or partial loss of memory as a result of drinking or using other drugs.	___	___
Drinking or using other drugs is affecting my reputation.	___	___
I have been in a hospital or institution because of drinking or taking other drugs.	___	___

College students who responded "yes" to these items from the Rutgers Collegiate Abuse Screening Test were more likely to be substance abusers than those who answered "no." If you responded "yes" even to just one of the 13 items on this drug-abuse screening test, you probably are a substance abuser. If you responded "yes" to any items, go to your college health or counseling center for help with your problem.

- **Listen to what others are saying to you.** Chances are that your roommate, a friend, or someone you have dated has told you that you have a substance abuse problem. You probably denied it. They are trying to help you. Listen to them.
- **Seek help for your problem.** There are lots of resources for students who have a substance abuse problem. These include Alcoholics Anonymous, Cocaine Anonymous (CA), Al-Anon, and Rational Recovery Systems. Most towns have one or more of these organizations, which are confidential and are led by people who

have successfully combated their substance abuse problem (Bennett & Miller, 1998). They can help you a great deal. Also, the health center at your college can provide help.

- **Use the resources at the end of the chapter.** Examine the Resources for Reducing Drug Use. They include phone numbers and information about organizations that can help you overcome your problem.

Make the Right Sexual Decisions

Making the right sexual decisions never has been more important than today. AIDS, other sexually transmitted diseases, and unwanted pregnancy pose life-altering challenges (Crooks & Bauer, 1999).

Sexually transmitted diseases (STDs) are diseases that are contracted primarily through sex. This includes intercourse as well as oral–genital and anal–genital sex. STDs affect about 1 of every 6 adults.

We do not recommend wasting time trying to diagnose what kind of STD you may have. There are many. With certain STDs, you may be showing no

If you have sex, be proactive rather than reactive. Use effective contraception and protect yourself against STDs. Promiscuity greatly increases your chances of contracting AIDS and other STDs. Think before you act. Too often enchanted evenings are followed by disenchanted mornings.

Surprised

How Much Do College Students Lie About Whether They Have an STD?

Just asking a date about his or her sexual behavior does not guarantee protection from AIDS and other STDs. In one study of college students, 33% of the men and 10% of the women said they had lied to their date about whether they had an STD (Cochran & Mays, 1990). Much higher percentages (47% of men and 60% of women) said potential sex partners had lied to them about not having an STD. Twenty percent of the men, but only 4% of the women, said they would lie about their AIDS blood test results.

immediate symptoms and yet still pass the disease on to someone else who will suffer. Here are some symptoms for which you should certainly see a doctor or visit a clinic as soon as you can.

Men:

- Foul-smelling, cloudy discharge from the penis
- Burning sensation while urinating
- Painless sore on the penis
- Painful red bumps in the genital region, usually on the penis, turning into tiny blisters containing clear fluid
- Warts in the genital area, either pink/red and soft or hard and yellow/gray

Women:

- Yellow-green discharge from the vagina
- Painless sore on the inner vagina wall or cervix
- Burning sensation during urination
- Painful red bumps on the labia, turning into tiny blisters containing clear fluid
- Warts in the genital area, either pink/red and soft or hard and yellow/gray

AIDS No single STD has had a greater impact on sexual behavior, or created more fear in the last decade, than AIDS. *AIDS* is caused by the human immunodeficiency virus (HIV), which destroys the body's immune system. According to federal health officials, 1 to 1.5 million Americans now are asymptomatic carriers of AIDS. This means they are infected with the virus and can infect others but show no clinical symptoms of AIDS. In 1989, the first attempt to assess AIDS in college students was made (American College Health Association, 1989). Tests of almost 17,000 students found that 30 were infected with the HIV virus. If the 12.5 million students attending college that year were infected in the same proportion, 25,000 students had the HIV virus.

Experts say that AIDS can be transmitted only by (Kalichman, 1996)

- Sexual contact
- Sharing hypodermic needles
- Blood transfusion (which in the last few years has been tightly monitored)
- Other direct contact of cuts or mucous membranes with blood and sexual fluids

The majority of AIDS cases in America continues to occur among homosexual males. However, AIDS recently has increased among female sexual partners of bisexual males or intravenous drug users. For example, in 1994, 18% of patients with AIDS were female, nearly triple the 1984 rate (Centers for Disease Control, 1995). This means that the risk of AIDS is increasing among heterosexual people with multiple sex partners.

It is not who you are, but what you do that puts you at risk for getting HIV. *Anyone* who is sexually active or uses intravenous drugs is at risk. No one is immune.

Beyond abstinence, there is only safer behavior to reduce the risk of AIDS. This includes having sexual intercourse only with an effective condom.

Protecting Against STDs What can you do to reduce the likelihood that you will contract an STD? First, recognize that the only 100% effective strategy is abstinence. But if you are going to have sex, the ways to reduce your chances of being infected are (Crooks & Baur, 1996)

- **Assess your and your partner's risk status.** If you have had previous sexual activity with others, you may have contracted an STD and don't know it. Have you been tested for STDs in general? Remember that many STDs don't produce detectable symptoms. If you care enough to be sexually intimate with a new partner, you should be willing to be open with him or her about your own physical sexual health.

  Spend time getting to know a prospective sexual partner before you have sex with him or her. Ideally, this time frame is at least 2–3 months. Use this time to convey your STD status and inquire about your partner's. Keep in mind that unfortunately many people are not honest about their sexual history.

- **Obtain prior medical examinations.** Many experts on sexuality now recommend that couples who want to begin a sexual relationship abstain from sexual activity until both undergo medical and laboratory testing to rule out the presence of STDs. If cost is an issue, contact your campus health service or a public health clinic in your area.

- **Use condoms.** When correctly used, condoms help to prevent the transmission of many STDs. Condoms are most effective in preventing chlamydia, gonorrhea, syphilis, and AIDS. They are less effective against the spread of genital herpes and genital warts. Recommendations for the effective use of condoms include the following: Put on a condom before any genital contact has occurred; make sure the condom is adequately lubricated; don't blow up the condom or fill it with water to test it for leaks (this stretching weakens the latex); don't unroll the condom first like a sock and then put it on but instead unroll it directly onto the erect penis; twist the end of the condom as it is rolled onto the penis to leave space at the tip; if the condom breaks, immediately replace it; and never reuse a condom.

- **Avoid having sex with multiple partners.** One of the strongest predictors of getting HIV, chlamydia, genital herpes, and other STDS is having sex with multiple partners.

Protecting Against Unwanted Pregnancy Most college students want to control whether and when they have children. That means either abstaining from sex or using effective contraception. Students who feel guilty and have negative attitudes about sexuality are less likely to use contraception than students who have positive attitudes about sexuality. Following are the main contraceptive choices:

- **Abstinence.** This is the only strategy that is 100% effective in preventing unwanted pregnancy.
- **Oral contraceptives.** Advantages of birth control pills are a high rate of effectiveness and low interference with sexual activity.

Women who miscalculate are called "mothers."

Abigail Van Buren
American advice columnist,
20th century

However, the pill can have adverse side effects for some women, such as blood clots, nausea, and moodiness.

- **Condoms.** A main advantage is protection against STDs. A small proportion of condoms break. Improve protection by using a spermicide with condoms.
- **Diaphragm.** This consists of a latex dome on a flexible spring rim that is inserted into the vagina with contraceptive cream or jelly. The diaphragm must be fitted by a skilled medical practitioner. The diaphragm has few negative side effects and a high effectiveness rate when used properly. A cervical cap is like a miniature diaphragm that fits over the cervix.
- **Spermicides.** These include foam, suppositories, creams, and jellies that contain a chemical that kills sperm. Advantages include a lack of serious side effects. Disadvantages include potential irritation of genital tissues and interruption of sexual activity. Most experts on sexuality recommend not relying on spermicide alone as an effective contraception strategy.
- **IUD.** The intrauterine device (IUD) is a small, plastic device that is inserted into the vagina. The IUD's advantages include uninterrupted sexual activity and simplicity of use. Possible disadvantages include pelvic inflammation and pregnancy complications.
- **Norplant.** Norplant consists of six thin capsules filled with a synthetic hormone that are implanted under the skin of a woman's upper arm. In 1991 it became the first new contraceptive system approved in the United States in 30 years. The implanted capsules gradually release the hormone into the bloodstream over a five-year period to prevent conception. Norplant works almost like a mini birth control pill. Norplant provides highly effective contraception. Its negative effects include potential bleeding and hormone-related side effects.
- **Depo-Provera.** Depo-Provera is an injectable contraceptive that lasts three months. Users have to get a shot every 12 weeks. Depo-Provera is a very effective contraceptive method but it can cause menstrual irregularities.
- **Tubal ligation.** This is the sterilization procedure most commonly done for women. It involves severing or tying the fallopian tubes.
- **Vasectomy.** This is a male sterilization procedure that involves cutting the sperm-carrying ducts.

Figure 12.3 summarizes the effectiveness of these contraceptive methods and lists some other ineffective choices. As it indicates, using no contraceptive method, trying to withdraw the penis just before ejaculation, and periodic abstinence are not wise contraceptive strategies. If you are sexually active, compare the various contraceptive methods and choose the method that is best for you based on safety and effectiveness.

Mental Health

It's important for your college success to be not only physically healthy, but also mentally healthy. What can you do for your mental health?

Contraception choices
The following are birth control methods and their failure rates in one year of average use:

Method	Unintended-pregnancy rate*
No Method (Chance)	85.0
Spermicides	30.0
Withdrawal	24.0
Periodic Abstinence	19.0
Cervical Cap	18.0
Diaphragm	18.0
Condom	16.0
Pill	6.0
IUD	4.0
Tubal Ligation	0.5
Depo-Provera	0.4
Vasectomy	0.2
Norplant	0.05

* Figures are based on women of reproductive age, 15 to 44. Rates vary with age. Failure rates with perfect use are lower, but people rarely use methods pefectly.

Figure 12.3 Contraceptive Choices and Their Effectiveness

Cope with Stress

According to the American Academy of Family Physicians, two-thirds of all office visits are for stress-related symptoms. Stress also is a major contributor to heart disease, accidental injuries, and suicide.

What are the most common stressors for college students? In a recent study, the academic circumstances creating the most stress for students were (Murphy, 1996)

- Tests and finals
- Grades and competition
- Professors and class environment
- Too many demands
- Papers and essay exams
- Career and future success
- Studying

In this same study, the personal circumstances creating the most stress for students were

- Intimate relationships
- Finances
- Parental conflicts and expectations
- Roommate conflicts

In another recent study, the first year was by far the most stressful year of college for students (Sher, Wood, & Gotham, 1996).

> *The ultimate measure of a man is not where he stands in moments of comfort and convenience, but where he stands at times of challenge and controversy.*
>
> **Martin Luther King, Jr.**
> **Clergyman and civil rights leader, 20th century**

Coping with stress is essential to making your life more productive and enjoyable. Coping means managing difficult circumstances, solving personal problems, and reducing stress and conflict. Not everyone responds the same way to stress. Some of us have better strategies than others. The good news is that if you do not currently cope with stress effectively you can learn effective strategies (DeLongis & Newth, 1998). Before we talk about the positive ways to cope with stress, let's look at some typically unsuccessful ways to cope with a stressful problem:

- Repress it so you won't have to think about it.
- Take it out on other people when you feel angry or depressed.
- Keep your feelings to yourself.
- Tell yourself the problem will go away.
- Refuse to believe what is happening.
- Try to reduce tension by drinking and eating more.

Fortunately, there are successful coping strategies as well.

Perceive Stress as a Challenge Rather Than a Threat Consider how first-year students view stress differently. Antonio sees an upcoming test as stressful; Anna sees it as a challenge. Greta views a D grade on a paper as threatening; Dion perceives the same grade as a challenge to study harder and take better notes. To some extent, then, what is stressful depends on how you interpret events.

To cope successfully we should appraise stressful situations in two steps (Lazarus, 1993, 1998):

Step 1: Is the event harmful, threatening, or challenging? First, we judge whether an event involves

- **Harm** or loss that has already occurred
- A **threat** of some future danger
- A **challenge** to be overcome

For example, if you overslept for an exam yesterday, then you already have done some *harm*. Missing the exam may lower the instructor's opinion of you and present a *threat* to getting a good grade in the course. Or you can appraise the event as a *challenge* and use the circumstance as an opportunity to become acquainted with the instructor. In this case, you may even benefit from what initially appeared to be a hopeless situation.

Step 2: What are our resources? Can we use them effectively to cope with the event? Your coping resources include your own personal coping strategies as well as other people who can help. Try to have a range of resources at your call. This can include friends, family, a mentor, and the counseling center.

Establish an Optimistic Outlook and Think Positively How important is it to be optimistic rather than pessimistic? In one study, college students were initially identified as optimists or pessimists (Peterson & Stunkard, 1986). Then their health was monitored over the next year. The pessimists had twice as many infections and doctors' visits as the optimists.

How can you develop a more optimistic outlook? Optimism expert Martin Seligman (1991) believes the key is to use positive thinking to challenge self-defeating thoughts. This strategy gets you to avoid ruminating and wallowing in self-pity when bad things happen. Another good strategy is to dispute your negative thoughts (Ellis, 1996). Pessimists tend to use absolute, all-encompassing terms to describe their defeats. They often use words like *never* and *always*. If this sounds like you, talk back to these negative thoughts in a self-confident, positive way that will get rid of self-blame and negative feelings.

Thinking positively helps to put you in a good mood and improves your self-esteem. It also gives you the sense that you are controlling your environment rather than letting it control you. Thinking positively improves your ability to learn. A negative outlook increases your chances of getting angry, feeling guilty, and magnifying your mistakes.

Talk positively to yourself. It can help you reach your full potential. Monitor your self-talk because uncountered negative thinking has a way of becoming a self-fulfilling prophecy. That is, if you tell yourself you can't do something well, you won't. How can you monitor your self-talk? At random times during the day, ask yourself, "What am I saying to myself right now?" Moments that you anticipate will be potentially stressful are excellent times to examine your self-talk. Figure 12.4 provides some examples of how positive self-statements can be used to replace negative ones.

Increase Your Self-Efficacy Self-efficacy is the belief that you can master a situation and produce positive outcomes. Albert Bandura (1994, 1998), a leading psychologist, has shown that self-efficacy is a key factor in solving many personal problems. These include improving low grades, developing better eating habits, and getting into a regular exercise routine.

How can you increase your self-efficacy? "Improving Your Self-Efficacy" gives some helpful steps (Watson & Tharp, 1996).

Seek Social Support Family members, friends, classmates, and coworkers can help us cope. In stressful times, they can reassure you that you are a valuable person who is loved. Knowing that others care about you can give you the confidence to tackle stressful circumstances.

Consider Juan, who was laid off from three jobs in three years. By all accounts he should be down in the dumps. Yet he says he is a happy person. When asked his secret in the face of adversity and stress, Juan says his secret lies in the support of a wonderful family and some great friends.

On Target Tips

Improving Your Self-Efficacy

■ *Select something you expect to be able to do.* Don't pick something you don't think you can accomplish. Later, as your self-efficacy develops and becomes stronger, you can tackle projects you previously thought were hopeless. For example, a person who wants to remain sober concentrates on not drinking for one day at a time. Twenty-four hours of sobriety is easier to attain than lifelong freedom from alcohol.

Do you have more than one problem you want to cope with more effectively? If so, make a list of the problems you expect to have the most and least difficulty with. If possible, start with the easier situations. Cope with the harder situations after you have experienced some success with a self-efficacy strategy. The list might include developing better study habits, reducing anger, and exercising more. If you think it will be easier to develop better study habits, then work on that first.

■ *Distinguish between your past performance and your present project.* You may have learned from past failures that you cannot do certain things. It is very important to remind yourself that past failures are just that: in the past. You now have a new sense of confidence and accomplishment.

The only value of looking at past failures is to develop a better strategy for now and the future. For example, a college student who repeatedly has failed to lose 30 pounds on a diet should avoid thinking, "I'll always fail; this weight is just me." On the other hand, the overweight student might recall that the failures came after a few days of starvation diets. The student then embarks on a more sensible, competent dieting strategy that includes exercise.

■ *Keep good records.* This helps you to be aware of your successes in a concrete way. Frustrated with being poorly organized and not studying enough, Dean tries to stay on a reasonable study schedule. After sticking to the schedule for four days, he doesn't make it on the fifth day. He labels himself a failure, but his recordkeeping shows that he actually has an 80% success rate.

Figure 12.4

Some Examples of How You Can Replace Negative Self-Statements with Positive Self-Statements

Situation	Negative Self-Statement	Positive Self-Statement
Having a long, difficult assignment due the next day	"I'll never get this work done by tomorrow."	"If I work real hard I may be able to get it done by tomorrow." "This is a tough challenge, but I'm up to it." "Look at all I've managed to accomplished so far."
Having to participate in class discussion	"Everyone else knows more than I do, so what's the use of saying anything?"	"I have as much say as anyone else in the class." "It's O.K. to be nervous; I'll relax as I start talking." "I might come up with a brand new idea."
Not getting into a social club or organization	"I guess they don't like me. I don't know what I will do."	"I guess a lot of students get turned down; it's so competitive." "I'm going to look at some other social groups that I might be able to get into." "I misjudged that group. I though they had good taste!"
Moving away from family and friends	"I'm leaving my whole life behind me. I'm so depressed."	"Just think of all the new people I'm going to meet." "I'll miss everyone but I can still stay in touch." "I'm likely to learn a lot about myself living away from home."
Breaking up with someone you love	"I don't have anything to live for. He/she was all I had."	"I really thought our relationship would work, but it's not the end of the world." "I'll just have to keep myself busy and not let it bother me." "There are a lot of other fish in the sea."

Recognize the potential support in your own life. Learn how to draw on these resources in times of stress. Sometimes you can improve your ability to cope by joining community groups, interest groups, or informal social groups that meet regularly (Taylor, 1995).

Relax We usually think of relaxation as something like unwinding in front of the TV set or taking a quiet walk in the evening. These activities can be relaxing. However, a different form of relaxation also can help college students to cope with anxiety and stress. It is called *deep relaxation*.

Try the following to attain a deep relaxed state (Davis, Eshelman, & McKay, 1995):

- In a quiet place, either lie down on a couch or bed or sit in a comfortable chair with your head supported.

- Get in a comfortable position and relax. Clench your right fist tighter and tighter for about five seconds. Now relax it. Feel the looseness in your right hand. Repeat the procedure with your left hand. Then do it with both hands. When you release the tension, let it go instantly. Allow your muscles to become limp.

- Now bend your elbows and tense your biceps. Tense them as hard as you can. After a few seconds, relax and straighten out your arms. Go through the procedure again. Tighten your biceps as hard as you can for a few seconds and then relax them. Just as with your biceps, do each of the following procedures twice.

- Turn your attention to your head. Wrinkle your forehead as tightly as you can. Then relax it. Next, frown and notice the strain it produces. Close your eyes now. Squint them as hard as you can. Notice the tension. Now relax your eyes. Let them stay closed gently and comfortably. Now clench your jaw and bite hard. Notice the tension throughout your jaw. Relax your jaw.

- Shrug your shoulders. Keep the tension as you hunch your head down between your shoulders. Then relax your shoulders.

- Breathe in and fill your lungs completely. Hold your breath for a few seconds. Now exhale and let your chest become loose. Repeat this four or five times. Tighten your stomach for several seconds. Now relax it.

- Tighten your buttocks and thighs. Flex your thighs by pressing your heels down as hard as you can. Relax and feel the difference. Next, curl your toes downward, making your calf muscles tight. Then relax. Now bend your toes toward your face, creating tension in your shins. Relax again. To avoid muscle cramping, don't overtighten your toes.

ZIGGY © 1982, 1995 ZIGGY AND FRIENDS, INC. Dist. by UNIVERSAL PRESS SYNDICATE. Reprinted with permission. All rights reserved.

Some students have limited success when they start to use deep relaxation. But with practice, deep relaxation usually works. Initially you may need 20–30 minutes to reach a deeply relaxed state, but eventually many students can become deeply relaxed in 2–3 minutes. The Resources section at the end of the chapter provides further information about deep relaxation. *Note:* If you have high blood pressure and are taking medication for it, do not do the deep relaxation exercise because it could lower your blood pressure too far.

Use Multiple Coping Strategies Sometimes a single coping strategy will make a big dent in your problems. However, don't hesitate to use more than one strategy.

Have High Self-Esteem

College includes many circumstances that can lower your self-esteem. *Self-esteem* involves your general evaluation of yourself. It is also called *self-worth* or *self-image*. Struggling with negative feedback or even outright failure can create a feeling of incompetence even in the most accomplished student. Most of

The time to relax is when you don't have any.

**Sydney J. Harris
English-born American
newspaper writer,
20th century**

the time these minor setbacks have only a temporary impact on our overall sense of well-being. However, chronic low self-esteem can result in anxiety, depression, and even suicide.

If you have low self-esteem, here are five ways to increase it (Bednar, Wells, & Peterson, 1995):

- **Identify the causes.** Identifying the sources of low self-esteem is critical to increasing self-esteem. Is your low self-esteem the result of bad grades? Is it a consequence of living with people who constantly criticize you? If so, then explore ways to change these sources.

- **Define important areas of competence.** Students have the highest self-esteem when they perform competently in the areas of their life that are important to them. If doing well in school feels important to you, then doing well academically will increase your self-esteem. If the social area is important to you, having a great social life will increase your self-esteem. Consider Arnold Schwarzenegger's example. He did not settle for physical superiority. He took college courses in business to give him added competence and self-esteem to launch a film career.

- **Get emotional support and social approval.** Emotional support and social approval can increase your self-esteem. When people say nice things to us, are warm and friendly to us, and approve of what we say and do, our self-esteem improves. Sources of emotional support and social approval are friends, family, classmates, counselors, and others we interact with.

Identify the causes of low self-esteem.

Perform competently in the areas of life that are important to you.

Get emotional support and social approval.

Achieve and learn skills.

Cope effectively with problems.

Figure 12.5 **How to improve your self-esteem.**

- **Achieve.** Achievement boosts self-esteem. The straightforward learning of skills increases achievement and self-esteem. For example, learning better study skills can improve your achievement and your self-esteem.
- **Cope.** Our self-esteem also increases when we tackle a problem. Coping makes us feel good about ourselves. When we avoid coping with problems, they mount up and lower our self-esteem.

Be Emotionally Intelligent

In his book *Emotional Intelligence*, Daniel Goleman (1995) argues that when it comes to predicting a person's competence, IQ as measured by standard IQ tests may matter less than what he calls emotional intelligence. Goleman says that *emotional intelligence* involves emotional self-awareness, managing emotions, reading emotions, and handling relationships. Emotional self-awareness is especially important in Goleman's view because it allows us to exercise some self-control. The idea is not to repress feelings, but become aware of them so that we can cope effectively. No emotional intelligence test has been devised along the lines of IQ tests, but Self-Assessment 12.3 will provide you with some insights.

The personal costs of deficits in emotional intelligence can range from problems in marriage and parenting to poor health. Lack of emotional intelligence can sabotage the intellect and ruin careers. The good news, says Goleman, is that emotional intelligence is not fixed at birth and can be nurtured and strengthened.

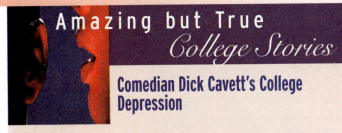

Amazing but True College Stories

Comedian Dick Cavett's College Depression

Comedian and TV talk-show host Dick Cavett has battled depression off and on in his adult life. His first encounter with depression was in his first year of college. Dick grew up in Nebraska and went to Yale. It was a difficult adjustment. He had been a star in high school but was behind a lot of his classmates at Yale, not only academically but also socially. There were times when Cavett felt like he was in a hole and never would get out. He felt like the world was caving in on him.

He got involved in the college's theater group and had a very supportive friend. Slowly, he began to catch up academically and socially. The confidence that he had in high school began to come back. He went on to become a famous comedian and talk-show host.

Watching Dick Cavett perform in front of audiences, telling jokes and interviewing famous people, it is difficult to imagine that he has had serious bouts of depression. He continues to take medication for his depression, which has kept the disorder in check.

Get Rid of Depression

Depression is all too common among college students. In one recent study, depression was linked with poor academic performance (Haines, Norris, & Kashy, 1996). Consider Sally. She was depressed for several months and nothing seemed to cheer her up. Sally's depression began when the person she planned to marry broke off their relationship. Her emotional state deteriorated to the point at which she didn't feel like getting out of bed most mornings. She started missing a lot of classes and got behind in all of them. One of her friends noticed how sad she was. She got Sally to go to the counseling center at her college for help.

Each of us feels blue or down in the dumps some of the time. These brief bouts are normal occurrences of sad feelings or discontent with the way our life is going. If the sad feelings last only for a few hours, a few days, or a few weeks, mental health professionals don't classify a person as depressed. But if the sad feelings linger for a month or more, and you feel deeply unhappy and demoralized, you probably are in depression. A person with depression often has

- Changes in sleep patterns
- Changes in appetite
- Decreased energy
- Feelings of worthlessness
- Problems in concentrating
- Guilt feelings

It is hard to make people miserable when they feel worthy of themselves.

Abraham Lincoln
U.S. president,
19th century

Self-Assessment 12-3

How Emotionally Intelligent Are You?

Goleman describes four important domains of emotional intelligence: emotional self-awareness, managing emotions, reading emotions, and handling relationships. Score each of the following items from 1 (very much unlike me) to 5 (very much like me):

	1	2	3	4	5
Emotional Self-Awareness					
I am good at recognizing my emotions.	__	__	__	__	__
I am good at understanding the causes of my feelings.	__	__	__	__	__
I am good at separating my feelings from my actions.	__	__	__	__	__
Managing Emotions					
I am good at tolerating frustration.	__	__	__	__	__
I am good at managing my anger.	__	__	__	__	__
I have positive feelings about myself.	__	__	__	__	__
I am good at coping with stress.	__	__	__	__	__
My emotions don't interfere with my ability to focus and accomplish my goals.	__	__	__	__	__
I have good self-control and am not impulsive.	__	__	__	__	__
Reading Emotions					
I am good at taking other people's perspectives.	__	__	__	__	__
I show empathy and sensitivity to others' feelings.	__	__	__	__	__
I am good at listening to what other people are saying.	__	__	__	__	__
Handling Relationships					
I am good at analyzing and understanding relationships.	__	__	__	__	__
I am good at solving problems in relationships.	__	__	__	__	__
I am assertive (rather than passive, manipulative, or aggressive in relationships).	__	__	__	__	__
I have one or more good close friendships.	__	__	__	__	__
I am good at sharing and cooperating.	__	__	__	__	__

Scoring and Interpretation:
Add up your scores for all 17 items. Total Emotional Intelligence Score:
If you scored 75–85, you are very emotionally intelligent. You probably are excellent at understanding your own emotions, managing your emotions, reading others' emotions, and handling relationships. If you scored 65–74, you have good emotional intelligence, but there probably are some areas that you still need to work on. Look at the items you scored 3 or below to see where you need to improve. If you scored 45–54, you have only average emotional intelligence. Give some serious thought to working on your emotional life. Examine your emotional weaknesses and work on improving them. If you scored 44 or below, you have very weak emotional intelligence. Your lack of emotional intelligence probably is interfering with your competence. If your emotional intelligence scores are in the average or very weak range, consider talking with a counselor at your college about ways you can improve it.

Depression is so widespread that it is called the common cold of mental disorders (Nolen-Hoeksema, 1998). More than 250,000 people in the United States are hospitalized every year for the disorder. Students, professors, and laborers get depressed. No one is immune to depression, not even great writers like Ann Sexton and Ernest Hemingway, or famous statesmen like Abraham Lincoln and Winston Churchill.

A man's lifetime risk of having depression is 10%. A woman's lifetime risk is much greater: almost 25%. Many people with depression suffer unnecessarily because depression can be treated effectively. To evaluate whether depression is a part of your life, complete Self-Assessment 12.4.

Understand Suicide

The rate of suicide in the United States has tripled since the 1950s. Each year about 25,000 people in the United States take their own lives. As many as two of every three college students say they have thought about suicide on at least one occasion. Immediate and highly stressful circumstances can produce suicidal thoughts. These include the loss of a partner, a spouse, or a job, flunking out of school, or an unwanted pregnancy. In many cases, suicide or its attempt has multiple causes (Maris, 1998).

Consider Brian, who just flunked two of his college courses. His parents had high achievement expectations for him, but his father was not supportive when the grades came in. He harshly criticized Brian and told him he had not put enough effort into his classes. This past weekend, Brian's girlfriend broke off their long-standing relationship. He became depressed and began to think about putting an end to his life.

If you know someone like Brian, what should you do? Some guidelines are offered in "What to Do When Someone Is Contemplating Suicide."

On Target Tips

What to Do When Someone Is Contemplating Suicide

- ■ *Stay calm.* In most cases, there is no rush. Sit and listen, *really* listen, to what the person is saying. Be understanding and emotionally support the person's feelings.

- ■ *Deal directly with the topic of suicide.* Most people have mixed feelings about death and are open to help. Don't be afraid to ask or talk directly about suicide.

- ■ *Encourage problem-solving and positive actions.* Remember that the person in the crisis is not thinking clearly. Encourage the person to refrain from making any serious, irreversible decisions while in the crisis. Talk about the alternatives that might create hope for the future.

- ■ *Get assistance.* Although you want to help, don't take full responsibility by being the sole counselor. Seek out resources, such as your college counseling center, for help. Do this even if it means breaking confidence. Let the troubled person know that you are very concerned. Say that you are so concerned that you are willing to get help beyond what you can offer.

- ■ *Emphasize that unbearable pain can be survived.* Say that the suicide crisis is temporary. Unbearable pain can be survived.

Seek Help for Mental Health Problems

When should you seek professional help? There is no easy answer to this question. However, as a rule, seek psychological help

- ■ If you are psychologically distressed
- ■ When you feel helpless and overwhelmed
- ■ If your life is seriously disrupted by your problems

Arizona State instructor Nancy Felipe Russo (left), shown here with a student she is advising, has been a leader in calling for greater attention to the roles of gender and sociocultural factors in depression. She has chaired the National Coalition of Women's Health. A man's lifetime risk of developing depression is 10%, a woman's 25%. Depression is the most common mental health diagnosis for white women and women of color in the United States. What factors do you think contribute to the much higher rate of depression in women than men?

Self-Assessment 12-4

Is Depression a Part of Your Life?

Below is a list of the ways you might have felt or behaved in the *last week*. Indicate what you felt by checking the appropriate box for each item, as follows: Column A for "Rarely or None of the Time (Less Than 1 Day)"; column B, "Some or a Little of the Time (1–2 Days)"; column C, "Occasionally or a Moderate Amount of the Time (3–4 Days)"; or column D, "Most or All of the Time (5–7 Days)."

DURING THE PAST WEEK: A   B   C   D

1. I was bothered by things that usually don't bother me.
2. I did not feel like eating; my appetite was poor.
3. I felt that I could not shake off the blues even with help from my family and friends.
4. I felt that I was just as good as other people.
5. I had trouble keeping my mind on what I was doing.
6. I felt depressed.
7. I felt that everything I did was an effort.
8. I felt hopeful about the future.
9. I thought my life had been a failure.
10. I felt fearful.
11. My sleep was restless.
12. I was happy.
13. I talked less than usual.
14. I felt lonely.
15. People were unfriendly.
16. I enjoyed life.
17. I had crying spells.
18. I felt sad.
19. I felt that people disliked me.
20. I could not get going.

Scoring: After completing the Depression Scale, for items 1, 2, 3, 5, 6, 7, 9, 10, 11, 13, 14, 15, 17, 18, 19, and 20 give yourself a 0 each time you checked Rarely or None, 1 each time you checked Some or a Little, 2 each time you checked Occasionally or Moderate, and 3 each time you checked Most or All of the Time. Then for items 4, 8, 12, and 16, give yourself a 3 each time you checked Rarely or None, 2 each time you checked Some or a Little, 1 each time you checked Occasionally or Moderate, and a 0 each time you checked Most or All of the Time. Total up your score for all 20 items.

Interpretation: If your score is around 7, then you are like the average male in terms of how much depression you have experienced in the last week. If your score is around 8–9, your score is similar to the average female. If your score is 16 or more, you might benefit from professional help for the depression you are experiencing.

Who are the mental health professionals you can turn to for help? A number of different professionals can help students with their mental health problems. They include clinical psychologists, counselors, social workers, and psychiatrists. Clinical psychologists, counselors, and social workers use a number of psychotherapy strategies to help students but they do not prescribe drugs. Psychiatrists are medical doctors who often prescribe drugs in treating students' emotional problems. They also can conduct psychotherapy.

The counseling or health center at your college is a good place to contact if you think that you have a mental health problem. The counseling or health center probably will have one or more counselors, clinical psychologists, social workers, or psychiatrists on its staff to help you, or they will refer you to a mental health professional in the community. Figure 12.6 shows the reasons college students on one campus sought counseling.

Some students may not admit that they have problems, or seek help for their problems, because they fear others will think they are weak. It takes courage to face your problems. Instead of a weakness, consider it a strength to admit that you have a problem and are willing to seek help for it. You will be doing something about a problem that is interfering with your college success.

Making changes can be hard. Be patient and allow some time for professional help to work. Part of the success of therapy involves developing a positive relationship with the therapist, so it may take several sessions for you to notice a change. Also, if you do seek professional help, continue to evaluate how much it is benefitting you. Not all therapists and therapies are alike. If you become dissatisfied, you always can ask to be referred to someone else. More information about mental health professionals is provided in the Resources section at the end of the chapter.

Feeling *Good*

By Putting the Ideas in This Chapter into Action

Of all the chapters in this book, this one spells out the specific strategies for feeling good. Put the ideas in this chapter into action and you will feel good physically and mentally. For example, regular exercise makes you feel good, both physically and mentally. Eating right makes you feel good physically and mentally. Using the strategies we described to cope with stress will make you feel good. Following the steps to reach a deep relaxation state will make you feel good. Reducing your anxiety will make you feel good.

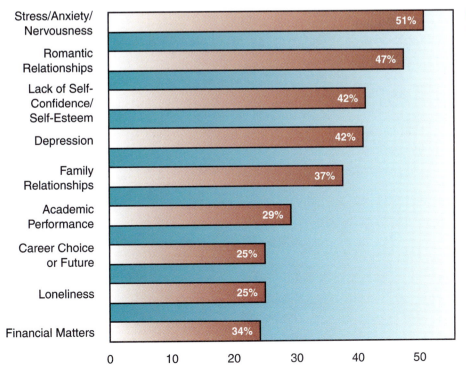

Figure 12.6 College Students' Main Reasons for Seeking Counseling

- Stress/Anxiety/Nervousness: 51%
- Romantic Relationships: 47%
- Lack of Self-Confidence/Self-Esteem: 42%
- Depression: 42%
- Family Relationships: 37%
- Academic Performance: 29%
- Career Choice or Future: 25%
- Loneliness: 25%
- Financial Matters: 34%

Summary Tips For Mastering College

Being Physically and Mentally Healthy

Being Physically Healthy

1. Know your body and the warning signs of bad health. Seek medical help immediately if you have a detectable problem. Lifestyle plays an important role in health. Know your lifestyle. Commit to a new style if you had any low scores on the health style test.
2. Make exercise a high priority.
3. Manage your time so that you get 7–8 hours of sleep a night.
4. Eat right. Know the dietary guidelines for healthful eating and follow them. If you diet, do it sensibly and combine it with exercise.
5. Don't smoke. Quitting is difficult but it can be done.
6. Avoid drugs. Watch out for the trap of using drugs to cope with stress.
7. Make the right sexual decisions. Increase your understanding of sexually transmitted diseases and protect yourself against them by assessing your and your partner's risk status, obtaining prior medical exams, using condoms, and avoiding sex with multiple partners. Protect yourself against unwanted pregnancy by abstaining from sex or using effective contraceptive methods.

Being Mentally Healthy

1. When you are stressed, recognize the stress rather than repressing your awareness of it, see it as your own problem rather than taking it out on others, express your feelings, acknowledge that the problem may not go away by itself, and notice whether the stress is causing you to eat or drink more and, if so, curtail these actions.
2. Perceive stress as a challenge rather than as a harm or threat. Evaluate your resources and determine how you can use them effectively to cope with stress.
3. Among the effective ways to cope with stress are to think optimistically and positively, increase your self-efficacy, seek social support, and learn deep relaxation. It is a good idea to use more than one coping strategy.
4. Have high self-esteem. You can increase your self-esteem by identifying the causes of low self-esteem, performing competently in the areas of your life that are important to you, getting emotional support and social approval, achieving, learning new skills, and coping.
5. Be emotionally intelligent. Become aware of your emotions and manage them. Learn to read others' emotions and to understand relationships.
6. Be aware of what depression is and how to cope with it. Know what to do if someone becomes depressed and contemplates suicide.
7. Seek help for a mental health problem. Do this if you are psychologically distressed, feel helpless and overwhelmed, or feel your life is seriously disrupted by a problem. The counseling center at your college is a good place to go if you have a mental health problem. Consider it a strength, not a weakness, if you seek help for a mental health problem.

College Success Checklist

Have your views changed since you completed this checklist at the beginning of the chapter? Place a check mark beside any item for which you feel good about your current practice. Also check any item for which you have new ideas about how to improve.

____ I have a healthful style of life.

____ I exercise regularly.

____ I get enough sleep.

____ I eat right.

____ I don't smoke.

____ I don't take drugs.

____ I make the right sexual decisions.

____ I cope effectively with stress.

____ I have high self-esteem.

____ I am emotionally intelligent.

____ I am not depressed.

____ I know how to talk with someone who is contemplating suicide.

____ I know how to seek help for mental health problems.

In the space below, list items that you still need to work on the most. This list may help you complete the goal-setting exercise in the Learning Portfolio.

Review Questions

1 When should students seek medical help? What is your health style?

2 What can students do to exercise, sleep, and eat better?

3 What are smoking's effects on health? Why do students take drugs? Are you a substance abuser?

4 What can you do to protect yourself from sexually transmitted diseases and unwanted pregnancy?

5 What are the most effective ways to cope with stress?

6 How can you improve your self-esteem, be emotionally intelligent, and get rid of depression?

7 How can you tell if you have a mental health problem? Who are the mental health professionals who can help you with such a problem?

Learning Portfolio

Learning by Reflecting... Journal Entries

Making Sexual Decisions

Think about the kinds of sexual decisions you have made:

- What is the best sexual decision you have made?
- What is the worst sexual decision you have made?
- What do you predict will be the most important sexual decision you will have to make in the next year? What will your choice be?

Examining Your Coping Style

This is a good time to take stock of your coping style. Think about your life in the last few months. When stressful circumstances have come up, how have you handled them in general?

- Did you appraise them as harmful, threatening, or challenging?
- Did you repress the stress or did you consciously make an effort to solve the problems?
- Did you refuse to believe what was happening?
- Did you try to reduce the stress by eating and drinking more?
- Did you call on effective coping strategies and have the resources necessary to deal with the problem? If so, what resources did you use?

Evaluating Your Self-Esteem

Examine the following aspects of your self-esteem.

- How high or low is your self-esteem? To help you answer this question, ask yourself the following:

    How much do I think I'm a person of worth?

    How much do I think I have good qualities?

    How positive or negative is my attitude about myself?

    How useless or effective am I?

- What factors contributed to your level of self-esteem?
- If you have low self-esteem, what will it take to improve your self-esteem? In answering this question, think about the description of ways to improve self-esteem in the text.

Learning by Doing... Action Projects

Keep an Eating Journal

Write down everything you eat for a week. Include when you eat (time of day), how much you eat, where you eat, who you are with when you eat, and the mood you are in when you are eating. At the end of the week, rate how good your nutrition style is (based on what you read in the chapter) on the following scale:

```
1  2  3  4  5  6  7  8  9  10
Bad Nutrition          Good Nutrition
Style                  Style
```

If you do not have a good nutrition style, map out a plan that you will commit to and follow it.

Use the Resources at the End of the Chapter

This chapter ends with a large number of helpful resources. Look them over, then

- Call one or more of the telephone numbers listed and find out what services, brochures, and advice are available.
- Read one of the books and write a summary of what you learned from it in your Learning Portfolio.

Visit the Health and Counseling Centers at Your College

Find out where the health and counseling centers are at your college. Record their addresses.

_____
_____
_____
_____
_____
_____

Stop by and find out what services and materials are available. Describe the services in your Learning Portfolio. Ask for copies of any health or mental health brochures that interest you.

Learning by Thinking Critically... Critiques

Examine Some Books on Dieting
Look through some popular books on dieting. The best place to find these is at a trade bookstore. Your college bookstore may have some dieting books and your library also may have some. Critically evaluate whether the program they recommend is safe and healthful. How much is exercise promoted as part of the weight loss strategy?

What Should You Tell Your Date?
If someone has herpes, should the person tell his or her date? Does the date have a right to know? If you think the person should tell his or her date, what is the best way to do this?

Becoming More Aware of Problems
Too many people are not aware that they have personal problems. How can we help people become more aware of their problems? What thinking strategies would you recommend to someone for becoming more aware of problems they need to cope with? Record some ideas here.

_____
_____
_____
_____
_____
_____
_____
_____
_____

Learning by Thinking Creatively... Personal Vision

Make Your College Healthier
Imagine that your college has just been given $100,000 to improve the health of its students. You are on the committee that decides how the money should be spent. Collaborate with several other students to create innovative ways to use the money effectively.

Become a Movie Producer
Imagine that you are a screenwriter with a major studio. Your task is to create a movie on coping and mental health. Describe the movie by writing a short treatment of it. Give it a title.

Develop Creative Slogans or Logos
Food and beverage companies often come up with creative ad campaigns to help sell their products. For example, think about Joe Camel, who is supposed to be a cool customer, and the Budweiser frogs and ants, who try to make you laugh and feel good. Get together with a group of other students and brainstorm about a creative campaign for encouraging students to quit smoking or quit drinking. Think of a logo or slogan to go with your campaign. Like the commercial companies, you might want to include animals in your creative venture. List some ideas here to take to the group.

_____
_____
_____
_____
_____
_____
_____
_____

Learning by Planning... Goal Setting

Review the results of the Self-Assessments you completed in this chapter. Also review the College Success Checklist. What can you conclude about things you need to do to improve your skills?

What goal do you want to select from this chapter for making positive changes that will help you master the college experience? *(Hint: Is your goal challenging, reasonable, and specific?)*

_____
_____
_____
_____
_____

What strategies will you use to achieve your goal? *(Hint: Can you organize your strategy into a series of smaller goals?)*

_____
_____
_____
_____
_____
_____
_____
_____
_____
_____

What obstacles may be in your way as you attempt to make these positive changes?

_____
_____
_____
_____
_____

What additional resources might help you succeed in achieving your goal?

_____
_____
_____
_____
_____

By what date do you want to accomplish your goal?

_____

How will you know you have succeeded?

_____
_____
_____
_____

Resources for Mastering the College Experience

Your Body and Health Style

American Public Health Association, 418 E. 76th Street, New York, NY 10021; 212-734-1114.
  Offers books, manuals, and pamphlets on many health topics.

The Psychology of Women's Health (1995) by Annette Stanton and Sherly Gallant (Eds.). Washington, DC: American Psychological Association.
  Explores many health issues—such as AIDS, smoking, exercise, eating disorders, heart disease, and alcohol use—from a woman's perspective.

Power Sleep: The Program that Prepares Your Mind for Peak Performance (1998) by James Maas. New York: Villard.
  This very recent book urges you to get the sleep you need to perform optimally as a college student.

Exercise

The Aerobics Program for Well-Being (1985) by Kenneth Cooper. New York: Bantam.
  Age-adjusted recommendations for aerobic exercise. *The New Aerobics for Women (1988)* by Kenneth and Mildred Cooper tailors aerobics activities for women.

Nutrition, Dieting, and Eating Disorders

The New Fit or Fat (1991, rev. ed.) by Covert Bailey. Boston: Houghton Mifflin.
  Ways to become healthy by eating sensibly and engaging in regular exercise routines. Solid, no-nonsense advice is offered.

American Anorexia/Bulimia Association, 418 E. 76th St., New York, NY 10021; 212-734-1114.
  Provides information and referral services related to anorexia nervosa and bulimia. Publishes the *American Anorexia/Bulimia Association Newsletter*.

Reducing Drug Use

Cocaine Helpline, 800-COCAINE (262-2463).
  A 24 hour-a-day hotline answered by former cocaine addicts. Refers cocaine users to treatment centers in many parts of the United States.

National Clearinghouse for Alcohol and Drug Information, 800-729-6686.
  Excellent information on alcohol and drug abuse.

National Institute on Drug Abuse Hotline, 800-662-4357.
  A hotline of immediate feedback about drug-related problems and crises.

Sexuality

AIDS Hotline and National AIDS Information Clearinghouse, P.O. Box 6003, Rockville, MD 20850; 800-342-AIDS, 800-342-SIDA (Spanish), 800-AIDS-TTY (deaf).
  A hotline responding to any questions from children, youths, or adults about HIV infection or AIDS. AIDS pamphlets and other materials are available.

Alan Guttmacher Institute, 111 Fifth Avenue, New York, NY 10003; 212-254-5656.
  An excellent source of information about sexuality. Journal *Family Planning Perspectives* includes a wide range of articles about contraception, pregnancy prevention, and sexually transmitted diseases.

Division of STD/HIV Prevention, National Center for Preventive Services, Centers for Disease Control, Atlanta, GA 30333; 404-639-2564.
  Very up-to-date information about sexually transmitted diseases.

For Yourself (1975) by Lonnie Berbach. New York: Signet.
  Rated by experts as the best self-help book on women's sexuality in a recent national survey. Explains to women how to attain sexual fulfillment.

The New Male Sexuality (1992) by Bernie Zilbergeld. New York: Bantam.
  An excellent, beneficial source of information for any man on male sexuality.

Permanent Partners (1988) by Betty Berzon. New York: Plume.
  Knowledge and understanding to help gay and lesbian couples make their relationships last.

Coping with Stress

Learned Optimism (1991) by Martin Seligman. New York: Pocket Books.
  Specific strategies for learning how to think optimistically. A positive message that because pessimism is learned, it can be unlearned. Includes self-tests to evaluate your optimism, pessimism, and depression.

Letting Go of Stress by Emmitt Miller. P.O. Box W, Stanford, CA 94305; 1-800-TAPES.
  An excellent audiocassette on how to cope with stress by learning how to relax.

The Relaxation & Stress Workbook (1995, 4th ed.) by Martha Davis, Elizabeth Eshelman, and Matthew McKay. Oakland, CA: New Harbinger.
  Many different exercises to help you learn relaxation techniques and improve your ability to cope with stress.

Recommended Music for Relaxation

Listening to soft music can create a relaxed feeling. The following instrumental music tapes are available in many stores:

Spencer Bower: *Emerald Portraits*

Michael Jones: *After the Rain* and *Pianoscapes*

David Lanz: *Nightfall*

George Winston: *Autumn* and *December*

Depression and Suicide

The Feeling Good Handbook (1989) by David Burns. New York: Plume.
Valuable for people who are depressed. Step-by-step exercises to improve your mood. Author is a psychiatrist at the University of Pennsylvania School of Medicine and a leading expert on coping with depression.

National Foundation for Depressive Illness, P.O. Box 2257, New York, NY 10116; 800-248-4344.
Provides information and education about recent medical advances in depression. Also a referral service.

Youth Suicide National Center, 204 E. 2nd Ave., Suite 203, San Mateo, CA 94401; 415-347-3961.
A national developer and clearinghouse for educational materials about suicide. Publishes *Suicide in Youth and What You Can Do About It*.

Self-Esteem

Women & Self-Esteem (1984) by Linda Sanford and Mary Donovan. New York: Anchor Doubleday.
Examines the causes of low self-esteem in women. Gives recommendations to women on how to increase their self-esteem.

Seeking Help for Mental Health Problems

National Institute of Mental Health, Information Resources Inquiries Branch, Room 7C-02, 5600 Fishers Lane, Rockville, MD 20857.
Government publications on many different mental disorders. Catalog available.

National Mental Health Association, 1021 Prince Street, Alexandria, VA 22314-2971; 800-969-NMHA.
Promotes mental health. Distributes pamphlets on mental disorders. Publishes *NMHA Focus* four times yearly to examine mental health issues.

Internet Resources

http://www.wellweb.com/preview/zpre.htm
Current medical research; lifestyle tips; information on diseases and medications.

http://www.plannedparenthood.org
Comprehensive resource on sexual health information; hundreds of indexed links for sexual health questions.

http://www.health.org
Prevention Online; latest information on research about substance use and addiction.

http://www.quitnet.org/quitnetta
Prevention strategies and current research on smoking. Massachusetts Tobacco Control Program.

http://www.io.org/-madmagic/help/help.html
Help! A Consumer's Guide to Mental Health Information on the World Wide Web.

http://www.mhsource.com
Mental Health InfoSource on the World Wide Web.

http://education.indiana.edu/cas/adol/adol.html
Gives referrals to counseling; describes issues affecting teen-age mental well-being.

http://www.somthing-fishy.com/ed.htm
Descriptions, resources, and links about anorexia, bulimia, overeating, and other eating disorders.

Pursuing Academic and Career Success

CHAPTER 13

 College Success Checklist

Place a check mark beside the items that apply to you. Leave the items blank that do not apply to you.

____ I am good at motivating myself.

____ I set realistic short-term and long-term goals.

____ I am an achiever but not a perfectionist.

____ I take responsibility for researching and planning my own academic schedule.

____ I meet regularly with an academic advisor to discuss my academic plan.

____ I have a mentor from whom I feel comfortable seeking advice about both personal and academic concerns.

____ I understand the value of beginning career planning early in college.

____ I have explored different career options.

____ I have talked with a career counselor about occupational choices.

____ I know what skills most employers are looking for in the ideal job candidate.

____ I know what work experiences during college can help me in my career.

Preview

The effort you put forth in college sets the tone for the degree of occupational success you will experience beyond college. Work is what most of us will do with about half of our waking hours for more than 40 years of lives. If you master the ideas in this chapter, you can make your career choices and work life more satisfying and successful.

Chapter Outline

Images of College Success: Bernard Shaw

Achieving

Designing an Academic Path
- Getting the Right Courses
- How Important Is the College Catalog?
- Majors and Specializations in Two-Year and Four-Year Institutions
- Finding a Mentor

Exploring Careers
- Occupational Outlook
- Finding the Right Career Match
- The Ideal Job Candidate
- Getting Positive Work Experiences During College

Self-Assessments
- 13.1 How Goal Directed Am I?
- 13.2 Am I a Perfectionist?
- 13.3 Planning Your Coursework for an Associate Degree or Certificate
- 13.4 Mapping Out a Four- or Five-Year Academic Plan
- 13.5 Matching Your Career Interests with the Fastest-Growing Jobs

On-Target Tips
- Getting Yourself Going
- Getting Rid of Perfectionist Tendencies
- Getting More Satisfaction Later
- Getting What You Want
- Knocking 'Em Dead in an Interview

Images of College Success
Bernard Shaw

Bernard Shaw is the principal Washington anchor for CNN and is one of the nation's most distinguished journalists. Bernard was born in Chicago, where his father was a housepainter and his mother a housekeeper. His high school grades were good and he was considered to be a bright student. However, his parents could not afford to send him to college, so he entered the U.S. Marine Corps.

When he was a 21-year-old marine stationed in Hawaii, he heard that Walter Cronkite, the famous news anchor for CBS, was coming to Hawaii to film a news special. When Shaw was a young boy he had always dreamed of being a major news anchor. He found out where Cronkite was staying and called his room "about 34 times," as he recalled. According to Cronkite, Bernard was the most persistent person he had ever encountered. Cronkite finally relented and gave Bernard five minutes of his time. They ended up spending half an hour talking.

Bernard Shaw's persistence helped him launch an award-winning career in journalism.

At 23, Shaw left the Marines and entered the University of Illinois, choosing history as his major. While carrying a full load of classes, he took an unpaid position at a rhythm-and-blues radio station. Within a few months, the station switched to an all-news format. Later in the year, when Martin Luther King, Jr. came to Chicago, Shaw talked the management of the radio station into hiring him for $50 as a reporter on the scene. Bernard continued to work hard in college and at the radio station, which finally put the relentless young man on their paid staff.

Shaw still abides by the advice his mentor Walter Cronkite gave him early in his career: Read prolifically and remain open and curious about all facets of human existence. Shaw has donated more than $130,000 to the Bernard Shaw Endowment Fund, which he established at the University of Illinois. Shaw also has earned many awards and honors, including a medallion from the University of Kansas for distinguished service.

Achieving

We began this book with a special focus on setting goals and planning. What you will achieve in life and how much you get out of life will depend a great deal on your ability to work toward goals (Harackiewicz, 1998). Your short-term goals can be steps along the way to reaching solid long-term goals. A short-term goal of earning a 3.0 grade point average this term can be part of a larger plan of rising to a 3.5 or 3.9 by the time you graduate from college.

This chapter deals with the long term goals of college and career. Now is a good time to stop and think more about your willingness to embrace big goals. Use Self-Assessment 13.1 to help you do this.

Motivation has been another key theme of this book. You can put yourself in command of your life. When the difficulties of college tempt you to say things like "I can't do this" or "I should never have taken this class," you can turn things around by thinking and speaking in more positive terms: "I'm going to make it." "This is a challenge I will overcome."

External motivation means doing things mainly to satisfy outer demands and other people's wishes–pressures from bosses, parents, society. Better perhaps is the view of an internally motivated person who chooses freely and sees the causes of success or failure in what he or she has done (Brophy, 1998). The internally motivated person sees solutions in the form of personal improvements: "I didn't study hard enough for the last test, but I'll study harder for this one." "I can manage my study time better." This frame of mind can serve you well. See "Getting Yourself Going" (page 347) for some tips on how to keep your motivation high.

Being motivated to achieve does not mean being a perfectionist. *Perfectionists* try to reach unreachable goals. They think in terms of "all or none." They convince themselves that they are never good enough. The result is often overwhelming anxiety, stress, exhaustion, and burnout.

Self-Assessment 13.2 will help you look at any perfectionist tendencies you may have. Of course you're not perfect; no one is. If perfectionism is a problem for you, consider the advice in "Getting Rid of Perfectionist Tendencies" (page 348).

Set realistic short-term goals. Tie them to realistic long-term goals. Be prepared to delay some gratifications for a few years until you have the education that you'll need to achieve your long-term goals. (See "Getting More Satisfaction Later" on page 350 for some delay of gratification strategies.)

Designing an Academic Path

You have a lot of choices to make in college. Some of these choices involve deciding which courses to take.

Getting the Right Courses

With a little effort, you can learn how to select courses that fulfill your requirements and that you really like. Some strategies for making sound course selections are as follows:

Whatever you can do, or dream you can, begin it. Boldness has genius, power, and magic.

Johann Wolfgang von Goethe
German playwright and novelist,
19th century

"When you have been second best for so long, you can either accept it or try to become the best. I made the decision to try to be the best."
–Florence Griffith Joyner, Olympic gold medalist

They can because they think they can.

Virgil
Roman poet,
1st century B.C.

Self-Assessment 13-1

How Goal-Directed Am I?

To find out how goal-directed you are, mark the answer that best describes your behavior in each of these situations. The columns are labeled as follows: Put a check mark in Column A if your answer is "Almost Always Like Me"; in column B if you'd say "Like Me Most of the Time"; column C for "Not Like Me Most of the Time"; and column D for "Hardly Ever Like Me."

	A	B	C	D
When I am faced with small tasks that need attention, I attend to them right away.	___	___	___	___
When I am involved in a project or task that is important to me, I take some time to clarify my objectives.	___	___	___	___
I'm good at not getting bogged down with inconsequential details.	___	___	___	___
When I write down a list of things to do on a given day, I manage to get all of them done.	___	___	___	___
My planning keeps me from saying or doing things I might regret afterward.	___	___	___	___
I can accurately project when projects will get done.	___	___	___	___
I develop both long-term and short-term goals for important things in my life.	___	___	___	___
My responsibilities don't overwhelm me.	___	___	___	___
Give me a deadline and I will meet it.	___	___	___	___
When I am under pressure, I still plan my days and weeks in a clear, logical manner.	___	___	___	___

Scoring: Give yourself 4 points for each time you answered "Almost Always Like Me," 3 points for "Like Me Most of the Time," 2 points for "Not Like Me Most of the Time," and 1 point for "Hardly Ever Like Me."

Total: _____

Interpretation:
35–40 points: You are definitely a goal-directed person. You organize your life and do a good job in planning. In some cases, though, you might be organizing your life to an extreme. Don't forget to smell the roses and take some time to enjoy your college life.
25–34 points: You are above average in being goal directed, although your goal-directed behavior may vary with the situation or activity. Think more about setting goals in all of the important areas of your life.
15–24 points: You need to work on becoming more goal directed. You probably are not reaching your full potential because of your failure to be goal directed.
14 points or below: You might consider yourself a spontaneous or free-spirited person, but you are jeopardizing your college success by not being goal directed. You probably are easily distracted and procrastinate too much. Make a serious commitment to becoming a more goal-directed person.

- **List your constraints.** You might have child care responsibilities or an inflexible work schedule. If so, block out the times you simply can't take classes.
- **Study your options.** Colleges have lists of classes that are required for various specialty diplomas or majors. Examine the college catalog to determine which courses are required for both general education requirements and specific courses in the specialty or major you want to pursue.
- **Register for a reasonable course load.** Many colleges do not charge for additional courses beyond a set number for being a full-time student. You might be tempted to pile on extra courses when you register to save time and money. But think again. By taking too many courses, you may spread yourself too thin.
- **Take the right mix of courses.** Don't load up with too many really tough courses in the same term. Check into how much reading and other time is required for specific courses. If you can't find anyone else who can give you this information, make appointments with the instructors. Ask them what the course requirements are, how much reading they expect, and so on.
- **Talk with your advisor.** Get an appointment with your academic advisor to talk about the courses you prefer. Put together a tentative schedule and questions before you meet with your advisor. Ask the advisor's recommendations about various courses and instructors.

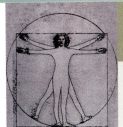

Feeling *Good*

Achieving Because of Me, Not Someone Else

Being internally motivated is a good feeling. Always trying to live up the standards of others makes us anxious and unhappy. When you achieve because *you* want to, not because someone else wants you to, you will be a happier person.

Anthony Taber © 1988 from The New Yorker Collection. All Rights Reserved.

Self-Assessment 13-2

Am I a Perfectionist?

As in Self-Assessment 13-1, Column A represents "Almost Always Like Me"; column B, "Like Me Most of the Time"; column C, "Not Like Me Most of the Time"; column D, "Hardly Ever Like Me."

	A	B	C	D
I am compulsive about keeping things in place and orderly.	___	___	___	___
I have very high standards for my academic work.	___	___	___	___
I have a lot of trouble relaxing.	___	___	___	___
I am afraid I will make a mistake.	___	___	___	___
When I think about things I have to do I get anxious.	___	___	___	___
I make sure every little detail is right in just about everything I do.	___	___	___	___
My standards are so high that I tend to procrastinate.	___	___	___	___
Sometimes I feel like I could cry but I don't want to.	___	___	___	___
I want to get everything right myself and don't like it when other people try to help me.	___	___	___	___
I worry about what will happen if I make a mistake.	___	___	___	___

Scoring: Give yourself 4 points for each time you answered "Almost Always Like Me," 3 points for "Like Me Most of the Time," 2 points for "Not Like Me Most of the Time," and 1 point for "Hardly Ever Like Me."

Total: _____

Interpretation:
35–40 points: You probably are a perfectionist. The anxiety you feel from striving to be perfect probably is interfering with your competence. Be sure to study the tips for reducing your perfectionism. If that doesn't work, contact a counselor at your college for some help.
28–34 points: You have some perfectionist tendencies that may be hampering your college success. Work on letting go of some of your compulsive tendencies.
21–27 points: You also may have a few perfectionist tendencies but they may not be interfering with your college success. Examine your responses to the particular items that you checked "Like Me Most of the Time" or "Almost Always Like Me" to determine the areas in which you can work on being a little less perfectionistic.
20 points or below: You are not a perfectionist.

Many academic counselors are specially trained to advise students about selecting the program that is right for them. They can help you examine a wide range of specialties or majors. They can talk with you about your abilities and interests, and help you find the one that matches what you want to do.

Before you see your academic advisor, make up a list of questions you want answered. These might include

- What classes should I take this term and next?
- What sequence of classes should I take?
- Am I taking too many difficult classes in one term?
- What electives do you recommend?
- What career opportunities are there if I study mainly _____ or _____?

■ **Ask the pros.** The pros in this case are more advanced students in your preferred program. Ask their advice about which courses to take and which instructors are the best. On many campuses, academic departments have undergraduate organizations you can join. If you want to be a biology major, you might consider joining something like the Student Biology Association. These associations are good places to get connected with more advanced students who can advise you about coursework in their area.

"Getting What You Want" on page 352 provides more tips on getting the right courses.

How Important Is the College Catalog?

A college catalog can be a valuable resource for you. If you don't have one, check with your advisor or the admissions office to obtain one. College catalogs usually are published annually or biennially. Be sure to save the catalog that is in effect when you enroll for the first time. Why? Because requirements for specific programs sometimes change and you usually will be held to the degree plan that was in place then. If you have decided on a field or have several fields in mind, turn to the part of the catalog that describes the area of study and the courses required for graduation. The catalog should tell you what the core requirements are for the fields you are interested in, whether there are any prerequisites for the programs, and whether there is a sequence of courses you should follow.

Majors and Specializations in Two-Year and Four-Year Institutions

Whether you are in a two-year or a four-year college, you will need to select a major or specialization.

On Target Tips

Getting Yourself Going

■ *Energize yourself.* Motivated people are energetic. They get things done. Examine your life. How energetic are you? Do you feel tired a lot? If so, an exercise program or healthier eating style might help you overcome your lethargy and give you more energy to achieve.

■ *Talk positively and enthusiastically to yourself.* Use self-talk to motivate yourself. Keep telling yourself that you can do it, that you are making progress, and that you are going to succeed.

■ *Be internally motivated.* You are responsible for yourself and your success. In high school, your parents or teachers may have motivated you. Now it's up to you. Accept the challenge. Be excited about the opportunity to control your destiny.

■ *Commit to effort.* Motivation takes a lot of effort. You can talk all you want about how successful you are going to be, but you never will reach your goals and dreams unless you commit to putting your heart into your work. And the effort is not just temporary. Giving all you've got one day and then slacking off for the rest of the week won't hack it. Being motivated means putting forth your best effort consistently over the entire term.

■ *Read about motivation.* The Resources section at the end of this chapter describes several books on motivation. If you have trouble getting motivated, read one of them to help get you going on the right track.

The world stands aside to let anyone pass who knows where he is going.

**David Starr Jordan
U.S. Senator and president of Stanford University,
20th century**

On Target Tips

Getting Rid of Perfectionist Tendencies

- *Realize that perfectionistic attitudes hurt you.* Challenge these self-defeating thoughts.

- *Set realistic goals that you can obtain.* Make sure they come from you, not someone else, such as your parents.

- *Instead of always aiming for 100%, try for 90% or 80% success.* This helps you to see that your world won't fall apart just because you are not perfect.

- *Emphasize the positives, not just the negatives.* Perfectionists tend to dwell on mistakes, especially small ones. Don't make mountains out of molehills. Toward the end of each day take stock of the positive things you have accomplished.

- *Focus more on the excitement and thrill of learning.* Perfectionists often dwell on the product, the final accomplishment. In learning and life, the journey is just as important as the destination.

Majors and Specializations in Two-Year Colleges

Some students enter a community college with a clear idea of what they want to major or specialize in, but many do not. Some students plan to obtain an associate degree, others pursue a certificate in a specialty field.

The Associate of Arts (AA) degree includes general academic courses that allow students to transfer to a four-year institution. If you plan to transfer, you will need to select that college and study its degree requirements as soon as possible. Students should consult regularly with an advisor at their community college and the four-year institution to ensure that they are enrolling in courses appropriate to their major.

In addition to a core of general education courses, obtaining an AA degree means taking either a concentration of courses in a major (or area of emphasis) such as history, English, psychology, and so on or taking a number of electives. In most community colleges, a minimum of 60 or more credit hours is required for an AA degree. A typical breakdown might be 45 credits in general education and 15 in your major, area of emphasis, or electives. Some community colleges also offer an Associate of Science (AS) degree that requires a heavy science concentration.

Many community colleges also offer certificate programs that are designed for re-entry into the job market or the upgrading of skills. There are many specializations: food and hospitality, graphic communication, press operation, medical record coding, word processing, building property management, travel management, vocational nursing, and others.

"Well, we've finally done it. We've listed two courses, each of which is a prerequisite for taking the other."

The coursework in certificate programs does not include general education requirements, as Associate of Arts and Science programs do. Certificate programs focus specifically on the job skills needed in a particular occupation. The number of credits required varies, but usually is fewer than for an associate's degree.

If you are a community college student, whether you are enrolled in an associate's or certificate program, it is a good idea to map out a plan that lists each of your courses until graduation. Studying your college's catalog and becoming familiar with the requirements for your degree will help you create the plan. With your college catalog in hand, complete Self-Assessment 13.3. Use the Self-Assessment as a starting point in discussing your plans with your academic advisor.

Majors in Four-Year Institutions A college major, or field of concentration, is a series of courses that provides a foundation in an academic discipline. Majors vary in the number of courses required. For example, engineering requires more courses than does history or psychology. They allow you to choose more electives.

Some graduate programs may prefer a specific undergraduate degree. Others may not. For example, law schools admit students from many different undergraduate majors. In contrast, graduate schools in physics require a physics undergraduate degree or a large concentration of physics classes. If you want to be an English teacher in a public high school, you probably need to major in secondary education with a concentration in English.

Many first-year students take a number of general education courses before they invest in courses in their specialty or major. This allows them to broaden their education and have more time to choose their focus.

If you are not certain what you want to focus on, you are not alone. More than two-thirds of first-year college students change their intended majors in the first year. If you are not sure right away, don't panic. When college administrators have you fill out forms during your first year, most let you write "undecided" or "exploring" in the column for a college major. Some four-year institutions have a one- or two-year general education curriculum you can study before you choose a major. But if you are in a four-year program and aren't sure about a major after two years of college, you will begin to find yourself taking extra courses that you may not need when you graduate.

Some students don't want to major in a specific area. They want to pursue a broad range of college courses. Many four-year institutions have individualized majors that allow this. Even individualized majors, though, usually require one or two concentrations of courses. With this constraint, the student's college coursework doesn't become a disconnected patchwork.

Mapping Out a Four- or Five-Year Plan Even though many first-year students do not know what to major in or change majors, it is still a good idea to map out a four- or five-year plan that lists each of your courses every term until

Amazing but True College Stories

It's Noon Thursday. Here Comes the Beer Truck.

One first-year student showed up at college motivated to do well. He never partied much in high school and really did not have plans to party and drink much in college. But things changed quickly. By the luck of the draw, his first roommate's father owned a major national brewery. The roommate conned one of the drivers who worked for his dad's company to deliver several kegs to him each week. Every Thursday around noon the beer truck pulled up and unloaded the kegs. And the party was on.

The student from the beer company family was a fun-loving, persuasive fellow. It didn't take long for him to convince his more naive, serious roommate that he was missing out on a lot of fun. How did it all end? Their parties went on several months before they got thrown out of the dorm. With all Fs at the end of the term, both were kicked out of school.

For several months, as they played and partied, their immediate gratification could not have been greater. But by the end of the term, their failure to delay gratification humbled them.

On Target Tips

Getting More Satisfaction Later

- **Be aware.** Evaluate your decisions over the last few months. Examine the choices you have made about delaying gratification or pursuing immediate gratification. Being aware that you need to delay gratification more is an important step.

- **Make a commitment to change.** If you tend to be impulsive and seek immediate gratification, make a commitment to change your behavior. Tell others about your decision to delay gratification more; they will help you stick to your commitment. You will be tempted to backslide. Plan ahead for ways to deal with the temptation to seek immediate gratification.

- **Monitor and talk to yourself.** Periodically monitor how you are doing with your new commitment to delay gratification. Keep reminding yourself about how good you will feel about yourself if you keep your commitment.

- **Make your commitment last.** Choose specific dates for checking your progress. If your progress isn't favorable, plan a course of action to improve your behavior.

- **Reward yourself.** Once you have successfully met your goals, reward yourself with something you enjoy doing, such as treating yourself to a movie or going out with your friends.

---

graduation. Studying your college's catalog and becoming familiar with requirements in a major that interests you will help you create the plan. You will need to know the general education requirements, required courses in the major, prerequisites for courses, restricted electives, free electives, and other requirements. By planning in this manner, you can take control of your academic planning and give yourself maximum flexibility toward the end of your four or five years of college. The risk in not doing a four- or five-year plan is that you will end up in your junior or senior year with too many courses in one area and not enough in another, which will extend the time needed to get your bachelor's degree. The four- or five-year plan lets you see which terms will be light and which will be heavy, as well as whether you need to take summer courses. It is unlikely that you will carry out the plan exactly. When you do have to make changes, the plan allows you to see the consequences of the changes and what you have to do to stay on track.

The four- or five-year plan is an excellent starting point for sessions with your academic advisor. The plan can be a springboard for questions you might have about which courses to take this term, next term, and so on. If you are contemplating several different majors, make a four- or five-year plan for each major and use the plans to help you decide which courses to take and when. If you are in a four-year institution, complete Self-Assessment 13.4 to map out your plan.

How Do You Know Whether a Major Is Right for You? Make a realistic assessment of your interests and abilities. Are you getting Cs and Ds in biology and chemistry, yet you honestly have put your full effort into those courses? Then pre-med or a science area may not be the best major for you. If you hate the math or computer science class you are taking, you may not be cut out for a career in engineering.

Be somewhat patient, though. The first year of college, especially the first term, is a time of exploration and learning how to succeed in college. Many first-year students who don't do well at first in courses related to a possible major adapt, meet the challenge, and go on to do extremely well in the major. A year or two into your college experience, you should have a good idea of whether the major you have chosen is the right fit for you. At that point, you will have had enough courses and opportunities to know whether you are in the right place.

A good strategy is to seek out students who are more advanced in the field you are considering. Ask them what it's like specializing in that particular area, and ask them about various courses and instructors.

Unfortunately, too many students choose majors for the wrong reasons. Some major in what their parents want them to study. Others major in the field that their friends are going into. Others choose a major because they hear it is easy.

Pursuing Academic and Career Success 349

Self-Assessment 13-3

Planning Your Coursework for an Associate Degree or Certificate

Examine the requirements for the major or certificate you are considering. Then fill in the blanks below with the courses you plan to take. Keep this Self-Assessment and use it to discuss your decisions about which courses to take and when with your academic advisor.

FALL	SPRING	SUMMER
First Year		
Second Year		
Third Year		

On Target Tips

Getting What You Want

- *Register as soon as you can.* Early registration improves your chances of getting the courses you want when you want them.

- *Use computer registration.* Many campuses encourage students to register directly using the campus computer system. This gives you immediate feedback about your scheduling. It may even suggest alternatives if you run into closed courses.

- *Have a backup plan.* Anticipate the courses that might close out (for example, preferred times or popular instructors). Have some other choices you can substitute to meet your requirements.

- *Explore the wait list option.* If you want to get into a closed class, find out your chances for getting into a class if you agree to be put on the wait list. If the odds aren't good, explore other options.

- *Plead your case.* If you get closed out of a class you really want, go directly to the instructor and ask for an exception. Base your request on your intellectual curiosity for the course content, not scheduling convenience. Some instructors may reject your request, but others will listen and try to help you.

What really interests you? It's your life. You have the right to choose what you want to do with it. What do you really want to major in? The courses in your major don't have to be easy for the major to feel right for you. They can be challenging. But you should have a good feeling about your match with the major program. You should be enthusiastic about it and motivated to learn more about the field.

What Do You Need to Know to Transfer to Another College? If you decide that you want to transfer to another college, you will want to know whether the credits you have earned at your current college will transfer to the new college. How well your credits will transfer will depend on the schools and on your major. If you do decide to transfer, be sure to talk with an advisor at the new college about which of your courses will transfer. You also should obtain a catalog for the new college and see how its requirements match up with those of your current college. The catalog will describe transfer requirements. Study it before you meet with an advisor there. Following are some questions you might ask the admissions advisor (Harbin, 1995):

- What are the minimum admission criteria that I have to meet in order to transfer to your college?
- Do I need a minimum grade point average for admission? If so, what is it?
- What are the important application deadlines for transfer admissions?
- Where can I get a transfer application?
- What else can you tell me about transferring to your college?

If you want to change colleges but aren't sure where you want to go, consult some general guides to colleges such as *Peterson's National College Data Bank* or *Barron's Profiles of American Colleges.* Try to visit several campuses that might meet your needs. Talk with students there, as well as an academic advisor. Walk around and get a feel for how you like it. Be clear about what aspects of your current life are unsatisfying and whether the new school will be better.

Finding a Mentor

A mentor is an advisor, coach, and confidant. A mentor can help you become successful and master many of life's challenges. A mentor can advise you on career pursuits, suggest ways to cope with problem situations, and listen to what's on your mind. A mentor might be

- An older student who has successfully navigated the first-year experience
- A graduate student
- An instructor
- Someone in the community you respect and trust

Self-Assessment 13-4

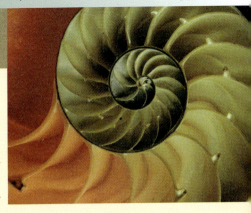

Mapping Out a Four- or Five-Year Academic Plan

Study your college catalog to find out what courses you will need to graduate with a particular major. If you have not selected a major, examine the requirements for the major you are considering. Then fill in the blanks below with the courses you plan to take. Keep this Self-Assessment and use it to discuss your decisions about which courses to take and when with your academic advisor. The plan below is for schools on a semester schedule. If your school is on a quarter system, create your own plan by listing four quarters for each of the four or five years and then filling in the courses you plan to take.

FALL	SPRING	SUMMER
First Year		
_____	_____	_____
_____	_____	_____
_____	_____	_____
_____	_____	_____
Second Year		
_____	_____	_____
_____	_____	_____
_____	_____	_____
_____	_____	_____
Third Year		
_____	_____	_____
_____	_____	_____
_____	_____	_____
_____	_____	_____
Fourth Year		
_____	_____	_____
_____	_____	_____
_____	_____	_____
_____	_____	_____
Fifth Year		
_____	_____	_____
_____	_____	_____
_____	_____	_____
_____	_____	_____

Staying Out of the Pits

A Mentor Saves the Day

Carla did not have much academic guidance while she was growing up. Neither of her parents went to college. Her grades in high school were OK but not great. She went to college mainly because her friends were going.

The first semester in college was eye-opening. Poor study habits and lack of motivation landed her on academic probation. At the beginning of the second term, she was talking with Marta, a third-year student. Marta told Carla that she too had low grades in her first term at college. She said that what turned college around for her more than anything else was finding a mentor. Marta explained to Carla what a mentor is. She told Carla that she would like to mentor her. They hit it off well and began studying together. Marta kept Carla on the right track. She convinced Carla that she needed to manage her time better and set some goals. Marta got Carla to begin thinking about what she wanted to do with her life.

An example of how Marta helped Carla involves the day Carla was sick and missed a test. Carla just was going to blow off the course and not even talk with the professor about making up the test. Marta had Carla call the professor at his office and explain her illness. He allowed her to take a make-up exam.

The mentoring paid off. Carla's second term grades were not earth-shattering, but they were good enough to get her off probation. Carla says that if she had not met Marta, she would have dropped out of college.

If you don't have a mentor, think about the people you have met in college so far. Is there a person you admire whose advice might benefit you? If you don't have anyone in mind right now, start looking around for someone. As you talk with various people and get to know them better, one person's competence and motivation can start to rub off on you. This is the type of person who can be a good mentor.

Exploring Careers

Examining different careers and making the right career choices are critical steps in our lives. Let's explore some different aspects of careers, beginning with the occupational outlook.

Occupational Outlook

It is a good idea to keep up with the occupational outlook for various fields. Get to know which ones are adding jobs and which ones are losing jobs. An excellent source is *The Occupational Outlook Handbook*, which is revised every two years. The following information comes from the 1996–1997 handbook.

Service-producing industries will account for most new jobs. Among service occupations, business, health, and education services are projected to account for 70% of job growth from 1994 to 2005. The goods-producing sector will decline, especially in manufacturing and mining.

Jobs that require the most education and training will be the fastest-growing and highest-paying. Jobs that require a bachelor's degree or more will increase by 23% from 1994 to 2005 (see Figure 13.1). Educational services are projected to increase by 2.2 million jobs and account for 1 out of every 8 new jobs from 1994 to 2005. Complete Self-Assessment 13.5 to see whether your career interests are in the areas with the fastest-growing jobs.

Finding the Right Career Match

Is the career you want to enter a good match for you? That is, do you have the skills, aptitude, and interests to be successful in the field? Career counselors at your college are trained to help you make a good choice. They can help you to assess your assets and to develop a list of occupations that could work for you.

If you have never sat down and talked with a career counselor about your career interests, make it a high priority to do so. You may find a new career, or several careers, that you never had thought about that would be worth exploring. Or you may discover that the career field you have wanted to go into for a long time really is the best match for you after all.

How much do you know about the career you want to pursue? Have you talked at length with people in that career about what a typical workday is like? Have you asked them how satisfied they are with the career? If not, arrange an appointment with one or more people in the field. Talk with them about their life and work. Ask them whether they would choose the field if they had it to do over again. If you don't know anyone in that field, ask the career center at your college or the department in which you plan to major to recommend someone you can talk with.

Also, be sure to scan the Resources at the end of this chapter. You will find some helpful books that describe a variety of careers in detail.

In a national survey of first-year college students, only 12% thought they were likely to change their major field of interest or career choice (Sax & others, 1995). In reality, far more will change. Thus, it pays to become knowledgeable about more than just one field. It also pays to develop skills that will serve you well across different fields.

Surprised

By How Many Career Changes the Average Adult Makes

The average adult makes three to five career changes over the course of a lifetime. What does this mean for you? It means that a good strategy is to acquire basic skills that will help you land jobs in a variety of fields. In this regard, communication skills are the most important.

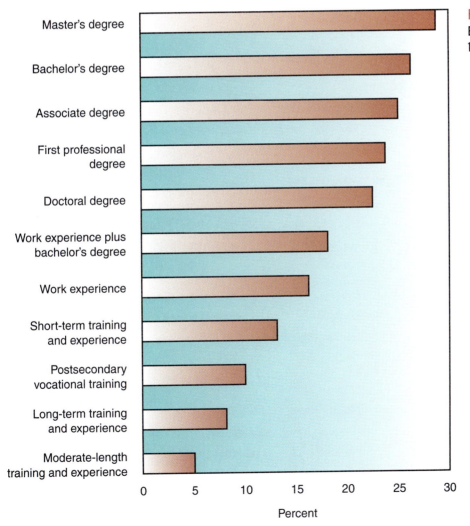

Figure 13.1 Projected Percentage of Growth in Employment by Level of Education and Training, 1994–2005

Self-Assessment 13-5

Matching Your Career Interests with the Fastest-Growing Jobs

All of the occupations listed below are in the fastest-growing category. They are organized by education level. The first column consists of occupations that will have the highest percentage of growth. The second column consists of occupations that will have the largest numerical increase in jobs. Place a check mark beside any occupations that interest you. See whether your career interests are in fields where an increase in jobs will occur.

Fastest-Growing Occupations	Occupations Having the Largest Numerical Increase in Employment
Professional degree	
❏ Chiropractors ❏ Lawyers ❏ Physicians ❏ Clergy ❏ Podiatrists	❏ Lawyers ❏ Physicians ❏ Clergy ❏ Chiropractors ❏ Dentists
Doctoral degree	
❏ Medical scientists ❏ Biological scientists ❏ College and university faculty ❏ Mathematicians and all other mathematical scientists	❏ College and university faculty ❏ Biological scientists ❏ Medical scientists ❏ Mathematicians and all other mathematical scientists
Master's degree	
❏ Operations research analysts ❏ Speech-language pathologists and audiologists ❏ Counselors ❏ Urban and regional planners	❏ Management analysts ❏ Counselors ❏ Management analysts ❏ Speech-language pathologists and audiologists ❏ Psychologists ❏ Operations research analysts
Work experience plus bachelor's degree	
❏ Engineering, mathematics, and natural science managers ❏ Marketing, advertising, and public relations managers ❏ Artists and commercial artists ❏ Financial managers ❏ Education administrators	❏ General managers and top executives ❏ Financial managers ❏ Marketing, advertising, and public relations managers ❏ Engineering, mathematics, and natural science managers ❏ Education administrators
Bachelor's degree	
❏ System analysts ❏ Computer engineers ❏ Occupational therapists ❏ Physical therapists ❏ Special education teachers	❏ System analysts ❏ Teachers, secondary school ❏ Teachers, elementary school ❏ Teachers, special education ❏ Social workers
Associate degree	
❏ Paralegals ❏ Medical record technicians ❏ Dental hygienists ❏ Respiratory therapists ❏ Radiologic technologists and technicians	❏ Registered nurses ❏ Paralegals ❏ Radiologic technologists and technicians ❏ Dental hygienists ❏ Medical record technicians

In making your career plans, it helps to be aware of the jobs that are growing the fastest and the ones where the most openings will be. If you did not place at least one check beside a job, you may want to go through the Self-Assessment again and think about whether any of jobs are attractive to you.

The Ideal Job Candidate

You might think it is too early to start considering how you will fare in the job market when you graduate from college. It is not too early. If you know what employers are searching for, you can work on developing these qualifications during college.

The National Association of College Employers recently conducted a survey of its members. The employers ranked oral communication skills, interpersonal skills, and teamwork skills as the three most important skills of a prospective job candidate (Collins, 1996). All of these skills involve communicating effectively. Employers also look for candidates to be proficient in their field, have leadership and analytical abilities, and show flexibility. Figure 13.2 (page 358) summarizes the skills that employers want in a job candidate.

An employer will look for evidence of your accomplishments and experiences. This evidence might include

- Leadership positions
- Activity in campus organizations or extracurricular activities
- Relevant experiences in co-ops, internships, or part-time work
- Good grades

Employers look for a combination of these characteristics. The more of them you have when you graduate from college, the better.

In the recent survey of the National Association of College Employers, employers said that first-year students need to realize that it's later in the job search than they think. Graduation and job hunting are only a few years away. Much of what employers look for in top job candidates (such as relevant experience) takes time to acquire. The employers especially recommend that first-year students get

- Work-related experience
- Involvement in campus/extracurricular activities

"I THREW IN A COUPLE OF PARAGRAPHS ABOUT MY LOVE LIFE TO MAKE MY RESUME INTERESTING."

Oral Communication Skills	4.7
Interpersonal Skills	4.6
Analytical Skills	4.5
Teamwork Skills	4.4
Flexibility	4.3
Leadership Skills	4.2
Proficiency in Field of Study	4.2
Written Communication Skills	4.2
Computer Skills	4.1

Figure 13.2 Desired Skills of an Ideal Job Candidate Rated by Employers
In a recent national survey of employers, desired characteristic of job applicants were rated on a scale of 1 = extremely unimportant to 5 = extremely important. Note how important communication skills were to the employers. Three of the four highest-rated skills were communication skills (oral, interpersonal, and teamwork).

- Good grades
- Computer skills

The employers point out that no matter what your career aspirations, you probably will need computer skills to perform your job competently. The reality is that computer skills are not just nice to have. These days they are a must.

An important aspect of getting the job you want is to perform well in an interview. For tips on how to stand above the crowd in an interview, see "Knocking 'Em Dead in an Interview."

"YOUR SON HAS MADE A CAREER CHOICE, MILDRED. HE'S GOING TO WIN THE LOTTERY AND TRAVEL A LOT."

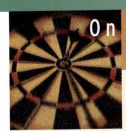

On Target Tips

Knocking 'Em Dead in an Interview

Martin Yate (1999) gives some great advice on how to get an interview and the job:

- Interviewers ask for detailed examples of your past experience. They figure you will do as well on the new job as the old one, so the examples you give can seal your fate.

- Résumés are important and you will need one. They are used by employers to decide whether they want to interview you in the first place. Organize your résumé, write it clearly, and don't use a lot of jargon.

- Don't wing the interview. Do your homework. Find out as much about your prospective employer as possible. What does the company do? How successful is it? Employers are impressed by applicants who have taken the time to learn about their organization. This is true whether you are interviewing for a part-time job at your college library or for a full-time job in a large company after you graduate from college.

- Anticipate what questions you will be asked in the interview. Do some practice interviews. Some typical interview questions include
  - "What is your greatest strength?"
  - "What interests you the most about this job?"
  - "Why should I hire you?"

  Also be prepared for some zingers. For example, how would you respond to
  - "Tell me something you are not very proud of."
  - "Describe a situation where your idea was criticized."

  These are examples of questions some interviewers ask to catch you off guard and see how you handle the situation.

- Ask appropriate job-related questions yourself. Review the job's requirements with the interviewer.

- Keep your cool. Always leave in the same mannerly and polite way you entered.

- As the interview closes, decide whether you want the job. If so, ask for it. Tell the interviewer that you are excited about the job and that it is a job you can do competently. If the job isn't offered on the spot, ask when the two of you can talk again.

- That's not all. Immediately after the interview, type a follow-up letter. Keep it short, less than one page. Mail the letter within 24 hours after the interview. If the decision is going to be made in the next few days, hand-deliver the letter or send a telegram. If you do not hear anything within five days, call the organization and ask what the status of the job is.

Getting Positive Work Experiences During College

Students can participate in cooperative education programs, internships, or part-time or summer work relevant to their field of study. This experience can be critical in helping students obtain the job they want when they graduate from college. Today's employers expect job candidates to have this type of experience. In the recent national survey of employers, almost 60% said their entry-level college hires had co-op or internship experience. Participating in these work experiences can be a key factor in whether you land the job you want when you graduate from college.

More than 1,000 colleges in the United States offer cooperative education (*co-op*) programs. A co-op is a paid apprenticeship in a career field that you are interested in pursuing. You may not be permitted to participate in a co-op program until your junior year.

Summary Tips For Mastering College

Pursuing Academic and Career Success

Achieving

1. Motivate yourself. Don't depend on others to motivate you. Be confident and enthusiastic. Commit to effort and read about motivation.
2. Be achievement-oriented but remember that being perfect is impossible.
3. Set challenging, realistic, and specific long-term goals. Become a master planner.

Designing an Academic Path

1. In making decisions about courses, list your constraints, study options, register for a reasonable course load, take the right mix of courses, talk with your advisors, and ask the pros (advanced students).
2. A college catalog is a valuable resource.
3. Whether you are in a two-year or four-year institution, you will need to select a major or specialization. Consult now with your academic advisor about your goals.
4. Be flexible and ask questions about what different majors are like. Find out what types of careers a major will prepare you for. It's okay to change majors. By the end of your second year, try to have your major pinned down. Map out a plan of your college years that lists each of your courses until graduation. Also be sure that the major you select is what you want, not what someone else wants for you.
5. If you are thinking about transferring to another college, do some exploring and planning. Find out which credits will transfer and make an appointment to talk with an advisor at the new college.
6. A mentor can be a key factor in your college success. If you don't have one, find one.

Exploring Careers

1. Learn more about which career fields are growing the fastest and which ones are losing jobs. A good source for this information is *The Occupational Outlook Handbook*.
2. Find the right career match for you. Talk with a professionally trained career counselor at your college.
3. Today's ideal job candidate has excellent communication skills. Regardless of the job you apply for after college, employers will want you have good speaking skills, interpersonal skills, and teamwork skills. Employers look for evidence of work-related experiences, activities, good grades, and computer skills.

College Success Checklist

Have your views changed since you completed this checklist at the beginning of the chapter? Place a check mark beside any item for which you feel good about your current practice. Also check any item for which you have new ideas about how to improve.

____ I am good at motivating myself.

____ I set realistic short-term and long-term goals.

____ I am an achiever but not a perfectionist.

____ I take responsibility for researching and planning my own academic schedule.

____ I meet regularly with an academic advisor to discuss my academic plan.

____ I have a mentor from whom I feel comfortable seeking advice about both personal and academic concerns.

____ I understand the value of beginning career planning early in college.

____ I have explored different career options.

____ I have talked with a career counselor about occupational choices.

____ I know what skills most employers are looking for in the ideal job candidate.

____ I know what work experiences during college can help me in my career.

In the space below, list items that you still need to work on the most. This list may help you complete the goal-setting exercise in the Learning Portfolio.

Review Questions

1 What are the best strategies for getting motivated?

2 How can you become more goal directed?

3 What is a perfectionist? Why is it not a good idea to try to be perfect?

4 What are some strategies for getting the right courses?

5 Why is your college's catalog important to you?

6 What are the most important things to know about selecting a major or specialization at a two-year or four-year institution?

7 What role can a mentor play in your college life?

8 What skills are employers looking for in job candidates?

9 What kind of work experiences during college can help you in your career?

Learning Portfolio

Learning by Reflecting... Journal Entries

Career Goal-Setting

As you would on a long journey, you need markers along your career path to tell you when you are on track. These are your goals, the specific things you will accomplish as your work life advances. Every dream and vision you might have about the future can be broken down into specific goals.

Keeping your career goals in focus, write down the specific career goals you have for the next 20 years, 10 years, and 5 years. Be as concrete and specific as possible. In constructing your goals, start from the furthest point and work backward. If you go the other way, you risk adopting goals that are not clearly linked to your dream.

My Ideal Job

Write down your #1 ideal occupation choice.

_____

Describe the preparation you will need for your ideal job, such as an AA, BA, Master's, or PhD. How many years will this preparation take?

_____

On a scale of 1 to 10, estimate your chances of obtaining your ideal job.

1 2 3 4 5 6 7 8 9 10
Poor   Excellent

Discuss these answers further in your journal.

My Work Values

A range of values can bring people satisfaction in their work. Following are 20 work values. Place a check mark next to the work values that are the most important to you:

- ___ Achievement
- ___ Advancement
- ___ Adventure
- ___ Caring
- ___ Competition
- ___ Creativity
- ___ Early entry
- ___ Health
- ___ High income
- ___ Home and leisure life
- ___ Independence
- ___ Interesting work
- ___ Leadership
- ___ Lifestyle
- ___ Location of work
- ___ Moral and religious concerns
- ___ People contact
- ___ Security
- ___ Status/prestige
- ___ Work environment

In your journal, describe how the work values that are important to you are reflected in your ideal job.

Learning by Doing... Action Projects

Examine Your College Catalog

Obtain a copy of your college's catalog if you don't have one. Your academic advisor can tell you where to get one. In most cases the admissions or registrar's office has the catalog.

- If you are not doing well in a particular class, you may want to consider dropping it. Look up the procedure for dropping a class and the latest date in the term you can do this.
- Look up the specialty or major you have chosen or that you are considering. What are the degree requirements for it? Is there a particular sequence of courses you should take?

Current Resumé and Future Resumé

Create a current resumé. List your education, work experience, campus organizations, and extracurricular activities. List any honors or awards you have achieved. Then write down what you would like your resumé to look like when you apply for your first job after college.

_____
_____
_____

Visit Your College's Career Center

Visit the career center at your college. Find out what materials and services are available. Describe them in your Learning Portfolio. Be sure to obtain brochures about the careers that you are interested in.

Learning by Thinking Critically... Critiques

Why Do People Pursue Particular Careers?
Get together with several other students. Critically analyze what influences people to pursue a particular career.

- Are people born to be engineers or nurses?
- Do their parents shape their career interests?
- Do teachers?
- What kind of an impact can mentors have on career choice?
- Are economic factors important?
- Are values important?

Explaining Career Change
Go to the library. Find evidence from recent books or journals about *why* and *how* people change careers. Before you go, write down here the reasons you expect. Compare your guesses with the documented answers.

_____
_____
_____
_____

How Good Are Your Communication Skills?
Among the skills that employers want college graduates to have, communication skills are the most important. Honestly examine your communication skills. Rate yourself from 1 to 5 (with 1 being weak and 5 being strong) on the following:

	1	2	3	4	5
Oral communication skills					
Interpersonal skills					
Teamwork skills					
Written communication skills					
Listening skills					

- What are your strengths and weaknesses in communication skills?

_____
_____
_____

- How important are each of these communication skills in the ideal job you want when you graduate from college?

_____
_____
_____

Learning by Thinking Creatively... Personal Vision

A Wish Box
Many creative people write down daily impressions, events, and feelings on index cards or in notebooks. These notes can be the raw material out of which creative ideas spring. Some artists tear out dozens of interesting images from magazines and newspapers, put them in boxes, and then return to them for creative inspirations. Start keeping a special box to store your impressions, feelings, and images related to your career interests and dreams. Come back to them from time to time for inspiration.

The Creative Job
- What type of job do believe would best unleash your creative skills?

_____

- What occupation would it be?

_____

- What characteristics would it have?

_____

- How much freedom would the job entail?

_____

Creating a Quotation
Thomas Edison once said, "Creativity is 1% inspiration and 99% perspiration." Think creatively and come up with your own quotation about the college major you are interested in or the career you want to pursue.

_____
_____
_____
_____

Learning by Planning... Goal Setting

Review the results of the Self-Assessments you completed in this chapter. Also review the College Success Checklist. What can you conclude about things you need to do to improve your skills?

What goal do you want to select from this chapter for making positive changes that will help you master the college experience? *(Hint: Is your goal challenging, reasonable, and specific?)*

_____
_____
_____
_____
_____

What strategies will you use to achieve your goal? *(Hint: Can you organize your strategy into a series of smaller goals?)*

_____
_____
_____
_____
_____
_____
_____
_____
_____
_____
_____

What obstacles may be in your way as you attempt to make these positive changes?

_____
_____
_____
_____
_____
_____

What additional resources might help you succeed in achieving your goal?

_____
_____
_____
_____
_____

By what date do you want to accomplish your goal?

_____

How will you know you have succeeded?

_____
_____
_____
_____

Resources for Mastering the College Experience

Achieving and Getting Motivated

Even Eagles Need a Push (1990) by David McNally. New York: Dell.
Inspiring and motivating. Stimulates you to think about what kind of life you want to live.

Flow (1990) by Mihaly Csikszentmihalyi. New York: HarperCollins.
Tells how to experience life optimally. Based on more than two decades of research on the concept of flow, the deep sense of happiness that people feel when they have been challenged and then mastered the challenge.

Mentors (1992) by Thomas Evans. Princeton, NJ: Peterson's.
Describes the enriching experiences of mentoring and how mentors can make a difference in a student's life.

Overcoming Student Failure (1996) by Martin Covington and Karen Teel. Washington, DC: American Psychological Association.
Up-to-date guidance on improving your motivation to learn.

Exploring Majors

College Majors and Careers (1993, rev. ed.) by Paul Phifer. Garrett Park, MD: Garret Park Press.
Provides extensive matching of your interests and college major with available careers.

Transferring to Another College

Your Transfer Planner (1995) by Carey Harbin. Belmont, CA: Wadsworth.
For students intending to transfer to another college. Includes many worksheets to help you make the right decision.

Exploring Careers

Encyclopedia of Careers and Vocational Guidance (1996, 10th ed.) by Holli Cosgrove (Ed.). Chicago: J.G. Ferguson.
Four volumes of information about a wide range of careers.

Journal of Career Planning and Employment.
A journal of articles on many of the topics in this chapter. May be available in your library. If not, the reference librarian may be able to help you locate it elsewhere or recommend similar journals.

Occupational Outlook Handbook (1998–1999). Washington, DC: U.S. Dept. of Labor, Bureau of Labor Statistics.
An excellent source of trends in job increases and decreases published every two years. Provides information about many different occupations.

Taking Charge of Your Career (1991, 2nd ed.) by Robert Lock. Pacific Grove, CA: Brooks Cole.
An excellent career exploration book with many self-assessments.

Career and Job Information for Different Groups

The Black Collegian (published each semester), 140 Carondelet St., New Orleans, LA 70130.
Contains features on top employers, graduate and professional opportunities, and career planning for African-American college students. Available on many campuses.

Job Opportunities for the Blind (JOB), National Federation of the Blind, 1800 Johnston St., Baltimore, MD 21230; 800-638-7518.
Gives information about the free national reference and referral service for the blind.

President's Committee on Employment of People with Specific Disabilities, 1331 F St. NW, 3rd Floor, Washington, DC 20004; 202-376-6200.
Provides information about career planning, training, and job opportunities for people with disabilities.

Wider Opportunities for Women, 815 15th St. NW, Suite 916, Washington, DC 20005; 202-638-3143.
An organization providing information about career planning, training, and expanded job opportunities for women.

Job Seeking and Interviewing

Knock 'Em Dead (1999) by Martin Yate. Holbrook, MA: Bob Adams.
An annually updated guide to job interviewing, subtitled "With Great Answers to Tough Questions." Pushes you to evaluate what your greatest weakness is, what decisions are difficult for you, and other difficult questions. Gives helpful suggestions on job search.

What Color Is Your Parachute (1999) by Robert Bolles. Berkeley, CA: Ten Speed Press.
A highly popular book, published annually. Demystifies job hunting, debunks myths, gives valuable advice about where the jobs are and what to do when you get hired. Also advises on how to use career counselors and how to find a mission in life.

Internet Resources

http://www.summerjobs.com
From jobs in your own back yard to opportunities overseas.

http://www.jobweb.org/catapult/Jobsall.htm
Job listings according to different fields and links to employment services.

http://www.careermosaic.com/cm/crc/crc15.html
Resumé Writing Center of Career Mosaic; help at every stage of writing a resumé.

http://www.d.umn.edu/student/loon/car/self/career_act_ii.html
On-line Act Interest Inventory and Student Profile to narrow down your vocational aims.

http://www.overseasjob.com
International database for jobs and career news.

http://www.interbiznet.com/hunt/tools.html
Career Mosaic; help at every stage of job search, from resumé writing through the interview.

Practicing Integrity

CHAPTER 14

 College Success Checklist

Place a mark beside the items that apply to you. Leave the items blank that do not apply to you.

____ I know what my values are.

____ I can describe the values of most first-year students.

____ I have explored religious and spiritual values deeply.

____ I can list the habits of highly effective people.

____ I know the right academic values and I practice them.

____ I know the "isms" associated with various academic disciplines and understand that these involve values.

____ Looking back over the term, I think that I have improved in a number of areas.

____ I feel confident about putting it all together in college and beyond.

Preview

Integrity has several important meanings. First, integrity means having and living by a positive code of values. Second, integrity means completeness and unity. Thus, this chapter is about values and about unifying the different parts of your college life into a meaningful whole.

Chapter Outline

Images of College Success: Emmitt Smith

Personal Values
- What Are Values?
- Value Conflicts
- Clarifying Your Values
- The Values of First-Year College Students
- The Right Values

Academic Values
- Academic Integrity and Ethics
- Disciplines and Values

Putting It All Together
- Looking Back
- Looking Forward

Self-Assessments
- 14.1 What Are My Values?
- 14.2 Where Am I Now? Re-examining My Identity
- 14.3 How Do I Resolve Value Conflicts on Campus?
- 14.4 Am I Mastering the College Experience?

On-Target Tips
- Covey's Strategy for Clarifying Your Values
- Putting It All Together Now and in the Future

Images of College Success
Emmitt Smith

Emmitt Smith, running back of the Dallas Cowboys, is one of the leading stars of the National Football League (NFL). His salary is approximately $6 million a year and he gets several million a year more in endorsement money. Emmitt has three Super Bowl rings and he owns three successful companies. But until May 1996, Emmitt Smith did not have something else that he always wanted and that most NFL players do not have: A college degree.

In high school, he promised his mother and himself that he would earn his college degree and decided to go to the University of Florida. Before completing his degree, he became a professional football player. However, in his mind that did not cancel the promise. He continued to think that if he did not go back to complete his degree, he would be letting himself down.

Emmitt Smith receives his college degree from University of Florida president John Lombardi.

After the NFL season was over each winter, Emmitt returned to the University of Florida to take classes, eventually graduating in the top one-fourth of his class. He also was involved in a number of in-class and out-of-class activities. For example, he sat in the hall for three days and sold tickets for an annual academic banquet.

Emmitt Smith often visited schools and talked with students about the value of an education. He always felt hypocritical talking with youth about education when he had not accomplished his own academic goals. He no longer has to feel this way. His values motivated him to persist and eventually earn his degree.

Personal Values

Values play an important part in helping us to lead exemplary lives. What do we mean when we say someone has good values?

What Are Values?

Values are our beliefs and attitudes about the way we think things *should* be. They embody what is important to us. For Emmitt Smith, persisting until he got his college degree was important. For David Starr Jordan, former president of Stanford University, there is no excellence without positive values.

We attach values to all sorts of things: politics, religion, money, sex, education, helping others, family, friends, career, cheating, taking risks, self-respect, and so on. Sometimes we are not aware of our values until we find ourselves in situations that expose our beliefs. For example, you might be surprised to find yourself reacting strongly when you discuss religion with other students.

People vary in how strongly they present their values. Two people may both believe that abusing our natural environment is wrong. One might campaign actively for keeping the environment clean by participating in campus protests. The other may just wear a pin that says "Keep the rivers clean."

Value Conflicts

College presents many opportunities to experience value conflicts. For example, if you see a student sitting next to you who is cheating on an exam, what will you do? A value of *integrity* may motivate you to report the cheating. By contrast, a value of *noninvolvement* might lead you to overlook it.

Some other value conflicts you might have to deal with include

- Abiding by your parent's values or a friend's, if they are in conflict
- Divulging aspects of your sexual history to a date (that is in the date's important interest to know) versus not disclosing the information
- Engaging in community action projects versus making money for yourself
- Pursuing leisure versus studying
- Trying to control someone to get your way versus acknowledging their needs and desires

As you make decisions about which way you are going to act when such conflicts arise, your values will become clearer.

Clarifying Your Values

What are the most important things in life to you? How do you think things should be? To examine your personal values, take Self-Assessment 14.1.

Are your values the right values? You probably think they are. That is why you chose them. Yet you may believe that getting good grades is a high priority while another student feels that a great social life is more important. You may think that having a good spiritual life is a very important value. Another student may believe that a healthful lifestyle is more important. The variation in values on

> *There is no real excellence in all this world that can be separated from the right living.*
>
> **David Starr Jordan**
> **Former U.S. senator and president of Stanford University, 20th century**

Self-Assessment 14-1

What Are My Values?

Look through and think about the following list. This list is not exhaustive but it captures a wide variety of values. Place a check mark in the spaces next to the 10 values that are the most important to you. Then go back over these 10 values and rank order the top 5.

- _____ Having good friendships and getting along well with people
- _____ Having a positive relationship with a spouse or a romantic partner
- _____ Self-respect
- _____ Being well-off financially
- _____ Having a good spiritual life
- _____ Being competent at my work
- _____ Having the respect of others
- _____ Making an important contribution to humankind
- _____ Being a moral person
- _____ Feeling secure

- _____ Having freedom and independence
- _____ Being well-educated
- _____ Contributing to the welfare of others
- _____ Having peace of mind
- _____ Getting recognition or becoming famous
- _____ Being happy
- _____ Enjoying leisure time
- _____ Being a good citizen and showing loyalty to my country
- _____ Living a healthful lifestyle
- _____ Being intelligent

My five most important personal values:

1. _____

2. _____

3. _____

4. _____

5. _____

As you review your analysis, think about how you got these values. Did you learn to appreciate these qualities from your parents? Teachers? Friends? Or from some events that happened to you? How deeply have you thought about each of these values and what they mean to you? Speculate about whether your actions support the values you describe as centrally important. Are you truly living up to the values you claim as important?

your campus is likely to be especially large if it has students from diverse ethnic and religious backgrounds.

It is important to remember that what people say their values are does not always coincide with their actions. Consider unethical politicians who use tax dollars for personal benefit, ruthless businesspeople who run roughshod over others, and corrupt ministers who fleece their congregations. Be motivated to have positive values and make your behavior match those values.

> *As long as you keep searching, the answers will come.*
>
> **Joan Baez**
> **Contemporary American folk singer**

The Values of First-Year College Students

During college is the first time that you probably will become conscious of many of your values. This is partly because, more so than in high school, you find yourself interacting with students and instructors whose values are different from your own. They will challenge you to think more deeply about what you believe. Maybe you believe the government should do more to control handguns, but you take a class in which the instructor says the government is too invasive in people's lives. You might think that homosexual relations should be prohibited but find your roommates vehemently disagree.

In a recent national survey, first-year college students were asked about their values (Sax & others, 1997). As can be seen in Figure 14.1, more than 75% of first-year college students strongly or somewhat agree that:

- A man is not entitled to sex on a date

First-Year Students' Views on Value-Related Issues

In a recent national survey, college freshmen were asked about their views on value-related issues. The following percentage of students strongly agreed or somewhat agreed that:

Statement	%	Statement	%
A man is not entitled to sex on a date	87%	It's okay for people to have sex if they like each other	42%
The federal government can do more to control handguns	82%	It's okay to disobey laws that violate your personal values	37%
The federal government is not adequately controlling pollution	81%	Marijuana should be legalized	35%
Employers can require drug tests	78%	Homosexual relations should be prohibited	34%
A national health care plan is needed	73%	An individual can do little to change society	32%
There is too much concern for criminals	70%	A married woman's best place is in the home	25%
Racial or sexist speech should be prohibited	64%	The death penalty should be abolished	24%
The wealthy should pay more taxes	63%	Taxes should be raised to reduce the government's deficit	22%
Abortion should be legalized	53%	Racial discrimination is no longer a problem	20%
Affirmative action in college admissions should be abolished	50%		
Legal status should be given to same-sex couples	50%		

Figure 14.1

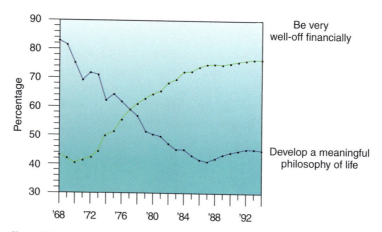

Figure 14.2 The Changing Life Goals of First-Year Students
The percentages indicated are in response to the question of identifying a life goal as essential or very important.

- The federal government should do more to control handguns
- The federal government is not adequately controlling pollution
- Employers can require drug tests

Compare your own views on these issues with how the students surveyed think about them.

Political Values More than half of first-year college students said that politically they are middle-of-the-road. Less than one-fourth said they were either liberal or conservative. A small minority said they were far left (3%) or far right (2%).

Self-Interest Over the past two decades, first-year college students have shown more interest in their own well-being and less concern for the well-being of others, especially the disadvantaged (Sax & others, 1997). As indicated in Figure 14.2, today's students are more motivated to be well-off financially and less motivated to develop a meaningful philosophy of life than their coun-

"I've got the bowl, the bone, the big yard. I know I _should_ be happy."

Mike Twohy © 1992 from The New Yorker Collection. All Rights Reserved.

terparts were 20 or even 10 years ago. Becoming very well off financially is a very important reason for attending college for three-fourths of today's first-year students, compared to only about one-half in the early 1970s.

Civic Concern Some signs indicate that today's first-year students are shifting toward a stronger interest in society's welfare. For example, between 1986 and 1995 an increasing percentage expressed strong interest in participating in community action programs (23% in 1997, compared to 18% in 1986) and in helping to promote racial understanding (32% in 1997, compared to 27% in 1986). In one recent study, students' participation in community projects stimulated them to reflect on society's political organization and moral order (Yates, 1995).

Spirituality and Religion In a national poll, 95% of Americans said that they believe in God or a universal spirit. About 60% said that they attend religious services ("Spiritual America," 1994). However, in the recent national survey of first-year college students, more students than ever said they have no religious preference (14% in 1997, compared to 8% in 1978) (Sax & others, 1997). Also in 1997, more students than at any time in the history of the survey said that they had not attended religious services during the past year (19%, compared with 9% in 1968). Despite these recent downturns, 86% of

> *Without civic morality communities perish; without personal morality their survival has no value.*
>
> **Bertrand Russell**
> **English philosopher,**
> **20th century**

College students are showing an increasing interest in society's welfare. For example, compared to college students in the 1980s, today's college students show a stronger interest in community action programs.

> *Religion enlightens, terrifies, subdues; it gives faith, inflicts remorse, inspires revolutions, and inflames devotion.*
>
> **John Henry Newman**
> **English churchman and writer, 19th century**

> *The religious need of the human mind remains alive.*
>
> **Charlotte Perkins Gilman**
> **American author, 20th century**

first-year college students continue to state a religious preference and 81% attend religious services (Sax & others, 1997).

College is a time when many people think in more abstract, logical ways about many issues. As part of their search for identity, college students grapple in more sophisticated ways with such questions as

- "Why am I on this planet?"
- "Is there a God or higher spiritual being?"
- "Have I just been believing what my parents and church socialized me to believe?"
- "What really are my religious views?"

Religion expert James Fowler (1981) believes that the late teens and early 20s are a special juncture in religious development. He says it is during this time that people become capable of taking full responsibility for their religious beliefs. They start to realize that their beliefs can be self-chosen and that it will take effort to follow a particular life course. Students come face to face with such decisions as

- "Should I consider myself or the welfare of others first?"
- "Are the religious doctrines that were taught to me when I was growing up absolute, or are they more relative than I was led to believe?"

The Right Values

As you read the results of the survey of students' values, you may have been surprised or even a little disappointed.

Is it morally acceptable to place a greater value on making money than developing a meaningful philosophy of life? Many new college students say it is. Most of us would agree that some values are right and some are wrong. When we talk about whether certain values are right or wrong, we are moving into the realm of morality.

In thinking about what the right values are, consider the following incident (French, 1996). In the Special Olympics several years ago, the nine contestants (each with a physical or mental disability) lined up to run the 100-yard dash. When the starter's gun sounded, each runner came out of the blocks hoping for a victory. However, one racer stumbled on the asphalt pavement, tumbled over a couple of times, and began to cry. The other eight contestants heard him cry.

> *The code of morality is to do unto others as you would have them do unto you. If you make that a central theme of your morality code, it will serve you well as a moral individual.*
>
> **Barbara Jordan**
> **American educator and congresswoman, 20th century**

"Sorry -- that's not on our list of approved churches."

They slowed down and paused for a second. Then all of them turned around and went back to console the fallen runner. They linked arms and walked together across the finish line. Everyone in the stands stood and cheered for ten minutes.

Most of us probably agree that the following are positive values that can serve as a moral code:

- Be honest
- Be responsible
- Show concern for others
- Don't be selfish

You probably can add to this list of commonly held positive values. As we see next, some popular writers have made similar recommendations about practicing the right values.

Covey's Seven Habits of Highly Effective People   Stephen Covey (1989, 1994) has helped many people to clarify their values. He stresses that each of us needs to identify the underlying principles that are important in our lives and then evaluate whether we are living up to those standards. Covey describes seven basic habits that he believes reflect and support good values.

- **Be proactive instead of reactive.** Anticipate problems before they appear. If they do crop up, take the initiative to fix them instead of waiting passively for others to act. For example, if you object to an assignment on moral grounds, voice your objections directly to your instructor rather than enduring the discomfort or complaining to your classmates. Also, when you make a mistake, admit it, correct it, and then learn from it.

- **Begin with the end in mind.** Covey asks you to imagine that you have come to attend your own funeral and are looking down at yourself lying in a casket. You then take a seat and four speakers (a family member, a friend, someone from your work, and someone from your church or a community organization) are about to give their impressions of you. What would you want them to say about you and your life? This type of exercise helps you to look into the social mirror and to visualize how other people see you. How satisfied are you with that image? Similarly, you can envision graduation day and think about what your family, friends, classmates, and teachers might say about your life as a college student.

- **Put first things first.** Covey asks you to think about the one thing you could do that you are not doing now that would make a major positive difference in your life. Putting first things first helps you to think about how you use your time in relation to your values. Do you find time for the things that matter most to you? See "Covey's Strategy for Clarifying Your Values" for some helpful tips.

- **Think win–win.** "Win–win" is about cooperating rather than being selfish. A win–win strategy seeks ways to obtain mutual benefits in all social interactions. Solutions to problems are mutually satisfying when a win–win strategy is involved. With this habit, one person's success is not achieved through another's loss. For example, you can learn to approach

The tissue of life to be
We weave with colors all
  our own
And in the field of destiny
We reap as we have sown.

John Greenleaf Whittier
American writer, 19th century

Stephen Covey. Which of Covey's habits do you think is the most important?

On Target Tips

Covey's Strategy for Clarifying Your Values

Stephen Covey and his colleagues (1994) recommend the following to help you clarify your values (use your watch to go through the timed exercises):

- First, take one minute and answer this question: *If I had unlimited time and resources, what would I do?* It's okay to dream. Write down everything that comes into your mind.

- Second, go back to Self-Assessment 14.1 and review the list of five values you chose as the most important to you.

- Third, take several minutes and compare your list of five values with your dreams. You may be living with unconscious dreams that don't mesh with your values. If you don't get your dreams out in the open, you may spend years living with illusions and the feeling that you somehow are settling for second best. Work on the two lists until you feel that your dreams match up with your values.

- Fourth, take one minute to see how your values relate to four fundamental areas of human fulfillment: physical needs, social needs, mental needs, and spiritual needs. Do your values reflect these four needs? Work on your list until they do.

- Fifth, identify which of the seven habits of highly effective people will produce the values on your final list.

---

inevitable conflicts with roommates in a way that helps everyone win.

- **Seek first to understand, then to be understood.** This habit is about developing good communication skills and empathic understanding of others. Covey says that communication is life's most important skill and that listening is key to communication. Yet few of us have been trained how to listen well. We usually seek to be understood rather than to understand people by actively listening to what they have to say. To interact effectively with others, we have to understand them. This strategy is especially helpful in group tasks or when you need help in interpreting assignment instructions.

- **Synergize.** Covey believes that the practice of the first five habits prepares us for habit six: synergy. *Synergy* is the idea that the result of two or more things can be greater than the result of each individually. Covey argues that when we faithfully engage in being proactive, begin with the end in mind, put first things first, and seek first to understand, a synergy takes place in which creative alternatives arise.

- **Renew yourself.** Covey's seventh habit involves what he calls "sharpening the saw," or renewal. It promotes preserving and enhancing the physical, mental, spiritual, and socioemotional dimensions of your life. Physical renewal includes caring for your physical body by practicing good nutrition, exercising regularly, and getting adequate sleep and rest. Mental renewal includes engaging in critical thinking, exploring new topics, continuing your education, organizing, and planning. Spiritual renewal includes clarifying your values and drawing on the sources that inspire and uplift you. Socioemotional renewal includes showing empathy for others and being oriented toward service. All four dimensions need attention to maximize your competence as a student.

Many people find Covey's seven habits attractive and say they have helped them to improve the quality of their lives. Whether you agree with his system or not, thinking about the seven habits provides a springboard for examining which principles you want to guide your life and your academic career. So do the ideas of M. Scott Peck.

M. Scott Peck's Values M. Scott Peck (1978, 1997) says that life is difficult. Each of us will suffer pain and disappointment. He counsels us to face up to life's difficulties and not be lazy. Peck also believes that people thirst for integrity in their lives. To achieve integrity, he says that we need to move spirituality into all aspects of our daily lives.

Peck also recommends four important tools to use in our search for a high-quality life:

- **Delay gratification.** The path to what we really want out of life is often a long one. We need to go to school day after day, year after year, to get the education we seek and possibly enter the career we want. It is easy to go astray—to skip a class or stay out all night—and seek immediate pleasure. However, Peck says that staying the course will make our future rewards much greater.

- **Accept responsibility.** Peck says that we might be right if we think some of our problems are caused by the way our parents brought us up. Nonetheless, we are not going to move forward in our life by continually blaming them. He urges us to take responsibility for ourselves and our behavior, attitudes, failures, and achievements. If you assume this self-responsibility, you will have a higher quality of life.

- **Dedicate yourself to the truth.** Peck advises us not to speak falsely, not to withhold the truth, and to make truth the cornerstone of our spiritual growth. He believes dedication to the truth involves never-ending self-discipline that frees us from fear.

- **Attain balance.** Peck argues that leading a good life means attaining balance. For example, you can't delay gratification for everything. You need to balance some delay with enjoying the present when it is not destructive to do so. To have freedom we have to assume total responsibility for ourselves, but in doing so we have to reject responsibility that is not truly ours.

Like Erik Erikson, Peck believes that forging a positive identity is a central part of being a competent human being. To re-examine your identity, complete Self-Assessment 14.2.

Since 1984, M. Scott Peck has devoted considerable time and money to the Foundation for Community Encouragement, a nonprofit organization that he and his wife, Lily, helped found. The Foundation has done considerable work in helping the poor and homeless.

Academic Values

In college your values will be challenged. Some challenges will leave you more firmly entrenched in your prior beliefs. Other challenges may transform your moral code.

Staying Out of the *Pits*

The Party's Over

Alex is a pleasure-centered first-year student who can't believe how much freedom he has. His world has become one instant gratification after another. He wants everything right now. When he has fun, he wants more. The next new pleasure has to be bigger and better, more exciting, a bigger high. He watches a lot of TV, plays video games for hours, shoots pool into the early morning hours, and lives for going to the best party each weekend.

Alex's life has become self-centered and pleasure-driven. Delaying gratification for something better down the road is not in his vocabulary. He wants it all right now, not tomorrow. But tomorrow comes and Alex's wasted days are catching up with him. Alex's parents just got his midterm grades, which are not good. His father is coming to meet with him and the undergraduate dean tomorrow to discuss Alex's academic problems.

The party is over for Alex. Don't put yourself in Alex's situation. You will not succeed in college unless you delay gratification. Have some fun but don't let it undermine your success.

M. Scott Peck. What do you think about Peck's recommendations for the kinds of values people should have?

Self-Assessment 14-2

Where Am I Now? Re-examining My Identity

In Chapter 1 we asked you to complete this assessment of your identity. This is a good time to re-examine your identity. For each area listed below, check your identity status as diffused (you have not yet explored meaningful alternatives and you have not made a commitment), foreclosed (you have made a commitment but have not adequately explored alternatives), in a moratorium (you are currently exploring meaningful alternatives but have not yet made a commitment), or achieved (you have adequately explored alternatives and have made a commitment).

IDENTITY COMPONENT	IDENTITY STATUS			
	Diffused	Foreclosed	Moratorium	Achieved
Vocational identity	____	____	____	____
Religious identity	____	____	____	____
Achievement/intellectual identity	____	____	____	____
Political identity	____	____	____	____
Sexual identity	____	____	____	____
Gender identity	____	____	____	____
Relationship identity	____	____	____	____
Lifestyle identity	____	____	____	____
Ethnic and cultural identity	____	____	____	____
Personality characteristics	____	____	____	____
Interests	____	____	____	____

Look back at your identity assessment you completed in Chapter 1. How much have you stayed the same? How much have you changed? Which areas of your identity are still the most puzzling to you?

Academic Integrity and Ethics

Although you are unlikely to register for a course called Character 101, your experiences in college (both in and out of the classroom) will contribute to your character and integrity. Let's explore the settings and circumstances in which you can strengthen your moral code.

In the Classroom Most instructors presume that you will behave in a way that promotes trust in the classroom. For example, they expect you to

- Complete and submit your own work on projects
- Refrain from cheating on exams
- Avoid plagiarizing the work of others
- Show respect for others' opinions

Practicing these behaviors helps to promote an atmosphere of respect and honesty.

With College Officials Maintaining high standards of conduct in other settings also is important. For example, when you deal with registration and financial arrangements, resolve problems in a civil way. By being reasonable, you encourage others to want to help you. By practicing civility in problem situations during your college years, you lay the groundwork for high standards of conduct in your postcollege life.

Feeling *Good*

About Practicing Integrity

You can practice integrity in many areas of your college life. It is not unusual to face temptations in college that challenge your personal and academic integrity. Not practicing integrity can bring forth a host of negative feelings: distress, misery, embarrassment, humiliation, panic, anxiety, anguish, shock, and shame. If you resist the temptations that challenge your integrity, you will feel much better about yourself.

With Campus Resources When you use your college's material resources, leave them in the condition that you found them. Unfortunately, stolen materials and articles that have been cut out of bound journals in the library are not only expensive to replace but will inconvenience others, like you, who need to use them. In the long run, abuse of campus resources raises tuition costs for everyone.

With Peers Integrity matters in the relationships you establish with friends and colleagues. For example, Self-Assessment 14.3 lists some typical moral challenges or value conflicts that you may face in college settings. Examine the problems and think about what you have done or what you would do when confronted with such problems.

As College Representatives To outsiders, you are now a representative of your college. When you wear campus sweatshirts or talk about your college experiences in public, you communicate something about the college. When you work as a campus volunteer or on an internship, your own practices and values (good or bad) reflect on the college. Make a commitment to represent your college in a positive way.

Disciplines and Values

Liberal arts courses expose you to diverse ideas and traditions that challenge the way you think and believe. The term *liberal arts* refers to a curriculum of studies that includes a balance of the arts, humanities, natural science, and social science. A liberal arts education provides information about general cultural concerns, in contrast to an education that focuses more narrowly on a profession.

The disciplines you study will foster different ways of thinking. However, they also will have some common features. For example, most instructors endorse the value of *rationalism* (using reason to arrive at conclusions). Notice that this value ends in the suffix *-ism*. Words that end in *-ism* often represent an abstract concept for a specific set of values or assumptions.

Table 14.1 summarizes many of the "isms" you will encounter in your first year of college. Your familiarity with the "isms" makes it easier to understand and appreciate the nature of certain disciplines. This list also alerts you that when instructors begin talking about this "ism" or that "ism," values probably are involved.

Moral courage is a more rare commodity than bravery in battle or great intelligence.

Robert F. Kennedy
U.S. attorney general,
20th century

Self-Assessment 14-3

How Do I Resolve Value Conflicts on Campus?

Examine the following moral dilemmas and make a judgment about which value you would practice.

	VALUES
Should I keep the secret my roommate told me or share the gossip with other friends?	_____ Privacy _____ Power
Should I keep my appointment with my study group or continue to watch the movie I started?	_____ Responsibility _____ Leisure
Should I give accurate feedback on a friend's bad work or minimize the problem to be encouraging?	_____ Honesty _____ Sensitivity
Should I agree to awaken my roommate each morning or insist that he or she operate independently?	_____ Friendship _____ Self-reliance
Should I stop to help pick up a stranger's books or hurry to get to class on time?	_____ Altruism _____ Efficiency
Should I join my friends in laughing at a sexist joke or take a stand against offensive comments?	_____ Cohesion _____ Equality

On Target Tips

Putting It All Together Now and in the Future

- **Understand that nobody's perfect.** Although we have encouraged you to improve in many areas, recognize that you are not perfect and never will be.

- **Recognize that you are unique.** No two people are exactly the same. You have your own strengths and weaknesses. The way you put it all together and maximize your skills will not be identical to the way other first-year students do it.

- **Put your heart into your college experience.** Make the most of college. You can't relive your life. Make every day count. Put your heart into your academic life. Face your problems and develop strategies to overcome challenges. Develop positive relationships.

- **You have a lot of change left ahead of you.** You have made it through an important first part of your college experience. You still have many beginnings, changes, and endings left. Expect that you will continue to change in many ways as you go through the remainder of your college years.

- **Keep the On-Target Tips, Summary Tips for Mastering College, and Resources for Mastering the College Experience handy.** You have read hundreds of tips throughout *Mastering the College Experience*. You also have read about many resources for mastering college and life at the end of each chapter. Keep these handy resources for college and beyond.

Table 14-1
Selected College Level "Isms" That Reflect Values

From the Arts and Humanities

Postmodernism	A contemporary perspective that emphasizes nonlinear thinking and subjective realities	Hedonism	The ethical doctrine that suggests that the pursuit of pleasure is the most important objective in life
Constructivism	A philosophical position that stresses the contributions of the perceiver in creating reality	Revisionism	The practice of reanalyzing historical information in light of subsequent knowledge
Realism	A preoccupation with factual representation	Egoism	The ethical and psychological doctrine that self-interest motivates all action
Materialism	A preoccupation with material objects rather than intellectual or spiritual pursuits		

From the Social Sciences

Humanism	A philosophy that rejects supernatural interpretations and promotes human interests	Liberalism	The view that people should have the freedom to act or express themselves in a manner of their own choosing; advocates change, progress, and reform
Behaviorism	The belief in the power of environmental influences in learning		
Collectivism	A preference for considering the good of the group over individual concerns	Conservatism	The view that favors preservation of the existing order and resistance to change or innovation
Individualism	A preference for placing value on individual concerns over collective concerns	Humanitarianism	The ethical belief that a person is obligated to work for the improved welfare of humanity
Egalitarianism	The belief that people should be treated as equals regardless of their characteristics or background	Feminism	The view that advocates the elimination of discrimination against females and promotes equality between the sexes

From the Natural Sciences

Evolutionism	The belief that life came about through evolution	Empiricism	The inclination to rely on experience and observation in understanding phenomena
Determinism	The belief that effects in nature happen as a result of natural law	Anthropomorphism	The tendency for human beings to attribute human qualities to animals and inanimate objects
Reductionism	The intention to reduce complex relationships to the simplest possible terms		

Putting It All Together

Each of us would like to "put it all together." We want to be academically competent and well-adjusted, and get along well with others. In this book and in this course, you have examined many different dimensions of your life. Let's evaluate how far you have come this term in reaching the objectives we discussed in Chapter 1 and then look to the future and think about what lies ahead.

Looking Back

In Chapter 1 we described a number of objectives that promote mastery in college. By completing Self-Assessment 14.4 you can evaluate how effectively you have met them this term.

How have you done? We hope that you have improved in many areas this term. Chances are, though, that you still think you need to improve in some areas. Some helpful strategies for thinking about how to put it all together are presented in "Putting It All Together Now and in the Future."

> *I'd like to know what this whole show is all about before it's out.*
>
> **Piet Hein**
> **Dutch poet and inventor, 20th century**

> *Life is lived forward, but understood backwards.*
>
> **Sören Kierkegaard**
> **Danish philosopher and theologian, 19th century**

Self-Assessment 14-4

Am I Mastering the College Experience?

In Chapter 1 you completed a Self-Assessment in which you rated yourself on which areas of college you needed to improve the most. How have you done this term? Rate yourself from 1 to 5 in the following areas, with 1 = no improvement at all, 2 = a little improvement, 3 = moderate improvement, 4 = quite a bit of improvement, and 5 = extensive improvement.

DEVELOP MY LEARNING AND THINKING SKILLS

- _____ Get motivated
- _____ Focus my talents and skills
- _____ Understand and use my preferred learning style
- _____ Make accurate assessments of my strengths and weaknesses as a learner
- _____ Cope effectively with stress

IMPROVE MY BASIC SKILLS AND WORK HABITS

- _____ Improve my ability to learn and memorize
- _____ Improve my reading, writing, and speaking skills
- _____ Identify available resources and use them to my advantage
- _____ Master technology
- _____ Manage personal resources, such as time and money, effectively
- _____ Develop effective classroom strategies
- _____ Adopt effective study and test-taking habits

DEVELOP MY COMMUNICATION SKILLS, RELATIONSHIPS, AND PERSONAL QUALITIES

- _____ Improve my communication skills
- _____ Develop more positive relationships
- _____ Connect with diverse people and ideas
- _____ Delay gratification
- _____ Practice positive values

We hope you have improved in a number of areas of college life this term. Think about the areas in which you still need to improve. Make a commitment to work hard to improve in those areas.

Looking Forward

What lies in your future? We hope that you will continue your education and obtain the degree you are working toward. Remember that college graduates make considerably more money in their lifetime and like their work better than students who do not graduate. College graduates also live a healthier life.

As you think about putting it all together, keep in mind some of the ideas we discussed earlier in this chapter regarding values. When you contemplate your future, examine the things that are important to you. Imagine where you want to be and what you want to accomplish

- 30 years from now
- 10 years from now
- 5 years from now

Think about how you will use these years to do the things that are most important to you.

We began this book by discussing endings, change, and beginnings. We asked you to think about what had ended for you. What changes were involved? What beginnings were you about to undertake in your new college environment? We hope that you feel invigorated about college as a place for many more endings, changes, and beginnings. We hope you will keep this book and refer to it when future questions or problems arise.

Surprised

By How Much You Have Changed and Learned

The end of your first term is a good time to reflect on how you have changed and what you have learned so far in college. As you look back, are you surprised at what you know now that you didn't know a short few months ago? Are you surprised at how much you have changed?

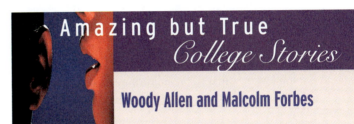

Amazing but True College Stories

Woody Allen and Malcolm Forbes

Academy Award-winning director, producer, and writer Woody Allen flunked motion picture production at New York University and the City College of New York. He also failed English at New York University.

Malcolm Forbes, the late publisher of *Forbes* magazine (one of the most successful business publications in the world) tried to get on the staff of the school newspaper at Princeton University as an undergraduate. He was turned down.

Allen and Forbes persisted and overcame their obstacles in college. So can you. Your college years will be filled with gains and losses. Learn from your losses. You have failed many times. You fell down the first time you tried to walk. You stammered and stumbled when you first learned to read. What counts is to keep after something you want.

Summary Tips For Mastering College

Practicing Integrity

Personal Values

1. Recognize that college presents many opportunities to explore your values.
2. Know your personal values. Think about whether they are the right values.
3. Be motivated to have positive values and make sure your behavior matches those values.
4. Examine your values in the following areas: politics, self-interest, civic concerns, and spirituality and religion.
5. The right values include being honest, being responsible, showing concern for others, and not being selfish.
6. Evaluate Covey's seven habits and M. Scott Peck's values. Do these habits and values characterize your life? Are these habits and values you want?

Academic Values

1. Recognize that your experiences in college (both in and out of the classroom) will contribute to your character and integrity.
2. Examine your integrity in the classroom, with college officials, with campus resources, with peers, and as a college representative. Make a commitment to have integrity in each of these areas of your college life.
3. Know the different "isms" and what they mean. Recognize that they are associated with various disciplines and involve values.

Putting It All Together

1. Evaluate how effectively you have mastered the college experience so far. Know which areas you have improved in the most and feel good about your progress.
2. Know the areas in which you still need to improve. Set some short-term and long-term goals for each of these areas. Make a commitment to attaining these goals. Review the goals periodically to see what progress you are making.

College Success Checklist

Have your views changed since you completed this checklist at the beginning of the chapter? Place a check mark beside any item for which you feel good about your current practice. Also check any item for which you have new ideas about how to improve.

____ I know what my values are.

____ I can describe the values of most first-year students.

____ I have explored religious and spiritual values deeply.

____ I can list the habits of highly effective people.

____ I know the right academic values and I practice them.

____ I know the "isms" associated with various academic disciplines and understand that these involve values.

____ Looking back over the term, I think that I have improved in a number of areas.

____ I feel confident about putting it all together in college and beyond.

In the space below, list items that you still need to work on the most. This list may help you complete the goal-setting exercise in the Learning Portfolio.

Review Questions

1. What are values?

2. What does clarifying your values involve?

3. What are the values of new college students?

4. What are Stephen Covey's seven habits of highly effective people?

5. What does M. Scott Peck believe are life's most important considerations?

6. How can you practice academic integrity and ethical behavior in different campus settings?

7. What are the different "isms" that you may encounter as a first-year student?

Learning Portfolio

Learning by Reflecting... Journal Entries

A Philosophy of Life

Developing a philosophy of life involves examining your values. This includes deciding what things are important to us. It also includes reflecting on how we believe the world should be. Get together with three to five other students and discuss each of your life philosophies.

- What do you agree on?
  _____
  _____

- What do you disagree about?
  _____
  _____

Exploring Your Spiritual/Religious Life

Think about the unique path your own spiritual/religious life has taken. Answer the following questions:

- When did you develop your spiritual or religious interest?
  _____
  _____

- What role did your parents play in your spiritual/religious interests?
  _____
  _____

- How important is your spiritual or religious life in your value system?
  _____
  _____

- Has your spiritual/religious interest become stronger or weaker since you started college?
  _____
  _____

Looking Back, Looking Forward

- Take a few moments to look back over this term. How effectively did you attain the objectives that were set forth at the beginning of the course for mastering the college experience?
  _____
  _____

- Also take a few moments to look to the future. In which areas do you need to improve the most to help you achieve success in college?
  _____
  _____
  _____
  _____

Learning by Doing... Action Projects

Wearing Your Values

- People vary in how much they advertise their values. Many college students wear T-shirts that give clear indications of the wearer's values. Notice the next 10 T-shirts you see on campus with emblems, symbols, statements, drawings, and so on. What can you infer from them about the wearer's values?

- Also examine your own wardrobe. What T-shirts do you own that reflect your values? Are they values that you want to display to others?

Analyze the Seven Habits

How do you stack up on Covey's seven habits? Are they a regular part of your life? Would any of the habits he described improve the quality of your life if you practiced them regularly?

Exploring the Rules on Your Campus

Look at your college catalog and examine what behaviors are and are not allowed. Sometimes students are unclear about what is considered cheating and what is not. The college catalog should spell this out.

Learning by Thinking Critically... Critiques

Using Values to Think More Deeply About Problems
Albert Einstein once observed that the significant problems we face cannot be solved at the same level of thinking we were at when we became aware of them. We need a deeper level of thinking to solve these significant problems. For example, people sometimes create a problem in either their academic or socioemotional life. Then they dismiss it at a superficial level. Describe an academic or socioemotional problem a person created and how he or she tried to solve it superficially. Then outline how the person can solve the problem with a deeper level of thinking. Hint: Think about how values might help the person solve the problem at a deeper level.

Compare Covey's Seven Habits and Peck's Values
Compare Stephen Covey's seven habits and M. Scott Peck's four values. How are they similar? How are they different? Which set do you prefer: Covey's or Peck's? Explain why you prefer one list over the other.

Explaining Gender Differences in Religious Interest
Women practice religion more, believe more in the presence of a higher power, and describe religion as more important to them than men do. Why does this gender difference exist? Generate two or more explanations for the difference. First brainstorm briefly here. Then analyze and expand.

_____
_____
_____
_____
_____
_____
_____
_____
_____
_____

Learning by Thinking Creatively... Personal Vision

Creating a Logo of Your Values
Go back and look at the five values you chose that are the most important to you. Put together a drawing or logo that reflects some or all of the values.

Creativity as a Value
We did not list creativity on the list of values earlier in the chapter. Do you think it should be on the main list of values? Some people believe that the excitement of creativity makes life worth living. Where does creativity fit in your value system? What is your best creative strategy?

Create a Quotation About Values
Think about the values that are most important to you. Select one of these and create a quotation that is meaningful to you. Place it in your Learning Portfolio. You also might want to put it on your bulletin board.

Learning by Planning... Goal Setting

Review the results of the Self-Assessments you completed in this chapter. Also review the College Success Checklist. What can you conclude about things you need to do to improve your skills?

What goal do you want to select from this chapter for making positive changes that will help you master the college experience? *(Hint: Is your goal challenging, reasonable, and specific?)*

_____
_____
_____
_____
_____

What strategies will you use to achieve your goal? *(Hint: Can you organize your strategy into a series of smaller goals?)*

_____
_____
_____
_____
_____

What obstacles may be in your way as you attempt to make these positive changes?

_____
_____
_____
_____
_____

What additional resources might help you succeed in achieving your goal?

_____
_____
_____
_____
_____

By what date do you want to accomplish your goal?

_____

How will you know you have succeeded?

_____
_____
_____
_____

Resources for Mastering the College Experience

Clarifying Your Values

The 7 Habits of Highly Effective People (1989) by Stephen Covey. New York: Fireside.
A book that has helped many people to clarify their values. Challenges you to live your life with fairness, integrity, honesty, and human dignity. Another Covey book, *First Things First* (1994), focuses on matching up your values with how you use your time.

Covey has a home page at www.covey.com and a toll-free number (1-800-255-0777) where information about worksheets pertaining to the seven habits is provided.

The Road Less Traveled (1978) by M. Scott Peck. New York: Touchstone.
A book and author that have inspired many young people to think more deeply about their values and how they want to live their lives. Suggests strategies for solving your problems and reaching a higher level of self-understanding. You also might want to read, *The Road Less Traveled & Beyond* (1997), which focuses on spiritual growth.

Values, Spirituality, and Religion

Invitation to Religion (1997, 2nd ed.) by Raymond Paloutzian. Boston: Allyn & Bacon.
Explores topics related to values, spirituality, and religion. Includes discussions of conversion, religious development, religious experience, religion and mental health, and the internal and external dimensions of religion.

Internet Resources

http://134.115.15.1/~winzar/Teaching/collude.html
Discusses potential negative consequences of colluding on writing projects. Murdoch University.

http://web.bu.edu/STH/Library/contents.html
Information on Asian religions, Christianity, Islam, and Judaism.

http://www.salc.wsu.edu/tlpub/index.html
On-line Learning Goals Inventory. Washington State University.

http://www.psych-web.com/mtsite/planpage.html
Mindtools; planning templates for managing change and overcoming resistance to it.

http://www.au.spiritweb.org/Spirit/impeccability-integrity-sasha-royal.html
Inspiring essay on living a responsible life.

References

A

Adler, R. B., & Towne, N. (1996). *Looking Out/Looking In*, 8th ed. New York: Holt, Rinehart, & Winston.

Alberti, R., & Emmons, M. (1995). *Your Perfect Right*, 7th ed. San Luis Obispo, CA: Impact.

Alverno College. (1993). *Writing and Speaking Criteria*. Milwaukee: Alverno Productions.

Alverno College Faculty. (1994). *Teaching Social Interaction at Alverno*. Milwaukee: Alverno Productions.

American College Health Association. (1989). *Survey of AIDS on American College and University Campuses*. Washington, DC.

Angelo, T. A., & Cross, K. P. (1993). *Classroom Assessment Techniques: A Handbook for College Teachers*. San Francisco: Jossey-Bass.

Appleby, D. (1990). Faculty and student perceptions of irritating behaviors in the college classroom. *Journal of Staff, Program, and Organizational Development, 8,* 41–46.

Appleby, D. (1994). *Liberal Arts Skills at Work*. Career Currents. Hanover, IN: Hanover College.

Appleby, D. (1997). *The Seven Wonders of the Advising World*. Invited address at the Southeastern Teachers of Psychology Conference, Kennesaw State University, Marietta, GA.

Armstrong, W. H., & Lampe, M. W. (1990). *Pocket Guide to Study Tips*, 3rd ed. Hauppage, NY: Barron's Educational Series.

Association of American Colleges. (1988). *Peer Harassment: Hassles for Women on Campus*. Washington, DC: Project on the Status and Education of Women.

Astin, A. (1993). *What Matters in College: Four Critical Years Revisited*. San Francisco: Jossey-Bass.

Astin, A. W., Parrott, S. A., Korn, W. S., & Sax, L. J. (1997). *The American Freshman: Thirty Year Trends*. Los Angeles: Higher Education Institute, UCLA.

Axelrod & Cooper (1993). *The Concise Guide to Writing*. New York: St. Martin's Press.

B

Bailey, C. (1991). *The New Fit or Fat*, Rev. ed. Boston: Houghton-Mifflin.

Bandura, A. (1994). Social cognitive theory of mass communication. In J. Bryant & D. Zillman (Eds.), *Media Effects*. Mahway, NJ: Erlbaum.

Bandura, A. (1998). Self-efficacy. In H.S. Friedman (Ed.), *Encyclopedia of Mental Health*, Vol. 3. San Diego: Academic Press.

Baumrind, D. (1991). Parenting styles and adolescent development. In J. Brooks-Gunn, R. Lerner, & A. C. Petersen (Eds.), *The Encyclopedia of Adolescence*. New York: Garland.

Baxter Magolda, M. B. (1992). *Knowing and Reasoning in College*. San Francisco: Jossey Bass.

Bednar, R. L., Wells, M. G., & Peterson, S. R. (1995). *Self-Esteem*, 2nd ed. Washington, DC: American Psychological Association.

Belenky, M. F., Clinchy, B. M., Goldberger, N. R., & Tarule, J. M. (1986). *Women's Ways of Knowing: The Development of Self, Voice, and Mind*. New York: Basic Books.

Benson, H. & Stuart, E. M. (1992). *The Wellness Book*. Birch Lane Press: New York.

Bem, S. L. (1977). On the utility of using alternative procedures for assessing psychological androgyny. *Journal of Consulting and Clinical Psychology, 45,* 196–205.

Bennett, M. E., & Miller, W. R. (1998). Alcohol Problems. In H. S. Friedman (Ed), *Encyclopedia of Mental Health*, Vol. 1. San Diego: Academic Press.

Bennett, M. E., & others. (1993). Identifying young substance-abusers: The Rutgers Collegiate Substance Abuse Screening Test. *Journal of Studies on Alcohol, 54,* 522–527.

Bernstein, D. (1993, July/August). Just when you think you've heard them all. . . . *Illinois Quarterly*, p. 2627.

Beyer, G. (1998). *Improving Student Thinking*. Boston: Allyn & Bacon.

Bloom, B. S., Englehart, M. D., Furst, E. J., & Krathwohl, D. R. (1956). *Taxonomy of Educational Objectives: Cognitive Domain*. New York: David McKay.

Bly, R. (1990). *Iron John*. New York: Vintage Books.

Bourne, E. J. (1995). *The Anxiety & Phobia Workbook*, 2nd ed. Oakland, CA: New Harbinger.

Bransford, J. D., & Stein, B. S. (1984). *The Ideal Problem Solver*. New York: W. H. Freeman.

Bridges, W. (1991). *Managing Transitions: Making the Most of Change*. Reading, MA: Addison Wesley.

Brislin, R. W. (1993). *Understanding Culture's Influence on Behavior*. Ft. Worth, TX: Harcourt Brace.

Brophy, J. (1998). *Motivating students to learn*. Burr Ridge, IL: McGraw-Hill.

Browne, M. N., & Keeley, S. M. (1990). *Asking the Right Questions: A Guide to Critical Thinking*. 3rd ed. Englewood Cliffs, N.J.: Prentice Hall.

Burt, C. D. B. (1993). Concentration and academic ability following transition to university: An investigation of the effects of homesickness. *Journal of Environmental Psychology, 13,* 333–342.

C

Canfield, J., & Hansen, N. V. (1995). *The Aladdin Factor*. New York: Berkeley Publishers.

Centers for Disease Control. (1995). *HIV/AIDS Surveillance Report*, Vol. 6, No. 2. Atlanta: U.S. Department of Health and Human Services.

Cochran, S. D., & Mays, V. M. (1990). Sex, lies, and HIV. *New England Journal of Medicine, 322,* 774–775.

Coles, R. (1989). *The Call of Stories: Teaching and the Moral Imagination.* Boston: Houghton-Mifflin.

Collins, M. (1996, Winter). The job outlook for '96 grads. *Journal of Career Planning,* 51–54.

Conner, J. E. (1984). The passionate pursuit of possibility. In J. Canfield & M. V. Hansen (1996), *Chicken Soup for the Soul.* Deerfield Beach, FL: Health Communications.

Covey, S. R. (1989). *The 7 Habits of Highly Effective People.* New York: Fireside.

Covey, S. R., Merrill, A. R., & Merrill, R. R. (1994). *First Things First.* New York: Simon & Schuster.

Crooks, R., & Bower, K. (1996). *Our Sexuality,* 6th ed. Pacific Grove, CA: Brooks/Cole.

Crooks, R., & Bower, K. (1999). *Our Sexuality,* 7th ed. Pacific Grove, CA: Brooks/Cole.

Csikszentmihalyi, M. (1995). *Creativity.* New York: HarperCollins.

Csikszentmihalyi, M. (1997). *Finding Flow.* New York: Basic Books.

Cutrona, C. E. (1982). Transition to college: Loneliness and the process of social adjustment. In L. A. Peplau & D. Perlman (Eds.), *Loneliness: A Sourcebook of Current Theory, Research, and Therapy.* New York: Wiley.

D

Davis, M., Eshelman, E. R., & McKay, M. (1995). *The Relaxation & Stress Reduction Workbook,* 4th ed. Oakland, CA: New Harbinger.

Davis, S. F., Grover, C. A., Becker, A. H., & McGregor, L. N. (1992). Academic dishonesty: Prevalence, determinants, techniques, and punishments. *Teaching of Psychology, 19,* 16–20.

DeLongis, A., & Newth, S. (1998). Coping with stress. In H. S. Friedman (Ed.), *Encyclopedia of Mental Health,* Vol. 1. San Diego: Academic Press.

Dobkin, R., & Sippy, S. (1995). *Educating Ourselves: The College Woman's Handbook.* New York: Workman Publishing.

Douglass, M. E., & Douglass, D. N. (1993). *Manage Your Time, Your Work, Yourself,* updated ed. New York: American Management Association.

Doyle. J. A., & Paludi, M. A. (1998). *Sex and Gender,* 4th ed. Burr Ridge, IL: McGraw-Hill.

Duffy, D. K., & Jones, J. W. (1995). *Teaching Within the Rhythms of the Semester.* San Francisco: Jossey-Bass.

E

Edelman, M. W. (1992). *The Measure of Our Success.* Boston: Beacon Press.

Ellis, A. (1996). A rational-emotive behavior therapist's perspective on Ruth. In G. Corey (Ed.), *Case Approach to Counseling and Psychotherapy.* Pacific Grove, CA: Brooks/Cole.

Erikson, E. H. (1968). *Identity: Youth and Crisis.* New York: Norton.

Evans, N. J., Forney, D. S., & Guido-DiBrito, F. (1998). *Student Development in College.* San Francisco: Jossey-Bass.

F

Fleming, J., & Morning, C. (1998). Adult students in higher education: Burden or boon? *The Journal of Higher Education, 69,* 65-88.

Fowler, J. W. (1981). *Studies of Faith: The Psychology of Human Development and the Quest for Faith.* New York: HarperCollins.

Frank, S. (1996). *The Everything Study Book.* Holbrook, MA: Adams Media Corp.

Frederick, P. J. (1991). The medicine wheel: Emotions and connections I the classroom. *To Improve the Academy, 10,* 197–214.

French, B. (1996). What's really important. In J. Canfield & M. V. Hansen, *A 3rd Serving of Chicken Soup for the Soul.* Deerfield Beach, FL: Health Communications.

G

Gardner, H. (1983, 1989). *Frames of Mind.* New York: Basic Books.

Gearheart, B. R., & Gearheart, C. J. (1989). *Learning Disabilities: Educational Strategies,* 3rd ed. Columbus, OH: Merril Publishers.

Gilligan, C. (1990). *In a Different Voice.* Cambridge, MA: Harvard University Press.

Goldberg, H. (1980). *The New Male.* New York: Signet.

Goleman, D. (1995). *Emotional Intelligence.* New York: Bantam.

Goleman, D., Kaufmann, P., & Ray, M. (1992). *The Creative Spirit.* New York: Plume.

Gordon, T. (1970). *Parent Effectiveness Training.* New York: McGraw-Hill.

Grabe, M. (1998). *Learning with Internet Tools.* Ft. Worth: Harcourt Brace.

Grandin, T. (1995). *Thinking in Pictures.* New York: Doubleday.

H

Haines, M. E., Norris, M. P., & Kashy, D. A. (1996). The effects of depressed mood on academic performance in college students. *Journal of College Student Development, 37,* 519–526.

Hallahan, D. P., Kaufman, J. M., & Lloyd, J. W. (1998). *Learning Disabilities.* Boston: Allyn & Bacon.

Halonen, J. S., & Santrock, J. W. (1997). *Psychology of Adjustment,* 2nd ed. Madison: Brown & Benchmark.

Halonen, J. S., & Santrock, J. W. (1999). *Psychology: Contexts of Behavior,* 3rd ed. Madison: Brown & Benchmark.

Hansen, R. S., & Hansen, K. (1997). *Write Your Way to a Higher GPA.* Berkeley, CA: Ten Speed Press.

Harackiewicz, J. M. (1998). Intrinsic motivation and goals. In H. S. Friedman (Ed.) *Encyclopedia of Mental Health,* Vol. 2. San Diego: Academic Press.

Harbin, C. E. (1995). *Your Transfer Planner*. Belmont, CA: Wadsworth.

Hellman, H. (1976). *Technophobia: Getting out of the Technology Trap*. New York: M. Evans & Co.

Hurtado, S., Dey, E. L., & Trevino, J. G. (1994). *Exclusion or Self-Segregation? Interaction Across Racial/Ethnic Groups on College Campuses*. Paper presented at the meeting of the American Educational Research Association, New York City.

I

Iacocca, L. (1984). *Iacocca: An Autobiography*. New York: Bantam.

Ishakawa, K. (1984). *What is Total Quality Control? The Japanese Way*. Englewood Cliffs, NJ: Prentice Hall.

J

Jendrick, M. P. (1992). Students' reactions to academic dishonesty. *Journal of College Student Development, 33*, 260–273.

Johnston, L. (1997). *Smoking, Drinking, and Drug Use in Young Adulthood: Impact of New Freedoms and New Responsibilities*. Mahway, NJ: Erlbaum.

Johnston, L. D., O'Malley, P. M., & Bachman, J. G. (1996). *National Survey Results on Drug Use from the Monitoring the Future Study, 1975–1994, Vol. 2*. Rockville, MD: National Institute on Drug Abuse.

K

Kalichman, S. (1996). *Answering Your Questions About AIDS*. Washington, DC: American Psychological Association.

Kantrowitz, B. (1994, May 16). Men, women, and computer. *Newsweek*, pp. 48–52, 54–55.

Kaplan, R. M., & Saccuzzo, D. P. (1993). *Psychological Testing: Principles, Applications, and Issues*, 3rd ed. Pacific Grove, CA: Brooks/Cole.

Keith-Spiegel, P. (1992). *Ethics in Shades of Pale Gray*. Paper presented at the Mid-America Conference for Teachers of Psychology, Evansville, IN.

Kennedy, M. M. (1998). *Learning to Teach Writing*. New York: Teachers' College Press.

Kerr, S. T. (1990). Technology: Education–Justice: Care or thoughts on reading Carol Gilligan. *Educational Technology, 30*, 7–12.

Kierwa, K. A. (1987). Note-taking and review: The research and its implications. *Instructional Science, 19*, 394-397.

Kinsey, A., Pomeroy, W., & Martin, C. (1948). *Sexual Behavior in the Human Male*. Philadelphia: Saunders.

Knox, D., Gibson, L., Zusman, M., & Gallmeier, C. (1997). Why college students end relationships. *The College Student Journal, 31*, 449-452.

Kolb, D. A. (1984). *Experiential Learning: Experience as the Source of Learning and Development*. Englewood Cliffs, NJ: Prentice-Hall.

Koss, M., & Boeschen, L. (1998). Rape. In H.S. Friedman, (Ed.), *Encyclopedia of Mental Health*, Vol. 3. San Diego: Academic Press.

L

Lage, E. (1991). Boys, girls, and microcomputing. *European Journal of Psychology of Education, 6*, 29–44.

Lakein, A. (1973). *How to Get Control of Your Time and Your Life*. New York: Signet.

Langer, E. (1989). *Mindfulness*. Reading, MA: Addison-Wesley.

Langer, E. (1997). *The Power of Mindful Learning*. Reading, MA: Addison-Wesley.

Lazarus, R. S. (1993). Coping theory and research: Past, present, and future. *Psychosomatic Medicine, 55*, 234–247.

Lazarus, R. S. (1998). Fifty years of the research and theory of R. S. Lazarus. Mahwah, NJ: Erlbaum.

Leatherman, C. (1997, November 7). Do accreditors look the other way when colleges rely on part-time instructors? *Chronicle of Higher Education*, XLIV. A12-14.

Lerner, H. G. (1989). *The Dance of Intimacy*. New York: HarperCollins.

Levine, A., & Cureton, J. S. (1998) *When Hope and Fear Collide*. San Francisco: Jossey-Bass.

Levinger, E. E. (1949). *Albert Einstein*. New York: Julian Messner, Inc.

Lin, J. G., & Yi, J. K. (1997). Asian international students' adjustments. *The College Student Journal, 31*, 473-479.

Lindgren, H. C. (1969). *The Psychology of College Success: A Dynamic Approach*. New York: Wiley.

Lorayne, H., & Lucas, J. (1996). *The Memory Book*. New York: Ballantine.

M

Maas, J. (1998). *Power Sleep: The Program That Prepares Your Mind for Peak Performance*. New York: Villard.

Maddux, C. D., Johnson, D. L., & Willis, J. W. (1997). *Educational Computing*. Boston: Allyn & Bacon.

Maimon, E. P., Nodine, B. F., & Finbarr, W. O. (Eds.). (1989). *Thinking, Reasoning, and Writing*. New York: Longman.

Marcia, J. E. (1980). Ego identity development. In J. E. Adelson (Ed.), *Handbook of Adolescent Psychology*. New York: Wiley.

Marcia, J. E.(1996, April). Review of Santrock, J. W., *Adolescence*, 7th ed. New York: McGraw-Hill.

Marcia, J. E. (1998). Optimal development from an Eriksonian perspective. In H.S. Friedman (Ed.), *Encyclopedia of Mental Health*, Vol. 2. San Diego: Academic Press.

Maris, R.W. (1998). Suicide. In H. S. Friedman (Ed). *Encyclopedia of Mental Health*, Vol. 3. San Diego: Academic Press.

Martin, G. L., & Pear, J. (1996). *Behavior Modification*, 6th ed. Upper Saddle River, NJ: Prentice Hall.

Marton, F., Hounsell, D. J., & Entwistle, N. J. (1984). *The Experience of Learning*. Edinburgh: Scottish Academic Press.

Matlin, M. (1998). *Cognitive Psychology*, 3rd ed. Ft. Worth: Harcourt Brace.

McDonald, R. L. (1994). *How to Pinch a Penny till It Screams*. Garden City, NY: Avery.

McLaughlin, M. L., Osborne, K. K., & Smith, C. B. (1995). Standards of conduct on Usenet. In S. G. Jones (Ed.), *Cybersociety: Computer-Mediated Communication and Community.* Thousands Oaks, CA: Sage.

McNally, D. (1990). *Even Eagles Need a Push.* New York: Dell.

Meltzoff, J. (1998). *Critical Thinking About Research: Psychology and Related Fields.* Washington, DC: American Psychological Association.

Michael, R. T., Gagnon, J. H., Laumann, E. O., & Kolata, G. (1994). *Sex in America.* Boston: Little Brown.

Miller, G. A. (1956). The magical number seven, plus or minus two: Some limits on our capacity for information-processing. *Psychological Review, 48,* 337–442.

Miller, J. B. (1986). *Toward a New Psychology of Women,* 2nd ed. Boston: Beacon Press.

Minninger, J. (1984). *Total Recall.* New York: Pocket Books.

Moawad, B. (1993). *Walt Jones.* Tacoma, WA: Edge Learning Institute.

Moses, H. C. (1990). *Inside College.* New York: College Entrance Examination Board.

Murphy, M. C. (1996). Stressors on the college campus: A comparison of 1985 and 1993. *Journal of College Student Development, 37,* 20–28.

Murray, B. (1998, March). E-mail bonding with your students. *APA Monitor,* 38.

Mussell, M. P., & Mitchell, J. E. (1998). Anorexia nervosa and bulimia nervosa. In H.S. Friedman (Ed.), *Encyclopedia of Mental Health,* Vol. 1. San Diego: Academic Press.

Myers, I. D. (1962). *Manual: Myers–Briggs Type Indicator.* Princeton, NJ: Educational Testing Service.

N

Newell, A., & Simon, H. A. (1972). *Human Problem Solving.* Englewood Cliffs, NJ: Prentice Hall.

Nichols, R. B. (1961, March). Do we know how to listen? Practical helps in a modern age. *Speech teacher, 10,* 122.

Nolen-Hoeksema, S. (1998). *Abnormal Psychology.* Burr Ridge, IL: McGraw-Hill.

O

Occupational Outlook Handbook (1998–99). Washington, DC: U.S. Department of Labor, Bureau of Labor Statistics.

O'Leary, M. (1995). *The Online 100: Online Magazine's Field Guide to the 100 Most Important Online Data Bases.* Wilton, CT: Pemberton.

P

Paludi, M. A. (1995). *The Psychology of Women.* 2nd ed. Madison: Brown & Benchmark.

Paludi, M. A. (1998). *The Psychology of Women.* Upper Saddle River, NJ: Prentice-Hall.

Park, C. L., & Stiles, W. B. (1998). Self-Disclosure. In H.S. Friedman (Ed.), *Encyclopedia of Mental Health,* Vol. 3. San Diego: Academic Press.

Peck, M. S. (1979). *The Road Less Traveled.* New York: Touchstone.

Peck, M. S. (1997). *The Road Less Traveled & Beyond: Spiritual Growth in an Age of Anxiety.* New York: Simon & Schuster.

Pennebaker, J. (1990). *Opening Up.* New York: Avon.

Perkins, D. N. (1984, September). Creativity by design. *Educational Leadership,* 18–25.

Perlman, D. & Peplau, L. A. (1998). Loneliness. In H. S. Friedman (Ed.), *Encyclopedia of Psychology,* Vol. 2. San Diego: Academic Press.

Peterson, C., & Stunkard, A. J. (1986). *Personal Control and Health Promotion.* Unpublished manuscript, Department of Psychology, University of Michigan, Ann Arbor.

Pleck, J. H. (1983). The theory of male sex role identity: Its rise and fall, 1936–present. In M. Lewin (Ed.), *In the Shadow of the Past: Psychology Portrays the Sexes.* New York: Columbia University Press.

Poole, B. J. (1998). *Education for an Information Age,* 2nd ed. Burr Ridge, IL: McGraw-Hill.

R

Reich, J. N. (1998, March). Technology's role in education. *APA Monitor.* 45.

Reid, E. (1995). Virtual worlds: Culture and imagination. In S. G. Jones (Ed.), *Cybersociety: Computer-Mediated Communication and Community.* Thousands Oaks, CA: Sage.

Rocheleau, B. (1995). Computer use by school-age children: Trends, patterns, and predictors. *Journal of Educational Computing Research, 12,* 1–17.

Rodin, J. (1992). *Body Traps.* New York: William Morrow.

Rodin, J., & Langer, E. J. (1977). Long-term effects of a control-relevant intervention with the institutionalized aged. *Journal of Personality and Social Psychology, 35,* 397–402.

Rogers, C. R. (1980). *A Way of Being.* Boston: Houghton-Mifflin.

Rosen, L. D., & Weil, M. M. (1995). Computer availability, computer experience and technophobia among public school teachers. *Computers in Human Behavior, 11,* 9–31.

Ruggerio, V. R. (1995). *Beyond Feelings: A Guide to Critical Thinking,* 4th ed. Mountain View, CA: Mayfield Publishing Co.

S

Sadker, M., & Sadker, D. (1994). *Failing at Fairness.* New York: Touchstone.

Salvia, J. & Ysseldyke, J. E. (1995). *Assessment,* 6th ed. Boston: Houghton-Mifflin.

Santrock, J. (1997) *Psychology,* 5th ed. Madison: Brown & Benchmark.

Sax, L. J., Astin, A. W., Korn, W. S., & Mahoney, K. M. (1995). *The American College Freshman: National Norms for Fall, 1995.* Los Angeles: Higher Education Research Institute, UCLA.

Sax, L. J., Astin, A. W., Korn, W. S., & Mahoney, K. M. (1997). *The American Freshman: National Norms for 1997*. Los Angeles: Higher Education Research Institute, UCLA.

Schacter, D. (1996). *Searching for Memory*. New York: Basic Books.

Schwartz, M. (1996, March 7). Medical student is realizing an impossible dream. *Dallas Morning News*, p. 1D.

Sears, D. O., Peplau, L. A., & Taylor, S. E. (1997). *Social Psychology*, 9th ed. Upper Saddle River, NJ: Prentice Hall.

Seligman, M. E. P. (1991). *Learned Optimism*. New York: Pocket Books.

Sher, K. J., Wood, P. K., & Gotham, H. J. (1996). The course of psychological distress in college: A prospective high-risk study. *Journal of College Student Development*, 37, 42–51.

Silverman, J. (1997). The aesthetic experience of learning: Stretching new boundaries. *Journal of General Education*, 46. 73-95.

Skinner, K. (1997). *The MSE Oracle System*. Dallas: Southern Methodist University.

Snow, R. E., Corno, L., & Jackson, D. (1996). Individual differences in affective and cognitive functions. In D. C. Berliner & R. C. Calfee (Eds.), *Handbook of Educational Psychology*. New York: Macmillan.

Smith, H. W. (1994). *The 10 Natural Laws of Successful Time and Life Management*. New York: Time Warner.

Spiritual America (1994, April 4). *U.S. News & World Report*, pp. 48–59.

Sternberg, R. J. (1988). *The Triangle of Love*. New York: Basic Books.

Sternberg, R. J. (1994, November). Allowing for thinking styles. *Educational Leadership*, 36–40.

Sternberg, R. J. (1997). *Thinking Styles*. New York: Cambridge.

Svinicki, M. D., & Dixon, N. M. (1984). The Kolb Model modified for classroom activities. *College Teaching*, 35, 141–146.

T

Tannen, D. (1990). *You Just Don't Understand!* New York: Ballantine.

Tannen, D. (1998). *The Argument Culture*. New York: Random House.

Tavris, C. (1992). *The Mismeasure of Woman*. New York: Touchstone.

Taylor, S. E. (1995). *Health Psychology*, 3rd ed. New York: McGraw-Hill.

Treagust, D. F., Duit, R., & Fraser, B. J. (1996). *Improving Teaching and Learning in Science and Mathematics*. New York: Teachers College Press.

Triandis, H. (1994). *Culture and Social Behavior*. New York: McGraw-Hill.

U

U.S. Bureau of the Census. (1990). *Current Population Reports*. Washington, DC: U.S. Government Printing Office.

University of Illinois Counseling Center. (1984). *Overcoming Procrastination*. Urbana–Champaign, IL: Department of Student Affairs.

V

Vickory, D. M., & Fries, J. F. (1996). *Take Care of Yourself*, 6th ed. Reading, MA: Addison Wesley.

W

Walters, A. (1994). Using visual media to reduce homophobia. A classroom demonstration. *Journal of Sex Education and Therapy*, 20, 92–100.

Waterman, A. (1989). Curricula interventions for identity change. *Journal of Adolescence*, 12, 389–400.

Watson & Tharp (1996). *Self-Directed Behavior*, 7th ed. Pacific Grove, CA: Brooks/Cole.

Weinberg, C. (1994). *The Complete Handbook for College Women*. New York: NYU Press.

Weinstein, C. (1987). *The Learning and Study Strategies Inventory*. Clearwater, FL: H & H Publishing.

Weinstein, N. D. (1984). Reducing unrealistic optimism about illness susceptibility. *Health Psychology*, 3, 431–457.

Whimbey, A., & Lochhead, J. (1991). *Problem Solving and Comprehension*. Hillsdale, NJ: Erlbaum.

White, J. L., & Parham, T. A. (1990). *The Psychology of Blacks*, 2nd ed. Englewood Cliffs, NJ: Prentice Hall.

Winston, S. (1995). *Stephanie Winston's Best Organizing Tips*. New York: Simon & Schuster.

Wolvin, A., & Coakley, C. G. (1995). *Listening*, 5th ed. Madison, WI: Brown & Benchmark.

Y

Yates, M. (1995, March). *Political Socialization as a Function of Volunteerism*. Paper presented at the meeting of the Society for Research in Child Development, Indianapolis.

Z

Zeidner, M. (1995). Adaptive coping with test situations: A review of the literature. *Educational Psychologist*, 30, 123–133.

Credits

Photo Credits

Chapter 1
1 (right) PhotoDisc, (left) Viesti Associates, Inc., Frank Siteman; 2 The Gamma Liaison Network, Theo Westenberger; 4 (top) PhotoEdit, Barbara Sititzer, (bottom) © Tribune Media Services. All rights reserved. Reprinted with permission; 5 Tony Stone Images, David Austen; Tony Stone Images, H. Richard Johnston; 6 Mal Enterprises, Inc.; 7 Edward Koren © 1988 from The New Yorker Collection. All Rights Reserved; 10 UPI/Corbis-Bettmann; 14 DILBERT reprinted by permission of United Feature Syndicate, Inc.; 17 © 1973 News America Syndicate, Mell Lazarus.

Chapter 2
25 (right) Tony Stone Images, Kevin Horan, (left) The Image Bank, Marvin E. Newman; 26 Barbra Witt; 32 DILBERT reprinted by permission of United Feature Syndicate, Inc.; 36 The Image Bank; 38 Third Eye Photography; 39 PhotoEdit, Gary A. Conner; 42 Reprinted by permission of Glenn Dines; 45 PhotoEdit, Robert Ginn

Chapter 3
53 Super Stock; 59 *Frank and Ernest* © 1990 Thaves/NEA, Inc.; 63 (right) PhotoEdit, Barbara Stitzer, (left) PhotoEdit, Gary A. Conner; 70 PhotoEdit, David Young-Wolff; 71 DILBERT reprinted by permission of United Feature Syndicate, Inc.; 73 PhotoEdit, D. Young-Wolff

Chapter 4
81 (right) Tony Stone Images, Jon Riley, (left) PhotoDisc; 82 Contact Press Images, Mark Richards; 83 ZIGGY © 1982, 1995 ZIGGY AND FRIENDS, INC. Dist. by UNIVERSAL PRESS SYNDICATE. Reprinted with permission. All Rights Reserved; 86 Reprinted by permission of Gahan Wilson; 91 Dana Fradon © 1991 from The New Yorker Collection. All Rights Reserved; 92 PhotoEdit, Mark Richards; 95 The Image Bank, Babriel Covian; 96 Reprinted by permission of Martha F. Campbell; 98 Reprinted by permission of George B. Abbott; 99 Courtesy of ERIC; 100 Reprinted by permission of Mark Litzler; 102 (top) Index Stock Photography, (bottom) Reprinted by permission of Carol Cable

Chapter 5
111 (right) Tony Stone Images, David Young-Wolff, (left) Viesti Associates, Inc., Greg Nikas; 112 Courtesy of Jane Halonen; 113 Reprinted by permission of Vivian Scott Hixson; 117 Doonesbury; G. B. Trudeau. Used by permission of UNIVERSAL PRESS SYNDICATE. All rights reserved; 124 Electronic Publishing Services Inc. NYC, Francis Hogan; 129 Reprinted by permission of Gahan Wilson; 135 The Image Bank, Flip Chalfant.

Chapter 6
143 (left) PhotoEdit, Mark Richards, (right) PhotoDisc; 144 Reuters/Corbis-Bettmann, Pete Souza; 146 PhotoEdit, Barbara Stitzer; 147 PhotoEdit, Gary A. Conner; 148 Reprinted by permission of Ravel Tate; 152 Reprinted by permission of © Sidney Harris; 157 The Image Bank, David De Lossy, 161 PhotoEdit, Cleo; 163 (left) Reuters/Corbis-Bettmann, (center) Courtesy of CBS, Cliff Lipson, (right) Reuters/Corbis-Bettmann, Fred Prouser

Chapter 7
173 (right) PhotoEdit, Gary A. Conner, (left) Viesti Associates Inc., Richard Pasley; 174 Corbis-Bettmann; 177 PhotoEdit, Gary A. Conner; 181 Reprinted by permission of Harold Bakken; 186 THE FAR SIDE © 1987 FARWORKS, INC. Used by permission of UNIVERSAL PRESS SYNDICATE. All rights reserved; 193 Reprinted by permission of © Sidney Harris

Chapter 8
203 (right) Index Stock Photography, (left) The Image Bank, Steve Dunnell; 204 © Rosalie Winard; 205 Reprinted by permission of Carol Cable; 207 PhotoEdit, Jonathan Nourok; 215 PhotoEdit, Gary A. Conner; 218 PhotoEdit, Mark Richards; 220 Courtesy of University of Chicago News Service; 221 (left) AP/World Wide Photos, (center) Courtesy of Nina Holton, (right) UPI/Corbis-Bettmann; 223 (left) Corbis-Bettmann, David Thomson, (right) Sigrid Estrada; 225 Rick Friedman/NYT Pictures

Chapter 9
233 (right) PhotoEdit, Michael Newman, (left) The Image Bank, Juan Silva; 234 Reuters/Corbis-Bettmann; 241 PEANUTS reprinted by permission of United Feature Syndicate, Inc.; 242 PhotoEdit, Myrleen Ferguson; 247 THE FAR SIDE © 1984 FARWORKS, INC. Used by permission of UNIVERSAL PRESS SYNDICATE. All Rights Reserved.; 248 CALVIN AND HOBBES © Watterson. Dist. by UNIVERSAL PRESS SYNDICATE. Reprinted with permission. All rights reserved; 249 FRANCIE reprinted by permission of United Feature Syndicate, Inc.

Chapter 10
259 (right) Index Stock Photography, (left) PhotoEdit, Bonnie Kamin, 260 UPI/Corbis-Bettmann; 261 PEANUTS reprinted by permission of United Feature Syndicate, Inc.; 264 (left) PhotoEdit, Bonnie Kamin, (right) PhotoEdit, D. Young-Wolff; 265 CATHY © 1993 Cathy Guisewite. Reprinted by permission of UNIVERSAL PRESS SYNDICATE. All rights reserved.

Chapter 11
283 (right) Contact Press Images, David Burnett, (left) FPG International, Gary Buss; 287 FPG international, Rob Gage; 288 FPG international, Bill Losh; 289 Reprinted by permission of Joel Pett; 294 PhotoEdit, Jonathan Novrok

393

Chapter 12

305 (right) Tony Stone Images, Brian Bailey, (left) Index Stock Photography; 306 Reuters/Corbis-Bettmann; 310 PhotoEdit, D. Young-Wolff; 311 THE FAR SIDE © 1982 FARWORKS, INC. Used by permission of UNIVERSAL PRESS SYNDICATE. All rights reserved; 315 The Gamma Liaison Network, Paula A. Scully; 317 PhotoEdit, Bachmann; 321 The Image Bank, David de Lossy; 322 Cheney from The New Yorker Collection. All Rights Reserved; 325 ZIGGY © 1982, 1995 ZIGGY AND FRIENDS, INC. Dist. by UNIVERSAL PRESS SYNDICATE. Reprinted with permission. All rights reserved; 326 The Image Bank, G&M David de Lossy; 329 Courtesy of Nancy Felipe Russo

Chapter 13

339 (right) PhotoEdit, Bonnie Kamin, (left) Tony Stone Images, Bob Torrez; 340 Black Star, Erica Lansner; 341 Corbis-Bettmann, David Boe; 343 Anthony Taber © 1988 from The New Yorker Collection. All Rights Reserved; 346 Reprinted by permission of Harold Bakken; 355 © Engleman/Rothco Cartoons; 356 (top) PhotoEdit; Mark Richards, (bottom) © 1998, Reprinted courtesy of Bunny Hoest and Parade Magazine

Chapter 14

365 (right) PhotoEdit, Rudi Von Briel, (left) Viesti Associates Inc., Richard Pasley; 366 University Photography; 370 Mike Twohy © 1992 from The New Yorker Collection. All Rights Reserved; 371 (left) Joel Gordon, (top right) PhotoEdit, Michael Newman, (bottom right) PhotoEdit, David Young-Wolff; 372 © National Review. Reprinted by permission of Rex F. May (Baloo Enterprises); 373 Courtesy of the Franklin Covey Co, Provo, Utah–1997; 375 Courtesy of M. Scott Peck

Text Credits

p. 12 "Amazing But True College Stories: A Remarkable Journey": Story of Mary Groda from J. E. Conner (1984), *The Passionate Pursuit of Possibility*, as found in J. Canfield and M. V. Hansen, *Chicken Soup for the Soul*. Copyright © 1984 by Health Communications Inc. Reprinted with the permission of Health Communications, Inc., Deerfield Beach, FL; *p*. 33 Table 2.2, "How to Get on the Wrong Side of an Instructor," after Appleby, D. (1990), "Faculty and staff perceptions of irritating behaviors in the college classroom" from *Journal of Staff, Program, and Organizational Development*, 8, pages 41-46. Copyright © 1990. Reprinted with the permission of New Forums Press; *p*. 63 Self-Assessment 3.3, "Are You a Procrastinator?" from M. S. Roberts, *Living Without Procrastination*. Copyright © 1995 by New Harbinger Publications, Inc. Reprinted with the permission of New Harbinger Publications, Inc., Oakland, CA, www.newharbinger.com; *p*. 68 "On-Target Tips": "Pinching Pennies" from R. L. McDonald, *How to Pinch a Penny Till it Screams*. Copyright © 1994 by Rochelle Lamotte McDonald. Reprinted with the permission of Avery Publishing Group, Wayne, NJ; *p*. 72 Table 3.2: "Sources of Funds for College Freshmen," after L. J. Sax, A. W. Astin, W. S. Korn, and K. M. Mahoney, *The American freshman: National norms for 1995*. Reprinted with the permission of Higher Education Research Institute, Graduate School of Education, University of California, Los Angles; *p*. 99 Table 4.1: "Popular Electronic Abstracts" from M. O'Leary, *The Online 100: Online Magazine's Field Guide to the 100 Most Popular Online Data Bases*. Copyright © 1995 by Mich O'Leary. Reprinted with the permission of Information Today, Inc., Medford, NJ, www.infotoday.com; *p*. 130 Self Assessment 5.2: "What's Your Reader Profile?" derived from V. Miholic (1994), "An inventory to pique students' metacognitive awareness of reading strategies," from *Journal of Reading* 38, no 2 (October 1994): 84-86. Copyright © 1994 by International Reading Association, Inc. Reprinted with the permission of the author and publisher; *p*. 133 Self-Assessment 5.3: "How Fast Do You Read?" from K. Skinner, *The MSE Oracle System* (Dallas: Southern Methodist University, 1997). Used by permission; *p*. 158 "On-Target Tips": "Deep Study Strategies for the Humanities" from B. S. Bloom, M. D. Englehart, E. J. Furst and D. R. Krathwohl, *Taxonomy of educational objectives: Cognitive domain*. Copyright © 1956 and renewed 1984 by Benjamin S. Bloom and David R. Krathwohl. Reprinted with the permission of Longman Publishing Group, White Plains, NY; *p*. 165 Self Assessment 6.4: "Could I Have a Learning Disability?" derived from B. R. Gearhart and C. J. Gearhart, *Learning disabilities: Educational strategies, Third Edition*. Copyright © 1989 by Charles E. Merrill Publishers. Reprinted with the permission of Prentice-Hall, Inc.; *p*. 207 Figure 8.1: "The Characteristics of Good Critical Thinking?" from V. R. Ruggiero, *Beyond Feelings: A Guide to Critical Thinking, Fourth Edition*. Copyright © 1995 by Mayfield Publishing Company. Reprinted with the permission of the publisher; *p*. 215 "On-Target Tips": "I Have a Question" from M. N. Brown & S. M. Keeley, *Asking the Right Questions: A Guide to Critical Thinking, 3rd Edition*. Copyright © 1990 by Prentice-Hall, Inc. Reprinted with the permission of the publisher; *p*. 222 Table 8.2: "Some 'Mental Locks' That Reduce Your Creativity — and What to Do About Them!" derived from Roger van Oech, *A Whack on the Side of the Head: How You Can Be More Creative*. Copyright © 1990 by Roger van Oech. Reprinted with the permission of Warner Books, Inc.; *p*. 224 Figure 8.3: "The Medicine Wheel" from "The medicine wheel: Emotions and connections in the classroom" from P. J. Frederick (1991), *To Improve the Academy*, 10, pp. 197-214. Copyright © 1991. Reprinted with the permission of New Forums Press; *p*. 243 Self-Assessment 9.1: "What are My Writing Strengths and Weaknesses?" adapted from *Criteria for Effective Writing*. Reprinted with the permission of Alverno College Productions; *p*. 250 Self-Assessment 9.2: "What Are My Speaking Strengths and Weaknesses?" from *Criteria for Effective Speaking/Media*. Reprinted with the permission of Alverno College Productions; *p*. 266 Figure 10.1: "A Bill of Assertive Rights" from Manuel J. Smith, *When I Say No, I Feel Guilty*. Copyright © 1975 by Manuel J. Smith. Reprinted with the permission of Doubleday, a division of Bantam Doubleday Dell Publishing Group, Inc.; *p*. 268 Self-Assessment 10.1: "Do You Blow Up, Get Down and Dirty, Cave In, or Speak Up?," after E. J. Bourne, *The Anxiety and Phobia Workbook, Revised Second Edition*. Copyright © 1995 by New Harbinger Publications, Inc. Reprinted with the permission of New Harbinger Publications, Inc., Oakland, CA, www.newharbinger.com; *p*. 275 Figure 10-2: "Strategies for Avoiding Settings in Which Rape Most Often Occurs" from WIN—Women's Issues Network, Dallas Working Against Rape brochure; *p*. 292 "Staying Out of the Pits": "Robert's Downward Spiral" from Joseph White and Thomas Parham, *The Psychology of Blacks, Second Edition*. Copyright © 1990 by Prentice-Hall, Inc. Reprinted with the permission of the publishers; *p*. 315 Figure 12.2: "The Trouble that 'Frequent Binge Drinkers' Create for Themselves and Others" from *Journal of the American Medical Association* (November/December, 1994). Copyright © 1994 by the American Medical Association. Reprinted with the permission of the publishers; *p*. 316 SelfAssessment 12.2: "Do You Abuse Drugs?" from M. E. Bennett, et al (1993), "Identifying Young Substance-Abusers: The Rutgers Collegiate Substance Abuse Screening Test" from *Journal of Studies on Alcohol*, 54, pages 522-527. Copyright © 1993 by Alcohol Research Documentation, Inc. Reprinted with the permission of the publishers; *p*. 321 Figure 12.3: "Contraceptive Choices" statistics from Susan Harlap, Kathryn Kost, and Jacqueline Darroch Forrest, *Preventing Pregnancy, Protecting Health: A New Look at Birth Control Choices in the United States*, Table 8.1. Reprinted with the permission of The Alan Guttmacher Institute, New York and Washington; *p*. 331 Figure 12.5: "College Students' Main Reason for Seeking Counseling" from "Client Problem Checklist," Student Counseling Center, Illinois State University. Reprinted by permission; *p*. 342 Self-Assessment 13.1: "How Goal-Directed Are You?" after K. Skinner, *How Goal-Directed Are You?* (Dallas: Southern Methodist University, 1997). Used by permission; *p*. 356 Figure 13.2: "Desired Skills of an Ideal Job Candidate Rated by Employers" adapted from M. Collins, "The job outlook for '96 Grads" from *Journal of Career Planning & Employment* (Winter, 1996), page 53. Copyright © 1996 by National Association of Colleges and Employers. Reprinted with the permission of the publishers; *p*. 357 "On-Target Tips": "Knocking 'Em Dead in an Interview" from Martin Yate, *Knock 'Em Dead*. Copyright © 1998 by Martin Yate. Reprinted with the permission of Adams Media Corp.; *p*. 369 Figure 14.1: "First-Year Students' Views on Value-Related Issues" from L. J. Sax, A. W. Astin, W. S. Korn and K. M. Mahoney, *The American Freshman: National Norms for Fall 1995*. Reprinted with the permission of Higher Education Research Institute, Graduate School of Education, University of California, Los Angeles.

Index

Note: Italicized letters *b*, *f*, and *t* following page numbers indicate boxes, figures, and tables, respectively.

A

Abbreviations, for note taking, 118t
Abstracts, electronic, 99t
Academic advisement, 90–91
Academic ethics, 376–380
Academic honor societies, 192
Academic integrity, 376–380
   cheating, 32, 193–195
   plagiarism, 244–245
Academic planning, 341–352
   calendars and time plans for, 56–58, 60–61
   college catalogs, 345
   course selection, 341–345
   four- or five-year degrees, 347–348, 351
   majors and specializations, 345–350
   mentors, 350–352
   transfers among colleges, 350
   two-year degrees, 349
Academic probation, 192
Academic problems, 28, 44–45, 91
Academic restrictions, 192
Academic skills
   improvement of, 13
   strengths and weaknesses, 160, 162
Academic success
   checklist, 339, 359
   learning portfolio, 360–362
   resources, 363–364
   review questions, 359
   summary tips, 358
Academic values, 376–380
Achievement, 341
Achievement identity, 6
Acronyms, and memorization techniques, 152, 153t
Activities
   for cultural enrichment, 88–89
   extracurricular, 88
Adapting to college, 1–23
   checklist, 1, 19
   learning portfolio, 20–22
   resources, 23
   review questions, 19
   summary tips, 18
   transition from high school, 3–4
Addiction
   to alcohol and drugs, 312, 314–317
   to computers, 101–103
Advisement, academic, 90–91
Age, diversity in, 295
AIDS, 318–319
Alcohol and drugs, 182, 184b, 312, 314–317
Andreessen, Marc, 82
Androgyny, 289–291
Anorexia Nervosa, 313
Anxiety, over tests, 27, 181–183
Assertiveness, 266–267, 269b
Assistance
   academic advisement, 89–91
   for mental health problems, 91–92, 329–331
   for physical disabilities, 92–93
   with resource accessing, 93–94
Attendance, 33–34, 113–114
Attitude, assessment of, 27
Auditory learning, 27
Austin, Alexander, 14

B

Bandura, Albert, 323
Banking, 70
Biological rhythms, 62
Birth control, 319–320, 321f
Bloom, Benjamin, 157, 205–208
   taxonomy of, 205–209
Boredom antidotes, 116b
Brainstorming, 38
Budgeting, 66–69
Bulimia, 313

C

Calendar, term, 56–58
Campus and community life
   college success checklist, 81, 105
   and diversity, 285–288
   familiarity with, self-assessment of, 84
   health care services, 83–85
   learning portfolio, 106–108
   living arrangements, 85–87
   resources, 109
   review questions, 105
   safety, 85
   summary tips, 104
Campus resources, 83–85
Career identity, 6
Career planning, 352–357
   interests, 354
   job candidates, ideal, 355–356
   job interviews, 357b
   job market, 354
   job search, 356f
   occupational outlook, 352
   work experiences during college, 357
Career success
   checklist, 339, 359
   learning portfolio, 360–362
   resources, 363–364
   review questions, 359
   summary tips, 358
Cheating, 32, 193–195
Checklist(s), college success. *See* College success checklist(s)
Child care, 87
Class attendance, 33–34, 113–114
Class participation, 34–35, 37
Collaboration, 37–39
Collectivist cultures, 285, 286b
College catalogs, and academic planning, 345
College experience, self-assessment, 379
College success checklist(s)
   academic success, 339, 359
   adapting to college, 1, 19
   campus and community life, 81, 105
   career success, 339, 359
   communication skills, 259, 277
   defined, 15
   diversity, living with, 283, 299
   health, 305, 333
   information processing, 111, 137
   integrity, 365, 383
   learning styles, 25, 47
   listening skills, 111, 137
   mental health, 305, 333
   money management, 53, 75
   note taking skills, 111, 137
   physical health, 305, 333
   reading skills, 111, 137
   relationships, development of, 259, 277
   speaking skills, 233, 253
   study skills, development of, 143, 167
   test-taking skills, 173, 197
   thinking skills, 203, 227
   time management, 53, 75
   writing skills, 233, 253
College success images
   Andreessen, Marc, 82
   Edelman, Marian Wright, 2
   Einstein, Albert, 174
   Espino, Ana Bolado de, 284
   Falkenstein, Talia, 112
   Fulghum, Robert, 26

   Grandin, Temple, 204
   Ma, Yo-Yo, 144
   Papczun, Eric, 54
   Schwarzenegger, Arnold, 306
   Shaw, Bernard, 340
   Smith, Emmitt, 366
   Tan, Amy, 234
   Winfrey, Oprah, 260
Communication skills, 261–265. *See also* Information processing; Listening skills; Speaking skills; Writing skills
   across ability levels, 296b
   assertiveness and, 266–267, 269b
   college success checklist, 259, 277
   for conflict resolution, 265–269, 297
   and cultural diversity, 286b
   development of, 14
   and gender, 264–265
   learning portfolio, 278–280
   and listener defensiveness, 262
   for negotiation, 267–269
   nonverbal, 263–264
   resources, 281
   review questions, 277
   summary tips, 276
   verbal communication barriers, 261–262
Community life. *See* Campus and community life
Commuting, 64, 86–87
Complaints, about instructors, 45
Computers, 95–102
   addiction to, 101–103
   avoidance of, 96–97
   and electronic mail (e-mail), 100
   and Internet, 95, 97, 99–101
   overcoming fears of, 96–97
   precautions for use, 242b
   purchase of, 95
   self-assessment, 103
   software for, 95, 97–98
   system components, 95
Concentration, 34–36, 113–114, 116b, 129–131, 184. *See also* Thinking skills
   assessment of, 27
Concept maps, for note taking, 119, 122f
Conflict resolution, 265–269, 297
Content-centered teaching styles, 43–44
Cornell System, for note taking, 121–124
Counseling
   academic, 90–91
   mental health, 329–331
Course selection, and academic planning, 341–345
Covey, Stephen, 373–374
Cramming, 147b, 175, 176b
Creative profile, self-assessment, 219
Creative thinking, 217–221
   brainstorming, 38
   Csikszentmihalyi's ideas, 219–221
   individual, 217–219
   mental locks, 220–221
   and motivation, 218–219
Creative writing, 236
Credit cards, 70–72
Critical thinking, 205–216
   Bloom's taxonomy, 205–208
   defined, 205
   keys to good, 208–216
   and problem solving, 208–216
   self-assessment, 209–210
Criticism, 261
Csikszentmihalyi, Mihaly, 219–221
Cultural identity, 6
Culture and ethnicity, 6, 285–288
   activities for enrichment, 88–89
   collectivists and individualists, 285, 286b
   diversity and communication skills, 286b

395

Index

D

Database management software, 98
Dating, 274
Deadlines, managing, 238t, 243
Dean's List, 192
Decision making, 217b
Deductive reasoning, 214–215
Deep learning, 27
Defensiveness, of learners, 262
Degrees, and academic planning, 347–349, 351
Depression, 327–330
Diagraming, and memorization techniques, 154
Diet and dieting, 62, 311–313
Disabilities, people with
   communication skills, 296b
   learning differences, 162–165
   overcoming limitations, 92–93
Distractions, from learning, 34–36
Diversity
   in age, 294–295
   on campus, 285–288
   in culture and ethnicity, 6, 285–288
   in gender, 288–293
   within groups, 285
   living with
     checklist, 283, 299
     learning portfolio, 300–302
     resources, 303–304
     review questions, 299
     summary tips, 298
   and relationships, 295–297
   in sexual orientation, 293–294
Drugs and alcohol, 182, 184b, 312, 314–317
Dyslexia, 163

E

Eating and nutrition, 62, 311–313
Eating disorders, 313
Edelman, Marian Wright, 2
Effective people, habits of, 373–375
Einstein, Albert, 174
E-mail (Electronic mail), 100
Embarrassing moments, while speaking, 251
Emergencies, on test day, 180–181
Emotional intelligence
   Goleman's theory of, 327
   self-assessment, 328
Employment. See also under Career
   and time management, 62–63
Erikson, Erik, 6–7
Espino, Ana Bolado de, 284
Essay tests, 178, 187–188, 189b
Ethics. See Academic integrity; Moral issues
Ethnic identity, 6
Ethnicity. See Culture and ethnicity
Exams. See Test(s)
Executive learning style, 28
Exercise, physical, 310, 311f
Experience, learning from, 12
Expressive writing, 236
Extracurricular activities, 88. See also Campus and community life

F

Falkenstein, Talia, 112
Family matters
   and college life, 87
   relationships, 270–272
   and studying, 125b
   and time management, 63, 87
Faxing software, 98–99
Feedback, learning from, 243–244
Fill-in-the-blank tests, 187
Finances. See Money management
Financial aid, 72–73
Financial success, achieving, 14–15
First impressions, instructors and, 30–32
Fishbone diagram, for note taking, 119–121, 122f
Foreign languages, study strategies for, 159–160, 161b
Foreign students. See Culture and ethnicity
Formal writing, 236–237
Fraternities, 86
Friendship, 272–274
Fulghum, Robert, 26

G

Gardner, Howard, 160
Gender
   androgyny, 289–291
   and communication, 264–265
   diversity in, 288–293
   and sexual harassment, 292
   stereotypes, 289
   and study success, 161–162
Gender identity, 6
Goal(s)
   changes in, 370f
   self-assessment, 342
Goal setting, and planning, 10–11, 55–56
Goleman, Daniel, 327
Grading systems, 192–193
Grandin, Temple, 204
Graphics software, 98
Groups
   and brainstorming, 38
   and collaboration, 37–39
   diversity of, 285
   effectiveness of, 38–39, 40t, 41
   for problem solving, 40t
   types of, 37–38

H

Health. See Mental health; Physical health
Health care services, on campus, 83–85
Health maintenance, 176
Heartbreak, dating and, 274
Help, obtaining, 89–93. See also Counseling
High school, versus college, 3–4, 32–34, 192
Holistic thinking, 221–225
   left-brained thinking, 222
   medicine wheel, 223–224
   mindfulness, 224–225
   right-brained thinking, 221–222
Homesickness, 87, 89
Honesty, in test taking, 32, 193–195
Honor societies, 192
Housing, on-campus, 85–86
Humanities, study strategies for, 157–158

I

Identity, development of, 6–9, 376
Images of college success. See College success images
Improvement
   of academic skills, 13
   areas needing, self-assessment of, 16
   of memory, 149–155
   of note taking, 134–135
   of reading skills, 129–131
   of work habits, 13
Individualist cultures, 285, 286b
Inductive reasoning, 214–215
Information processing
   checklist, 111, 137
   efficiency in, 113–141
   learning portfolio, 138–140
   resources, 141
   review questions, 137
   summary tips, 136
Instructors
   problems with, 44–45
   relationships with, 30–32, 33t, 39–45
   roles of, 40–42
   and seniority, 42
Integrity. See also Value(s)
   academic, 32, 193–195, 244–245, 376–377
   checklist, 365, 383
   learning portfolio, 384–386
   resources, 387
   review questions, 383
   summary tips, 382
   in test taking, 32, 193–195
Intellectual identity, 6
Interests, 7
International students. See Culture and ethnicity
Internet, 95, 97, 99–101

J

Job search. See Career planning
Judicial learning style, 28–29

K

Kinesthetic learning, 27
Knowledge, expansion of, 11–12
Kolb, David, 29

L

Lakein, Alan, 59
Langer, Ellen, 224–225
LASSI. See Learning and study strategies inventory
Learning
   and defensiveness, 262
   differences in, and study success, 162–164
   disabilities, 162–165
   from experience, 12
   from feedback, 243–244
   hindrances to, 35–36
   from mistakes, 180
   self-assessment, 156
Learning and study strategies inventory (LASSI), 27
Learning portfolio
   academic success, 360–362
   adapting to college, 20–22
   campus and community life, 106–108
   career success, 360–362
   communication skills, 278–280
   defined, 15–17
   development of, 29
   health, 334–336
   information processing, 138–140
   integrity, 384–386
   learning styles, 48–50
   living with diversity, 300–302
   mental health, 334–336
   money management, 76–78
   physical health, 334–336
   relationships, 278–280
   speaking skills, 254–256
   study skills, 168–170
   test-taking skills, 198–200
   thinking skills, 228–230
   time management, 76–78
   writing skills, 254–256
Learning styles, 12, 27–29, 30t
   adapting, 29
   auditory, 27
   checklist, 25, 47
   deep versus surface, 27
   executive, 28
   judicial, 28–29
   kinesthetic, 27
   Kolb's, 29
   learning portfolio, 48–50
   legislative, 28
   Myers-Briggs Type Indicator, 28
   resources, 51
   review questions, 47
   self-assessment, 31
   sensory styles, 27
   Sternberg's Thinking Styles, 28–29
   summary tips, 46
   visual, 27
Lectures
   boredom antidotes, 116b
   tape recording, 118b
Left-brained thinking, 222
Legislative learning style, 28
Library resources, 4, 93–94
Life goals, changes in, 370f
Limitations, with physical disabilities, overcoming, 92–93
Listening skills. See also Information processing
   as an audience member, 247
   in the classroom, 113–116
   college success checklist, 111
   defensiveness of learners, 262
   development of, 261, 262b
Living arrangements
   on campus, 85–86
   off campus, 86–87
Loneliness, 272–274
Longevity, of college graduates, 14–15
Long-term memory, 149–150

M

Ma, Yo-Yo, 144
McNally, David, 11
Magolda, Marcia Baxter, 157
Majors, and academic planning, 345–350
MAMA cycles, 9
Marcia, James, 7, 9
Mathematics, study strategies for, 158, 159*b*
The Measure of Our Success (Edelman), 2
Medicine wheel, 223–224
Memorization
    Bloom's taxonomy, 205–206
    techniques, 150–155
Memory
    decay, 150
    improvement of, 149–155
    interference, 150
    long-term, 149–150
    self-assessment, 156
    short-term, 149
Memory aids, 149, 151–153
Mental health, 91–92, 320–331
    campus services, 83–85
    checklist, 305, 333
    counseling and assistance, 91–92, 329–331
    depression, 327–330
    emotional intelligence, 327
    learning portfolio, 334–336
    resources, 337–338
    review questions, 333
    self-assessment, 308–309
    and self-esteem, 325–327
    stress management, 12–13, 321–325
    and suicide, 329
    summary tips, 332
Mental locks, 220–221
Mentors, 350–352
Method of loci, 152–153
Mindfulness, 224–225
Mnemonics, 149, 151–153
Money management, 65–73
    banking, 70
    budgeting, 66–69
    checklist, 53, 75
    credit cards, 70–72
    financial aid, 72–73
    learning portfolio, 76–78
    resources, 79–80
    review questions, 75
    summary tips, 74
Moral issues, 32, 193–195. *See also* Academic integrity
Motivation, 9–10, 345*b*
    assessment of, 27
    and creative thinking, 218–219
Multiple choice tests, 185–186
Myers-Briggs Type Indicator, 28

N

Natural sciences, study strategies for, 158, 159*b*
Negotiation, 267–269
Nonverbal communication, 263–264
Note taking, 114–115, 117–124, 127. *See also* Information processing
    abbreviations for, 118*t*
    college success checklist, 111
    Cornell System, 121–124
    formats for, 119–124
    improvement of, 134–135
    marking text, 133–135
    self-assessment, 120
    strategies for, 117–119
Nutrition, 62, 311–313

O

Objective tests, 177–178
Occupational outlook, 352
Outlining, for note taking, 119

P

Papczun, Eric, 54
Participation, class, 34–35, 37
Peck, M. Scott, 374–375
Perfectionism, self-assessment, 344
Personal concerns, 91–92
Personality
    characteristics, 6–7
    development of, 14
    factors, 28
Phobias, about speaking, 249–250
Physical disabilities
    and communication skills, 296*b*
    limitations of, 92–93
Physical health, 307–320
    biological rhythms, 62
    campus services, 83–85
    checklist, 305, 333
    and drugs and alcohol, 182, 184*b*, 312, 314–317
    eating and nutrition, 62, 311–313
    and exercise, 310, 311*f*
    learning portfolio, 334–336
    maintenance of, 176
    personal, 307
    resources, 337–338
    review questions, 333
    self-assessment, 308–309, 316
    and sexual issues, 317–320, 321*f*
    and sleep, 62, 310–311, 312*b*
    and smoking, 313–314
    summary tips, 332
Plagiarism, 244–245
Planning
    academic. *See* Academic planning
    and goal setting, 10–11, 55–56
Political identity, 6
Pregnancy, unwanted, 319–320
Presentation software, 98
Priorities, setting of, 59–62
Probation, academic, 192
Problem(s), academic, 28, 44–45, 91
Problem solving
    academic, 28, 44–45, 91
    brainstorming for, 38
    creative thinking for, 217
    critical thinking for, 208–216
    in groups, 40*t*
    self-assessment, 213
    skills for, 212
Procedural tests, 178
Procrastination, 64–65, 66*b*, 66*t*, 244
Professors. *See* Instructors
Psychological assistance, 91–92, 329–331. *See also* Mental health
Punctuality, 113–114

R

Rape, 274–275
Reading materials, 127–128
Reading skills, 124–131. *See also* Information processing
    checklist, 111
    for different disciplines, 128–129
    improvement of, 129–131
    marking text, 133–135
    self-assessment, 130
    speed, 131, 133
Reasoning
    and critical thinking, 212–216
    deductive and inductive, 214–215
    systematic, 28
Records, release of, 88*b*
Reference materials, 237*t*
Relationship(s)
    with children, 271–272
    dating, 274
    development of, 14
        checklist, 259, 277
        learning portfolio, 278–280
        resources, 281
        review questions, 277
        summary tips, 276
    and diverse groups, 295–297
    with family members, 63, 87, 270–272
    with friends, 272–274
    with instructors, 30–32, 33*t*, 39–45
    with parents, 270
    with partners, 270–271
    with roommates, 272
Relationship identity, 6
Relaxation, 182*b*, 184
Religious identity, 6
Remembering. *See* Memorization; Memory
Resources
    on academic success, 363–364
    on adapting to college, 23
    campus, 83–85, 93–94
    on campus and community life, 109
    on career success, 363–364
    on communication skills, 281
    on diversity, living with, 303–304
    on health, 337–338
    on information processing, 141
    on integrity, 387
    learning portfolio and, 15–17
    on learning styles, 51
    library, 4, 93–94
    on mental health, 337–338
    on money management, 79–80
    on physical health, 337–338
    on reference materials, 237*t*
    on relationships, 281
    on speaking skills, 257–258
    on study skills, 171
    on success, academic and career, 363–364
    on test-taking skills, 201
    on thinking skills, 231
    on time management, 79–80
    on writing skills, 257–258
Responsibility, personal, 32–34
Restrictions, academic, 192
Retrieval strategies, and memorization techniques, 154–155
Review questions
    academic success, 359
    adapting to college, 19
    campus and community life, 105
    career success, 359
    communication skills, 277
    diversity, living with, 299
    health, 333
    information processing, 137
    integrity, 383
    learning styles, 47
    mental health, 333
    money management, 75
    physical health, 333
    relationships, development of, 277
    speaking skills, 253
    study skills, development of, 167
    success, academic and career, 359
    test-taking, 197
    thinking skills, 227
    time management, 75
    writing skills, 253
Right-brained thinking, 221–222
Rodin, Judith, 224–225
Rogers, Carl, 5–6
Roommates, 85–86, 272

S

Safety, on-campus, 85
Schwarzenegger, Arnold, 306
Self-assessment
    academic planning
        four- or five-year degrees, 351
        two-year degrees, 349
    androgyny, 290–291
    Bloom's taxonomy, 209
    budget preparation, 67, 69
    campus knowledge, 84
    career interests, 354
    class participation style, 37
    college experience, 379
    computers, addiction to, 103
    conflict management, 268
    creative profile, 219
    critical thinking, 209–210
    defined, 15
    depression, 330
    drugs and alcohol, 316
    emotional intelligence, 328
    gender diversity, 290–291
    goal orientation, 342
    group effectiveness, 41
    health, 308–309, 316

Self-assessment (continued)
  homesickness, 89
  honesty, in test-taking, 195
  identity, 8, 375
  improvement, areas needing, 16
  job market, 354
  learning and memory, 156
  learning disabilities, 165
  learning styles, 31
  library resources, 4
  mental health, 308–309
  note taking styles, 120
  perfectionism, 344
  physical health, 308–309, 316
  problem solving, 213
  procrastination, 65
  reading profile, 130
  reading speed, 133
  speaking skills, 250
  strengths and weaknesses profile, 162
  study timing, 148
  term planner, creation of, 57
  test anxiety, 183
  test-taking, 190
  time plans, 60–61
  value conflicts, 377
  values, 368
  writing skills, 243
Self-esteem, 325–327
Seligman, Martin, 323
Sensory styles, 27
Sexual acts, unwanted, 274–275
Sexual harassment, 292
Sexual identity, 6
Sexual issues, and physical health, 317–320
Sexual orientation, diversity in, 293–294
Sexually transmitted diseases (STDs), 319
Shaw, Bernard, 340
Short answer tests, 187
Short-term memory, 149
Skipping class, 33–34, 113–114
Sleep
  deprivation of, 62
  and physical health, 310–311, 312b
Smith, Emmitt, 366
Smoking, 313–314
Social sciences, study strategies for, 159, 160b
Software. See Computers, software for
Sororities, 86
Speaking skills, 235, 245–251
  checklist, 233, 253
  embarrassing moments, 251
  for formal presentations, 246
  for informal situations, 245–246
  learning portfolio, 254–256
  and listening skills, 247
  and phobias, 249–250
  for problem solving, 249–251
  resources, 257–258
  review questions, 253
  strategies for good speaking, 247–249
  strengths and weaknesses, self-assessment, 250
  summary tips, 252
  verbal communication barriers, 261–262
Specializations, and academic planning, 345–350
Spreadsheet software, 97–98
STDs, 319
Sternberg, Robert J., 28–29
Stimulants. See Drugs and alcohol
Strengths and weaknesses profile, self-assessment, 162
Stress management, 12–13, 321–325
Student-centered teaching styles, 43–44
Study aids, 180
Study groups, 38, 175
Study skills
  assessment of, 27
  development of
    checklist, 143, 167
    learning portfolio, 168–170
    resources, 171
    review questions, 167
    summary tips, 166
Study strategies, 145, 146b
  for complex ideas, 155–160
  cramming, 147b, 175, 176b
  for foreign languages, 159–160, 161b
  for humanities, 157–158
  last-minute, 179–180
  for natural science and math, 158, 159b
  sensible, 175–178, 179t
  for social science, 159, 160b
Studying
  effectiveness of, 145
  environment for, 145–146
  and family matters, 125b
  objectives of, 145
  successful, factors influencing, 160–164
Success. See also Academic success; Career success; College success checklist; College success images
  financial, achieving, 14–15
  study, factors influencing, 160–164
  on tests, 175–201
Suicide, 329
Summary method, for note taking, 119
Summary tips
  academic success, 358
  adapting to college, 18
  campus and community life, 104
  career success, 358
  communication skills, 276
  diversity, living with, 298
  health, 332
  information processing, 136
  integrity, 382
  learning styles, 46
  mental health, 332
  money management, 74
  physical health, 332
  relationships, development of, 276
  speaking skills, 252
  study skills, development of, 166
  success, academic and career, 358
  test-taking skills, 196
  thinking skills, 226
  time management, 74
  writing skills, 252
Support groups, 91–92
Surface learning, 27
Syllabus, course, 32
Systematic reasoning, 28

T

Tan, Amy, 234
Tannen, Deborah, 264–265
Tape recording, of lectures, 118b
Task-oriented groups, 38
Teaching styles, content-centered versus student-centered, 43–44
Technology. See Computers
Term planner, creation of, 57
Test(s)
  anxiety over, 27, 181–183
  checklist, 173, 197
    learning portfolio, 198–200
    resources, 201
    review questions, 197
    summary tips, 196
  emergencies on test day, 180–181
  failure to take, 180–181
  formats for, 177–178, 185–188, 189b
  general strategies for taking, 184–185
  grades on, 191–193
  integrity in taking, 32, 193–195
  make-up, 181
  preparation for, 147b, 175–182
    assessment of, 27
  reviewing, 191
  skills effectiveness, self-assessment, 27, 190
  succeeding on, 175–201
Testing
  benefits of, 175
  conditions for, 176
Text, methods of marking, 133–135. See also Note taking
Textbooks, 127–128
Thinking
  convergent, 38
  divergent, 38
  left-brained, 222
  right-brained, 221–222
Thinking skills
  Bloom's taxonomy, 205–208
  college success checklist, 203, 227
  for college work, 205–208
  creative. See Creative thinking
  critical. See Critical thinking
  expansion of, 11–12
  higher order, 157
  holistic, 221–225
  learning portfolio, 228–230
  resources, 231
  review questions, 227
  summary tips, 226
Thinking styles, 28–29
Time management, 56–65
  checklist, 53, 75
  and commuting, 64
  and employment, 62–63
  and family matters, 63, 87
  learning portfolio, 76–78
  pattern assessment, 27
  and priority setting, 59–62
  resources, 79–80
  review questions, 75
  set time approach, 59
  summary tips, 74
  Swiss cheese approach, 59
Time plans, 56, 58, 60–61
To-do lists, 59–62
Transferring to another college, 350
Transition to college, from high school, 3–6
Treisman, Philip, 38
Triandis, Harry, 285
True-false tests, 186–187
Tutoring. See Academic problems

V

Value(s)
  academic, 375–377
  and academic disciplines, 377
  clarification of, 367–369
  defined, 367
  of first-year college students, 369–372
  of highly effective people, 373–375
  Peck's, 374–375
  personal, 367–377
  positive, 372–377
  self-assessment, 368
Value conflicts, 367
  self-assessment, 378
Van Oech, Robert, 220–221
Verbal communication, 261–262. See also Speaking skills
Visual learning, 27
Visualization, and memorization techniques, 153–154
Vocabulary, enhancement of, 131
Vocational identity, 6

W

Waterman, Alan, 7–8
Weight maintenance. See Physical health
Winfrey, Oprah, 260
Winston, Stephanie, 59–62
Word processing software, 97
Work experiences, career planning, 357
Work habits, improvement of, 13
World Wide Web, 95, 97, 99–101
Writer's block, 244
Writers, habits of effective, 237–244
Writing skills, 235–245
  acquiring, 235–236
  checklist, 233, 253
  for creative writing, 236
  effectiveness of, 237–244
  for expressive writing, 236
  formal writing, 236–237
  learning portfolio, 254–256
  managing deadlines, 238t, 243
  organization strategies, 240b
  problems encountered with, 244–245
  resources, 257–258
  review questions, 253
  strengths and weaknesses of, self-assessment, 243
  summary tips, 252
  writing-to-learn, 235–236